The Manufacture of Evil

Also by Lionel Tiger

MEN IN GROUPS (1969)

THE IMPERIAL ANIMAL (with Robin Fox) (1971)

WOMEN IN THE KIBBUTZ (with Joseph Shepher) (1975)

FEMALE HIERARCHIES (editor) (1978)

OPTIMISM: THE BIOLOGY OF HOPE (1979)

CHINA'S FOOD (with photographs by Reinhart Wolf) (1985)

MEN IN GROUPS, second edition (with an introduction by
   Desmond Morris) (1985)

To JR, and to my friends

The Manufacture of Evil

Ethics, Evolution and the Industrial System

Lionel Tiger

Marion Boyars
New York · London

First published in paperback in 1991
by Marion Boyars Publishers
237 East 39th Street, New York, NY 10016
24 Lacy Road, London SW15 1NL

Distributed in the United States and Canada
by Rizzoli International Publications, New York

Library of Congress Cataloging-in-Publication Data
Tiger, Lionel, 1937–
    The manufacture of evil : ethics, evolution, and the industrial
system / by Lionel Tiger.
    Originally published : New York : Harper & Row, c 1987.
    Includes bibliographical references and index.
    1. Good and evil.   2. Man.   3. Civilization, Modern.   I. Title.
[BJ1406.T64   1991]
170--dc20

                                                        91–8381

British Library Cataloguing in Publication Data
Tiger, Lionel 1937–
    The manufacture of evil : ethics, evolution, and the
    industrial system.
    1. Ethics
    I. Title
    170

ISBN 0–7145–2929X

Contents

Introduction: Point of Entry

Imagine a triangle.

One point of it is a complex and bustling species, ourselves, perhaps four million years in the making, largely as a hunter and gatherer, as a creature that scrutinized nature and other creatures and then acted with burgeoning and more elegant skills as the centuries flowed. This way we lived for all but the last ten thousand years of our history. At the time of Christ half the planet's people were still hunting and gathering. We are a complex primate with special adaptation to a special way of making a living, and a special way of living as we made it.

The second point of the triangle is our industrial system, a way of earning a living based on denying nature's inevitability, a method of aggressive managerial penetration of the world's surfaces, appearances, and routines. A method which makes night day, day night, fast slow, and slow fast. A way of life with enough leverage to jump to the moon, with enough technique to produce complex things in factories peopled by robots. A system so pervasive and seemingly logical we have virtually equated it with progress and evolution. A system which advertises itself through its own bulging cornucopia of products and processes.

And it lays claim to our consciousness. The industrial style has made more converts more quickly than any brigade of priests or preachers. It beguiles those in and out of it alike with the lure and convenience of membership. A species newly united by a web of electricity shares respect for the scheme that makes the spark and carries the message for miles and miles.

The third point of the triangle is our ethics, our codified ways

1

of deciding about right and wrong, good and bad, acceptable ecstasy and dire evil. The Bible, the Koran, the Buddhist creeds, the definitions and assertions of Confucius, these and other famous front-line manuals of behavior are in varying ways the products of agricultural and pastoral societies. These were groups concerned with radically different numbers and arrangements of people than either hunters or ourselves, and with differently derived notions of nature, life's process, and how much option there really is about managing social arrangements.

This book is about that triangle.

Triangles are eternally tense forms. This one is, also, under particularly interesting strain because the industrial age has yielded no commanding ethical scheme with which to operate our social lives. Apart from Marxism, which can be seen as an antagonistic response to the crisis of industrialism, no widely accepted positive ethics has yet emerged. We struggle to adapt the new efficiency of laboratories and factories to the eternal verities of shepherds. Not without results. If it is possible to say, as I think it is, that the industrial system has provided an unparalleled opportunity to enjoy a startling array of products and experiences, it is also possible to claim that the impact of the system has been largely benign and highly agreeable to those who receive its bounty. More ambiguous has been the system's impact on civic satisfactions—on what members of industrial communities think about the grace and fairness of their experience as citizens. Is there clear-cut enjoyment of the moral and aesthetic quality of their lives outside their immediate circles or even within them? It seems not, since more or less passionate and political concerns have been endemic as our system has gained sway. Complaints abound about impersonality, alienation, the coldness of the iron law of bureaucracy, the strangely willful impact of large-scale structure on small-scale needs and wants, a host of complaints which, while they echo some similar ones in the past, are currently identified as pathologies of *our* way of life, as problems for *our* solution, as dilemmas of *our* creation.

So we develop mighty organizations to accomplish ambitious tasks and then regret that they seem so impersonal, so heartless. We invent spectacular machines which allow us to see the most minute operations of our bodies and then complain that the doctors who know how to use them could not care less about our stormy emotional needs. We generate corps of experts to analyze

2

what we do and why but then resent losing our autonomy to their expertise. We create a plethora of interesting objects but then deplore materialism. There is a clear link between the benefits of chemistry and cancer.

For a system founded on firm management of the relationship between means and ends, the huge industrial arrangement appears often to yield vast outcomes no one wanted. This is the subject of my book. Those miserable outcomes nobody desires I want to examine as an especially characteristic modern form of evil. They may result from incompetence or ignorance or casual negligence rather than from outright malevolence. But for those who have to endure the consequences, the result is the same as if there had been a well-worked-out conscious plan to do bad things. Inadvertence is no balm. I suspect it is also a chronic feature of a system of life so elaborate and potent that assessing its effects at the same time as they are being produced is evidently extremely difficult. Various forms of "risk assessment" and of ethical consultancy have become voguish. But this is relatively new and somewhat exceptional and therefore puzzling. Operating an industrial community without such monitors is like creating a swift strong tank without steering. The newness of the effort to monitor it reflects a characteristic of the system itself worth exploring in depth.

Then why do I call this "evil"? Partly of course because the term is showy. It attracts attention. It conveys the scale of the issue. It suggests the almost classical nature of the subject. But that is only the beginning of it.

The duality of good-evil occurs everywhere and throughout time. Exposés are principally about evil, not goodness. The former compels our attention, the latter is a less successful lure. We remain fascinated by malefactors and malfeasance, outraged at the incidence of evil in the world, surprised and shocked when it touches us. Perhaps this has always been so. But once upon a time, evil was personified. Evil was Mephistopheles or the Devil. Colorfully costumed. Almost flavorful, altogether identifiable, a clarified being from another world. But in the industrial system evil has become systematized. The production of it has become technologized, internationalized, multinationalized, and especially in times of war and high zealotry, officially rhapsodized. Just as industrialism has radically altered the ways and means of making and distributing, it has also altered the moral structure within which we live. Yet malefactors are harder to spot. They no longer boast horns and wear suits with tails, but rather three-piece suits and sometimes turtleneck sweaters of cashmere wool or magenta blouses of tailored silk.

My problem is this. I want to learn more about how a particular species of primate coexists with a particular system of economy which it made but which is different from the kind of economy which in the past made it. How does the creature respond to industrial food, industrial space, industrial smells, industrial groups, the industrial model of existence? There is a quality of stark drama to the historical situation in which we find ourselves, the most drastic and compelling element of which is the capacity of nuclear weaponry to destroy life as it is currently known. We have made machines of such astonishing power that if they are used, they can destroy or poison all other matter with which they come into contact.

For an exuberant primate, the problem is breathtaking. The political challenge is profoundly troubling. The whole situation is at the poetic extreme of any possible consciousness of evil. There must be an essential truth about the industrial system revealed by its ability and apparent readiness to destroy itself and everything else in a flash flood of nuclear fission. Since this flood would not be an act of nature but rather an act of *our* nature, what does this mean about our nature?

*　　　*　　　*

A question: Has all this to do with the development of industry and the corporation? Surely this was a pivotal social invention since it permitted individual people with fully fledged private moralities to conduct business without personal liability. Or so it seemed, for decades. The American publisher of this book is a group of people who appear to be very decent and who try to do decently the widely esteemed task of causing information and reflection to be gathered and made available. But it is a "limited company" with limited liability, like all others of the genre an innocent bride still wearing what lawyers call "the corporate veil." In France it is all even starker somehow—the letters after the official names of businesses are frequently "S.A.," which stands for *Société Anonyme*. Really limited? Really anonymous? Does this make any sense whatever? Are we still sure that legal forms provide freedom for one's personal moral account? Is it useless to try to adapt ideas of good and evil etched with small-scale clarity to situations where sheer mass and impersonality mitigate against moral accountability? Does not the very fact of membership in a group allow an individual to submerge private moral decision making within a reassuring consensus? Does the industrial system provide a uniquely efficient lubricant for moral evasiveness? Presumably this is not its point, nor should it be. Presumably it is also true that the rules of accountability appropriate to it are in a deep sense quite unclear and still emerging. One of my responsibilities in this book is to try to make them clearer and more useful to an animal basically ethical but frequently baffled about right and wrong.

Once I had the privilege and fun of being seated at a dinner party next to one of society's surgeons, the nonpareil cartoonist Saul Steinberg. We talked for a while, in particular about his very fine book *The Passport,* and then he asked me what work I did. "I'm an anthropologist." He smiled. "Oh, that's a good alibi." Then what is a professor of anthropology trained as a political sociologist and lured by biology doing in a book like this? Herewith my alibi: First of all, though anthropologists have traditionally focused their attention on small-scale, relatively exotic societies, it is timely and necessary that we focus on our own industrial pattern. I hope to show that this pattern is a fascinatingly exotic one; but practically speaking, it is the dominating system that threatens with extinction most, if not virtually all, of the technologically simple societies in the world. Since its military habits also threaten itself with extinction, it is worthwhile to seek as impartial and skeptical an insight into the system as human wit and the tools of cultural analysis permit.

Thus, anthropology. The role of biology should be as obvious. I foresee that the future task of the science of social behavior is to generate a science of skillful human husbandry, to teach us how to organize ourselves to maximize our contentment, pleasure, productivity, conscious reproductivity, and health, just as veterinarians and biologists do for animals in captivity and also those in the wild we are seeking to protect from various threatening forces. To do this, we have to know who and what we are, what we need and why, and what common circumstances attract and repel people no matter what their tribe or continent.

Of course there will always be some variation. But tropical medicine is part of medicine and the musicology of the Andean people is still musicology. The variations in human arrangements are like that, too.

The clear common humanity of all people, whatever their economic style, has focused attention on what we share as a species as well as on how we differ. The addition of modern biology to the scientific mix provided a new sense of the complexity of analyzing human behavior, a basis of real comparability, and an elegant awareness of mechanism and process. Using biology makes the work of social scientists more difficult—it is certainly not "reductionist," as some would claim. It offers a generous perspective with which to work. It allows and even compels us to pay attention to the forces of nature which the industrial system has so ingeniously permitted us often to overcome.

Nevertheless my approach will be reductionist, in the sense that I will seek explanations for behavior at the species level—at the level of saying: it is likely that a group of humans faced with a or b circumstances will respond in x or y manner. This will happen because all people share—by virtue of our common human genetic inheritance—a finite set of ways of perceiving the world, and then responding to it. Now there is no question that there will always be variations in all these factors. I or any other student claiming to see consistency across cultures in any important area of life run a considerable risk of simply being wrong. But unless we all abandon ourselves to the analytical despair of saying, "We can only understand a little bit of the picture at once," the risk must be taken for at least two reasons. The first is simply because in other disciplines such as history—e.g., Toynbee, Durant, Muller, Shorter, Schlesinger—or sociology—Wallerstein, Goffman, Lasch —large themes indeed are announced and then followed, and the evidence of many often widely disparate kinds of facts is accommodated within a large framework. If *they* can do it, why not we? Why should the introduction of biological data and theory immediately cause that special indignant outcry from wounded, relatively punctilious scholars who see in biosocial explanation a specially grievous ruination of thought and lapse of academic integrity? As I've acknowledged, sometimes their wounded cry may have been and still be legitimately evoked. But there also is an important version here of that old argument about our human exemption from the laws of biology—a claim carried to the most ludicrous extreme by the so-called Creationists, who defy the sturdiest understandings of our human place in the antiquity of cold time.

Introduction: Point of Entry

My second reason is I hope more interesting and also more relevant to my overall argument: the industrial system has been hugely successful. It has caused millions of people and dozens of countries to scorn or downgrade agriculture and pastoralism as livelihoods. An important reason for this is that it involves emotional and social processes sufficiently similar to the hunting-gathering way to make it the system of choice, the one with the most punch, the readiest zest, the most provocative and seemingly achievable dreams, and the most readable scenario. This same system also produces the burden of evil which this book is about.

When individuals create situations that cause them real grief and problems, there are medical psychiatric diagnoses and ways to begin treating them. And when a species does the same? Who's the doctor?

Industrialism appears to be not only effective but also persuasive. Mephistopheles reenters here, in the global guise of "life style" or way of life. The industrial way has been so influential, in part, because it appeals to people for the very same emotional and other psychological reasons that made the hunting-gathering way a well-balanced and integrated scheme for so long, for hundreds of thousands of years, in fact. But the industrial pattern is no holding pattern. It is an explosive eruption, so that what was initially intriguing, stimulating, and gratifying becomes seemingly unmanageable, distracting, irritating, and not what we meant at all.

Everyone and his rebellious sophomore nephew has sounded off about this or that aspect of the industrial system, in earnest complaint about what element particularly offends their political, moral, aesthetic, or social sense. My task here is to try to produce a catalogue of complaints particular to the industrial system, or at least thoroughly integrated with it, and to show how the items in the catalogue are generated, what their impact and use are, how much they cost, and to whom.

In the name of protecting our safety, our species has with spectacular design produced the means to destroy ourselves. That is all too obvious. If it took our system a surprising span of years —decades!—to become first aware of and then convinced by rumors of pollutions caused by acid in the rain, asbestos in the mine, chemicals in the water, even devils in health-giving drugs, what new forms of pollution may be discovered? It is difficult yet crucial to know. My concern is principally with behavioral pollution, with

7

the way in which the natural behavior of our species is restricted, thwarted, distorted, stretched, disallowed, or otherwise harshly and uncongenially molded by a way of living and earning. This may be as damaging to human social life as it has been to water, soil, bones, arteries, birds, and even our huge air. So my method will be to examine the body social for what may be bruises or tumors, to assess its temperature, its circulation, its productivity and reproductivity, its fear and trembling, even the sparkle in its eye and the spring in its movement or its slouch.

Consider this curious fact. While people are intensely gregarious and members of a species in which solitary confinement is the most feared punishment next to physical torture and execution, nevertheless the legal system of the industrial countries principally focuses on the acts and motives of individuals. This raises intriguing questions because the system may be screening behavior in an inaccurate way. By analogy, classical economics employed Adam Smith's general notion that people are coolly maximizing creatures who possess a calculating zeal which will draw them faithfully to an economically optimal course. Now we know that this is not how people behave. Economics theorists have had to come to terms with a greater set of operating considerations than Mr. Smith had expected.

Is a comparable error being made in the assumption that people have the moral equivalent of a calculator and act accordingly? Has the individualist assumption ill-served us in ethical theory, in particular when individuals may have to make moral decisions as members of large and perhaps comfortably integrated work groups? The broad emergent fact is that work becomes more important to people and kinship less. So do we have to recognize that to protect their jobs and the gregariousness they deliver, people may bend the rules for coworkers as it is frequently assumed they will try to do for members of their family group?

After all, we now treat with great caution—or refuse it altogether—the testimony in court of one close relative about another. The bonds of family are said to hold even in the face of morality. Abraham himself, faced with the literal order of God, hesitated before preparing the knife for his son Isaac's heart. Why not recognize then that a new family—at work—may offer an equally powerful vindication for acts of wrongdoing?

I know this is a very large question with possible answers of major import. Yet our plight as a relatively kinless species is so new, and our emotional and social needs so old, that we must ask how and why we do what we do because of what we are.

So in the first part of this book, I want to consider the implications of the possibility *that in an intensely gregarious species such as man, moral autonomy may be more difficult to achieve than moral consent.* This will form part of a general discussion of the relationship between the elements of the triangle with which I began this chapter. That is, between a hunting-gathering species formed in prehistory, the pastoral and mini-agricultural communities that produced our regnant ethical theories, and the grandly effective but brand-new industrial system which has evidently failed to generate any appropriately capacious and broadly satisfying ethical system of its own.

Any success such a discussion may have will partly depend on trying to come to terms with what may be the "moral human nature" of *Homo sapiens.*

Large task. But it is relieved somewhat by exploring consistencies across cultural lines, and by estimating the extent to which human beings, while variable and even quirky, are nevertheless similarly constituted in substantial ways. Hence it seems reasonable to suggest such possibilities as that shopping is emotionally equivalent to gathering, which helps explain the ferocious force and spread of industrial materialism in the world, or that the spread of literacy created a massive problem for our species because it has permitted the managers of the world to find distance from life and from each other through words; it produces the illusion that describing the world in writing actually reflects its reality.

Of course science has been a prime mover in the development and spread of the industrial system. It is a form of perception as powerful for making ideas about reality as the lever is for moving bits of reality, such as huge stones, up or down. It can protect or assault the welfare of the public. What specialists in gathering and using information think about human beings is central to the conduct of modern life. But they may think erroneously, or not eagerly or specifically enough, about the impact of applied knowledge. For example in the form of drugs. Chemistry has produced ever more drugs, for which there have been wonderful uses, but also abuses. The question of how drugs are tested and with what sensitivity to their social and psychological impact remains, in my view, inadequately answered in significant respects. A reason for this is that

9

scientists have broadly speaking seen humans as relatively passive pieces of physiology, whose emotional and social responses to drugs are of far less interest than impacts on the pancreas or the middle ear. So for two decades, for example, Valium and Librium were the most widely distributed psychiatric drugs in North America, even though there was no generous body of knowledge about their impact on the social, economic, reproductive, and ethical lives of the users. It is rather startling that the drugs were considered useful enough to have an immediate intimate impact but with little expectation of broad social impact. Why did no one question this until many millions of pills later? Why was so much attention given to the social impact of illegal drugs such as marijuana and heroin and so little to legal ones, such as Valium and the contraceptive pill?

A chilling if speculative case in point: Over the past thirty years at least 22 million American women were prescribed barbiturates to soothe them during pregnancy. Only now is it discovered that among small mammals, females carrying males given barbiturates produce males who are relatively feminized—the extra male ingredients a female has suddenly to produce from her own body that are needed to produce males are evidently inhibited by the tranquilizing drug. Does this mean that some 12 million American males experienced some possible impact? Is this related to what seems to be an unexpectedly rapid growth in at least the prominence if not the numbers of homosexual men? Again, did no one creating drugs with one behavioral effect suspect there might be another? And what technical theories underlie the whole method of testing, anyway? What theories about human nature?

Other medications, those surrounding contraception, have had striking impacts on the core human process, reproducing life itself, yet without adequate inspection of possible consequences. Not only chemical medications but also surgical interventions such as the IUD, vasectomies, and sterilization are likewise volatile intruders. What happens when the body itself becomes industrialized, a weapon of the industrial way of controlling nature? Is this why, at the time of writing, birth rates in the mature industrial societies are below replacement? Why many men and women regard sexual congress as a discrete and isolable unit independent of the larger biological event of which it is the consummatory shiver? Why, in that acme of modern settlement, Manhattan, do 30 percent of people who rent shelter live alone?

Not that this is either good or bad. But it is strikingly different from the ubiquitous form of extensive human domestic affiliation of the past.

Some countries are unexpectedly nonreproductive, such as wealthy West Germany. Others are both expectedly and unwantedly nonproductive, such as poor Bangladesh. Why? The colonial system of political and economic control of some countries by others has segued into a fully developed and highly turbulent system of global inequality, in which the richest and poorest are linked by a common regard for many common products, services, and processes. The dual convulsions of the Second World War and the rapid death of political colonialism united the planet in enthusiasm for the general spread of industrially produced wealth virtually everywhere. Rapidly and pervasively, an eventful commitment to the artifacts and ways of life of the industrial system has so beguiled the world that it comes to seem wholly reasonable to those communities without wealth to ask wealthy ones simply to give them some. Remarkable! Hence, in the spring of 1982, the countries of the South, meaning the poor ones, demanded of the cultures of the North, the wealthy ones, that they transfer wealth according to rules of equity, and quickly. What a change from the colonial days or before, when the whole *point* was to maintain poor countries poor—they were markets, clients, laborers, in any event backward, inept, and placid.

Gone are the colonial officers in pith helmets—those somewhat bewildered second sons of the middle classes who were sent out to exotic places to plant the flag and control the future. In their stead are economic development officers of individual governments and global agencies who roam the world to bring information and theory about the knack of making wealth. An industry of industrial promotion, of lore about the right way, forms a lattice around the real globe like the Mercator projection lines on the model of it. AID, the Development Decade, or whatever, are more or less zealous efforts to apply information about the experience of the rich to the facts and plight of the poor. That it all has not worked is reiterated with dolorous formality whenever comparative GNP statistics are issued and whenever some new General or some new Leader ambitious for dignified equity moves into Government House brandishing new plans and abjuring the thread-bare past.

Has the world ever been so united and so disunited by the things it makes? By salt, pepper, cumin? Perhaps by gold, as Pizarro thought? Certainly sugar and tobacco—those ubiquitous addictions—made a global difference. The illegal drugs and their entourage have generated their own multinational elaboration. But still the motorcar, the tin can, the airplane, the radio, the TV, the camera, the computer, the refrigerator and stove, have con-spired better than any apostles, any dealers or pushers, any bul-lion pirate, to engross *Homo sapiens* in a network of making, consuming, craving, and connoisseurship so self-evidently worth-while that governments and institutions even give away money to abet it. Now of course I am not concerned here with medical measures against infant mortality, the care of the foolish and un-well, or with the education that should be of the young and old. I am concerned with the big bamboozle—that industrial objects and the good life go together. Once when I was affiliated to the University of Ghana, a new American came to teach at the Busi-ness Administration School. One of the magical items he and his wife imported from the United States for their work in Ghana was an electric punch bowl!

*   *   *

Now we—ex-hunters—can manufacture our own prey!
Has any hunting species ever endured such provocation?

*   *   *

While there remains immense absolute poverty in the world and seemingly endless relative poverty even in rich communities, a form of deprivation derives from abundance itself. There is a relationship between diet and disease, between what we eat, how well we are, and of what we become ill or die. This is by now a banal and pervasive problem, widely recognized and explored. But it may be worth a fresh glance at the corner grocery and supermar-ket to realize how successfully human neo-addictions to sugar, tobacco, and caffeine are served by our system, and how the meats we eat and the prepared foods we purchase may violate good rules of nutrition because of the food industry's great skill in producing flavors and textures an omnivorous primate finds wholly appealing. An old story, and portentous. The discovery of neat sugar caused an explosion—it was mainly for sugar and tobacco that slavery became a world-embracing pattern. A civilization is not just the food it eats. Once there exists some freedom to choose its diet, that diet becomes part of its morality.

Just Another Product?

Because we can create so many interesting things, we seem to believe that we are products ourselves. At the heart of much of our social science, which explains our industrial culture to ourselves, lies the conviction that we are socially natureless, creatures of circumstances, like trained pigeons products of the world around us and client to its schemes. Attitudes, role models, stereotypes, the mistakes or triumphs of history—these are the building blocks of our convivial lives. Not our inner gusto and ancient path.

But is it really possible that such a glum cultural form is the direct outcome of the psychology of the industrial way? Other features of modern life pertain centrally to this and are parts of the larger picture. For example, the legal system which permitted industrialization rests upon several salient features. What C. B. Macpherson in a profound book has called *The Political Theory of Possessive Individualism* (1962) was necessary to atomize communities sufficiently to make their heartless rules and often exploitative management and use of property legally acceptable. This was one element. The other was the seemingly contradictory emergence of the impersonal corporation in which possessive individualism existed at a remove, principally for the purposes of ownership. Meanwhile corporate conduct permitted a screen between individual and action, person and performance. The "corporate veil" masked varying degrees of slyness and candor. The robust decisions of individuals alone or in groups could become absorbed by the implacable intricacy of the corporate entity as a legal mechanism. Thus did people become denatured again, perhaps as persuasively as if they were inhabited by Buddhist karma or Puritan witchery or saintliness. The evidence of the eye becomes subordinate to the interest of the law. So in an absolutely stunning rendition of this concerto, in 1982 the then-Johns-Manville Corporation declared bankruptcy to avoid a future of legal suits about asbestos, bankrupt in the very season its coffers bulged, its order books were thick, and its dividends comparatively generous. This is such a specialized and interesting way of dealing with reality, even the opposed realities of rotting lungs and corporate prosperity.

*　　　*　　　*

Before we embark on the long straight line that a book is, let me describe how the material is organized.

The first chapter is essentially about the question of whether or not ethics are natural. Is part of human nature that we are moral and cooperative, or coolly self-interested, without the imagination for the uses of generosity? Or both? And this can be usefully reviewed in the context of what is known about our history and prehistory—about our history as an animal and about our history of self-description and self-accountancy.

The second chapter is a brief description of how the social sciences have been formed in relation to the industrial system, and what this has meant for the communal self-consciousness of our societies—in particular for the difference that seems to emerge between those systems that existed before industrialization and those that accompanied and followed it.

The third shows that the idea of management is surprisingly new. It has its origins in engineering and the military, with considerable consequence for the forms of modern social organization. In the fourth chapter, I try to show that the psychological sciences have conspired with the needs of industry to produce a psycho-industrial complex every bit as distinctive and every bit as formidable—and even more basic—as the military-industrial complex of which President Dwight Eisenhower warned his people. The fifth chapter is an analysis of literacy as a central feature of the industrial system. I try to show how significant it is for the way in which work and communication occur. Related to literacy is ideology, and some discussion of that is what the second half of the chapter is about.

The sixth chapter focuses on family life and how the productive system affects the reproductive, while the seventh goes into some detail about the way in which feminism and other views of gender relate to our economic system. The eighth chapter is about how we deal with the material world—how and why we make things and places by design, and then how we plan to defend our own and destroy other people's, again by plan. The inevitable concluding chapter suggests what all this may mean for those who try to create and execute social policies, and for the sense of fun which industrial citizens are able to enjoy.

How do I propose to discuss all this in the context of the triangle of forces with which I began? There is most knowledge about industrial people, who have produced information as profusely as everything else. So a scholar looking at all this must decide that "less is more." As to agricultural and pastoral ethics, these have been the subjects of priests and scholars and universities for as long as the idea of disciplined formal thought has existed. Consequently, anyone writing now about all this has to accept in confident humility that there is too much to do. Which should not however mean doing nothing.

*   *   *

Does the persistence of the ethical question and the almost extravagant attention paid to it reveal the possibility that ethics are unnatural to humans? That is, paradoxically, do we engage in such long-standing controversy about this issue precisely because *Homo sapiens* is not *Homo ethicus,* is not a species endowed with a full-fledged natural morality and so must struggle anew each generation, each New Year's Day, perhaps each hour, to find and refine the right way of doing social life and being a person? This is the third part of the triangle, about our hunter-gatherer nature, and it is totally impossible to write with any conviction about whatever happened in our groups in the millions-years-old past. We are in a condition of dire speculation here. We have to face this fact.

Nevertheless humans naturally seem to make pronouncements about human nature as predictably as we sweat during long footraces. Surely the assertion, "Humans have no behavioral human nature whatsoever," is the most extreme possible statement about our behavioral biology. Obviously there are some conclusions we can draw from the fossil record, from knowing about primates and other animals. And we can use the comparative methods in social science, which can at the very least tell us what kind of human behaviors happen the most, and possibly why, and what normal inner mechanisms of brain and body are mobilized to achieve normal outcomes. But again, the data are considerable, and considerably heterogeneous. It is a troubling challenge to make sense of them.

But we must try. One of my favorite replies to critics of this

15

sort of theorizing or, sometimes, of any theorizing, is to quote the English economist Alfred Marshall, who informed us, "The most reckless theorist is he who presumes to let the facts speak for themselves." We have some facts about the past. Our present lives bristle with facts of all our events, utterances, and experiences. There has got to be a connection between now and then. Whichever poet it was understood something serious when he said, "To the blind everything is sudden." Are the moral and procedural uncertainty and controversy we now endure the sudden result of our blindness to our past? What is the link between the productive system we have produced, our flair and failings as a species, and the myriad disagreeable facts we are obliged to inspect if we are to be fair to ourselves, each other, and the universe?

What is the moral missing link?

1. The Moral Missing Link

Embrace the force and detail of our evolutionary social history and you will find that moral missing link. This is the argument of this chapter. Biological evolution produced the real beginning of real ethics. "Good" and "bad" as ideas are rooted in bodily tissue as realities. Recall that throughout most of our history we lived in small groups of 25 to 200. Many if not most of the people who lived around us were near or distant relatives. What we did unto others to some real extent we did to ourselves. In other animals, this centrality of family life has provided scientists with the basis for developing the powerful new tool called "the genetics of altruism" —about which more later.

In the human case, this centrality is as compelling as can be. We are the family animals par excellence, given how much we have to learn and how long it takes to learn it, and how directly and elaborately family members are involved in this extensive process. It provides nothing less than a direct and full refutation of Hobbes's grim opinion that every man's hand was raised against every other man's and that life was necessarily nasty, brutish, and short.

So long, that is, as we remain encircled by family and committed principally to the family circle, to its protection, expansion, to enjoying and enduring it. So long, that is, as we don't have to emigrate to the land of strangers, in the endless vista where people are not family. That is, not familiar. In another chapter I will discuss the profound implications of the dichotomy made by the industrial system between productive and reproductive elements of life, and I will try to show how this affects modern *Homo sapi-*

17

ens's capacity for ethical behavior. But now I want to explore the origins of ethics. I do not think that human ethics arose full-blown from the imaginations or certainties of priests or philosophers or gangsters. Then there has to be some other origin. Since people appear to be so concerned with who is good and who bad and why things go wrong, and since people are so soothed by stories of triumphant justice, let's speculate there is a kind of gene for moralizing.

Or is there? The controversy is ancient. For example, even those ancestral protagonists Plato and Aristotle took clear sides early on. Plato claimed that human beings created moral laws and then lived up to them with varying degrees of success. The laws themselves varied in quality. So the overall quality of moral life could be judged by the quality of a community's laws and by how well it observed them. How well was the morality play written? How well was it played?

Aristotle on the other hand asserted that human morality was a natural phenomenon. Therefore good communal life had to express the natural characteristics appropriate to our kind of creature. A long time later, his point was boosted by Darwin's fierce placement of man in nature, and particularly by the explanation of how natural selection operated on function as well as structure —on behavior as well as bodies. But the controversy remains unsettled. At the same time as Darwin described the roots of human behavior, the industrial system was permitting people substantial emancipation from their circumstances—which had been seen as rather immutable by medieval eyes. Were we now free? Or still constrained? Once again, the lines were sharply drawn in this analytical contest, the stakes higher than ever.

For their part, Aristotelian naturalists found support for their conclusions in the seamless connection between then and now, between people and other animals, and between our nature and our action. In Aristotle's famous sentence, "Man is by nature a political animal," aside from his prescient use of the word "animal," his phrase "by nature" is central. It suggests the bias in enthusiasms and skill toward that endless chronic ruckus, politicking, which we know happens as vivaciously among marmosets as among royalty, in typing pools as in laboratories, in families as in armies. More correct than he knew or than we mostly still acknowledge, Aristotle defined our principal product as process, as the process itself. Perhaps he even thought politics was fun, perhaps even that living itself was fun.

By contrast, the apparently more open-ended Platonist position was vigorously strengthened by the success of the industrial system in stimulating vast and genuine changes in ways of human life. Was it not the case that we suffered from few constraints when we could move rapidly by machines, make goods easily and quickly, could communicate instantly through the air much beyond the reach of eye and ear? Did not the power of science and technology take us far from our indigenous human frailty and offer us options so formidable that anyone who focused on limits not opportunities was out of touch with the real forces of contemporary life? Republican emancipation accompanied industrialization in many societies. More or less radical reforms secured a sturdy place in the system of the world. So why not assume change as the constant, and, true to Plato, assume that form follows decision, that *will* determines, that *is* can follow *ought?* Science at once offered an insight into the fixity of biology but also the promise of possibly limitless technological liberation from any fixity at all.

The durability of both Plato's and Aristotle's positions suggests there is some value in each, of course. My own effort in this chapter will be to suggest that Plato's enthusiasm has falsely overwhelmed Aristotle's empiricism, and that despite, and even because of, the success of the industrial way in producing a sense of emancipation, nevertheless there remains a basic human moral nature which finally must be taken into any account of human possibility.

But how are Plato and industrialism particularly compatible? The clearest index of this I believe is the character of the preeminent psychological theory associated with the industrial pattern—behaviorism. Essentially, behaviorism favors the environment of an animal, and particularly of humans, as the predominating influence over what happens in a being's life. This is in effect John Locke's *tabula rasa* proposal that at birth the mind is a blank slate, to be filled in by ideas and impressions. Industrial success improved the circumstances of life, which was a persuasive practical inducement to forego contemplation of the primordial and instead to emphasize potential. Why bother about the past when the present was intriguingly fulsome and when it promised such an elaborately enhanced future?

In retrospect, the alliance of environmentalist behaviorism with industrial technology was almost inevitable. It is not surprising that in both the United States and the USSR the work of Pavlov was so influential. In both these massive industrializing communities, the open-ended view of human character was so much more attractive than any view limited by the intransigence of our species's character. The roots of this go deep. As Klaus Sherer commented in 1980 to a scientific meeting in Bad Homburg, West Germany, "Plato's early division of the human psyche into cognition, emotion, and conation has profoundly affected virtually all scientific approaches to the study of human nature and human behavior. . . . The appropriateness of this . . . has seemed so readily apparent that its adequacy has been rarely challenged. . . . Emotion . . . is seen as a regrettable imperfection in an otherwise perfect cognitive machine." (Scherer, 1982, p. 507) It is in keeping with the behaviorist canon that B. F. Skinner, its most prominent modern exponent, should have said clearly if also somewhat shockingly in his autobiography: "I . . . do not think feelings are important. Freud is probably responsible for the extent to which they are taken seriously." (Skinner, 1983, p. 24) Even in Freudianism, the psychological theory perhaps most attentive to the primordial, the principal endeavor was therapeutic. The individual by introspective analysis could become emancipated from the inner forces of psychological nature. Clients of this method could "work through" whatever dolors and meannesses their flesh and spirit were heir to. They could "shrink" their past. Then they could face and embrace the world with a conviviality and self-knowledge triumphantly geared to a process of constant improvement of the self and the wider social context.

Would Freudianism have become so influential had it not a therapeutic "get-out clause" that mitigated its somber picture of the human condition? In anthropology, too, the dominating theme of ethnographic work was: how different are different people; how variable the ways of mankind; how responsive we are to outside forces; how little inner constraint there is of culture; how firmly determinant is the force of culture! In the now famous, still controversial case of Margaret Mead and Samoa (Freeman, 1983), her assertion that the fortunate Samoan adolescents suffered little of the trauma and confusion of their Euro-American age-mates has been described as a complex if understandable error. Nonetheless it helped produce a heretofore accepted basis for a view of human behavior: that it is so variable we may share no important natural patterns at all.

I draw an extreme picture. But the picture is really a cartoon, very sharply drawn, extreme in itself, of the conception the dominant group of social scientists have maintained of human culture for half a century. I am reminded of a line uttered by W. C. Fields: "Hugh Briss is back in town." Hubris has been intellectual mayor of the college town for decades and it has only recently become clear that he is not up to the job. If all this seems rather tinged with bitterness, it is, because the struggles within science over how social nature could be described have been fueled not only by the usual wholesome disagreements over data and their interpretation but also over approaches to experience that lurch from sophisticated ideologies to banal and simple prejudices to wishful thinking, energized always by the exemplary power of the economic engine. After all, if man can make so many things in so many different ways, and produce so many styles of dance and cut of hat, then is he not truly almost limitless in his estimate of himself and his collective future?

For anyone familiar with the recent twenty-five years of discussion of human nature, all this will seem highly familiar and uninterestingly tedious. And so it is. But perhaps more interesting is the curiously durable relationship between biology and ethics, a link firmly drawn by John Stuart Mill, who announced that any recognition of a biological "is" could hinder the opportunity to achieve a sociological "ought." An old story, that continues to vex practitioners of the arts of the discernible on the one hand—scientists—and of the arts of the possible—politicians—on the other.

Let us consider the proposition that we are a self-mistrusting species—that a persistent feature of our philosophical concern has been about sin original and sin conventional, about renunciation and forgiveness, about the embrace of spirituality and the rejection of animality, even about the odd fact that, as for unfortunate Adam and Eve, knowledge itself is evidently corrupting. Do we attend to ideologues and follow gurus, worship saints and make pilgrimages, because of an almost cellular dismay about ourselves? In other words, is the fall from grace the same phenomenon as species-dismay?

In an earlier book, *Optimism: The Biology of Hope* (1979), I put the case that as a species we evolved a pattern of moderately overestimating the odds in our favor in a whole variety of situations, from love to war, or investment to the lottery, or religion to cheerleading. In part, this was a profound pattern related to organic health, and certainly to the neurophysiology of the brain. Now it seems it is also intertwined with the immune systems which have come to loom as such a large mystery in the study of disease and cure. Other animals, too, needed optimism. Their organic health, reproductive success, and general efficacy were in some sense imbued with an optimism-like tone. Knowing the odds is a cognitive business. So the brain of even simple animals must be involved in assessment, and then discouragement or satisfaction. Humans are supermuscled as to brain, so the matter is endlessly more complex. Not only can we assess the real odds pro or con an action, but we also can create fictitious odds about fictitious situations; can create Heaven and Hell, Brahmans and Untouchables, Café Society to which few are called but many find beckoning.

When the brain considers the future with congenial expectation, it produces optimism. When it faces the present and assesses the past, it loses courage. It develops fear. It produces ethics. When we are not convinced that life *will* go well, we set about insisting how it *should* go well. Ethics are intrinsic to how we confront reality. Far from being a luxurious flower of economically or politically developed cultures, the ethical impulse seems more likely one predictable outcome of a sense of skeptical despair an imaginative animal has had good and frequent reason to experience.

At any level of technology or organization, people generate rules. From early childhood on, as Piaget among others has shown, the rule-making animal fusses about what is right, what is wrong, who is right, who is wrong—the good guys and the bad guys. Ethical behavior is a primitive behavior. Even though it calls us all to the highest standards and lays claim to the most generous of human purposes, it is as basic a business as suckling or stalking. It involves ancient social responses which we share with other creatures.

In a very interesting essay, the anthropologist Christopher Boehm has argued that we share morality with the other primates. But, compared with other primates, humans are less well adapted to tolerate submission than dominance. For other primates, being number two or three or ten is a relatively comfortable and stable situation. But not for us. Thus we have had more need than the other primates to generate moral structures to alleviate the stresses and strains of inequality and to keep all members in the group with reasonable contentment. In particular, Boehm argues, early hominids developed skills at deliberate, moral, third-party interference. We invented the referee, whose novel achievement was to prevent interference with the group solidarity necessary for cooperative hunting and gathering, and with the group effectiveness we needed when we lost the protection of living in trees and became watchful tenants of ground-level real estate. (Boehm, 1982) Whatever one thinks of this bold assertion about the chronological depths of our legal knack, what is certainly new in the human story is the codification and interpretation our great brain permits. It has also magnified the importance of ethics through our development of a corps of priests, philosophers, lawyers, and now folk activists (sometimes also called terrorists), whose work is to take simple, small, or singular ideas and lever them into practical politics as effectively as they can.

Let me describe an experiment of significance for understanding where social structure comes from. It pertains to a broad central question in social science: Is society in the genes, or principally the result of external (such as economic) circumstances which coerce organized social endeavor? This is a question of very fundamental philosophical concern. Is social behavior a higher-order or lower-order function? Does it require active, thoughtful planning and consideration? Or does it emerge with generous spontaneity as a feature of life itself?

Three researchers from the Laboratory of Brain Evolution and Behavior of the U.S. National Institutes of Mental Health in Maryland removed the neocortex from newborn hamsters, leaving intact the more primitive striatal complex of brain elements and the even more primitive limbic system. The point of the experiment was to determine if development of a relatively familiar array of hamster behavior was possible, despite the absence of the higher-order cognitive functioning associated with the neocortex. The neocortex, the most recent evolution of hamster brain, and of other animals too, would be metaphorically most likely essential for complex social behavior. This brain tissue was probably developed specifically to cope with complexity.

The hapless animals were operated on a day or two after birth, while a control group was given similar treatment but without destruction of brain tissue. After surgery, the animals were returned to their habitat and their behavior observed:

Hamsters devoid of neocortex grew at the normal rate and resembled their litter mates with respect to the time of development of hamster-typical behavior. The list of observed behaviors included thermotaxis (seeking comfort in heat), play-fighting, digging, seed cracking, food pouching, hoard and nest building, tunnel blocking, scent marking, aggression, territorial defense, circadian activity rhythms, species preference, mating, and breeding. . . . Although males without neocortex had some motor difficulty during mating and required twice the usual number of intromissions to achieve ejaculation, they displayed normal sexual arousal, performed the complete copulatory act, and successfully impregnated females. The experimental females showed an estrus cycle, readily copulated with males, conceived, gave birth, successfully reared their young. (Murphy, et al., 1981, p. 460)

A surprisingly complete inventory of the behaviors of normal animals was produced by these tissue-deprived creatures. Despite one further experimental piece of surgery, the loss of the mid-line limbic structures, the hamsters continued to show the behavior already indicated, with the important exception that they "displayed no play-fighting during development and exhibited severe deficits in maternal behavior." In addition, "the animals without neocortex were generally more difficult to handle than the controls; but those with additional loss of the midline limbic structures exhibited a ferocity that led their handlers to refer to them as 'wild.' " *(ibid.)*

This experiment is intriguing because it shows how much of a relatively normal hamster existence is possible even with the amount of brain loss described here. The authors assert that the evolution of nursing, maternal care, and play were important to the shift from reptile to mammal existence, and the role of the damaged limbic system suggests how deeply involved in producing relatively highly sociable behaviors are even ancient neural structures.

Even if hamster social life seems simple to us, nevertheless it is highly complex and interactively dense, from the hamster's point of view at least, and broadly speaking as a phenomenon of nature also. But it can be generated by relatively primitive parts of these animals' cognitive instruments. We need not assume that hamsters possess "will." Under normal circumstances they will try to avoid disruption, aggression, and antisociability. And they probably have no moral or ideological perception—that hamster social life is more moral than hamster antisocial life, or to rear one's pups adequately rather than cruelly, and so on. The absence of tissue to process higher-level information reveals that the emergence of social behavior can occur with a mysterious and primitive clarity; the underlying story of hamster sociability is clearly told. It is as if we were watching a ballet, perhaps without hearing the music.

This is rather far away from problems of human peace and war and matters such as equity, dignity, crime, and so forth. Yet the experiment, and other work comparable to it, suggests that there is a force to the social impulse which is profoundly ancient —millions and millions of years in development. As the animal with what appears to be the most complex social behavior, it may be that, as the early psychologist McDougall opined, we may have more "instincts," not fewer. That is, more elements of our behavioral process are firmly rooted in the selected experience of our species and reflected anew in each generation.

Let's assume for a moment that this is so, and that we come equipped—wired—with a relatively elaborated set of social propensities, needs, skills, and enthusiasms. Why then are we so furiously interested in and so furiously concerned about rectitude? If our social natures could once carry us along, why now do we have such a problem getting along? Or at least, why do we think that we do? If hamsters can demonstrate a quite full sample of their normal behavior even without their neocortical tissue, why can't we, with it, also find some sense of appropriateness and fit?

But this might be itself part of the problem. Perhaps the very existence of our cortically based understanding of the world compels us to produce ethical systems—because we are smart enough to know what to fear or suspect, or what we are unable to avoid. Perhaps the special case of the industrial system is marked by an unusually great difficulty of taking ethical care and making ethics an ambient part of both intimate and public experience. Perhaps the industrial way does not reflect and does not stimulate that ethical knack which was part and parcel of our existence over the generations, with the exception of the most recent few.

The steps of my argument are as follows. A highly sophisticated animal prospered and grew more populous, in part because of the development of intellect. But he had a rather well developed social inventory beforehand. Out of the interaction of rules, emotions, sexuality, and kinship, and the development of formal social institutions, emerged the likely development of ethical systems in human groups. This was particularly marked in the most recent phases of the movement, from hunting and gathering to pastoralism and agriculture. During this period there was a rush of ethical creativity, most likely because we needed new ethics, and fast. Then the industrial system interposed a new set of barriers between individual and community, between intimacy and the public. Now this ethical passion founders, or is in any event muted. The consequence is a world experienced by many as ethically problematic, if not almost beyond control. In essence this is all a classical philosophical question, and yet a prior question must be put. Not which philosophical ethics should apply, but why do we have philosophers at all? and philosophy? Why do we have such a population, small but influential, and as oddly but firmly esteemed as philosophers finally are? Is it because they are supposed to know something about this Eternal Triangle of the Three Ethics?

*   *   *

I am making the claim that ethics have a broad biological base, and therefore must explore how this could be so, and try to show the history and prehistory of the various elements of moral action with which I am concerned. So it is necessary to begin at the beginning, at the first analytical principles.

Darwin's basic question was: How do variations in body, physiology, and behavior reflect themselves in reproductive success, and thus in the origin of species? The red breast of the robin works. The peacock's plume apparently does, too. Did Paleolithic ethical behavior have some sexual allure? The suggestion has been made—and pop singers seem to prove it in various ways each generation—that the evolution of language owed much to the songs of courtship and the reproductivity of skillful speakers. Even in songbirds, researchers at Rockefeller University recently have shown that there is a clear and significant relationship between male singing, the ability to learn it, the hormone testosterone, and male reproductive success. (Nottebohm, 1982) An inner physiological environment appears to affect how successfully an individual bird manages to make the largest possible individual statement: reproducing itself. And that this is related to something as literally lyrical and interactive as singing suggests the hard connection— even if it's variable—between courtship, communication, the body, and the origin and continuation of species.

Among humans the matter is hardly as simple, just as the

26

relationship between song, speech, and courtship cannot be reduced to trite formulae. There is a provocative mystery here nonetheless, particularly if one begins with a reductionist position about language such as Noam Chomsky's, for whom "language is divorced from other (and earlier) forms of thinking. . . . [Chomsky] repeatedly invokes the striking, if somewhat bizarre metaphor of the mind as a collection of organs, rather like the liver or the heart. We do not speak of the heart as learning to beat but rather as maturing according to its genetic timetable . . . we should conceive of language (and other 'organs of the mind' . . .) as mental entities that are programmed to unfold over time." (Piatelli-Palmerini, 1980) Should language as a piece of a person's life unfold in this way, there is a reasonable authority to the suggestion that at adolescence with all its shift in reproductive potential, something happens also in the relationship between what is said, what and who are desired, and how all this is phrased. Troubadours play to willing listeners.

There is another part of the puzzle of how life is formed, too, which is being slowly but surely solved by biological scientists, and that is how kinship—"genetic relatedness" is the technical term—appears to affect the social behavior of even creatures as simple as tadpoles and as exotic as hordes of bats. This will prove important for the argument of this book. It is enough here to note that with almost wholly unexpected predictability and logic, biological creatures act differently toward kin than to non-kin, even when it is difficult to know how on earth they can make this distinction in the first place—for example, all those clamorous bats in a cave. And why, in the second, should they act in ways apparently contradictory to those broad notions of self interest that have supported theories of nature red in tooth and claw, applied across the board from hunting dogs to entrepreneurs. We know that many species of animals conscientiously attend to the needs of their own offspring even when this may be "costly." But the new elaboration of extensive kinship behavior must give pause to anyone who still insists that the only natural ethic is based on individualism.

Let me linger on this for a moment. What has essentially happened in biology is that there now exists a genetic basis for altruism—behavior of animal A that appears to benefit animal B more than A itself. The reason is by now well known and relatively simple. Let's assume a brother and sister of the same parents. They

27

share 50 percent of their specific genes. (Only identical twins would share 100 percent.) If Brother requires assistance, for example, with securing resources appropriate to successful courtship, it is reasonable for Sister to help out because any help she gives may be rewarded with offspring boasting 25 percent of her own genes —in a metaphorical sense, half as much as if she'd reproduced herself. Now if her new niece is up to reproduce, it will reward Sister with 12.5 percent of genetic reproduction if she contributes effort and resources to her niece's courtship. In fact, if she has enough brothers and sisters who reproduce, her own "genetic fitness" may be as well or better served by her total devotion to her family's reproductive life rather than to her own.

This whole process, called "inclusive fitness" and first described by the Englishman William J. Hamilton in 1964, has been shown to be an organized form among animals as various as songbirds and wild horses, jackals and lions, wolves and baboons. (Fox, 1979)

Mysteries remain. The behavior of animals lacking human-like consciousness and cognitive skill appears to follow principles requiring quite complex calculations of relationship and something like investment. The creatures act *as if* they were conscious calculators, even though it is unlikely they are able to perform such demanding mental operations. Yet they are doing something, and the implication is that a heretofore unknown, presumably very subtle mechanism is at work. Of course it is relatively easy to understand the unambiguity of connection between mother and offspring and between littermates. It is easy to comprehend how even simple animals could conduct themselves according to such bold kinship patterns. It is the first and second cousin kind of relative that poses the problem; but even in the close kin, the question remains: what, actually, is the family mechanism? Smell? The knowledge of the eyes? Habituation to physical closeness? A mystery ray?

Not that understanding and explaining these mechanisms is simple and uncontroversial, even if the patterns themselves may stand in quite bold relief. Since members of species overall share nearly all of their genes anyway, compared with the possible ones related to characteristics of any remote species, it makes genetic sense for all members of species to be as altruistic to all other members as to their own kin, since their long-run genetic benefit is virtually the same. But the theory is really about particular genes, which may not be radically important for the species's success but which do play a role in sexual and hence natural selection—characteristics such as appearance, pace of movement, size, song quality, and so on. That is, families exist; resemblances between family members are real; this is the limited element of the large picture of concern here. I recall a line from William F. Whyte's classic *The Organization Man:* "The more exquisite distinctions are, the more important they become." (Whyte, 1956) This is really what the kin selection story is about. What *were* the differences between those Montagues and those Capulets?

The consequences of the mechanism of exquisite distinction can be enormous, "the more important they become." My son conducted an experiment for his seventh-grade science class. He acquired four male gerbils—two pairs, each pair of a different litter—and then examined the impact on their behavior of light-colored as opposed to black paper covering their cages. (As predicted, the darker the cage, the less of all behavior except sleep.) The two cages were side by side, equally well provisioned, and out of visual contact with each other. In neither cage did the brothers ever fight so far as we could see. They huddled and cuddled and slept in one fur ball. While there was no occasion for them to share any mutually rewarding or interesting cooperative behavior, nevertheless they lived in a pacific manner belying the grim reputation gerbils endure at least among the parents of their potential custodians. Until the moment when, for the first time, one each of the two pairs were let out of their cages. Within seconds these well-fed, heretofore agreeable animals were literally locked in viciously violent combat and could well have produced one dead gerbil quickly had not my son pulled their clutching nails from each other's fur.

Why? Of course, "that's how gerbils are," and the response was to have been expected. Yet why does a species possess a mechanism that could yield murder among unrelated adult males and comity among brothers? Since so many more male gerbils are not brothers to each other than are, is this not a species-destroying adaptation? But murder on one side is mitigated by a famously high birth rate on the other.

However, I want to urge an aggressively naive perspective on the question, why don't the brothers kill each other? Since they live in the same cage, there could be more food, twice as much room by definition, no potential competition for mates should any come into the picture, no disturbance from the squeak of the exercise wheel, unlimited access to the few facilities of the cage, and at the very least a sense of autonomous control over one's circumstances. Yet the animal who really does interfere with the gerbil's life is left unharmed, while a total stranger is savagely and dangerously attacked. By any conventional economic or psychological calculation, this is senseless. But by the genetic calculation I described above, it is not senseless and is rather the contrary. Two small but potentially fierce animals find each other melded into comity by their close connection in a system which is essentially about their futures—about their family-based genetic futures. It is the most seemingly fugitive connection, for animals are presumably ignorant of genetics and ideas of reproductive success, and yet it is formidable enough as an inhibitor at least to prevent murder and preserve the peace. I happen to think that knowing about this pattern of the social world is as important as knowing about the law of gravity in the physical world.

My friend and colleague Robin Fox has written what I regard as a very significant paper in which he is able to show that those kinship categories anthropologists have always studied in fact correspond to biological categories. Fox made his reputation in anthropology as an analyst of kinship, and his *Kinship and Marriage* (1967) is an enduring contribution to the field. His more recent work is more directly about biology and evolution, in particular about the evolution of mind. What he tries to show in this paper (1979), and in his book *The Red Lamp of Incest* (1980) (which is about the evolution of inhibition, of the brain, and of categorizaton), is that there is a thorough interpenetration of the reproductive system, the way and rate in which the brain evolved, and for humans, in the relationship of all this to those often gorgeously elaborate family systems which have intrigued and sometimes dazzled anthropologists since the profession became self-conscious.

Let Fox speak for himself here: "There exists no human society which does not have classification of kin; it must therefore be accepted as a universal human attribute in the same way as language, of which, of course, it is a part. . . . Kinship grouping and kin-derived behavior do not make us unique; the naming of kin does." (Fox, 1979, p. 132) Because *Homo sapiens* moved relatively rapidly into varied and challenging environments and had to generate ways of responding to other groups of people, "it selected for speaking, classifying and rule-making creatures *who could apply these talents directly to the breeding system."* (p. 132) Later on, Fox adds another feature to this: "whatever it was that was succeeding became *built into the cortical processes.* This included the intellectual and emotional apparatus that we have been discussing. . . . This went together with an *anxiety* about the whole process. . . ." (p. 180, his italics)

The business of anxiety is particularly interesting. Given what is known about the widespread relationship of sexuality to guilt, uncertainty, insecurity, social control, taboo, and so on—as well as to joy, affirmation, fun, fulfillment, and so on—it is reasonable to expect close connection between sexuality and ethical or normative concerns. It seems Freud was quite right in placing sexual anxiety and concern at the core of his explanatory system. Finally a species's most important decisions are about its reproductive future. Because humans have an enormous consciousness of all these matters, the decision about with whom or when or whether to reproduce is both important and vastly ramified by the rules we produce, by the in laws and the outlaws, and by the overwhelmingly ambient impact on people's lives of the various moral interdictions that apply to their sexual lives.

For example, it is always important for males to believe that the offspring defined as theirs which they are helping raise and to whom they are providing goods, services, and time, are indeed their own. "Paternity certainty," this is called.

With humans, the matter is of course very complex. It was Othello's problem, in a nutshell, and various mechanisms are brought into play to offer fathers confidence about their offspring. There are very complicated ways of trying to ensure this, but one simple, charmingly simple, way is for people merely to announce to the father, "Oh, it looks just like you." This was shown clearly in a study of utterances surrounding newborns in hospitals; mothers and other relatives far more than by chance noted resemblance between baby and father, much more frequently than for example the baby was said to look like the mother: "Mothers were entirely responsible for the bias toward allegation of paternal resemblance." (Daly and Wilson, 1982) Even where it is claimed people do not know about the carnal origins of children and attribute them to various spirit-like machinations, among the Trobrianders studied by Malinowski (1929): "It is an offense to remark similarity to uterine kin and polite to assert resemblance to the father, who is said to influence the child's appearance in utero by his association with the pregnant mother." (cited in Daly and Wilson) So even here ideas about family life are molded to the reality of biological continuity. In a way this is hardly surprising, given how important a sex organ is the brain.

Let me review the steps so far.

The substantial points are (1) that other animals orient their behavior toward kin. In varying degrees they act as if they understand genetic principles, even if in our cognitive terms they do not. (2) Humans also are deeply affected by kinship, and while there is no direct link between culturally developed and assigned kinship terms and biological relationships, nevertheless there is a powerful association between the laws of genetics and the rules of kinship. (3) Insofar as this is deeply linked to the very evolution of the brain and to the human capacity for culture itself, then altruistic behavior toward members of one's family is probably as immutably and quintessentially human as bipedalism. With other animals, the mechanism of kin recognition is not always evident and often downright mysterious. With people, the definition of who is familiar is often very clear indeed. But evidently the whole matter is too important to be left to whatever subcortical mechanisms other animals use because it is commonplace in human cultures for the members and rules of kin group to be specified with relative precision—often, indeed, with quite striking detail and care.

The core of my argument is that biological evolution produced the real beginning of real ethics, in part because throughout most of our history we lived in small groups of 25 to 200, many of whom around us were near or distant relatives—"familiar." Hence the importance of the genetics of human altruism, and of what people think is good or bad.

This point of departure here may even be a comfort. It implies that the ethical passion and the sexual shiver are linked, that the very act of categorization and the process of thinking itself are inevitably rampant on an ethical field. It implies that the very basic fact of human gregariousness is a reflex of some moral knack. So if the circumstances of our time lead many people to doubt the reliability of this capacity, perhaps we must look to the circumstances, not to ourselves. Even if we produced the circumstances, we may with T. S. Eliot's Prufrock lament, "That is not what I meant at all. That is not it, at all."

It is possible we have been systematically misled about our

morality from the very beginning. Why should God have interfered with Eden as he did, evidently for the dual offenses of sexual awareness (sexual anxiety again!) and empirical skepticism, that forbidden fruit? And why blame poor Adam, whom after all God made? And why was what happened in Eden the "Fall"? And why were Adam and Eve so harshly and disproportionately ridiculed for their sexual frisson? Were not those perplexingly pleasurable nerve endings in their genitalia there for a purpose? Was orgasm an accidental spasm, which happened to be so mightily pleasing that (later on, when churches got going) its occurrence or not could be held up as a measure of obedience to God?

This is mad. No wonder practitioners of the morality trades have so enthusiastically separated man from animal, culture from nature, devotion from innocence. If morality is natural, then you don't need priests as much as you're likely to enjoy being informed by scientists. If morality is a biological phenomenon, then it is merely insulting to harass mankind for its current condition because of an historic Fall in the past and a putative Heaven in the future. When spirituality became a special flavor and ceased being fun, when mystical congregation and speculation became instead a matter of bare knees on cold stone and varying renunciations; when involvement with the seasons and the other subtle rhythms of nature became formalized into arbitrary rituals governed by functionaries, then the classical impulse for moral affiliation became translated into something else: into a calculation of ethical profit and loss supervised by an accountant Church and a demanding God. A new tax was born. The tithe. Ten percent for the first agents.

And yet by this same argument, the story of Genesis is an appropriate marker. Wrongly called "Genesis," it is more accurately an index of the end of one way of life and a shorthand description of the newly augmented involvement of God with His flock as it moved from the paradisaical rural ways of the hunter-gatherer to the more sedentary and populated forms of pastoralists and agriculturalists. It should have been called "The Book of Transition." New density, new forms of property, new population levels —an eruption.

Perhaps most important, there was the utterly new force of leverage. Two sheep produce many, a few seeds bear many fruit. For the first time multiplication tables and what appeared on the dining table were related. The uncertainty, promise, and openness of the new economic form almost paradoxically generated a cast of religious characters to reduce uncertainty, define promises, and constrain infinity. In our book *The Imperial Animal* (1970), Fox and I called agriculture "the great leap backward" because it separated *Homo sapiens* from the satisfactions and symmetries of the hunting-gathering life and produced that characteristically miserable figure, the peasant—whose long workday and remorseless commitment to work necessary to feed his face was like the obligation of our primate ancestors and cousins to forage at length for quickly digested fruits and vegetables which kept them on the job nearly all the time. On the other hand, eating meat is luxurious because it involves the consumption of another creature's food gathering and digestion. The cow's endless cud-chewing becomes our leisure time, our post-roast snooze. And hunting if not gathering remains a popular and prestigious activity in wealthy societies in which, obviously, it is the social action and the private emotion —the fun—not the protein, that induces otherwise often sedentary people to endure the effort, cost, and to some extent dangers of hunting.

Perhaps because of its association with landed elites among whom modern intellectual and scientific commentators rarely find themselves, and certainly because of antipathy to blood sports, hunting endures a poor reputation these industrial days. I share this general disaffection, but a strong mystique nevertheless persists about the sport and perhaps explains why it remains an activity involving countless people. For example, in an essay of quite wonderful verve and natural compassion, Spain's outstanding modern philosopher Ortega y Gasset offers an eloquent analysis and defense of hunting. While he identifies it as clearly, now, an activity for relatively privileged people because of the scarcity of animals and the crowding of our planet, his case about the philosophy and aesthetics of hunting is fascinating, if controversial. Not controversial at all is his rich understanding of even contemporary hunting compared with its Paleolithic form; his opinion is that we would all find Paleolithic hunting life as familiar as cool water were we back in it. "When we leave the city and go upon the mountains it is astonishing how naturally and rapidly we free ourselves from the worries, tempers, and ways of the real person we were, and the savage man springs anew in us. Our life seems to lose weight and the fresh and fragrant atmosphere of an adolescence circulates through it. We feel . . . submerged in Nature

. . . when the hunt places us in it we have the impression of returning to our old homestead. The hunting ground is never something exotic . . . but . . . something known beforehand, where we might always have been. . . ." (Ortega, 1972, p. 136)

Perhaps hunting and gathering were congenial ways for human beings to earn a living when the game was running, population was low, when there was an agreeable balance of needs and resources. And perhaps the reproductive system and the ethical system were also well suited to this deeply embedded adaptation. As John Pfeiffer (1977) has written, "For some fifteen million years, members of the family of man foraged as animals among animals. . . . The world was a wilderness 10,000 years ago. . . . There were fewer people in the whole world than there are now in New York City and they were all hunter-gatherers." (pp. 28–29)

Then why change? After all, the shift to agriculture was rapid and extensive. As Mark Cohen (1977) has observed: *"The most striking fact about early agriculture . . . is precisely that it is such a universal event.* Slightly more than 10,000 years ago, virtually all men lived on wild foods. By 2,000 years ago the overwhelming majority of men lived by farming. In the four million year history of *Homo sapiens,* the spread of agriculture was accomplished in about 8,000 years." (p. 5, his italics) Were people pushed onto the farm or pulled? The answer is of course uncertain. John Pfeiffer's suggestion is that the Neanderthals knew about agriculture 75,000 years ago, that the transition to agriculture occurred as early as 9000 B.C. in the Near East and as late as 8500 B.C. in the eastern United States and Southern Africa, and furthermore, that "early moves toward agriculture were probably made on a small-scale family basis." (*op. cit.,* p. 74) And yet, as Cohen indicates, many of the world's people chose agriculture during a relatively brief time span, whether or not they invented it and however they learned the techniques. (*op. cit.,* pp. 5–6) Did they do so because they wanted to? Or did they have to because of population and other pressures? Perhaps hunting and gathering were hardly as agreeable, and reliable, and productive as some anthropologists have claimed. For example, in an analysis of plant food collecting among the Alyawara, a hunting group in central Australia, Kristen Hawkes and James F. O'Connell suggest that the subsistence economy is difficult and demanding indeed, far more so than the theory of the vaunted affluent hunter would have us assume. (Hawkes and O'Connell, 1981)

There is a problem here, in that they focus on a hunter-gatherer group living in arid terrain where the game is poor and to which, presumably, these groups have been forced by pressure from possessors of more fruitful lands or because they elected to stay where they were despite ecological change over an extended period. It is difficult to infer from contemporary hunter-gatherers who live in very marginal lands what the prototypical "hunting life" was like in the Paleolithic and before. (Cohen even suggests that "contemporary hunting and gathering groups are anomalous simply by virtue of the fact that they are still hunters and gatherers. [They may even have genetic peculiarities which affect population growth. . . .]") (Cohen, *op.cit.,* p. 47) In general, I accept Cohen's proposition that population pressure was central in coercing the shift from hunting, a view shared by John Pfeiffer (1982) in his thorough speculation about the origins and function of art, particularly the cave paintings of the Upper Paleolithic. He sees the problem of declining or unreliable fauna as central not only to the emergence of art forms but to the maintenance of social bonds themselves. "We can imagine that a band which had always enjoyed success in the hunt may have suddenly encountered a dwindling of herds in its range and goaded by the prospect of starvation, joined up with other bands which meant wider sharing and less meat for its members." (Pfeiffer, 1982, p. 123) Interesting about the art of this period is the firm pattern of gradual increase in incidence and sophistication, which began about twenty thousand years ago and was probably related to the problem of sustaining social life in larger and larger groups with an increasingly unreliable supply of edible prey. Pfeiffer sees these symbolic artifacts as ways to remember, teach, learn, bear witness, instill fear and reverence in the young, immortalize the dead, and somehow incorporate untamed animals into the managed world. The success of the creators of these works is apparent from the immediacy of their impact even today. If they had a role in facilitating intergroup contact, it seems likely on the ground of our own response that they achieved their purpose. They *connect.* And they had, presumably, to function in this way until the next major innovation in communication, writing, which began its slow (and still incomplete) impact on our own species some 5,500 years ago.

But let us stand back for a moment and ask why larger and larger groups had greater and greater requirements of communication. In one sense, the answer is obvious: more people had to receive standardized information quickly, reliably, and inexpensively. In another sense, though, there is also a more interesting function being served: communication on a large scale permits the communicators to act as if they were making intimate exchange. "Good evening," says the newscaster, as if dropping in for coffee. His ratings in effect depend on whether you answer back. The essence of the interaction is, can a sense of real contact be made? "The camera doesn't lie," and the problem faced by public figures is, regardless of the number of their viewers or receivers, to replicate private straight talk in some acceptable manner. This is of course the principal reason the modern television TelePrompTer is far more reassuring than the earlier prompters, which were off to the side and made the reader shifty-eyed, or sheets of paper on a desk, which required the reader to look down rather than straight on. And not only does the through-the-lens device apparently have an impact on the viewer, but on the reader too; having had the opportunity to try both methods while doing a television series in Canada, I know that the sense of relief I felt with the through-the-lens method was so clear to me it must also have been to viewers. However uncomfortable I might have been with the camera altogether, the shifty-eyed mode exaggerated the difficulty of achieving some sense of congenial familiarity in the artificial, almost religious, environment of the TV studio. In any event, for political and marketing purposes the large scale is critically important, but for the communication itself the small scale is paramount.

Let me put this in a larger context. There is a law in biology called "Romer's Rule," developed by Alfred Romer, a former chairman of biology at Harvard and a theorist of evolution, which announces that animals change to remain the same—that they undergo minor mutations to avoid enduring major evolutionary adaptations. So an animal will evolve a shift in skin color, for example, which is a minor genetic change, in order to be able to achieve camouflage from a newly arrived predator in its homeland, instead of undergoing more direct but more demanding change such as in its mode or rate of locomotion. It is genetically easier to turn green when your territory becomes grassy than to develop wings or the speed of a panther. Similarly, it is easier when climate changes to accumulate the genetic basis for more body hair and then fur, rather than to move altogether to a warmer place or produce changes in the fundamental method of internal temperature control—this would require extremely complicated adjustments of metabolism, diurnal cycles, digestion, etc. So the small mutation permits the animal to adjust to changes in its social or physical environment without major biological change.

My adaptation of Romer's Rule for human culture is that human cultural differences are the equivalent of small mutations. They permit us to retain basic human patterns, ranging from internal temperature control to the support of important social bonds. These can be such as between mother and offspring or between interdependent coworkers—"This Bud's for you"—even in situations quite removed from the ancient hunting-gathering circumstances in which they evolved. So, "Good evening," says the cordial anchorman to 25 million people. However dazzling and extensive the technology, the core function of the newscaster is the fireside accounting of the events of the day and the fears and possible frolics of the morrow. As the Pope is just Father, the priest just Brother, the powerful nun Mother Superior, a large structure is functionally reduced to the psychological scale with which the human animal is comfortable. Perhaps one community places a high value on work as redemption, in the American Protestant or Swiss Calvinist setting, while another prefers the values of meditation and spiritual action, as among some Buddhists. The resulting differences will be in the amounts of extra wealth in the communities. But survival as a basic business will have to be attended to in both cases. So will child rearing, producing shelter and clothes so that the normal body temperature of 98.6° can be maintained relatively predictably. So will some rather formal and generally known relationships between fun and responsibility.

Of course not all adaptations to climate, neighboring groups, or general ecology will prove equally successful in terms of maintaining population or the sense of well-being, of the ability to adapt to new circumstances. I have already implied that agriculture placed greater burdens on the indigenous skills and vulnerabilities of *Homo sapiens* than hunting and gathering had. Now I am suggesting that an important force which helped produce the ethical codifications accompanying agriculture and pastoralism was precisely the one that could adjust a species with a certain behavioral grammar to a new set of requirements arising out of new and more crowded conditions of social life. These new schemes of ethics and laws were examples of Romer's Rule at work in the social world.

Needless to say, the industrial transformation has been even more dramatic (but with some "redeeming social value" I'll come to later) and my version of Romer's Rule has had barely any opportunity to find its application. Perhaps, even, our agri-ethics have been interfering with our freedom of creative, industrial maneuver! And the problem of scale seems as difficult to solve as it is ceaselessly invoked as a cause of our malaise—a virus bigger than its victim.

Los Angeles is a metaphor-city of the modern industrial age. Its emergence as a major metropolis *after* the widespread diffusion of automobile transportation has yielded an urban pattern of great novelty and comparative drama. As David Brodsley has written in his elegant book, "The freeway is literally a concrete testament to who we are, and it continues to structure the way we live. . . . [The freeways] rank with the mountains and the rivers in influencing the organization of a changing city, and uncontestably [sic] they are the single most important feature of the man-made landscape." (Brodsley, 1982, p. 2) "Every time we merge with traffic we join our community in a wordless creed: belief in individual freedom, in a technological liberation from place and circumstance, in a democracy of personal mobility." (p. 5) Each car-owning citizen is theoretically in a space capsule, though earth-bound, and able to negotiate life and time with the relative freedom of movement within a region offering perhaps forty miles of options in any direction.

Yet what happens, even in the free L.A. of the freeway? In a study done among three hundred white middle-class women of Los Angeles, Drs. Michael McGuire and Susan Essock-Vitale of the UCLA Medical School asked questions about patterns of help-giving and help-receiving when illness occurred or help was needed for whatever reasons. As the researchers predicted, and hardly a surprise, helpful behavior was strongly correlated with kinship and the reproductive patterns associated with it. Relatives with younger children received more help than those with older; parents of older children were more likely to give help than those with younger. "Patterns of helping among a sample of Los Angeles women appear to have underlying regularities which are not obvious to the subjects themselves." (McGuire and Essock-Vitale, 1982, p. 9) In essence, relatively primordial emotions and arrangements persist in the sampled group even in Los Angeles, even among the freeways, even with the forty-mile radius of option, even without the cosy small-scale neighborhood of the traditional city in other parts of the world. The biology of reciprocity overcomes even the often beautiful lines of concrete which appear (perhaps falsely) in texture and force so antithetical to the stirrings of private inner needs and desires.

Even in déracinée Los Angeles, a predictable and stolid familism continues to create a sense of meaning and haven for mortals with cars when they or their kin grapple with a problem. Perhaps this study is misleading about the wider population and may principally reflect the patterns of middle-class life in which personal transport is readily available. Nevertheless, it suggests how recalcitrant even under relatively inhospitable conditions may be those social predispositions which I have claimed have been of crucial importance to maintaining human solidarities throughout our evolution. Of legend, Southern California is the fount of divorce and remarriage. But this does not drastically affect the McGuire–Essock-Vitale results because they focus in good measure on kinship reckoned through blood and not marriage. The difference is quite critical because while the nuclear family as an institution may be unstable, the wider system of blood relatives may become even more significant and durable given the fragility of marriage —marriage is after all optional kinship. Indeed, one of the chronic difficulties inherent in discussing kinship in current society is precisely the confusion between the nuclear family and marriage, and the wider network of blood relationships marked by genetic proximity. It is mainly the latter that will display those durable processes of affiliation based on increasingly well-known principles common to a host of species. Obviously the late twentieth century in Los Angeles or elsewhere in the industrial world is not exactly hospitable to familial existence. Yet there remains a family-oriented reciprocity, a symptom of general moral capacity.

But wait. Isn't family-oriented behavior selfish? Isn't it far from free-floating generosity of resource and spirit? Hasn't the durability of family-linked property and privilege been an anguishing cause of countless revolutions in the name of generosity against the inequities caused by family ownership?

Yes, and this is precisely a core problem which radical groups and social movements must address, and usually do—as for example in the original Israeli kibbutz movement, in which even child rearing was to be communal, let alone property, lest the bourgeois style infect children with the virus of its sweet and selfish particularity. The reiterated conflict endures between private familial enthusiasm, as a source of nepotism, and wider community equity, surely an important source of anonymously prepared and administered college admissions exams, for example. Later I will try to show how profoundly influential this conflict has been. Here my point is that it depends for its intensity on the recurrence in each generation—in each of the ten or so of the industrial period—of the kin interest to which I've referred.

There is one very important reservation about all this which we'll return to but which must be noted here, and that is: for biosocial reasons as basic as kin interest itself, there is likely to be an intransigent difference between how males and females respond to kinship, and how this affects their moral sense.

In a recent book describing her patient and probing research on how males and females view moral and social dilemmas and act on them, the social psychologist Carol Gilligan has broken new ground in respectfully addressing the question of gender difference and concluding that differences there are probably profound, but that these should not be viewed as invidious, nor of course employed for inequitable purposes. Among other things, she considers that females more than males see personal power as rooted in nurturance rather than aggressivity and demonstrating an enhanced concern with affiliation and attachment to others. Speaking broadly, she says, "My research suggests that men and women may speak different languages that they assume are the same, using similar words to encode disparate experiences of self and social relationships. . . . In the different voice of women lies the truth of an ethic of care, the tie between relationship and responsibility, and the origins of aggression in the failure of connection." (Gilligan, 1982, p. 73) While her technique of extrapolation from a relatively small sample has given some scholars pause, Gilligan's conclusions have seemed convincing to many commentators in the field, and at least resonate with some sense of truth to her readers. Though she does not link her proposal to a theory of sex differences rooted in any basic sense of biology, and may overgeneralize from a rather small sample, the emphasis of her work is congruent with developments in more frankly biologically based investigations, to some of which I have already referred.

Let us recall that the McGuire–Essock-Vitale study was of women. Would men have responded differently? Someone will have to find out, but there is good theoretical reason to believe, yes they will, reason outlined in a boldly speculative article by Jonah Western of the New York Zoological Society and Shirley Strum of the Department of Anthropology at the University of California in San Diego. They have assessed recent work on the biological evolution of social behavior and as a result suggest that if for no other reason than that males are far less likely (particularly in the primates, including ourselves) to know who their kin and offspring are than females, then since "a male has less certainty of kin and, in many cases, few or none available to him within a social group, he will be unable to favor kin or benefit from them as reliably as will a female. It is predicted, therefore, that social strategies involving unrelated individuals will be more common among males than females. . . ." (Western and Strum, 1983, p. 19) I find this argument particularly reassuring because it provides a basis for a hypothesis I published many years ago in *Men in Groups* (1969), which contained the assertion that human males and females with differential frequency formed one-sex bonds and that this pattern in fact occurred in other primates, too. At the time I did not have the benefit of the new work which Western and Strum employ. The relative crudeness of my argument in part at least reflected the state of the biosocial art in the late sixties. But the new material bolsters the case. The unexpected connectedness between, for example, the Gilligan work, the Western-Strum hypothesis, and my own much earlier one suggests that slowly but very surely a coherent picture is being drawn of the deep sources of human social affiliation.

If there are differences in how males and females respond to some similar social, environmental, and inner states, then this clearly means that the problem of relating female "is" to female "ought"—and ditto for males—will have to face this added complication. Does this mean there is or must be a war between the sexes? Why have the preeminent Utopias been written by men and largely pursued by them? If there is a war between the sexes, is it between two groups employing different rules in service of different strategies and who in effect are not engaged in the same confrontation? Is this why the recent disarticulation of the productive and reproductive systems is so emotionally fraught—because it reflects the even more basic differences I have alluded to? And does the consistently and persistently acrimonious debate about nature, nurture, feminism, anatomy, destiny, and cultural stereotyping in fact reflect a more portentous differentiation between male and female strategies toward the broad processes of social life? So that resolving the attendant controversies is even more problematic than the complexity and ruckus imply?

I think so, and think also that inattention to the factor of gender in the evolution of ethics has had the same misinforming impact as, earlier in scholarly time, the study of politics was impoverished because when political scientists wrote of people, they invariably meant men. The same applied for most economists. Even sociologists and psychologists hardly assumed any significant possibility of sex difference in their subjects, and talked confidently about populations, classes, ethnic and occupational groups, and so on. They assumed gender was at best a highly limited source of behavioral difference. If social and behavioral differences did occur, they were in turn caused by other social and behavioral differences; it was unnecessary to go deeper. Modern feminist scholarship and the array of other disciplines focusing on inner and outer sex differences have shown plainly that the assumption of similarity, whatever its cause, is wrong. Therefore we must look again, and again, at the impact of sexuality on ethics.

I wrote of the "moral missing link." Is one feature of this missing link an increasing disconnection between male and female ethical circumstances because of the changes wrought first by agriculture and now industry? In *Men in Groups,* I argued that the movement to hunting and gathering from predominantly gathering widened the behavioral differences between males and females as humans evolved in the context of differential tasks and opportunities. Have agriculture and industry in their turn also widened the differences, since they in themselves are so different from the original point of departure? It is worth considering, and so are the eventful and problematic existences of some young women of Sri Lanka who have been given coveted jobs as factory operatives in "Free Trade Zones" designed to bring foreign earnings into the country, jobs which so isolate them from their families' and lives' traditional trajectories that the areas are colloquially known as "Free Prostitution Zones." Such is the general enthusiasm for the productive aspects of this scheme that scant attention is paid by the (principally male) planners and managers to its broad reproductive implications and the concomitant emotional fallout. What may be seen as an ethical violation from the women's viewpoint is an ethical success from the men's. This is characteristic of an overall problem, not however one widely recognized as such, as for example, the matter of using or rejecting gender as a factor in determining pay-out schedules of pension schemes. Should they be different, for all males and for all females? Because as a group women live longer than men, should they receive lower payments over a longer time to ensure an equal amount for men who receive more per month for the six or seven years less they live on average? Whatever one's opinion on this, at least the issue is being directly joined. But in the behavioral sphere, as in the Sri Lanka case, the issue is evaded, in good measure because those framing the case do not recognize the factors that stem from gender and produce questionable impacts on people's lives—Sri Lankan women in this case.

A feature of modern moral theory is of course its endless controversiality. Writers such as Nozick, Rawls, MacIntyre, to say nothing of classic thinkers on the subject, have all sought to deal with the issue of what constitutes equity. Is the amount of controversy a measure of the complexity of the community itself—a *ragoût* with many flavors? Yes, almost inevitably; so first let's glance at some problems and solutions of a society that is far smaller than our own and technologically very simple by comparison.

The !Kung Bushmen are classical hunter-gatherers, living in relatively small communities with a high degree of communal self-consciousness. The need for companionship and cooperation among them is striking—neither an individual nor a single nuclear family lives alone. This is necessitated in part by the arduous hunting-and-gathering way of life. Also, the ownership of such resources as plant foods and waterholes is organized through band structure. An individual's right to these comes from band membership. Belonging to the band is in effect the only source of security and comfort. Lorna Marshall has pointed out that "their security and comfort must be achieved side-by-side with self-interest and much jealous watchfulness. Altruism, kindness, sympathy or genuine generosity were not qualities that I observed often in their behavior. However these qualities were not entirely lacking, especially between parents and offspring, between siblings, or between spouses." Further, "their desire to avoid both hostility and rejection leads them to conform in high degree to the unspoken social laws. . . . I think that most !Kung cannot bear the sense of rejection that mild disapproval makes them feel. If they do deviate they usually yield readily to expressed group opinion and reform their ways. They also conform to certain specific useful customs that are instruments for avoiding discord." Obviously people living in small-scale communities can have no impersonal focus of griev- ance—the system, the government, or some other similar human force. They must accept that the various elements which affect their lives are produced by them, and therefore to some extent, anyway, influenceable by themselves and their community mem- bers.

The same is true with a much-desired principal resource, meat. This is invariably shared according to clear rules about which person's poisoned arrow actually first contributed the poi- son that killed the animal, and then to other patterns in an elabo- rate network of reciprocity and obligation. Without refrigeration or other storage, meat has to be eaten quickly. Yet there must be some patterned and perceived equity to all this. In the long run the risks and benefits of an unpredictable form of securing food must be shared to maximize the survivability of the entire group.

This appears to happen. "The !Kung custom of sharing meat helps to keep stress and hostility over food at a low intensity. The practical value of using up meat when it is fresh is obvious to all, and the !Kung are fully aware of the enormous social value of the sharing custom. The fear of hunger is mitigated; the person with whom one shares will share in turn when he gets meat; people are sustained by a web of mutual obligation. If there is hunger it is commonly shared; there are no distinct haves and have-nots. One is not alone." (*ibid.*, p. 357)

In this kind of community also, of course, theft is extremely difficult if not impossible. Marshall records one case of a person who stole honey from a tree marked as the property of another, and the owner of the tree, in fury, killed the thief. Everyone knows everyone else's economy, and therefore there is relatively tight social control.

The important point is that equity and probity not only exist but are seen to exist—an important principle of course of all law. Here, what is seen to exist is not an impersonal force or a rectitudi- nous theory. It is a real, known process.

The old assertion about justice is that it not only be done but that it be seen to be done. This is the stuff of the great courtroom dramas. It fuels mystery stories and cowboy films with good guys and bad ones. The essence of the matter is that evil, once committed, has to be identified, its perpetrator uncovered, tried openly, judged, and punished. Not only is this often a technically interesting exercise—do the ballistics of the unusual Italian Beretta handgun exactly match the damaged and also unusual bullet lodged in the body of the dead investigative reporter? But also, again, as producers and consumers of courtroom drama know, it is all highly satisfying emotionally.

And why should it satisfy? Once again I suggest that this art is the handmaiden of that illusion. What we now regard as "emotional response" is no more nor less than an evolutionary memory, the reflection of countless similar events which have happened before and which have had impact on who we thought was good, who bad, who desirable, who an outcast, who an outlaw, who an in-law. If in the beginning (and really for the longest time), ethics and kinship were related, then all the emotionality associated with family, courtship, reproduction, parenthood, and so on would also enter into calculations of a wider sort later on, even in those larger or more contemporary structures in which family and polity are separated. The goings-on of familiar strangers now occur most overwhelmingly on television—Perry Mason, and others of a seemingly inexhaustible supply of heroic managers of morality who arrive weekly as apparently welcome guests to millions of homes. And before that, they were at home, too, in the book, either as the Three Musketeers, or Maigret, or Hercule Poirot.

And about the enemies of morality there is deep emotional interest too, in the outlaw, either putatively provident such as Robin Hood, or gratuitously antisocial, such as the great murderous Jack the Rippers, Sons of Sam, Boston Stranglers. It seems clear that their wide appeal taps an emotional system connected to those feeding all the love stories of the whole world. There is surely no real difference between a medieval morality play shown to illiterates in a tutorial or uplifting mode in a church, and any weekly television detective drama in which finally and inevitably the benefactor wins, though after varying degrees of challenge to the mores of the community. Malefactors may get away with, *only for a time,* clearly intriguing and in some sense exciting aberrant acts. Even if such productions are by the standards of high art clichéd and predictable, nevertheless they are working with something real and indigenous. They are not breaking new emotional ground; they are taking advantage of an audience prepared by prehistory for prime-time morality. And when, as in for example the *Dallas* saga, malefaction and kinship are frankly united, as they have always been in *Homo sapiens,* then—if the creators of the work somehow catch that old mode accurately—the mix of kinship and judgmentalism seems irresistible, even to people whose familiarity and connection with Dallas may be no greater than common use of the electric current which unites them with other viewers in a web of canned meaning.

Justice must not only be seen to be done, but people will try to see it being done, even when they are not involved. It is satisfying in some way we might be tempted to call primordial. With more information and a wiser eye, we can see it as in continuity with the past. Yet in how many law schools are courses given about the relationship between equity and emotion? Are lawyers trained to understand the phylogeny of probity? Are they provided any appropriate information about the possible role of justice in early formative hominid societies?

More than inadvertence or ethnocentrism may be involved here. When the goddess holding the scales of justice sports her blindfold, is she suggesting more than that she seeks to be impartial? Like a child who covers his face and assumes he is not seen, is the goddess of justice assuming that we can't see her inner turmoil, her concern about death, her fear of favor, and even her passion for justice? If not this, what *is* the goddess of justice hiding or revealing with her blindfold? The obvious point is: she operates without fear or favor. But then to do this, does she feel that she must not feel? Compare her to the three monkeys who perform the charade of "Hear no evil, see no evil, speak no evil," who must abandon three sensory modalities to avoid what is bad.

Why does the goddess of justice have to lose even one modality in order to confront what is good and fight what is bad? And are not the symbols of justice—the enormous steps and porticos of the Supreme Court Building in the United States, or comparable structures elsewhere—plainly meant to reveal the impersonality and size of the institution of justice, not its sense of intimacy, of connection and scale? Obviously government buildings are made to impress, and they are big particularly when they reflect the self-conscious pride of large communities. Nevertheless these monuments concretize a community's self-conception. They are effective. That shiver of awe, that sense of one's own almost unimportance in the presence of such a structure, clearly works through cognitive, almost visceral stimuli, which say, "I am so small and

I am to see this as a system which operates without the confusions of private pettiness. I am as important as anybody else to this building and what it means—and as unimportant. When the judge sits up high and I stand down low and must say, 'Yes, your Honor,' and, 'No, your Honor,' and look at the judge to affirm the honesty of my reply, this is how I felt when my parents said, 'Now you look at me, you look me straight in the eye,' when I had done something punishable." There is perhaps deliberate confusion here between the almost hypnotic impersonality of buildings and rooms larger than all but mythical life, and the use of relatively primitive responses to authority. A confusion which may require a cadre of practitioners called lawyers who are themselves uninvolved in any but a finite and technical way. Perhaps lawyers should be able to remain physiologically, that is emotionally, unperturbed (other things being equal) by the processes of the court and the events of the law's activity—surgeons of social pathology, with surgeons' remove.

Do I make all this seem too exotic? Let's consider the matter from the point of view of another species, let's say Mr. See No Chimp Evil. Say events occur in this individual's community which are immensely disturbing to its members—perhaps a female with young is beaten by a male emerging into adult status who wishes to find a reproductive life of his own. In nature, the issue will usually find some relatively quick resolution: either he secures the consent of the female and drives away an opponent male, or he is himself beaten, either by the female or more likely a coalition of females, or a male or males of the group. But in the human case, the action is freeze-framed. There is no immediate resolution. A uniformed individual chimp, wearing a cap, who has not been party to this action, enters the situation and essentially immobilizes the aggressive chimp, by force if necessary. He is kept away from kin and acquaintances for a time, and then required to appear before yet other chimps where he is accused of violating chimpanzee civil order. He is asked to describe the events in dispute. Various other individuals offer their versions. As a result of careful and overt discussion of the actual matter, perhaps of his motive, a decision is reached, and if he is found guilty, he is kept away from his kin and associates for an even longer period. Otherwise he is released to his normal life.

Consider what remarkable emotional adaptations are involved in all this for everyone concerned. The quite staggering

48

sophistication of the mechanisms of this action becomes all the more clear when viewed with the eyes of a chimpanzee. Bizarre though it may seem to compare a major law court with a primate altercation, if we understand how another primate might be baffled by such events, then we may appreciate how these same events may still seem odd to those enduring elements of our own being, those old brains, old nerves, old needs, which we retain as much as the chimpanzee has them. If a chimpanzee and a human are both living in a cruel dictatorship and are both in cold poor housing, only the human will understand that he is in a dictatorship. But both creatures will understand that they are cold. Both will avoid the dominant figure as much as possible.

The difference between a system of ethical relationships that depend on personal encounters and one that has an arbitrary formula, to which individual cases are applied, may be considerable. A personal example: When I was working at the London School of Economics and Political Science on my doctoral dissertation, my fieldwork took me to Ghana. There I studied the impact of independence on the civil service administration which had under the colonial system been the actual government. It was most convenient for me to live at the University of Ghana just outside of Accra, the capital, and I was given relatively inexpensive housing. And, as was the custom of both expatriates and Ghanaian members of faculty, I hired a servant who attended to the many chores required in tropical countries in addition to those of running any household. The man who worked for me was named Kofi; he had a wife and three children, and was a respected member of the community in which he lived, which was composed of his fellow Ewe people, not far from the university area. Kofi was an excellent cook, cheerful, and at about thirty-five years of age warmly knowledgeable about the byways of his community and the wider new Ghana of 1960–61, still emerging from an untested chrysalis.

One day he arrived for work drawn and bitter and explained that all his possessions had been stolen. Everything. "Oh," I quickly exclaimed, "you must go to the police." Since I had a car, I would drive him to the station, and he would make a report and the police presumably would deal with it all. No, he said, rather than that, could I kindly let him have six pounds—a huge sum, half a month's salary—so that he could go the next day to a ju-ju man who was exceptionally powerful, who lived on the other side of the

Volta River and was known far and wide for the potency of his magic.

I regarded this plan as likely to prove wholly ineffective. I confess to the youthful condescension of a formally schooled North American social scientist who concluded sadly that this was one more example of the morass of ineffective and incompetent superstition from which communities such as Ghana would have to emancipate themselves before achieving the reasoned clarity of a world like mine. Nevertheless, because Kofi had asked, because I was very fond of him and thought that at the very least this expedition would make him feel efficacious even if it were, as I expected it to be, ineffective, I provided the funds and he took the next day off. When he returned the day after his visit, I asked how had everything gone. Oh fine, he said; he had got all his things back.

"How?" Then he told me his reasoning and the story. Anyone who stole his intimate things must know him well and would be a part of his world and thus subject to the forces which an intimate world contained. Therefore the ju-ju man had simply insisted that all members of the community gather in a circle. Kofi would tell of his visit to the potent ju-ju man and then announce that the ju-ju man had asserted that a spell had been cast, and whoever was guilty had to rise in the circle and lead Kofi to his belongings. This happened. A man rose who had in fact been living in one of the rooms in Kofi's establishment and was an unfamilied man who had come into the community through a minor connection some time before. Neither there nor evidently anywhere else had he secured an adequate life. Precisely because of Kofi's generosity of spirit, he had taken the drastic action of absolute theft. He had taken all the things and hidden them in a forest, and when these were returned to Kofi, the man had to leave the town where he had tried to make a home and failed. Now he was imprisoned just as assuredly by his loneliness and the utter formlessness of his new life as if by steel prison bars.

Needless to say, this was a rapidly instructive and sobering episode for me, and underlined the extent to which my fourteen months in Ghana would instruct me about the relative narrowness of the social concepts I had so proudly and enthusiastically gleaned from my teachers and synthesized from my experience.

This is a case in which an external agent, a ju-ju man rather than a judge, was necessary for the solution of the problem; yet the system was able to work, presumably because everyone in the group believed in the power of the ju-ju man's expensive spell. The force of the whole group drawn around the social circle compelled the miscreant to acknowledge his violation of the group by leaving it. Of course it was also in a way a jury, though one that caused the suspect to judge himself. In Western courts, we may still use a jury, a jury of one's peers, in effect a version of what worked to produce justice in simpler times. Is not the foreman of the jury who enters the courtroom and announces to the judge, "Guilty, your Honor," or, "Not guilty, your Honor," as much symbol of an ancient ethical process as when Romeo and Juliet exchanged rapturous vows in the name of all impolitic lovers who preceded and followed them? We respond and understand because in both cases they reflect a common experience.

In an early film of Jane Goodall's with her chimps, there was an extraordinary scene involving a female with young who had attached herself to the outskirts of an existing group and clearly wished to join it. She sat quietly for some considerable time, at least as depicted by the film, untroubled by the inhabitants and not troubling them, but going about her business while, as it were, facing into the group, wanting into the group. Eventually she was permitted to enter when she was physically touched or groomed by one of the senior females. Thus acknowledged, she made her rounds of the adult males of the group, being touched on the neck or the back or the palm of the hand.

Then she took her place inside the group. Obviously group membership is not a random thing. It matters to Goodall's chimpanzees. It matters to exiles. Evidently it mattered to the man who sought the vigorous warmth of Kofi's life. The depth of response to membership is evident, at no time more than when vindictive groups try to preserve what they have by persecuting those they regard as deeply unfit for membership or confining them in solitary, the worst punishment which does not damage skin.

The perfect exercise of rationalism, even by conscientious and skilled jurists, for example, will not provide the emotional satisfactions that human beings require. Contemporary social groups may not provide such satisfactions, but this does not mean that the individuals working in them remain content. They may not even appreciate that they are malcontent or less than content—it has taken scientists decades to appreciate the depth and order of even children's emotions. People may display characteristics of alienation both from the process of securing a living and living a life in its social and convivial aspects.

The brain did not evolve as an organ exclusively or perhaps even principally for formal thought. It became the increasingly skilled accomplice of action. (Stebbins, 1982, pp. 372–78) We will turn later to the so-called scientific management movement, which tried to reduce industrial work to emotionless time-and-motion studies and to impose organization charts on work groups that were logically defensible but that as a matter of policy assumed emotions were not part of work. This tradition has in the long run failed to prove competitive with management theories such as the Japanese, which take for granted that webs of social solidarity will emerge in human groups, and that as careful attention must be paid to the theme and content of social and psychological intercourse as to the movement of materials for energy and the use of time. I may make rather much of this. However, I will try to show that the effort to quarantine the emotional life away from the economic has much more consequence than we think.

With important interim steps along the way, the movement to the industrial mode of life has been marked by efforts to reduce the importance of passionate encounter and reward official impersonality as a means of conducting predictable and equitable social life. This is of course uninterruptedly entangled with ethical behavior. The image remains haunting of the blindfolded goddess of justice.

Why do I emphasize the emotions quite as much as this, when I'm interested in discussing forms of social life that appear to be as removed from emotional interchange as can be—technological, financial, and so on? Why focus on the blindness of the goddess of justice?

The answer is that the emotions are guides to behavior. They summarize assessments of situations and are a creature's estimate of what its broad circumstances are—fear, safety, love, uncertainty—which lead to the choice of possible behaviors—flight, embrace, aloofness, and so on. Such assessments may be critical not only to enjoying life but to surviving. An animal required to operate without its emotional equipment is like a tourist in a foreign country who doesn't understand the language, the script, the meaning of signs, the colors and tastes of foods, or the implications of gatherings of people. Restricting appropriate material for communication—for example, emotional state—clearly may lead to nonunderstandings, if not misunderstandings. Consider the futility of trying to comprehend the needs and experiences of a child without attending to its emotional display: a smile, a cry, edginess, and so on. Should it be easier with adults, who retain the same emotional capacity but made more complicated, more based on emotional and other experience? In part this is the message of Carol Gilligan, that the modes of discourse which males and females use may be rather sharply marked by how differently they encapsulate and respond to emotional content—how adequate these are to reflect the logic or turbulence of inner experience, as well as to anatomize the discernible facts of the outside world.

Perhaps removing emotional information from a situation necessitates even more false diagnosis of it, most likely by precisely those "rational" procedures that gave rise to the lack of information in the first place. Trying to simplify makes things harder. In a way it is as if we are on an extremely complex ocean liner. The vessel has highly sophisticated and formally predictable internal systems—heating, cooling, etc. But it also has very poor navigation devices to help orient it as it makes its clever way . . . where? It is hardly surprising that people may become disoriented like a ship when they are expected to ignore or inhibit elements of their social lives that are in effect irreducible. The emotions may be channeled or denied, identified or scorned and arbitrated. Nonetheless they recur and recur. Take the by now almost universal understandings of the realm of experience Freud and his colleagues describe. Add more recent understandings of the importance of neurotransmitters and other chemical features of human experience. Now we can be certain that the effort to engage in social behavior without emotion is an extraordinarily exotic endeavor. Not that the effort is necessarily doomed to failure—even circus animals can be trained to perform unexpected tasks on schedule and on demand, and presumably without disruptive emotional display or experience. Nevertheless, that they do the tasks, as it were against their nature, is why we go to the circus to see them. That's how exotic that is. It is tempting to ask if there is a relationship between the extraordinary emotional and sexual denial of Victorian England and that country's innovative commitment to the Industrial Revolution it was so firmly abetting.

Let me consolidate for a moment. I am trying to draw a picture of a creature, man, living in a kind of new zoo ill-adapted to his basic behavioral nature. Nevertheless it also reflects important

53

elements of this nature. I am implying that something curious has happened—that a natural animal has produced an unnatural system. One important cost of this is rather profound ethical confusion. We are by nature committed to distinguishing between right and wrong. But we currently inhabit socioeconomic circumstances that make it difficult if not sometimes impossible to draw satisfying moral distinctions. The conditions which produced this dilemma were first directly related to the movement to agriculture, and more recently of course to the massive conquest of the planet and human species by the industrial way. So this argument has an element of economic determinism. But with a difference—that we take account of biosocial data and theory which pertain directly to our nature, a nature both compelled and released by genetic tradition.

In turn, this is a tradition mediated through that family life within which the act of reproduction usually occurs; a whole set of emotional connections are established and continued through kinship arrangements. It is a pattern located in small-scale social groups, from 25 to about 200.

But there was a break to the larger system, from the personal to impersonal, from status to contract, from the intimate to the official. What was required was a new set of ways of interacting with people who were strangers and therefore threatening, but who had to be treated evenly and without disruptive or alarming emotional display. One good ritualization of this is what happens when a head of state visits a foreign country. Often the first thing he does is review troops who do not attack or kidnap him. Sometimes cannon shots are fired, not at the visitor but out to sea.

In the literature of social science, two formidable German words have been used for decades to distinguish between the personal style and the impersonal one, the dread duo: *Gemeinschaft* and *Gesellschaft*. The first refers to what I take to be the evolutionarily natural state of human society, while the second refers to the modern form, which is inextricably tied to the industrial world. People who have traveled in Germany may recall that signs outside businesses may actually have one of these G words following the name of the business itself. The legal status of the enterprise is being defined, either as a closely held, family-based matter, or as an impersonal corporation in which responsibility is located in the enterprise, not in the people who work in it. Later I want to deal more fully with this dichotomy. It is enough to comment here that the sense of connection among people in *Ge-*

meinschaft derives from their unchangeable connectedness to the people around them—just as you cannot ever totally resign from your family. But in the *Gesellschaft* form, there is much more option and possibility of variable social grouping. Not incidentally, there is also far more opportunity for individuals to plan and control their own destiny. They can become independent contractors of their own lives.

The *Gemeinschaft* way was based on an immediate and reciprocal interaction of people and nature, and also on the obligation of members of groups—as among the famous !Kung Bushmen —to share goods and services on an open and definable basis. There was no impersonal "system" to rip off, no possibility for "the tragedy of the commons" in which what no one owned everyone could despoil because the scale of responsibility was beyond any individual's ken. People's social lives were rooted in ethical behavior involving emotionally flavored responses to others they almost invariably knew and probably knew well. Fine adjustments of often highly nuanced behavior would permit social life to carry on with at least some congeniality. People were committed to each other with almost implacable certainty, unless they left their own group, to live among strangers. The time scale in which events occurred was the life cycle itself. Longer than that even, because not only were the sins of the father visited on the son, and vice versa, but all other manner of influence crossed generations in a relatively seamless flow of causes and effects.

Compare that with what confronts modern industrial people: the opportunity to bomb total strangers half a planet away. To export to poor countries drugs ruled unsafe in wealthy ones. To exterminate whole peoples for the sake of the master race. To divide the world up into impractically vast and heterogeneous power blocs which are linked with almost farcical looseness to superpowers whose own internal politics are marked by conflict and contrast. Once upon a time we had the knack of managing intimate disagreements because there was broad equity between the social tasks to be accomplished and the tools available for the purpose. A nutcracker with which to crack nuts, not a power hammer. Now people may have relationships with people the other side of the globe with whom they are locked in cold and theoretical embrace.

So a military planner in Washington will with perfect logic lobby for a weapons system to respond to one proposed or achieved by the perceived enemy in Moscow: he has little choice so long as he stays in the system. But the consequences, military, economic, psychological, of the operation of his logic are not his responsibility. If they are anyone's responsibility, it is to politicians we must turn. Yet they in turn routinely argue, "We have no choice, we are bound by the logic of the preexisting analysis." The technologic implacably overwhelms intimate confidence or knowledge. I know a Russian philosopher who lives in Moscow and I have no more reason in my heart to blow him up with a bomb than I do my cousin Rhoda who lives in Washington, D.C.; yet in the set-up of my life, money extracted from me by my government is designated precisely to do Vladimir in. His government has a similar investment in Rhoda's military death.

Are the people making these decisions unethical, bad people? I know a few and I don't think they are. Their problem is our problem. The system is beyond individual people's confident knowledge and accurate control. Formal logic as an innovation was bad enough, but formal technology produced problems of unprecedented portent, to say nothing of vast benefit and chronic danger. The new tragedy of the commons is that what we share in common is a tragedy.

And the tools which we can use to analyze this dilemma are at the same time the product and the tools of the problem itself. For example, literacy has been essential to the development of the industrial system. Yet as anyone knows who has received a government form to complete or a document made by lawyers, reading may increase confusion and uncertainty. In addition, the world which is to be analyzed depends so thoroughly upon literacy that it seems impossible to separate the diagnostic tool from the disease to which it is directed. A more recent version of the same issue exists in the world of computers, where it is possible almost instantly to exchange sets of numbers summarizing huge numbers of events. There is little distance between life and its record, between what people do and the accounts of what they do. Practical action becomes immediate data; in a newly built pulp and paper mill in Wisconsin, the operations of every machine and person in the plant are monitored *four times a second.* All the information about everything is available to everybody at the same time and in the same way. Every quarter-second is Inspection Day.

The impact of this is not yet clear; among others, a psychologist at the Harvard Business School, Shoshanna Zuboff, is trying to determine how this fierce blitz of information affects the human beings both producing and consuming it. It is fascinating. Everyone must conform and inform at once. And everyone has grown a third eye as in the Cubist Picasso painting—to inspect the self as well as the world around. Andy Warhol once announced that in the future everyone would be famous for fifteen minutes. But in new-fangled factories everyone is being interviewed all the time, is famous right through the whole shift. What changes when a machine with eyes is one's colleague? Anything? Nothing?

Whatever the answer, major exotic innovations clearly affect increasingly large numbers of people. These changes are of often remarkably precise delicacy, nevertheless they will cumulatively matter. In a tiny case, I am able to report on the difference between typewriting with a manual and with a computer. The latter is faster and has more swoop. But it lies in wait once switched on. It hums impatiently when only its heart, not its keys, is activated. To end this provocation it is necessary willfully to halt the action, to shut down one's instrument, in itself a denial of literary life force. Writing being an unnatural act anyway, anything, even a machine that will stimulate it, is presumably a good thing for writers. A machine makes a difference for even the most solitary and reflective of jobs, writing. Obviously a symptom of larger processes affecting more social and complex endeavors.

Even if machines are born of economic sense and geared to achieve specific tasks, nonetheless they make an aesthetic and social impact too. The robot and its image suggest the extent to which machines may be endowed, however monstrously, with intimations of human meaning. Not that such intimations are necessarily monstrous, necessarily depressing, necessarily dehumanizing. There is of course a whole art of industrial design which I will describe as the true folk art of our time. There is also a deep interest in both mature and newly industrial economies in the frank form of machines and other made things. But it is with their impact on behavior and emotional experience that I am concerned here.

Machines are aesthetically important if only because they are new in the world. The human central nervous system must respond to them without the preparation that probably exists for dealing with trees, grass, water, the human face, sharp loud noises—the whole range of stimuli which have existed in our human world forever and in terms of which we moved around, ate and drank, relaxed and became frightened, in the deep context of which we lived. I think that it is this very novelty of machines—the fact that there is no set-up in our nervous systems for approaching them which has been tried and tested for literally generations—that allows them to be potentially more destabilizing or shocking or stupefying than natural things.

A very practical matter, this. Once when I was research director of the Harry Frank Guggenheim Foundation, there was a lunch of the board of directors and we were all in an elevator en route to the dining room. One of the members of the board in the elevator was William Baker, who for many years was director of the highly fertile Bell Laboratories of the AT&T system. Presumably because too many people were threatening to invade the elevator, it gave a loud, unpleasant, rasping warning buzz. Baker asked me, "Why in evolutionary terms is this noise unpleasant?" On the spur of the moment I could think only that the sound might remind us of a large breaking and falling tree—Get away!—or that it also had some characteristics of the roar of a large cat, a tiger, for example. Get away! again. Who knows why the buzzer was unpleasant; but then Baker provided a fascinating description of the problems the phone system had in dealing with bells and other signals—how do you fashion a signal that will be sufficiently stimulating so that you will actually respond to it as you are supposed to, but not so irritating that you pull wires out of walls or pour maple syrup onto the bell? Perhaps the human sensory system can tolerate a lot; but given the range of possibility, that still may not be very much.

Nevertheless, machines have been remarkably effective in intruding themselves on our social schedules. Because machines possess emotional heat and are usually expensive by comparison with natural things and people's time, they have been able to coerce human schedules so that people have to serve them. We work in the dead of the night even though it is dangerous and disruptive of the natural bodily and familial scheme. In Dickensian times we even forced young children to serve machines in ways wholly shocking and in retrospect morally incomprehensible. Most extremely in the forms of weapons but also as factories and for a while automobiles, machines have been able to override with their sheer, almost magical force our better judgment about their potential impact on our well-being. Virtually regardless of which system they're in and who owns them—U.S. Steel or U.S.S.R. Steel—the medical and safety impact of machines has taken hard years to acknowledge and to discipline. Even now there remain strong ob jections—obviously on economic grounds, but I suspect also for more emotional ones—to efforts restricting the use of machines which foul the air of employees and citizens, which may affect even the chromosomes through mutagenic chemical or radiation stimuli, and which will certainly (as I've noted) affect the circadian rhythm of a night-sleeping creature by requiring it to work at night.

I propose that machines have a unique capacity to violate moral human nature, whatever that is, and that their induction into the world has been so effective because we are aesthetically and ethically unprepared for them. We may master them when we make them and feel masterly when they are finished. But we are far less masters of their use than of their creation. This is most obvious with weapons, so obvious as to cause self-conscious communities paroxysms of communal self-doubt about what they are paying for and what their weapon machines may reap and destroy. But it happens with other machines, too, with impacts more intimate than jet fighters and more selective than atomic bomb–tipped rockets. The sleek invaders are not just at our gates but in our homes and plugged in.

Controversies remain about just how old is *Homo sapiens*. The most recent major finds that affect our estimate of this have placed us 400,000 years earlier in the hominid line than Lucy, the Ethiopian skeleton dated at 3,600,000 years ago, and found by Don Johanson and his colleagues.

Even about Lucy, the controversies swirl still. Did she walk as we walk, or with a bent-hip, bent-knee stance such as chimpanzees use? Do signs from the hand bones of Lucy suggest that she and her kind were occasionally partially arboreal as they strode about? (Roger Lewin, 1983) Whatever the detailed answers to such fascinating questions, the broad fact remains that our basic patterns of locomotion and perception were in place forever ago, before screaming jets, pneumatic drills, fluorescent lighting, cement right angles, and sixty-story buildings which have to sway a little to stay put.

Another cross-species comparison may visualize the point. An enduring and at first exciting discussion in primatology focused on whether or not man was the only toolmaker and how knowingly, if at all, other primates could use objects as tools. The upshot of it all is that, yes, chimps can poke twigs into tree trunks to which ants adhere, which the chimps then eat. They have used water to cleanse potatoes of sand. Many primates will use sticks as bats to threaten with, and they will hurl objects in a fairly effective way. But to them a car is merely shelter or a mirror or a bench. It is difficult to know what they would achieve with bombs or missiles or even rifles. Had a dominant terrestrial baboon male a pistol and a lesson in how to use it along with a box of bullets, rival males would be very likely killed. In short order the group would be driven away from its area or taken over by a rival group, unless the leader used his magic gun to try to control other groups as well. And unless he shared his gun and rotated with a colleague to keep guard over the situation, he would be soon deposed, most likely at first by his harem of females who would hardly be pleased at the carnage made possible by the small metallic machine.

And what if a chimp could drive or a spider use a fly-magnet or poisonous snakes produce killing gas instead of bites? Again I exaggerate perhaps, but we can recall that the owners of circus bears are well paid to teach them to ride cycles, throw balls, and perform a few other tasks with objects. And as we will see, even with humans instruction in technical tasks is no simple matter; military groups in particular appear in various countries to experience difficulty in turning over machines to persons who were not raised in cultures specifically committed to them. (In New York City in 1983 a police officer said that one of the few discernible problems with hiring more females and members of minorities for the force, rather than suburban white males, was that they drove poorly, having little experience; one recruit totaled two cars in three days.) This all becomes mightily significant when we consider the role of machines in modernization, and the worldwide fascination with that form of wealth and way of life associated with the industrial pattern. My suggestion is hardly novel: that like any other cultural artifact, machines are rooted in the milieu which produces them, and that they are translatable elsewhere only with some consciousness and perhaps difficulty. Nevertheless, it relates to a dual assertion: that machines may be interestingly unsettling even within the cultures that produce them because they have shapes, make noises, motions, and remove things out of our natural realm. Secondly, they may be doubly devastating in cultures foreign to the machine-making ones because they are not only intrinsically odd but also introduce almost virally the impact of social patterns from powerful but alien lands.

What is particularly effective about the industrial system and its artifacts is that par excellence it is the scheme which makes graven images. It does not leave proof of personal success to private Buddhist-like contemplation or Confucian sagacity or Muslim rectitude. In the formative period of industrialization, wealth was a sign of God's choice and satisfaction. A person could see his collection of things as proof not of selfishness but its opposite, of connection perhaps with God himself. Many have remarked on the link between Protestantism and capitalism. Industrialization follows right along. The bourgeois virtues could not have been more fulsomely rewarded than by a richly productive apparatus embedded in a scheme of authoritative possessive individualism. Small wonder it all convulsed the world. Small wonder perhaps the most broadly innovative urban architectural form of the twentieth century is the shopping mall. Small wonder economic development became a moral imperative. Perhaps the *Lares* and the *Penates,* the household and personal Roman gods, were reduced to a crucifix or two, if that; nevertheless the inner spaces of houses were enshrined with objects—many highly useful to be sure, but also of vivid symbolic value, some so much that when advertising as an art form got into its stride, it could induce buyers to replace otherwise adequate objects because of their obsolete symbolic value. Of course houses always boasted objects before industrialism; but the scale and emotional intensity of consumption of them seems new.

However, my main concern is not with the objects or even with the specific factories, devices, or processes that gave them rise, but rather with the array of social forms and expectations associated with them, and how in turn the new conditions had impact on an old species. I began this discussion by trying to show how important kinship was in the development of ethics and how small-scale reciprocity was likely to have been the customary formula for getting along. Unlike the other primates, *Homo sapiens* shares food extensively. The significance of this cannot be over-estimated. Mealtimes matter; they always did, they still do. With whom one shares food is sufficiently charged emotionally so that in some cultures, such as the Dutch or Japanese, a dinner invitation to the home is a major index of a close or important relationship. Even in cultures which are casual in this respect there is still awkwardness when, in a crowded restaurant, for example, strangers find themselves having to share a table for the period of a meal.

Certainly this seems related to the two major kinds of food sharing in which the human primate pioneered: between adults and young once they are weaned, and between males and females. Among the other primates, everyone gets their own food once they are no longer suckling. But among humans, few people get all their own food. With his vaunted picture of independence, Thoreau at Walden Pond was a cartoonist, an unwitting satirist. From babyhood on we depend upon others for something, sometime. The habit of this, the need for it, the expectation of it, and the pleasures and rewards of it make the endless matter of eating intrinsic to the equally recurrent process of exchange. Insofar as we are mammals anyway—defined by the fact that we get our food from another's body after birth—all the wired-in emotional components of mammalian feeding are extended and generalized to the wider social network. Why else should "homecooked taste" be a selling point for a bottled spaghetti sauce when most cooks in most homes lack the formal expertise of professional managers of industrial catering? Who would buy "guaranteed machine-made spaghetti sauce" in preference? Obviously freshness and direct knowledge of the diner will, among other factors, provide an advantage for the home cook. Yet there is an undeniably tangible additional ingredient: the reality of personal exchange.

This is the positive element. The negative one, particularly in small-scale societies, involves an injunction against the selfish use of food. As Audrey Richards writes, "The sharing of food is one of the first lessons in social behavior learnt by children in societies of this type. In a Bemba village in Zambia, in which education was of a most permissive type, the only thing for which children were punished was for eating food alone." (Richards, 1969, p. 30)

The whole question of transfer payments has come to vex economists galore, and also politicians concerned with flows of money mediated through the government from one group of people to another—for example, from wealthy orthodontists to welfare mothers or from industrial workers to pensioners on Medicaid. On the one hand writers such as Gilder argue that these payments are counterproductive, while others such as Galbraith see them as necessary civilizers of a rough and inefficient system. But important or wasteful as they may be, these impersonal transfer payments are much less interesting to an understanding of human ethics than the private ones which still constitute the primary arena of interchange between people—between parents and children, and among spouses or people living together.

The most obvious is between parents and children, a transfer that in industrial communities continues almost universally until puberty and frequently much later. Endlessly expensive, relentlessly diurnal, with neither season nor option, children must be fed and clothed, housed and amused, taught and circumscribed. And it all begins intensely. As Nicholas Blurton-Jones of the UCLA Medical School has indicated, we are a species whose infants prefer to feed frequently and modestly, and who must not therefore be left apart from their mothers for very long.

This is the traditional pre-bottle-feeding situation. Modern formulas provide richer milk than mothers do and thus permit longer intervals between feedings. But the possibility remains that frequent feeding is not only nutritionally advantageous to the infant but behaviorally also, and perhaps for the mother as well. I know many will protest that contemporary technology should free both mothers and infants from the coercive closeness of the mammalian beginning—that both might be better off for this emancipation. I doubt it, but this is another issue, except in the context of the spread of bottle feeding under the stimulus of forceful advertising in poor countries by Western manufacturers; the case of Nestlés is perhaps most prominent, and has involved efforts to induce that Swiss-based food company as well as others to stop advertising their bottle-milk formulas to new mothers in poor countries. In a very balanced review of the nutritional and contraceptive effects of breast feeding, in *Scientific American,* the reproductive biologist R. V. Short concludes: "It would be wrong to blame the manufacturers of powdered milk for having initiated the trend away from breast-feeding; it began centuries ago. They must bear much of the responsibility . . . for perpetuating and facilitating the trend in developing countries today, to the detriment of maternal and infant health. The fact that the U.S., where many of the powdered milk companies are based, was the sole nation in 1981 to refuse to endorse the WHO's recommended International Code of Marketing of Breast Milk Substitutes, which would limit the aggressive advertising and sale of powdered milk and condensed milk, tells its own story." (Short, 1984) Tells the story, that is, of a nation whose policy makers appear committed to the dual enthusiasms of supporting private business and consumer choice and of stimulating "modernity."

The importance of how, where, and with whom one feeds obviously extends beyond nutrition. This feeding is not merely metaphorical; the preoccupation with dieting in rich countries where—except from over-, not under-eating—food is not generally a life or death problem betrays the depth of the zest for intake. And not only intake but also presumably its accompaniment, giving. The wiring for exchange is wound up and ready to be used. In the United States it is estimated there are nearly 50 million each of dogs and cats, all principally dependent on humans for their food and care. While there are numerous flagrant cases of animal abuse and abandonment, overwhelmingly people accept their obligation to their pets. They operate as mammalian parents to creatures who have been withdrawn from their natural cat or dog mothers in order to serve human purposes. North American supermarkets appear to devote as much aisle space to pet foods as to biscuits! As far as the transfer from parent to child is concerned, in my experience this can only be understood fully by parents. Perhaps there is too much vitality and complexity in the interaction for its generosity to be apprehended theoretically. Of course people who adopt children or step-parents will also experience what I am writing about. The relationship of needer and provider is the core of the business. It is the quintessence of human generosity. A human breakthrough.

Primates are such competent creatures that they can feed themselves. But virtually everywhere until very recently in a few societies humans have split the work of acquiring food. The most salient split has been between what men and women did. Males hunted, females gathered. The ratio of overall foodstuffs might vary from society to society. But whatever the fraction, reciprocity was critical. The controversy over which was more important is by now tedious and for another place. There is no controversy about the interdependence of males and females during virtually all of our species's history. As Conrad Arensberg said in his presidential address to the American Anthropological Association in 1980, "the defining question is the form the sharing behavior takes," not whether it takes place at all. (Arensberg, 1980, p. 570)

We may also surmise that along with the food is shared an extensive set of feelings and sympathies. The stereotype of the newly minted couple eagerly planning to build a life together must have roots in a general capacity for intersexual reciprocity. This may take the form of the nuclear family, an extended one, or some other plan. Whatever the form, perhaps socioeconomic connective tissue exists between the collaborating males and females as emotionally and practically vital as the sexual attraction between the sexes.

For example, in an unusually explicit speculation about a critically important link between then and now, two experts on Peking Man describe their view of the social patterns which marked the 230,000 years of cave dwelling of *Homo erectus Pekinensis*, a period beginning 460,000 years ago:

> ... Peking man was a cave dweller, a fire user, a deer hunter, a seed gatherer and a maker of specialized tools. . . . Hunting of large animals is so complicated, difficult and hazardous that the cooperation of numerous individuals is needed. . . . Peking man was more likely to have been living in a group than in solitude when he began to hunt deer ... thousands of fossils of prey species found in the cave suggest that these primitive hunters may have preferred to bring back to the cave and share the meat with others rather than to consume it where it was killed. . . . The hunting of large and fast-moving animals may have been difficult for women because of physiological limitations (such as pregnancy and child rearing). It is thus possible to speculate that the hunting behavior of Peking man may be caused [by] or contributed to the sexual division of labor within the group. The pattern of male hunters and female gatherers, which is common in hunting and gathering societies today, may have already been established. (Rukang and Shenglon, 1983, p. 94)

The implication is that there exists a compatible duality between males and females, which in the procedural matters of daily life, as far as sharing resources, work, time, and space are concerned, is of the same order and status as the eroticism that both reflects and ratifies this. I am presupposing that there exists sexual difference in more than solely erotic-reproductive matters. But if there is wonderful natural balance, why so many divorces? Because of our strange way of life. We will have to come back to that, too.

This is a model of morality from the inside out—that is, beginning with the individual and stressing the small, nonideological scale first. Clearly I am convinced that it is necessary to develop notions of ethical adequacy working out from the intimate, particularly familial situations. There seems to be some good ground for this. For example, in an intriguing study of family and public life in five cultures—in Mombasa, Kenya; Seville, Spain; La Jolla, California; Demonte, Italy; and Kahl, West Germany—responses to questionnaires about social life suggested that families are more like each other than members of particular similar professional or occupational statuses are like each other. Even the structural comparability of jobs, training, professional perspectives—say of accountants or dentists—is less influential in producing a common pattern of response than family membership. Hence, "societies are similar, families are distinctive. . . . Within societies as wholes, about half the cultural elements are shared, but within families this sharing is somewhat greater." (p. 324) "It seems quite possible that mothers play a distinctive part in family life; that is, independent of the particular cultural elements the mothers in different societies share. . . . We found . . . that fathers share the cultural elements concerned with family life more fully with their own family members than they do with other fathers." (*ibid.*, p. 322)

Ethics do not just arise from an acceptance of sacred texts or from adherence to extant ethical systems, religious ones, or ideological universes in which all events are valued by how they advance the esteemed purposes of the framers and believers of the credo. At the beginning of this chapter I referred to the problem of natural ethics; I want to conclude by underscoring the relevance of ethical naturalism to what follows in this book. With force and succinctness Robin Fox has summarized the argument that environmentalism and modern social science, and the potential manipulation of the public by an elite, are all tightly linked: "purveyors of either progressive-liberal or revolutionary-socialist solutions have to adhere to a doctrine of human perfectibility as a matter of principle. There is no 'old Adam' in this philosophy, no original sin. There is only an infinitely perfectible human machine and totally unoriginal virtue that will be implanted by the benign, self-appointed mentors." (Fox, 1982, p. 72) "Why this environmentalist doctrine should be so deeply entrenched in both communist and capitalist ideologies is . . . easy to see . . . both are concerned to remold man in accordance with the dictates of a new environment, be it a socialist utopia or an affluent capitalist production line. Both wish to erect an 'unnatural' order; that is, an order made according to rational decision, not an order evolved from the needs of 'human nature.' To this extent, then, 'human nature' must be denied, at least insofar as it appears to stand in the way of rational reformist action." (*ibid.*)

Finally, he identifies as a possible program: "to understand the parameters which define our humanity, we must explore our evolutionary history to ask what are our inbuilt potentials? and what is the necessary environmental input for the realization of that humanity?" (p. 75) Back to Aristotle, and back away from Plato.

It is not easy to assess the natural state of human ethical society. I have already noted that as hunter-gatherers we evolved under circumstances drastically different from those we now confront. Furthermore, our movement to agriculture did not solve this problem. It compounded it—the possible explanation for the eruption of ethical system-making during that period. The industrial way seems at first much more congenial than the earlier forms, if only because it is so remarkably efficient. The manifestation of human will in action and artifact is extravagant and there are so many more options to be seized or rejected. Yet the problems created by industrial opportunity are so massive, penetrating, and novel that it is scarcely a surprise that full confidence about solving industrial problems is enjoyed mainly by the simple-minded or the mindlessly zealous. Not to say that there are no solutions. Not to say that Jeremiah is the only accurate guide for commentators on the industrial system. If nothing else, this way of life has produced perhaps the largest cadre of theoreticians, experts, investigative reporters, historians, seers, printouters, and simple hecklers of any comparable civilization. Surely they will in sum produce something. So the personnel, the talent, and the capacity are there. But, as always, first assumptions and points of departure may be the least carefully examined features of the situation. It is these which a reductionist anthropological lens may usefully inspect. Therefore I want to turn next to the central matter of how evil emerged as a significant product of industrialism, and how the function of moral judgment and the moralists had to change—or at least did change—under the impact of the scale, complexity, and clatter of the new productive mode.

2. Mephistopheles Become Machine

Believe it or not, when I was a young child I entertained the view that if I washed my hands sufficiently often—or at least as often as instructed by supervisory adults—eventually all the dirt in the world would swirl down the basin drain. We would all be spared this pointless ablution. The recurrent existence of evil presents a similar problem to mature people, and appears to be exceptionally irritating to people who adhere to religious systems and therefore have reason to expect helpful support from their God or gods. "Theodicy," which amalgamates the Greek *theos,* or god, and *dike,* or justice, is the word that refers to the vexing problem of explaining the existence of evil and the reason for glaring imperfections in a world supposedly subject to the will of God. The discussion of this has been understandably chronic. The modern British writer C. S. Lewis has offered his estimate of the nature of God's concern for the happiness of his subjects: "If God were good, He would wish to make His creatures perfectly happy, and if God were almighty He would be able to do what He wished. But the creatures are not happy. Therefore God lacks either goodness, or power, or both." (Lewis, 1957, p. 14) In bleaker contexts, Job's dolorous experience represents one effort to explain grievous features of life while still retaining the hope that enduring suffering proves faith in God; it will be rewarded by an effortless life without pain in Eden regained or Heaven achieved. The philosopher Leibnitz was an influential inspector of the problem, and in a commentary from 1710 identified the core of his view:

... the best plan is not always that which seeks to avoid evil, since it may happen that *the evil is accompanied by a greater good.* [my italics] For example, a general of an army will prefer a great victory with a slight wound to a condition without wound and without victory. . . . I have followed the opinion of St. Augustine, who has said a hundred times, that God has permitted evil in order to bring about good, that is, a greater good, and that of Thomas Aquinas . . . that the permitting of evil tends to the good of the universe. I have shown that the ancients called Adam's fall *felix culpa,* a happy sin, because it had been retrieved with immense advantage by the incarnation of the Son of God, who has given to the universe something nobler than anything that ever would have been among creatures except for it. (Leibnitz, ed. Weiner, 1951, p. 510)

This all seems almost dazzlingly simple-minded. But it reflects the strong need to explain the existence of evil. After all, if a person decides that the world is not, or should not be, planless, formless, and unpredictable, then some principle of causality and effect must apply, however tentatively. Hence it becomes appealing to try to say why things go wrong, why people go rotten, why dreams are dashed. Perhaps the explanation is easier for agnostic people. If there is no God, the world might as well be evil as good, abrasive as enjoyable. If the world is fully secular, and if there is no overriding benign point to it all, then any unwanted irruption is as appropriate and predictable as any happy one. The cycle of birth, growth, decay, and death is closed and self-contained. It is its own justification. Since it doesn't serve God or another larger principle, then it is just another event of the universe.

Obviously this can induce passivity, as for example in extreme monastic Buddhism. But even nihilists needn't be passive. They may respond to disease, say, with research on causes and cures and more general techniques of amelioration. Furthermore, it is possible for the agnostic to treat seriously a distinction between evil that occurs for natural cause, such as flood, typhoons, unexpected epidemics; and evil clearly caused by human action— by cruel or anti-social motives or even by the inadvertent error of the knowledgeable or powerful. Obviously, for the religious person the latter form of evil is easier to understand than the former. In religions which enthusiastically link human imperfection with observance and penitence, frail and erring sinners are to be expected. Indeed, they even affirm the need for God and for God's remedial direction and salvation. More problematic are the impersonal events that result in nothing gained, except in the minds of such fruitcakes as Dr. Pangloss of Voltaire's *Candide* as he considered the Lisbon earthquake.

In essence the problem of theodicy stems from human beings' intelligent ability to identify pain and trial, and from our insistence on linking an effect with a cause. Therefore we reject the idea that suffering is random and we try to find its cause, or at least its source.

Herein lies one of the implicit obsessions of this book: when the industrial system produces undesirable consequences, who or what is responsible? How can we locate the culprit? Is someone in particular responsible for pollution, urban noise, traffic jams, birth defects, unemployment? Who? The bosses, the workers, the government, engineers, cooks?

This book is part of an effort at secular theodicy: to identify the source of evil but without recourse to the supernatural. As such, it falls into an extensive tradition of scholarly and philosophical work broadly concerned with the reasons for what is often seen as man's fall from grace—with the reasons why bad things happen that displease the people who must endure them. Clearly there is not that severe a difference between religious and secular theodicies. One can even see the modern tradition of muckraking journalism or investigative reporting—call it whatever—as a secular version of the theological disputation about the origins and causes of evil. Perhaps the first exposé dealt with the Devil or some other malefactor; the tradition of lighting up dark and evil places is hardly new. As we will see, a thread of substantial disaffection runs through a surprisingly heterogeneous array of writers, ranging from Plato to Lévi-Strauss. They appear to harbor some sense of a Golden Age gone lost, a time of history when lives were fuller, more integrated, people less thwarted by the very circumstances they themselves created. In general, the imputation is that in the past there was greater harmony with the essence of humanity than in the miserable circumstances of the present. One is reminded of Marshall McLuhan's fragrant apercu that one generation's technology is the next's art form. So people of the computer age buy model steam engines to perch on their coffee tables. The "high-tech" notion of design exaggerates mechanical primitiveness when the economy no longer operates with it. A certain nostalgia for a half-remembered, half-accepted past is apparent in the objects symbolizing it. If the future is uncertain and the present boasts too little of joy and conviction, then the bits and pieces, literally, of the past will somehow spice today's bland taste.

But what is the truth of all this? Was the past better? Is there the remotest possibility that, with the exception of better health, faster and cosier transport, much more food, and all the various telecontacts, the stuff of human experience has declined in real value for those of us alive now, compared with our ancestors?

This must be an illusion. Or is it? Modern veterinary medicine is excellent. Elegant dog foods are advertised on color television. Still, what does it feel like to a natural dog to walk the streets with a chain around its neck, a perpetual convict? Has the fun of dogs improved now that they have become tiny pools of manageable emotion in a wealthy factory universe? There is no question that in terms of vital statistics and the various measures it is customary to use in officially assessing the welfare of populations, dogs are doing well. There are those almost 100 million household pets in America, and even if their reproductive system is broadly managed to provide the people, not the animals, with the provocation of sexual selection, nevertheless the group prospers as a whole and it is a growing group. But do individual animals on a restrictive chain care about the numerical triumph of their own kind in Indiana? Does an evolutionary biologist's estimate of the meaning of it all enhance the taste of a soft kiss celebrating a love affair? That is, are we merely using the rhetoric of manufacture, of GNP, of cross-national comparative tables about indoor plumbing and the production of lawn furniture to define private experience in a manner frankly irrelevant to the participants in it? Are we once again defining "the people" or "the dogs" from what has to be described as an elitist managerial perspective? Another tiresome "State of the Whatever" address read to the crowds bused in on government transport, given a day off from office and school to have their lives anatomized by officials?

I try to characterize a shift in consciousness from the intimate to the general which is part of the hankering for the golden past. That golden past in which there was direct relationship between experience and its description, between a life and its public record, when little or nothing got lost in translation. The harkening back, the sense of loss of the past, poignantly reveal the incompleteness and emotionally unsatisfactory quality of modernity. And this perception preceded modern modernity. It existed in the days of Confucius, and before, and after. It exists because the circumstances of life drastically changed after agriculture enlarged the scale of human community; when, once and for all, was lost the emotional certainty of the small scale.

So there *was* a golden past. It was our period of biological evolution, when we became human. We cannot fully recapture it. But secular theodicy requires us to compare our knowledge of human evolution with what it may mean for how we are and live today. This is important because it enables us to find a basis in some relatively rich scientific materials for our opinions about the suitability of the world we have wrought. We can for example inspect the industrial system, as I intend to do, in order to learn how it suits our species, given our evolution, and then pass some judgment about what we may want and what we may not want. We can confidently improve on Confucius and Plato and others because we have better information than they had, though we may still share with them the same perception of what is wrong, even if we can now better know why what is wrong, is wrong.

Why am I going on so about Confucius? Because so long ago he established a contrast that is enduring and rather typical in social analysis between the small scale and the large scale in social organization—between *Gemeinschaft* and *Gesellschaft,* which let us now refer to as Community and Society. Confucius called the former the "Great Similarity" and the latter the "Small Tranquility." In the former, the five fundamental social relationships Confucius valued highly were maximized: father-son, elder brother and younger, husband wife, ruler-subject, friend-friend. As Pitirim Sorokin indicates, Plato too favored the personal character and social pattern of the society of the Guardians. (Sorokin, 1963) And to go on with it, religious thinkers, notably St. Augustine, distinguished invidiously between the City of God and the city of man; the former is Community/*Gemeinschaft,* the latter Society/*Gesellschaft.* The dichotomy persists in Western thought, and not only there—for example, Ibn Khaldūn also perceived it as a central feature of his history of Arab life and of social structure in general.

The distinction is almost as if between prose and poetry, black-and-white film and color, a motorcycle roar and a flute's song. Community ways are warm and soft; Society demands straight lines, rigor. You are not supposed to have nostalgia about Society even though you might find some of its machines pleasing to look at. Community is about trust, Society about contracts, about enthusiasm freely shared rather than formal obligation dutifully fulfilled; the obvious difference between the small town or village in which everyone knows everyone's business and pleasure, and the hard-driving metropolis, where much work may get done but at the cost of the affections. A caricature, but still a common picture of the world people carry in their wallets.

Ferdinand Tonnies's *Community and Society* (*Gemeinschaft and Gesellschaft* in the original German) remains the central statement in sociology about the subject. I would like to explore it a little because it is so revealing of the elements of the overall perception of that old lost Golden Age. Tonnies's book appeared in 1887, and though it was at first little known, it finally achieved six editions and enormous influence. In their Introduction to the English edition (1963), Loomis and McKinney note the "romantic characteristics and ominous prophecy" of the book (p. 1) and that while Tonnies was obviously more favorably inclined to the *Gemeinschaft* pattern, nevertheless he believed that *"Gemeinschaft* represented the youth, and *Gesellschaft* the adulthood of society," and that individuals could become freed from the demands of *Gemeinschaft* and enter the *Gesellschaft* with a healthy dose of rational will. (p. 2) This is likely to be difficult to achieve, however, because *"Gemeinschaft* among people is stronger and more alive; it is the lasting and genuine form of living together. In contrast . . . *Gesellschaft* is transitory and superficial. Accordingly, *Gemeinschaft* should be understood as a living organism, *Gesellschaft* as a mechanical aggregate and artifact." (pp. 33–35)

The assumptions behind all this recall our earlier discussion of emotions. There are two broad kinds of will, natural and rational, which correspond to Community and Society. Rational will leads to instrumental social behavior, not necessarily based on affection or warmth. While natural will is not necessarily irrational, it is less concerned with systematic exploitation of the environment or other people than is rational will, leading to Tonnies's remarkably quaint announcement that "the businessman, scientist, person of authority, and the upper classes are relatively more conditioned by rational will than the peasant, the artist, and the common people who are more conditioned by natural will. In general, women and young people are conditioned predominantly by natural will, and men and older people by rational will." (p. 5) And now, enter the machine, which destroyed "the previous unity of blending of the three elements—man, instrument, and work.

74

. . . When people are used as mere means to ends, even as 'inanimate things' such usage is governed by rational will. . . . It was Tonnies's belief that it remained for the scientific man to devise means of freeing the majority from the role of mere machines or puppets." (p. 6)

The chase for the core assumptions about human nature narrows as we read about a distinction between rational law and "original natural law." "Tonnies assumed man to be, in part at least, a social animal by nature. This led him to conceive a system of law which stood in direct contrast to the individualistic rational law." (pp. 8–9)

Now we see how explicit this is and how explicitly it relates to the proposal here. There is a natural law, rooted in the past and in some sense in animality. From *this* has man fallen—fallen into rationalism, manipulation, exploitation, the loss of craftsmanship and family integrity—even before the full force of the industrial system made itself felt. Once the rule of this form of law is established, it is heartless. We are given no comfort: "It extinguishes diffcrences and inequalities, gives all the same behavior, the same way of speech and expression, the same money, the same culture, the same cupidity, and the same curiosity. It forms the abstract human being, the most artificial, regular, and unscrupulous type of machinery, which appears as a ghost in broad daylight." (p. 202) And in a final alarming quotation here, Tonnies claims: "In the real and organic world there is no dichotomy of cause and effect as between the pushing and pushed ball. . . . But a rational and scientific and independent law was made possible only through the emancipation of the individuals from all the ties which bound them to the family, the land, and the city and which held them to superstition, faith, traditions, habit and duty." (p. 202)

Very serious, this, because it asserts that while there were obvious advantages of the changeover, there were also important depredations that people suffered from this quite radical shift from the Great Similarity—from that secular Eden which preceded this troubled time. Could it have been just any troubled time? Remember that I am claiming the rot set in with agriculture. But wait, here is Tonnies saying the rot set in when people were forced off the land and into secular association, when they could no longer do agriculture. He is certainly right, and I hope I am right too, because in both cases our arguments depend upon changes in scale and the introduction of contract relation, not blood relation, as the way of ordering the world. In particular, I think we're both right because the shifts which were associated with the origins of industrialism and hence the decline of agricultural society as the center of the social world were epochal indeed. Once one refuses to accept automatically that progress is inevitable with industry and that there may be human losses possibly overshadowing economic gains, then the specific timing of the Fall is perhaps less important than this realization: man has a certain nature and it is now being traduced by social arrangements forced upon him willy-nilly by economic modes that may be useful but are, well, soul-destroying. Had Tonnies had information about the specific path of human evolution and the possible impact of genetics on behavior, might he have pushed the Fall back in time, into prehistory, as I have? Who can know? But my case for similarity rests not on the reasons for the diagnosis but its conclusion: there is a profound distinction between the social circumstances modern man has made, and those which made him.

If my argument is right, what went wrong? If we identify the economic system as the principal location of the problem, then which element or elements of it are likely to be the most significant factors? Let's simply begin with a broad given: that our species, like so many others, is a gregarious one; that solitary confinement is the direst of punishments short of death, so that when we come home at night and there is no one there, we are very likely to turn on television or open a book in order to remain in quite direct contact with other human beings and their stories. We are so gregarious we insist on having social contact even with people who are not there, people made up to seem real, people we pay to encounter in the cinema or theater or opera. We make parties and go to them, to heighten the gregarious stimulus, and the party may reverberate in the inner personal circuits for hours or days. Much technology is used to create ways of memorizing social moments, in photography for example, or making them possible despite distance, with the telephone for example. So there is an overwhelming urgency to social connection and we literally move mountains to reach one another.

A salient feature of our modern history is that we have as a community not only permitted but encouraged the break-up of the natural gregarious group into individual units who are permitted to hold property and who constitute the real blocks of the society. In economic terms, we have deconstructed the body social.

Through what C. B. Macpherson called "possessive individualism," we have linked the tantalizing aesthetic, reproductive, and
psychological individualism that emerged from the ferment of the
European Renaissance with the rockhard reality of how wealth is
owned and how therefore it is used and constrained. The marriage
of money with relative emotional freedom has been durable and
fecund. Its offspring is nothing less than the modern world. To
paraphrase what they say in the movies, money that travels alone
travels fastest and evidently farthest.

A note about this possessive individualism. Macpherson is a
Canadian political scientist who wrote a genuinely original book
which demonstrated the depth and meaning of that departure from
medieval concepts of society that yielded modern beliefs about
political value. Let Macpherson himself describe the core assumption of that seventeenth-century individualism which has provided
the basis for even contemporary practice:

> . . . possessive quality is found in . . . [the] . . . conception of the
> individual as essentially the proprietor of his own person or capaci-
> ties, owing nothing to society for them. The individual was seen
> neither as a moral whole, nor as part of a larger social whole, but
> as an owner of himself. . . . The individual, it was thought, is free
> inasmuch as he is proprietor of his person and capacities. The
> human essence is freedom from dependence on the wills of others,
> and freedom is a function of possession. Society becomes a lot of
> free equal individuals related to each other as proprietors of their
> own capacities and of what they acquired by their exercise. Society
> consists of relations of exchange between proprietors. Political soci-
> ety becomes a calculated device for the protection of this property
> and for the maintenance of an orderly relation of exchange. (Mac-
> pherson, 1962, p. 3)

Macpherson sees this remarkable theory as essentially operable in
England and similar societies through the nineteenth century because, by and large, "the individuals of whom the society is composed see themselves, or are capable of seeing themselves, as
equal in some respect more fundamental than all the respects in
which they are unequal." (p. 272) Of course once an industrial
working class emerged, this no longer applied, and much of the
convulsion of late nineteenth- and twentieth century politics has
to do with seeking some remedy for the fundamental incompatibility between the notion that every person is an equal market

77

player and the patent inequality in a system in which various individuals begin with different opportunities to play. The problem of ensuring social cohesion while also providing social equality is at the heart of the dilemma.

I cannot emphasize enough how important such *ideas* about social life were for the *practice* of that life. New notions of the social order animated a new social order as well as reflected it, just as in the late twentieth century controversies about public policy are quite directly linked to conflicts between political philosophies. Sir Henry Maine, the pioneering English scholar of comparative law, recognized the shift from the community-based economic system, which he summed up in his famous phrase "from status to contract." This was a convenient theory for a legal philosopher of Victorian England. Maine's biographer has commented about Maine's idea "that the legal development of progressive societies involves the movement of the position of the individual in private law 'from status to contract,' a thesis that was understandably well received in the great age of *laissez-faire* liberalism, but which has become more controversial in this century of growing government regulation of the traditionally private sector. . . . Maine . . . provided an authoritative legal rationale and the guiding academic spirit of the middle-class entrepreneurial attitude." (Feaver, 1969, p. xvii) He represented the practical spirit of his time and of his peers, who were creating and managing an empire and knitting the world together in industrial interdependence:

> Starting as if from one terminus of history, from a condition of society in which all the relations of persons are summed up in the relations of Family, we seem to have steadily moved towards a phase of social order in which all these relations arise from the free agreement of individuals. . . .
>
> The word Status may be usefully employed to construct a formula expressing the law of progress thus indicated, which, whatever be its value, seems to me to be sufficiently ascertained . . . we may say that the movement of the progressive societies has hitherto been a movement from Status to Contract. (cited in *ibid.,* p. 53)

Maine is acknowledged as an innovator in legal theory; but while ahead of it in this regard, he was also very much of his time. The Victorian period was a time of intellectual synthesis, the time of the origins of systems theory. For example, the great triumvirate, Freud, Marx, and Darwin, were all representatives not only of their particular intellectual, political, and scientific forces but also of a period of history which permitted and stimulated thinkers to see human actions as systematically linked to each other, not necessarily to an external force such as God. The system could be analyzed with complexity and of course challenged. As Marx wrote confidently to the German magazine editor Arnold Ruge in 1843: "The philistine world is the *political animal world*.... Centuries of barbarism have produced it and formed it, and here it stands now as a consistent system whose principle is a *dehumanized world*. . . . [my italics] The old world must be fully dragged into daylight and the new, positive one created. The longer the time that events allow for thinking humanity to ponder, and suffering humanity to assemble, the more completely will the product, which the present carries in its womb, enter the world." (Marx, ed. Padover, 1979, pp. 27–29)

A free-floating optionality enters here. Though the Freudian and Darwinist insights suggest the prehistoric rootedness of human social life (and of that of other animals too) in their legacies from their species's past, nevertheless in the context of the time their contribution offered an organized picture of the shape of human reality which could mean the beginning of change, not its barrier.

Obviously, of this trio Marx was the most politically energetic and has had endless impact on the conduct of modern society. As Paul Heyer has shown in his excellent study of this period (1982), both Tonnies and Marx were influenced by biological thinking, Marx most directly by his reading of Darwin and because of his voracious scholarship in general. In particular, Heyer shows how Marx's concept of alienation reflects his belief that the conditions of the industrial capitalism he saw were essentially and almost literally unnatural, and that workers were "voting with their feet" by resenting it as much as he thought they did. I have already noted my belief that the Fall concept in general reflects a perception of discontinuity between man's evolved nature and his new circumstances. Even Darwin alludes somewhat whimsically to this in a cryptic comment in his "M" Notebook for August 16, 1838: "Origin of man now proved—Metaphysics must flourish.—He who understands baboon would do more towards metaphysics than Locke." (Darwin, ed. Barrett, 1974, p. 21) Nor were politics likely to turn out less well than the progress of science. For example, Darwin commented on the slave population he observed in Rio de Janiero in

1832: "I cannot help believing they will ultimately be the rulers. I judge of it from their numbers, from their fine athletic figures (especially contrasted with the Brazilians) proving they are in a congenial climate and from clearly seeing their intellects have been much underrated; they are the efficient workmen in all necessary trades. If the free blacks increase in numbers (as they must) and become discontented at not being equal to white men, the epoch of the general liberation would not be far distant. . . . I hope the day will come when they will assert their own rights and forget to avenge their wrongs." (p. 175)

And once again, that Victorian English optimism. On September 25, 1836, on the *Beagle*'s voyage home: "From seeing the present state, it is impossible not to look forward with high expectation to the future progress of nearly an entire hemisphere. The march of improvement, consequent on the introduction of Christianity . . . probably stands by itself on the records of the world. . . . Yet these changes have now been effected by the philanthropic spirit of the English nation." (pp. 175–76)

The significance of this sense of possible new departures is that it freed thinkers from the restraints of theological, feudal, and in the case of Freudianism at its more daring, conventional familial traditionalism. As a result, there could develop relatively confident and self-conscious experiments in Utopian communities which sought to change conventional patterns of sexual and family life. (The kibbutz case is a good one in point, uniting as it did around the turn of the century radical efforts in political, economic, and family life, and all with rather new theoretical confidence.)

This made systems theory possible. It stimulated a host of developments ranging from scientific management to forcefully directed notions of economic development to clear expectations of political progress. In a word, modernization. Where technology and theory meet the art and logic of the possible. The sociological equivalent of the perpetual motion machine. A body politic and economic of eternal youth. Enough leverage literally to jump into space and around and back. Everyone knows what this means. A television studio is modern but a vestry isn't. The cockpit of a beautiful Boeing 747 is modern but a saddle isn't. Deciding what to do with money by listening to an economist equipped with financial records and a computer is modern but going to a fortune teller is not. It is more modern to have a nuclear reactor producing electricity than a factory packing cans of anchovies. It is more modern to send a worried or aberrant child to a psychiatrist than to an uncle. It is by and large more modern to have a factory or a dentist's office than a farm or a set of trap lines. It is modern to expect that the amount of general wealth will continue to increase and so a recession is defined as the absence of growth for two quarters while a depression is a decline.

For a long time it was considered modern to take newborn babies from their mothers and in perfect sanitation keep them in a barracks room with some twenty other newborns, under skilled supervision by trained medical personnel. It is becoming altogether clear what a disruption this can cause. Even in a simpler animal, the monkey, Vogt and Levine (1980) have shown how mother and infant squirrel monkeys respond to separation with measurable psychological changes related to anxiety and distress, while Penman, et al. (1983), have found that human mothers and infants may be affected by separation, losing some of the ability to synchronize their behavior, again with a physiological result that can be measured. "This raises the possibility that the chaotic asynchrony observed in clinically diagnosed mother-infant disturbances may have a neurophysiological base." (p. 1) One wonders whether postpartum depression among mothers of newborns is related to such a disruption of bonds, too.

Just as it is assumed that the modern system will produce ever greater wealth, there is also a commitment to the self-generating, self-satisfying nature of that system, "autonomous technology," as Langdon Winner calls it. (Winner, 1977) There is a genie or genius in the bottle which continues to spin out the heterogeneous products of a system that is driven by its own assumptions. These are clear and coercive, such as the importance of annual rate of return on investment. Managers of the system will continue to see its path as correct unless it is challenged on its own fundamental terms. That is, it is easier to claim that placing a factory in a particular place will yield inadequate profit than that a profitable factory should not be built because of its impact on the surrounding environment or people. At least, this has been the position of some political and business figures who assert that measures supporting occupational or environmental safety may produce a competitive international disadvantage for the enterprises subjected to them. Hence, those who support such measures are "soft" rather than "hard."

The burden of interfering with the technological processes of

81

production is generally on the shoulders of the interferers, not on those who share the assumptions and rewards of the system. Poor, unindustrialized countries have been willing to endure relatively polluting and otherwise disturbing factories because they decide the benefits of the system outweigh what may be quite demonstrable deficits for health and environmental welfare. Even such clearly avoidable pathologies as black lung disease and asbestosis were too little and too late taken into direct account when investments and production were planned. It would be foolishly naive to ignore the obvious role here of simple thoughtless greed, or complex and thoughtful greed. But some other less patent impulsion and permission seems to be involved also, and we will have to examine what that is.

*   *   *

Let me sketch out what I want to do now. I want to show that sociology developed independently and even in opposition to the natural sciences. For various reasons, this permitted a sense of emancipation from biological nature which stimulated the ardor and imagination of the ideologues and planners I described briefly in the last chapter. The sense of emancipation was also shared by the engineers, technical scientists, and other managers of the emerging industrial world. This synthesis of technological and sociological forces has produced a delightful and irritating system whose members obviously enjoy its almost wildly provident productivity but also question its wider impact on the planet and on their own inner worlds. Yet the system continues to grow. In the space program, for example, it has been shown how with excellent precision it is possible to carouse through incomprehensibly vast areas—an analogue "out there" of the processes "down here"—one reason why the launching and advertising of missiles is of such importance politically, and perhaps why military programs based on space receive such extravagant funding. The future has become the present, we have seen it, and it usually works. Or so it seems. Leaders and followers alike are linked in formal appreciation of the community's overall technological genius, a communal technological narcissism. Each blast-off and each new technical achievement is tied also to a notion of social progress—first woman in space, first black in space, first schoolteacher in space. The technique works, when it works.

Sometimes, and spectacularly, it does not work—Chernobyl,

spaceship Challenger, the *Titanic*, a long list. Then there is stunned disbelief at the betrayal by ourselves of our most reliable verity. As if the gods for whom were made the thousands of sacrifices on the pyramids of Teotihuacán in Mexico had suddenly revealed: "No, we said kissing, not killing." Other forms of doubt remain. As there was a first man on the moon, there lurks the specter of the last man on earth. In any heavenly scheme with a Sun, there is night and day, light and dark. Having created this new world, the uprooted human race must surely seek some accountancy for it all. But where to look? If we ask the folks who operate the system, will we find out anything we don't now know? Are we so integral with, committed to, and almost devoted to our system that we are unlikely to be able to inspect it? Possibly, but not necessarily. Obviously it is understandable. But more easily so if we untangle our way back to first principles. One of these, as I have already suggested, is, oddly enough, the existence of sociology as the most characteristically modern of the social sciences. So let us explore this briefly.

An influential book in early sociology was Emile Durkheim's *The Rules of Sociological Method.* Durkheim was a Frenchman who taught at the University of Bordeaux and was particularly influential and productive in the years around the turn of the century, until his death in 1917. He wrote widely, vividly, and well, and thought deeply about the possible ways of explaining and describing human social behavior. For example, his pioneering study of suicide (Durkheim, 1952, for the English translation) showed the interdependence of even such a private act as suicide with wide social, economic, and religious circumstances. But I am principally interested here in his commentary on sociological method. This both reflects and was a stimulus for separating sociology from the natural sciences. In turn he abetted a *sense* (not necessarily the reality) of the emancipation of modern society from old nature.

Durkheim said the realm of social life was autonomous. It should and could be viewed as a collection of social facts as tangible and discernible as the facts of geology, physics, or other science. The particular role of sociology was to master these facts. This it had to do as autonomously from other sciences as the facts themselves were autonomous. Therefore it was necessary for sociologists to develop an independent body of expertise, and to perceive their subject matter on its own terms and from their own vantage point. For example: "Social facts do not differ from psychological facts in quality only: *they have a different substratum. . . .* [my italics] The mentality of groups is not the same as that of individuals . . . the two sciences are hence as clearly distinct as two sciences can be." (Durkheim, 1972, p. 70) Durkheim was particularly set against any form of reductionism, that is, explaining one phenomenon by invoking a mechanism that was simpler, perhaps more physiological or psychological. You do not explain the behavior of the judge by what he ate for breakfast and therefore by the state of his digestion. You do not explain a journalist's anger at a public figure by endocrinological analysis, or even a person's system of symbols by the patterns of function of the human brain. Therefore Durkheim issues the rule: "The *determining cause of a social fact must be sought among antecedent social facts and not among states of individual consciousness. . . .* Psychological training, more than biological training, constitutes . . . a necessary preparation for the sociologist; but it will not be useful to him *except on condition that he emancipates himself* [my italics] from it after having received it, and then goes further by special sociological training." (*ibid.,* pp. 74–75)

This had academic and practical implications. It encouraged a strong separation between the natural and social sciences. By the 1950s, in the United States, for example, it was not only possible but almost certain that persons receiving doctorates in sociology, economics, political science, and many anthropologists and psychologists too, would focus on one animal, the human, and largely within the twentieth-century industrial framework. In sociology, this was a virtual certainty. In the early days of sociology there had been some interest in biological explanation, but it languished almost totally. By the 1950s, everyone involved was set in their ways. When in the sixties and seventies the emergence of newly sophisticated social biological explanations had to be confronted, the response was hot and widespread, and reflected the Durkheimian point of departure which was now elevated to a fact of nature. The argument does not let up, to the present.

In Durkheim's specific case, there was an important direct reason too for his position. The French educational system is traditional and highly centralized. Change does not come lightly. Durkheim understood that to create a niche for his new science in that system, he had to make a clear separation between it and the competing academic bureaucracies that would try to keep it within their spheres of control. The prestigious natural sciences must not be allowed to overwhelm the sciences of human social behavior. This is all the more intriguing in view of the fact that Durkheim's main teacher was a biologist named Alfred Espinas, who wrote *Des Sociétés animales,* and from whom Durkheim undoubtedly understood the power of the biological approach. Rosemary Zumwalt (1982) reveals how fiercely Durkheim fought on behalf of his discipline and his journal, *L'Année sociologique,* and describes his almost messianic conception of his role in French sociology. By contrast, Van Gennep, who wrote a classic work on *The Rites of Passage* and espoused "la biologie sociologique," was rather severely ostracized from the French sociological picture. So was his method and perspective.

Durkheim had to contend with other major difficulties. He was Jewish, at his intellectual and professional peak during the Dreyfus Affair, which could not have been reassuring to French Jews. He was also something of a Socialist. Finally, he was of the provinces, just a provincial, unable to claim that special sense of efficacy which attaches to Parisian citizenship.

Durkheim fought with integrity and success to establish sociology in the French system and elsewhere. He left a large and fertile legacy of fine work. He was a worthy challenger to the muddle-headed instinctivists who sought to explain elaborate forms of social behavior by an ever-increasing list of "instincts," which ranged from attitudes to cleanliness to needs for dominance and abasement to the final disastrous Nazi corruption of biology into a metaphor for rampant murderous xenophobia.

A cost of this success was that the social sciences and sociology, in particular, remained substantially uninformed about the natural sciences, which were conclusively changing our understanding of the complexity and yet reducibility of behavior. Not that introducing biology into social science is easy or simplistic. On the contrary, it makes scientific work harder. For too long the traditions of work in the natural and social sciences have skillfully developed apart from each other and hence contributed little to each other's strengths.

As always, academic ideas about life had an influence well beyond the academy. A denatured science of human social behavior permitted us to think that our behavior was denatured, too. If the experts told us that we needn't take biology into account when we studied our behavior, then there was no need to consider it in planning our behavior, in conducting it, and in evaluating it. I think this is as important a conception as the medieval religious one which saw so much of our behavior as an outcome of the force of God and the energies of the heavens. The earlier view tied our behavior to a wide scheme, in which humans were only one factor, and a partly dependent one at that. The more recent one liberated us from any such coercive determinant. And modern sociology was central to this liberation.

Soon I will examine the working assumptions of "scientific management theory," and of visionaries and Utopians who had an interest in retaining flexibility in their plans. This was something John Stuart Mill himself asserted—that reformers had to resist efforts to delineate human nature. Any such delineation could impede the progressive changes he desired.

This was not an altogether unreasonable position. How many times has it been said: "You can't do this, it's against human nature"? The obvious relationship between "is" and "ought" is ancient in philosophy. There ought to be some connection between what *is* behaviorally and what *ought* to exist in ethical terms but there is no point taking this too far. It may quickly become an adventure in tacit ideology. It may be possible and prudent, even reassuring, to treat the matter with a kind of wholesome or positive negativity. As Heyer notes: "a biosocial approach can be relevant, not if it advises us regarding what to do, but if it charts limits by suggesting or warning us of things we should refrain from doing. In this area we cannot derive 'ought' from 'is,' to recycle David Hume's famous terminology—but we may be able to discern 'ought not.' " (Heyer, 1982, p. 227)

This is the crux of the matter with the industrial system—its workings generate outcomes which no one or few people want. With relative inadvertence, it may generously produce "ought nots." Some are obvious, such as pollution and the effects of loud industrial noise on the central nervous system and hence on health. But many are not obvious. My task will be to highlight these. My basic point is that since we were told, as a civilization, that we were emancipated from our behavioral biology, then we could do as we pleased. We could nurture or just concoct whatever social schemes we fancied or that suited our economic and political theorists and decision makers.

The idea of autonomy from biology and nature is an old one. A legion of scholars including Max Weber, Durkheim himself, R.

H. Tawney, Joseph Schumpeter, and many others have sought the origins of capitalism and/or industrialism in particular religions, in other world views, and their values. Perhaps the most aggressive, brilliant, and to my mind explanatory proposition of this kind is from Peter Berger, who associates modern notions of natural independence with ancient Israeli theological theory: "Biblical religion polarized God and man. One of the essential experiences of ancient Israel was that God is distinct from the rhythms of nature, the rhythms of the world. . . . Ancient Israel thus effected two separations . . . of God from man . . . and of man from the world. . . . The idea of the autonomous individual, who can step outside of his community and even turn against it, is an essential feature of modernity. An autonomous nature, not subject to the gods and their intervention, is a presupposition of modern science and . . . of modern technology." (Berger, 1982, p. 65)

For Berger, this has explicit and contemporary social consequence. As he plainly announces in the first sentence of a book he co-authored: "The basic contention . . . of this book [is] . . . that reality is socially constructed." (Berger and Luckmann, 1967, p. 1)

First God, then Man, is deconstructed, then created. Managers arise. A whole new world, a world of contingency, relativism, and pragmatic response, a new occupational specialist emerges. A specialist in the secular as the priest was in the sacred. From God to Man. From Man to manager.

Then wherein lies the source of industrial evil? In the hearts and minds of managers? This would seem to be the inescapable conclusion. Yet it is not only too simple an accusation but does no justice to the *sui generis* effectiveness of the system itself. The system has achieved the autonomy from God and nature which the sociologists have identified. It is for this reason that we face a new moral problem.

Berger and Luckmann go on: ". . . there is no human nature in the sense of a biologically fixed substratum determining the variability of socio-cultural formations. While it is possible to say that man has a nature, it is more significant to say that he constructs his own nature, or more simply, that man produces himself." (*ibid.*, p. 49) Breathtaking!

I cite from a relatively early work. I have discussed with its authors their appreciation of the possible impact of new work on their own. But their statement stands as a fair and representative one of a position which grows out of Berger's own analysis of the roots of sociological consciousness and of modernity itself. It is vitally interesting that Berger's location in time of the Fall is precisely the Bible's. He sees the Hebrews responding to an historical situation with a sociological innovation that has had immense resonance, perhaps because of its accurate analysis of the convulsive shift to agriculture and pastoralism. Does the Judeo-Christian tradition rest on a sharp awareness that we had to reject our own human animality at just the time our hunting and gathering had been so overly successful that there were too few wild animals to ensure the dinners of too many of us? So that we had to grow our own beasts in herds and gather our food where we planted it? So that we tamed ourselves and our own wildness when we did the same with other animals and plants? An idea whose time had come? Yes, the end of hunting was the beginning of industry and of officialdom.

The conception of evil being described here is different from one involving a bogeyman, or a twistedly efficacious pervert, or utterly frank greed, sadism, misanthropy, or any other identifiably malign behavioral characteristic. I am locating the source of what is defined or felt or in the long run realized as evil in the system itself. In the nowhere and everywhere of it, in the ambient array of geared ins and outs, ups and downs, of situational certainties and conventional practices, of outcomes that emerge from no one's clear intention. It is not that evil is banal, but that it emerges from the profound exoticism of a system *Homo sapiens* is ill-equipped to discipline even though it was easy to make. The system domesticates us more easily than we domesticate it. This creates a difficulty for moralists and managers alike. Hence we produce schools for both. Not until recent years has it become clear that both cadres shared at least some concerns. Now the trickle of interest with ethics in business has become a flood.

For illustrative contrast, we can see that this is all quite different from the Hindu theory of "karma," which essentially explains current suffering by an antecedent moral deficiency. It also offers the prospect of improved circumstances at rebirth if the individual leads a morally fine life. In any event, being born human is achievement enough in the Hindu belief since there are far lower beings one could have become and may have been in the past. And in the present, "sin may occur without the will of the sinner in Indian thought, so that a sense of personal repentance is rare, and one may pray for deliverance from sins committed by others in the same way as for those committed by oneself. . . . The evil which we do commit is the result of delusion . . . or deception . . . and it is God who creates these. . . ." (O'Flaherty, 1976, p. 7)

So in the Hindu concept, evil-doing is not located within the system itself; it stems from God, a fixed point. Therefore it cannot be the system itself which produces evil. In addition, the current age is condemned at least in a temporary sense, because Hindus believe we suffer from a Fall to begin with. There have been according to the Hindu texts four Ages, of which this is the fourth. The first was of course the Golden Age. The second (Treta yuga) and third (Dwapara yuga) have led us to our present, the morally poorest of the lot, Kali yuga. How strange. Why would people *ever* conclude, despite plainly increasing control of food supply, health, transport, and so on, that their lives were ethically collapsing, that their social arrangements were in decline? If they dislike the present so, why not do something about it other than complain? For example, by reducing material needs or moving to environments offering simpler ways of life such as the deep countryside, or by electing to do an untroubling provident routine job such as driving a school bus.

What is pertinent here is the notion of the Fall, in four stages to be sure, but Fall nonetheless. In a most curious way, this is another version of that kind of optimism I sought to describe in my earlier book (1979)—a pattern which was species-specific, and which resulted in a persistent if moderate overestimate of the odds in one's favor, in endeavors of all sorts. This overestimate permitted an animal with a huge brain and hence a huge imaginative capacity to envision disaster, and with the knowledge of death already in hand, to perdure nonetheless. To turn the other cheek to reality, to continue the good fight though in practical terms the outcome, death, is bound to be bad, at least on the face of it. Doesn't the myth of the Fall provide an omnibus optimism, an analogue of Heaven, demonstrating that life *can* be better because it *was* better? That therefore the present is not only endurable but there is even a possibly noble aspect of it—that is, if it helps us better prepare through our trials and travail for a better future. "Nostalgia for the future," I called it.

In Indian society this is a very practical matter. A formal justification offered for severe caste distinction in the present is that it legitimately reflects virtue or evil in the past. The sins of the father and all that. As O'Flaherty indicates, in the Golden Age, the beliefs generally go: "men were happy and equal. *There was no distinction between high and low, no law of separate classes.* [my italics] Then after some time, people became greedy, and wishing trees [to satisfy man's food needs] disappeared, and passions arose." (*op. cit.,* p. 20) No improvement in this scheme, no need for it. But once the Fall occurs, human beings become enmeshed in real time not eternity, and what they manage to achieve is simply an unhappy process. People are left doomed to their perfectionless legacy. Eventually they are to be rigidly segregated into castes. The highest Brahman caste so vividly understands the frailty of its claim on virtue that it must perform highly elaborate, almost crazed, protective rituals. It has to quarantine itself in what it eats, touches, and who it relates to with relentlessly fierce fastidious-ness. For their part, as Michael Moffatt has shown in his sensitive ethnography, the Untouchables validate, almost embrace, the sys-tem which places them at the bottom of the social ladder by them-selves, creating a replica array of fine gradations within their own pariah group. (Moffatt, 1979, p. 58; see also Dumont, 1970)

This is weird and disturbingly brutal to the delicacy of human dignity. So it has appeared also to many members of Indian society who have sought to change their community. Gandhi and Nehru come to mind. Still, the system exists, it is massive, it continues, and it betrays the human animal as a possessor of major imperfec-tion, which stigmatizes human beings because of profoundly wrong analysis. (Could it be the result of the Fall, after all? Was this why the Fall involved the apple of Enlightenment—the fruit of mind-work?)

Nevertheless there is an important difference between the Hindu conception of evil-as-legacy but remediable within clear guidelines and over time and lifetimes, and the Judeo-Christian modern pattern. In the latter, it is possible finally to alter the whole system. There is a protean quality to it. It is hardly surprising that it relies so much on science and technology, which turn informa-tion about what exists in the physical universe into ways of chang-ing and adding to it. The same applies to the social universe. While it is true that throughout history there are many cases of organized heretics, crackpot self-help theories, and other bizarre recipes for moral betterment—Aldous Huxley's *The Devils of Loudon* comes to mind—it seems reasonable to suggest that never before has a population of the species been so much subject to the theory and practice of self-help, self-improvement, self-management, and various other forms of transcendence and renovation.

Presumably this as much reflects a dismay about the present, a dissatisfaction with life as it is being lived, as it betrays a vision of a golden future. Whatever the reason, the psychological trades place so much emphasis on human "potential" that even the promises of politicians and ideologues seem colorless and workaday by comparison. Possible consumers of various nostrums are urged to "express their potential," as if this were some form of secretion lurking just under the skin awaiting liberation by the right course, guru, manual, therapy style, whatever. But these are industrial citizens, for all their ardor.

It is appropriate that the first written constitution should have been the American, ten generations ago. This was a bulletin that man was the center of the universe. We were in control. We would and could write our own ticket. We could and would determine what arrangements would be suitable, pleasing, and fair. No more interference from the Monarch or any monarch. The Church was cordoned off on the other side of the Church/State barrier. This was a profound declaration of independence far beyond the political. Whether forced to or not, the New World "made it new" as its relatively newly arrived citizens took a giant step. The political theory of exiles is characteristically bold. Though industry grew in other countries as effectively and inventively as in the United States, there seems little question that the particular mix of republican political experimentality, pan-geographic wealth, and the industrial spirit yielded a psychological and practical result which has preeminently defined the system in its present worldwide form.

*   *   *

I have related contemporary notions of policy and public freedom to classical notions of the origin of evil. I have claimed that the new consciousness, codified and encouraged by the social sciences, contained a strong presumption that human social arrangements need not be held down. We should be able to do what we please. Achieve the sociological equivalent of weightlessness. Fly above our history, cosseted by technology and reassured by dreams of limitlessness. Reason, science, research show the way.

When even in Paradise evil rears its ugly head, there are explanations at hand. The traditional one was that *the inner man has failed the outer system.* Eaten a forbidden apple, committed sins great or grubby, done something bad. But in the modern mode, the answer is that *the outer system has failed the inner man.* Man, the People, the Community, are good. However, a few especially potent and effective villains have manipulated the whole system against the interest of all or most of its members—the wicked capitalists, the evil Communists, the pagan chieftains, the zealous holy warriors, capricious devotees of terror, whoever. In our fall from Grace or primatology, we have been temporarily misled by bad people. We wouldn't even know if and how we had created a pathological system because we do not believe in and therefore do not explore what is normal, what is natural. If conquering pathology requires lucid knowledge of normality, there is no one around to say what that is because this normality is partly ancient —and the ancient days are gone.

The Durkheimian lens could not provide a clear enough snapshot of what was normal because it looked outward, not inward. This was an opportunity because it emancipated people from nature. Allowed us to fly. But who was to navigate? Managers, that's who.

3. From Man to Management:
Ten Generations That Shook the World

The United States of America is a huge country with much open space. Still, the finding of the 1980 Census is startling, that the average American traveled 21.7 miles to work and 21.7 miles back. That is a long way to go and it's a long way from living above the store. This average distance is a real fact. It is not a phenomenon of consciousness. It is not an attitude. It is not the result of conspiracy. It is a length of ground a body must cross every working day. It is also a fact about a wealthy society that is a highly desirable place in which to live, to judge from the legal and illegal immigrants who hover round its borders, and the minuscule number of indigenous Americans who elect to leave. Think also about what that fact presupposes. A way of transversing 21.7 miles twice daily. Presumably a car or commuter train or other mass transit or a car pool or a bike or moped—anyway using roads or roadbeds, a machine, and of course using time. So a great deal of the wealth of the community, what gets reckoned in its gross national product, is an artifact of the productive system itself, a tax on itself as it were, what has to be produced to make production possible. Still, 21.7 miles is a long distance there and a long distance back, even if it is considered just a normal daily passage.

If this extensive travel is not the result of a conspiracy, then who started it? Who is responsible for it? Unclear. Obviously it is intrinsic to the system itself. Again, it is a real fact, as real as the countless other features of the industrial way which, when we stop to think about it, are as exotic as the distance it takes to get to one's job.

How did something so exotic come to seem so normal?

I have already mentioned a friend, Vladimir Denisov, who is a philosopher at Moscow University and a member of the Academy of Sciences of the USSR. One day when he was in New York, we talked about the relationship between industrialization and Marxism. He felt that industrialization was inevitable. From his reading of Marx, he thought Marx foresaw the process of industrialization as progressive, ineluctable, and desirable. There was little doubt in his mind that the laws of history would in the end yield the way of life which now exists, with the important difference that the capitalist pattern temporarily associated in much of the world with industry would yield to the fairer, more agreeable Communist way. When all was in place, a law of human social nature would join with machines and techniques and be fully and healthily manifested. There was symmetry between machines and human needs and capacities. He was untroubled in his confidence that this was so. There might be perversities such as capitalism and anomalies such as pollution. But these were transient and controllable, and the laws of human destiny were fixed.

This is a controversial assertion, particularly for those who do not see in the Communist imperium a signal of human perfection. But, ideology aside, is not Professor Denisov's point of view widespread, which is that the power and virtues of industrialization are self-evident and implacable, and that there is no way and no value in trying to stop history? Face it: modern is better, and modernity is highly spiced with machinery. As Siegfried Giedion tells it in his striking book *Mechanization Takes Command* (1969), the Greeks lived in a world of constants, and durable forms. Their temples reflected a world of stability and repose—compared, say, with the Gothic cathedral, where there is turbulence and action. The notion of movement as a regular part of the world became widely accepted. Muybridge recorded the human body in photographic motion. Among many others Kandinsky and Duchamp in painting captured the notion of life in motion, of life on the move and life getting better. "In the nineteenth century the creed of progress was raised into a dogma . . . belief in progress is replaced by faith in production. . . . Mechanization . . . is the end product of a rationalistic view of the world." (Giedion, 1969, p. 30) But mechanization depended for its reception on a willing and able population; for example, eighteenth-century France could boast of the technical skills appropriate for industry. However, as Giedion reminds us, because of a still-feudal rigidity under the *ancien régime* in Cathollc France, they could not take root (*ibid.,* p. 36). However hardy the industrial plant, it appears to require a particular soil at least at first.

Volumes have been written about this subject and volumes about the volumes. Acres of paper have been covered with facts and opinions about modernization and economic development. Scholars from Weber to Marx to Tawney to Parsons—on and on —have speculated about the connection between ideas about society, spirit, wealth, the afterlife, reward and punishment, etc., and the process of earning a living—of saving, investing, producing, consuming, and sharing. Now I want to explore a variety of ways in which the industrial pattern interacted with family life, with attitudes toward the organization of work, the nature of colonialism, the aesthetic impact of machines, and how individualism and theories of management joined to produce the world we know. I want to show how individualism and behaviorist psychology relate to the surprisingly recent discovery of management theory— at around the beginning of the twentieth century. We will see that a movement from man to management obscured the moral accountability of people working in organizations animated by an overriding collective purpose. The individual became subservient, responsibility was diluted. And while there is an implicit claim here that technology has a logic of its own, which limits the range of what its masters choose to do, nevertheless the social world in which technology must live may or may not support it well or at all.

For example, it seems the Chinese had a fairly firm grasp of scientific enterprise before the fifteenth century. They had notions of industrialized architecture even as early as the fourteenth. But something about the particular history and social structure of China stopped the process of which they had both the basis and beginning. Were the lords of China too preoccupied with warlordship and too little with expanding markets for products they had the knack of making? Were they territorially defensive rather than entrepreneurially aggressive? Was the climate wrong or the country too crowded or the Han dynasty too self-absorbed? Was there simply no *need* for a sense of technical savoir-faire since those who would principally benefit from it were established lords otherwise absorbed in more traditional and bellicose encounters? Was the origin of industry a one-time, one-spot event, which then swiftly crossed border after border?

Perhaps so. Perhaps the singularity of the specific historical process is as palpable as the 21.7 miles the average American has to cover to claim his job. Obviously industrialization did not happen everywhere all at once. When and where it did emerge must be at least a little different from where it didn't. Or, more likely, a lot different.

Is Modernization Just a Tribal Theory?

Let's now explore the particular history in which people cohabited happily with machines and collaborated to produce a world of system and relative order. It is now difficult to imagine a time when time wasn't the same everywhere. But before 1883, in the USA, the clocks in Albany might be set twelve minutes earlier than those in New York City, while Macon, Georgia, could enjoy its midnight twenty minutes later than a community down the road. Government intervention finally relieved everyone of the inconvenience of this pre-technological lackadaisicality. The control of time itself through the emergence of clocks and watches had quite profound impact on how easily people could relate their specific lives to an outside secular force and coordinate their activities with high precision. (Landes, 1983) It is significant and interesting that so many people carry readings of the time on their wrists, now even to the split second. There is obviously a need for such information in order to function in a systematized society. It is difficult to think of another device which so firmly makes people responsible for their own individual actions and rhythms, and yet also commits them to be aware in detail of what everyone else is doing.

This suggests an eagle's-eye view of two apparently contradictory processes linked up with economic development. On the one hand, the rise of possessive individualism made it possible for people to be regarded as free agents, as independent contractors. In effect, they could lease their life cycles to the productive apparatus in return for enough goods and services to survive and reproduce. As Marx claimed, this was the minimum overall obligation the system had to the wage worker, and could well be the only one. For the entrepreneur, the removal of fixed responsibility for workers was even more significant. Now he could move capital and people wherever it seemed profitable and adventurous to do so. With Adam Smith's permission, this could be anywhere and with whatever impact. The emergence of centers of international trade and banking meant that the stored skill, energy, and resources of one society—capital—could be intruded into another. Often, as in colonialism, this could have considerable, even drastic impacts on local life and culture. Capital itself was atomic, in the senses of being both self-contained and explosive. The pressures for free trade and investment that accompanied the growth of industry in Euro-America permitted the rapid diffusion of the ways of life that produced the wealth in the first place.

On the other hand, given all these forces, there also emerged a means for articulating and ordering them. This was called management. It seems significant that the first professional managers emerged from engineering, and many from the military, West Point in particular. Was there the same attitude to people as to things? Were all forces, real and human, alike? Individuals became free agents and might be loosed from the bonds of community. But there was a new way of calling them back and domesticating them. It eventually became almost an autonomous, science-like profession on its own: management. In the United States in particular, it was so professionalized that it threatened to become almost abstracted from the real endeavor that was being managed. Since management was everywhere, a good manager could go anywhere. It was an autonomous skill, wielded by mercenaries crusading for efficiency.

Two trends converged: the strong individualism which arose in England perhaps as early as the thirteenth century, as the English historian Alan Macfarlane (1978) has suggested, and the American response to its huge market and the challenge it posed, which yielded American corporate management. "The Visible Hand," Alfred Chandler called it, and a strong hand it was. Based on examination of the surprisingly good records available about social and economic life of the period, Macfarlane claims that even in the thirteenth century, England had "a capitalist market-economy without factories." (p. 106) This was part of a pattern of activity which included primogeniture. It provided emotional permission for people to focus on the trade or the task or the estate rather than on the kin or other local group. In quite striking contrast, for example, to the Ghanaian civil servants I interviewed in the early sixties, who would routinely complain that when they replaced English officials, they (Ghanaians) might suddenly find themselves having to support a half-dozen relatives, who as a matter of right saw the official's good fortune as to some extent theirs—they might just move in with him. Needless to say, this produced pressure on time and money at the very least, and was obviously not in the proper individualistic style of traditional English civil service practice.

I am not making a value judgment about this, but asking whether the overwhelming force of the industrializing process depended at its onset, and may still, upon basic attitudes to social life and property of a particular tribal group rooted in Saxon England. Can it be that modernization is a tribal theory and economic development the result of tribal envy? Is management theory the gussied-up version of Saxon lore? Is laissez-faire economics the general version of a cool or cold familial style in which emotion is constrained and children obligated to make do on their own—life being essentially a struggle? Was a possessive individualism rooted in English history necessary for the development of successful, integrated impersonality? Does it take a particular tribal personality to succeed in the impersonal mode? Did a special alchemy of Protestantism and Anglo-Saxon ways of living family life yield the germ of industry?

Of course other groups than Anglo-Saxons had prospered mightily in preindustrial worlds. Catholic Italian merchants of the great Italian city-states, Jewish bankers, Dutch and Belgian merchants, Hausa and Han traders, Inca, Mayan, and Aztec oligarchs had all somehow calculated to generate economic activity and to profit fully from it. Two days of Tuscan tourism will instruct anyone about the profound force of familism underlying virtually all major Florentine or Sienese economic and political endeavor. The Jewish merchant and banker families were families first, which evidently provided them the organizational freedom and certainty that was such an advantage in dealing over long distances and with many non-kin strangers. In the United States, as Alfred Chandler points out, even after 1840 the partnership remained the basic business unit and was usually a family affair involving two or three close colleagues. (Chandler, 1977, p. 36)

But then he describes the shift from general merchandizing and trade to the highly specialized version demanded by America's role as the principal supplier to the United Kingdom of raw materials for its industrial plant and a major market particularly for its textiles: "The coming of these new trades was the most important single factor in bringing specialization to business enterprise and impersonalization into business activities. . . . The specialized impersonal world of the jobber, importer, factor, broker and the commission agent of the river and port towns replaced the personal world of the colonial merchants, caught in transformation." (ibid., pp. 19–27) A striking index of how important personal ties were in the initial stages of this economy was that the U.S. government issued hardly any paper money before 1862. (ibid., p. 29)

In his important *Thought and Change* (1965), Ernest Gellner of Cambridge University describes the close relationship of early industrialism and sociology. He relates both to a radical individualism necessary for the new system: "the shrinking of the ego to a hard, ultimate kernel which provides the basis, or at least the touchstone for everything." This is strong stuff indeed, a hard, ultimate atom from which the rest of the world can be reliably constructed. With this "hard, ultimate kernel" or atom as a self-centered fiscal rationalist, economic decisions can be expected to show the good sense they require. The overall impact is firmly useful; it all works out efficiently in the end. And again, this kernel is sensibly committed to the general scheme, not the familial one. As Max Weber strikingly wrote: "the greatest achievement of ethical religions, above all of the ethical and asceticist sects of Protestantism, was to shatter the fetters of the kinship group. These religions established the superior community of faith and a common ethical way of life in opposition to the community of blood, even to a large extent in opposition to the family." (cited in Macfarlane, op.cit., p. 50)

If this is so, is it strange that this social equivalent of atomic energy should have proved itself so effective? Of course there were significant technical and juridical features of all this, for example, primogeniture, which meant if nothing else that landholdings were maintained as efficiently large units and not broken up between offspring—a clear sign of favor for the productive as opposed to reproductive modes (and presumably a wet blanket on family affections).

A graphic instance of the importance of this pattern or its absence is to be seen still along the banks of the St. Lawrence River in Quebec. There, the precious fertile land which fronted on the river was cut up generation by generation, strip by strip, to provide inheritances for all. The result was that the increasingly narrow farms barely supplied wherewithal for anyone. This was no doubt to some extent responsible for the relative slowness of French-Canadians to form industrial capital and the large enterprises common in North America. The whole question of the difference between French and English Canada, and the impact of Catholicism in contrast to Protestantism, remains intriguing for historians. And in view of contemporary French-Canadian politics, to politicians and citizens too. The Quebec case seems an almost clear-cut vindication of the thesis about Protestants and money, perhaps too clear-cut for analytical comfort, but nevertheless provocative. Of course the French-speakers lost the colonial war with the British, and they were relatively isolated from North American economy. Strict ecclesiastical control and until the 1960s almost untroubled political dictatorship did not conspire to yield a nimble economy either. (Quinn, 1965)

There was in Quebec until the early sixties what amounted to a conspiracy between English-speaking industrialists and financiers, and the French-speaking churchmen and politicians. Both groups were able to maintain their respective power and interests with considerable cooperation and little difficulty. As a student editorial writer at the McGill *Daily,* I wrote a righteous editorial on the subject in 1958 called "The Shame of English Canada" in which I accused English leaders, including the Senior Governor of McGill University (who was the publisher of the major English paper), of collusion in corruption and irresponsibility to the people of Quebec. In a scholarly article he wrote several years later, Pierre Elliott Trudeau, then a law professor in Montreal, said that this was the first such assertion in the English press. This was hardly surprising since the ruling political party controlled the allocation of newsprint in the province. In any event the situation is interesting because it reveals in relief the process of economic specialization I am concerned with in this chapter.

As Macfarlane shows, in England even the lower strata of English society abided by the practices of primogeniture. (*op. cit.*, pp. 87–88) For some reason, English social life was particularly well adapted to the patterns that would best suit high-achievement, high-accumulation industrial forms. Had this to do with the emotional choices English people made about their families? Macfarlane cites an Italian ambassador, Andrea Trevisano, who in 1497 wrote of the English that "Each individual was out for himself and trusted no one else." Trevisano also described how "the want of affection in the English is strongly manifested towards their children; for having kept them at home until they arrive at the age of seven or nine years at the utmost, they put them out, both males and females, to hard service in the houses of other people, binding them generally for another seven to nine years, and these are called apprentices." (*ibid.*, p. 174) In addition, research by Valerie Fildes has recently revealed that during this period—and for two hundred years more—wealthy and influential English women sent their new infants to wet-nurses, who could live miles away, with who-knows-what impact on the children's sense of psychological comfort and security. (Fildes, 1986)

In addition to whatever emotional consequences there were, primogeniture was another factor. If only one child could work with any zeal or sense of prospects in the family enterprise, whatever it was, then the others must leave. Where to? Later on, luckily, the Empire had to be supervised. Was it not George Bernard Shaw who called the Empire "a vast system of outdoor relief for the second sons of the English middle classes"? To complete the picture, the existence of nannies and then boarding schools helped ensure the development of youngsters, males in particular, who would be accustomed from their youngest days to an implacable independence or at least forced self-sufficiency. (Wilkinson, 1964) In any event, the extraordinary possibility for lonely self-sufficiency (if that and not despair is what it is) in the English upper- and middle-class scheme of life is reflected in the case of Winston Churchill, whose parents visited him all of once during his years at boarding school. "In his ten years away at school, whether in health or in dire sickness, he had only one visit from each parent." (Pritchett, 1983, p. 89)

In a real psychological sense this justifies the term "public school." The effective platform on which life was lived *was* public. The private innerness and flow of family privacy was a matter for vacations and other respite from the more serious concerns of the public world. How different from the contemporary North American pattern in which skill at conducting intimate relationships, as in families, is accorded high priority in contrast to that British pattern.

Is there a real connection between how parents and children live with each other and the commanding forms of economic method. Why not? I have already suggested how forcefully the industrial mode has separated the productive and reproductive systems. Didn't this come from somewhere? If the family and factory became disassociated, surely it is a plain possibility that the reason for this is that the Founding Family, the First Industrial Family, was already a broken family. The first rules against nepotism were promulgated within the family itself, against the younger brothers and sisters, and of course against the wives.

Consider again the remarkable emotional impact of primogeniture. Sunday dinner, rich glow of silver, warm aromas of beef and claret, Father, Mother, two sons, two daughters. All of them equally favored, equally comfortable with the Wedgwood plates bearing the family crest. It is *their* family. But then the scene is shattered. The father dies. One son inherits the mill or lands or partnership at Lloyd's of London. Under these circumstances it is better that everyone keep to himself. Since they run so deep, feelings could run too high.

In the tradition about which I am writing, it happens and is even prestigious in some circles that a male child is called by the father's name with "Jr." added. I noticed when astronauts were still principal planetary heroes that three of the first seven U.S. astronauts were Juniors. Could this be accidental? Or did it suggest that these men had the kind of central nervous systems that were disciplined enough and yet confident enough to be willing to leave earth in a tin can? Had they a special kind of forceful childhood which produced a character able and willing to obey others and believe in oneself under the most remarkably demanding circumstances, one "hard, ultimate kernel" flying in another?

Perhaps I make too much of this, which is however no more mistaken than making too little. Machines weren't made by magic. Their requirements and routines were not ordained by tables of random numbers. People had to make decisions about what machines do and what people should or could do about them. Particularly at the beginning of something, when the first cuts are being made, when the trajectory starts, when the basic assumptions are being formed and accepted, how people feel about discipline, sang-froid, hardness, and so on may make a decisive difference in what then becomes the norm, the only game in town—technology. Once expensive machines get going, a rather firmly defined route is inevitable. Not that change is impossible. But, for example, in order to use expensive machines as much as possible, people have to fit in around them and work all night.

I am proposing an almost melodramatic scheme here: Once upon a time, a relatively small group of people lived in a particular community and over a long period developed a way of life. It was reflexively individualistic and apparently easily suited to the adoption of industry and its machines and rigamaroles. Born, bred, and refined in the United Kingdom, the syndrome was also given hospitality in the United States, where it not only grew in impor tance but was further developed and specified by the particular problems and opportunities of markets and management in a vast country. It was also stimulated, if gruesomely, by a civil war that was to a significant extent focused on the difference between an industrial, individualized, monetized economy and a rural, traditional, feudal agriculture. Again, I am not gainsaying the immense moral issues involved here, slavery in particular, and the whole issue of equity in general. But the clash was real and large, and it signaled the end of a way of life as well as the emergence of an attitude to work and wealth.

That battle had been fought in England before, in bloody terms. King Charles I was beheaded in part to satisfy the interests of individualist protagonists unconvinced by theories of divine right which did not include or even truncated their own freedom of maneuver. The expansions of Empire, the peculiarly inconsistent way in which free trade was associated with imperial preference, the literally explosive growth of the industrial system, depended on social values and people who lived by them. Once started, perhaps all this was implacable. Was it inevitable to begin with? Of course not. But again, given that even thirteenth-century England may have been, as Macfarlane describes it, "a capitalist-market economy without factories" (*op. cit.*, p. 196), there was a deep preparation for what subsequently happened so forcefully and influentially.

The anthropologist Kenelm Burridge has described this tradition's strong connection to Christianity and individuality. He claims that "the most obvious exponent of individuality is the Christian missionary" (Burridge, 1979, p. 236). The Western notion of individualism is finally "an essentially religious stance." The individual "is the agent for . . . new rationalization and new moralities." (pp. 48–49) The soul-bearing individual is the stuff of morality. Burridge regards Christianity as "anti-structural, anti-organizational." (pp. 54–55) I will later try to show that the elaborately coercive industry of psychological and competence testing, in the United States in particular, is an outgrowth of the basic Christian notion of the lone soul in search of expression, release, vindication

103

THE MANUFACTURE OF EVIL

—in search of a sign of value and calling. Tests are supposed to uncover qualities as generic as the soul itself, immune to environmental suasion, unrelated to time and place. The computer grades and scores and prints out a modern form of Calvinist destiny. "What's your score?" and "What's your sign?" are two questions about modern essence, both taken very seriously in some disparate circles. If the concern about "signs" is merely idiotic, the concern about "scores" is crucial to operating our whole shooting match. Possessive individualism extends to owning one's own skills and characteristics. Curious.

The modern end product of the process of Christian individuality is the bureaucracy. This is not only an instrument of work but provides a new kind of moral option: bureaucracies "appropriate that burden of moral choice, which is the prerogative of the human." In bureaucracies, "the moralities are buried even deeper in the interstices of procedure." (pp. 107–09)

We are at the very heart of the problem of moral choice with which I am concerned in this book. Once the bureaucratic scheme is on the scene, do the basic conditions for choice change rather fundamentally? The extreme challenge—extreme in the subject matter of the controversy—was made by Adolph Eichmann, who persistently evaded all admission of guilt for extermination of European Jews by repeated references to exculpatory bureaucratic clauses, misunderstandings, and inequities. Witness the diligence, almost ecstasy, with which he challenges any accusation in the edited transcript of his lengthy interrogation before his trial in Israel: " . . . killing wasn't in our department. . . . I have to say these things, because as head of Bureau IV B4 I wasn't responsible for everything, only for a rather narrowly circumscribed field. . . ." (cited in Von Lang, 1984, p. 165) This material, and the trial itself, among other considerations of course, led Hannah Arendt to her famously controversial "banality of evil" proposition about Eichmann's guilt, namely, that Eichmann was a relatively ordinary man whose monstrous actions were in no way matched by the quotidian pettiness of his motivation and comportment. A prudent victim of a desperately immoral system. If no punishment could fit his crime, no symmetry existed between the man and what he did.

The broader point. We are a gregarious species, always affected by what other people say and do to us. We are never alone, even if we are isolated. Any decisions we make are taken in a social context. Yet legal culpability is determined principally on an individual basis. The basic presumption endures that human cognitive and analytical skills are such that individual people are able to penetrate to the moral center of an issue. Under extraordinary circumstances people may even analyze events and conclude that they must deliberately break rules of an organization to which they have been regularly loyal—what Mortimer and Sanford Kadish call "discretion to disobey." (Kadish and Kadish, 1973)

But the idea of accurate, autonomous, legal rationality may be as erroneous for describing the law as the belief in perfect rationality is for classical economic theory. People are subject to a host of "irrational" factors when they decide economic matters. Any economic theory or government plan that assumes the contrary will fail to predict or influence in the direction it wants. An example is the failure of tax cuts initiated by the Ronald Reagan administration in 1983 to stimulate the saving and investments which theorists predicted would flow from greater cash balances among consumers. Rather than save and invest the extra money, people by and large spent it, an evidently ambiguous boon in an economy straining to reduce inflationary pressure. The predictors were wrong because they employed inadequate theory. Their only consolation must be that they are hardly alone in their misapplication of misconceptions to real events. This is not to say that economic ideas are avoided in high-level discussion. Senator Patrick Moynihan, who has served in the cabinet or sub-cabinet of four U.S. presidents, has commented that at no cabinet meeting did he ever hear a "serious discussion of political ideas—ones concerned with how men rather than markets behave. . . . The lesser coin of economics drives all else out of circulation, save only foreign policy, about which there is neither an economic or political science." (Moynihan, 1981, p. 103)

Money Made That World Turn Round

If people are not "rational" when they make decisions about work or money—say about whether or not they buy sneakers or a new tablecloth, or a ticket to a cousin's Colorado wedding rather than a vacuum cleaner—why should they be expected to act rationally when they are involved in deep issues of major right and major wrong? Bear this question in mind while I return to another aspect of economic activity: the effects of money. Money is the unit of exchange of *Gesellschaft,* par excellence. It permits and stimulates the adoption of the impersonal style in social relations. Burridge again: "Money opens the moralities to shades of meaning making them susceptible to qualification and change. . . ." (*op cit.,* p. 96) Money is the primary distinction between complex and subsistence economies, and hence presumably between the moralities appropriate to each. (*ibid.,* p. 97)

Further: "Money encourages ego-centered social relations, loosens group and moral allegiances, invites the person to be an individual; its atomizing effects can only be reined in by rigorous traditional moralities such as the caste system, or by overarching and tightly knit bureaucracies." (p. 188) Burridge suggests money has become synonymous with bureaucracy by integrating the diverse moralities permitted by money. (p. 233) But he does not amalgamate the two elements of the problem at its most hazardous: if money is impersonal and bureaucracies are impersonal, then how on earth can individuals in bureaucracies be personally accountable in communities which are totally monetized and predominantly bureaucratized? How, in effect, can most of the people making most of the significant decisions about most of the most salient public matters in industrial societies be held directly and precisely accountable?

I've suggested that the recurrent dichotomy between community and society reflected a real sense of social decline—of how some rich kind and quality of human encounter has been replaced by poorer and thinner contemporary experience. There is a real difference between sticking a plastic card in a machine and receiving cash with which to buy a cough medicine at a supermarket, and asking the local herbalist what to chew or breathe for a painful throat. The impersonal monetized economy permits a different way of life for people in it. This autonomy is sufficiently luxurious so that many people will endure the difficulties of dense urban life in order to achieve the ease of social distance. Much has been written about this quality of money, in particular by Marx of course. Less well known is *The Philosophy of Money* (originally published in German in 1907) by the sociologist Georg Simmel, who addresses the question of its impersonality in a very searching and influential way. (Simmel, 1978)

Simmel wants to "illustrate and clarify the nature of money by two processes that are almost endemic to the heights of a money culture—cynicism and a blasé attitude—both of which are the results of the reduction of the concrete values of life to the mediating value of money." (p. 255) As to the blasé attitude: "The decisive moment . . . is not the devaluation of things as such, but indifference to their specific qualities from which the whole liveliness of feeling and volition originates. Whoever has become possessed by the fact that the same amount of money can procure all the possibilities that life has to offer must also become blasé." *(ibid.)* The triumph of the money economy permits participants in it to become déracinée with respect to "liveliness of feeling and volition." Money eases the shift from emotionality to rationality in the conduct of economy (even though emotion is a constant and rationality is a fantasy, almost a kind of emotion itself). The new world of market economy becomes possible once the abrasions and affections of personality can be avoided in the supposedly pure exercise of economic rationalism.

And not only in the economy, but in any system which says that people can operate as officers rather than individuals with color and partisan crankiness. It is significant that the immense analyses of Weber, Marx, Simmel, Durkheim, and others appeared during those great changes producing the modern scheme. A Rutgers graduate student of Nigerian origin once quipped that the mighty German thinkers such as Marx and Weber wrote about ponderous and enormous subjects because "they enjoyed it." If they did, the humorous content of their remarks verges on the invisible. Nevertheless, they turned their attention to central issues and it was timely that they did so.

The changes in the world were indeed immense. Daniel Headrick has shown that the people who ended up owning empires depended on the new technology of the industrial pattern to expand and maintain their territories. (Headrick, 1981) Heady racial supremacy and confident Victorian progressivism were necessary ingredients in the imperial endeavor. Headrick cites the explorer and shipbuilder MacGregor Laird: "We have the power in our hands, moral, physical, and mechanical, the first based on the Bible; the second upon the wonderful adaptation of the Anglo Saxon race to all climates, situations, and circumstances . . . the third bequeathed to us by immortal Watt . . . carrying the glad tidings of 'peace and goodwill toward men' in to the dark places of the earth which are now filled with cruelty." (p. 17)

Of course, without Watt's legacy, the steamboat, even with the best and most will in the world the "glad tidings" could be carried slowly with difficulty. The attractions of Empire did not wholly depend on the steamboat; governments long before the 1800s had expanded reigns—the Romans had after all ranged as far as England itself in their day. Their Holy successors were not and are not without massive acreage to claim as their own. But the scale was different. So were the size and sophistication of the populations to be subdued. So were the rewards in trade, supplies, and markets. There was a difference in the scope and scale of what the new imperialists could extract and sell from their charges. The ante was higher, the pace far more rapid, and the geographical range vast—the difference between the balloonist and the astronaut. Not only was it important to secure colonial possessions for resources, services, and markets, but these were also significant counters in the struggles between the dominant powers of Europe and Asia. "Losing China" to the British was important to the French, let alone to the Chinese. The meaningful political world expanded drastically. The tools of expansion were available.

But which came first, the people or their tools?

The basic nonsocial components of colonial expansion were productive and military technology, the fast and extensive transport permitted by rails, steamships, and roads, by submarine telegraphy and comparable communications, and by some mastery of particular tropical diseases—quinine as protection against malaria was probably the most important. These developments helped increase the distance between people, permitted impersonality, expanded social networks. They allowed people to move away from their natal homes with little danger. Those technologies worked best which most efficiently stimulated the impersonal industrial mode. The technology was a stimulant. It was also an amplifier. It took the reigning social forces of the moment, expanded their impact, and broadcast their message.

I am reversing the usual explanation of these events. The usual one is that technology caused the new world. But I am speculating that there was a willing and able body of "buyers" for the new technology. A cadre of people psychologically and socially adjusted to the kind of performances necessary to acquire and operate the machines and systems without trauma and with confidence. Confidence was important. Political control was usually backed by minuscule military threat. Inducing "the natives" to produce and consume the products of the system didn't happen without effort and sometimes struggle. The numerical odds against the colonizers were great. But because they represented the industrial system, the colonizers had the psychological odds on their side. This is one explanation for their one-sided dominance for so long. They owned the magic of mechanism.

There has been much discussion of the motives of the colonizers—the will to power, to dominate, to proselytize, to dramatize beliefs of racial superiority, and so on. Even the colonized, as Mannoni (1956) and Fanon argued some time ago, grew to depend on their subordinate posture in face of the ardent and encompassing skill of the conquering agent of the Metropolis. In Mannoni's image, it was how Caliban yielded to Prospero. The reasons to him are fundamental, and they echo Burridge's: "The personality of the occidental was long ago transformed by a breaking with the ancestral customs and the removal to heaven of a universalized paternal authority. That . . . was how Europe was converted from paganism to Christianity." (p. 52) The colonial arrangement particularly suited a European psychological style: " . . . colonial life is simply a substitute to those who are still obscurely drawn to a world without women . . . who have failed to make the effort necessary to adapt infantile images to society." (p. 105)

The inheritance of early colonialism remains even after one or two generations have come and gone. For example, the "dialogue between the North and the South" in which the South requests funds and aid from the North, while the North wants austerity, discipline, productivity, and reliability from the South, harkens back to Mannoni's theme. A melange of feelings, of anger, outrage, betrayal, bafflement, may be masked by negotiations about hard economic realities and concrete units of currency. Nevertheless, an emotional ocean supports the calm talk—supports it unsteadily and unpredictably. A carefully litigated near-madness covers over the almost unbelievable financial facts which resulted from a foolish belief in the inevitability of productivity. How else explain how supposedly sensible bankers offered loans of vast proportion to countries in which as individuals they would not make even minimal investments? Their greed in making loans and their clients' shortsightedness in applying for them have yielded a financial and human disaster for poorer countries which must endure the demoralization and poverty debts confer. The magnitude of the miscalculations suggests forces hardly taken into account and into the accounts—those forces which freshly recall the whole story of industrial expansion and colonial control. It may be small comfort that in the new version both rich and poor partners are losers, that both rich and poor partners experience comparable confusion about what went wrong. Insofar as grievance is the lingua franca of our political time, everyone can satisfyingly blame everyone else for the situation. But this changes nothing, except to harden psychological attitudes into even firmer perceptions—firmer but not necessarily better understood.

Recall that my task in this chapter is to account for the development of the special forms of production and organization which are the sine qua non of the industrial way. I have extended this to colonial expansion too. Hence Mannoni's comment is haunting, about the particular personality of the colonial agent or officer who sought distance both from home and also from the local people which his status as stranger provided. Yet at the same time that he was a stranger, he was also a superior, a boss really, accustomed to the responsibility for managing everything from the road and wireless systems to teaching Latin to the spiritual welfare of his luckless pagan charges.

Power and apartness in the same man. His very existence was a tribute to his function. The colonial individual enjoyed automatic high status and social effectiveness. A racially or ethnically based aristocracy and elite, the colonial group magnified the separation of status and function of managers from managed.

It is also significant that the British style of colonial administration depended on what was called "indirect rule." Yes, the British were the undisputed rulers. But they permitted and even encouraged local chiefs and satraps to maintain their local powers and administer often complex and certainly exotic territories in the name of the Crown. This was cunning, cheap, and reinforced the special elevated character of the Monarch's manager. So it was taken as perfectly in order, by the English anyway, for a brand-new Oxford graduate with the appropriate social style to be given authority over elderly and seasoned leaders of complicated communities who had to kowtow to a kid to have their durbars undisturbed.

This aggressively confident "managerial style" had hardy roots in the English social world at the beginning of the global expansion of everything associated with industrialism. It was almost reflexive, so that not until decades and decades later, in the late 1950s, did the United Kingdom begin serious efforts to train managers in schools of business. Why teach anyone to do what comes naturally, what is part of the order of nature? When I was a Ph.D. student at the London School of Economics, I took advantage of a program which existed for the benefit of Commonwealth students who were invited to the home of an English family for a country weekend, presumably so that we could experience congenially an excellent official version of English values. I had a delightful time, but was startled when I was chatting with the hostess in the kitchen of her large and agreeable home while she prepared afternoon tea. Suddenly the confident tranquility of the whole soft late afternoon was shattered as she raced into the dining room to retrieve the jacket of her suit and install herself in a very easy chair. Guests were arriving in the driveway and, as she said, "I can't let them see me in my kitchen." The marriage of the managerial assumption and class structure had found its way into the kitchens of people confronting the beginnings of the "servant problem."

There is no easy way to identify precisely how important were different elements in the relationship between industrialization and colonialism. After all, the age of steam is reckoned to have begun with Robert Fulton's steamboat *Clermont*, which harmlessly plied between New York City and Albany—hardly a colonialist sashay. Nevertheless, we have to assume from the effectiveness of the duet of colonialism and industrialization that the mix was relatively volatile at the time. Knowing about machines was somehow proof of moral, social, and actually genetic superiority. Very stimulating and satisfying. As Headrick asserts, "The age of the new imperialism was also the age in which racism reached its zenith. Europeans, once respectful of some non-western peoples—especially the Chinese—began to confuse levels of technology with levels of culture in general and finally with biological capacity. Easy conquests had warped the judgments of even the scientific elite." (*op. cit.,* p. 209)

I stress the British approach to all this because it so clearly depended on notions of racial difference. The French had a rather more encompassing view of their colonial territories and actually formulated their own version of the great chain of being. For example, a French-speaking West African, say from Senegal or Togoland, could receive education and metropolitan socialization, be elected to the French Assembly, and in general be regarded as possessing the high standards of native-born white Frenchmen. A black man from the Ivory Coast could carry a French passport and he would be called, unbelievably enough, *"un évolué."* Once I was interviewing a black senior civil servant in Abidjan, the capital of the Ivory Coast. To show how enthusiastically he admired the French colonial arrangement, he suddenly reached into his desk drawer and proudly pounded his French passport down on the desk: "Voilà! Je suis français!" He appeared to mean it. This is not to claim that the French were any less racist than the British or any other European country (with the probable exception of the Portuguese). But they structured the whole relationship differently, with much more explicit attention to the connection between personal quality and the achievement of modernity. But the implicit paternalism of the French pattern could be dangerous, too. So when the government of Guinea, led by Sekou Toure, voted against formal association with France after it achieved independence, it suddenly found virtually the entire cadre of experienced French officials, business people, and others gone, often with essential files, and clearly intent on punishing their recklessly ungrateful black client-state. Nor could it be claimed that the early record of the French in the struggles for Algerian independence was benign and charming. Nor was the struggle to regain Vietnam after the Second World War a sign of French compassion for the peasantry.

The claim that racism and technology are strongly, even inextricably, related is controversial. But I can find no more charitable interpretation of a persistent theme in modern thought. Even in anthropology, which should have known better, only recently has all talk more or less ceased of "primitive" or "backward" people. And what the hell do notions such as "modernization" or "development" imply if not some new great chain of being with industrializers at the top and poison-arrow hunters with paint on their faces at the bottom? (Somehow it seems an important index of the primordial when men paint their faces. Women can do it anywhere, all the time, without getting called pagan.)

So not only did machines permit a massive expansion of the effect of impersonality on human persons, but they also made possible and passable a quite astonishing conceit about human value and its relationship to artifacts and money. Machines and management became more important, men less.

Colonialism permitted white people to leave their homes with cold confidence. It also stimulated local people to confuse personal betterment with emancipation from the shapes of life from where they came. One could become an *évolué* in French Africa. This was explicit. But the subtler forms of "evolution" elsewhere in the colonial scheme equally disrupted integrated community. The Barbadian writer George Lamming, in the Introduction to a book by Walter Rodney, who was assassinated in a Guyanese prison where he was held for active politicking against Forbes Burnham's government, points out that "what began as a necessary strategy of self-emancipation would become, in our time, a major obstacle to national liberation. . . . Education was a means of escape from the realities of labor, a continuing flight from the foundations of society. To grow up was to grow away." (Lamming, in Rodney, 1981) Migration—geographic, ethnic, religious, political—is a constant feature of modern literature and social science. Once the feudal system collapsed, mobility became possible and often necessary.

However, the case of the migrant from indigenous culture to metropolitan sophistication who had also the barrier of race to surmount was particularly drastic. The barriers could be threefold: getting out of a culture spiced with paganism perhaps a generation away; overcoming the sense of racial deficit hammered home by all the powerful molders of opinion; and simply not knowing how to do the work and penetrate the mysteries of the new industrial way of life. In Ghana, a major source of agitation for independence were the black troops who had served in the war against Germany in the Commonwealth brigades. They *knew* they could do as well as white people. In fact they had helped beat the Germans. But war is very straightforward; there are few mysteries to it. It is practical to the point of smashing kitchens and destroying flesh. Whereas complicated machines may remain threatening still. It is no accident that at a time when computers are entering small offices and now homes, the most successful computer company in the world, IBM, uses as the principal figure in its ads a harmless, somewhat foolish clown, wholly reminiscent of Chaplin (the Chaplin estate was asked for permission) and thus of *Modern Times*. Suddenly a tramp makes good. Innocence is rewarded by brilliant technology and life made better even down to the fine red rose. So don't be frightened; even the simple little tramp can handle it. The machine is his friend and can be yours. Take the machine home.

To extend the colonial metaphor: you're just a colonial too, just like a tramp, but we understand your timidity and will help you just as we did the sweet clown. Self-government is just around the corner. Even the clown is not altogether reassuring, however.

I was told by my lecture agent, who has extensive contacts with hundreds of educational, business, and other organizations, that his most frequently requested subject matter for lectures was the impact of computers. Will they solve all our problems? Will they deprive us of freedom and reduce the quality of our lives? One presumes people think they know little about technology and its limits and possibilities, otherwise they would not spend funds to hear lecturers discuss a highly effective but still manipulable tool. Come to think of it, perhaps that is the problem.

Or do those who fear the machine not know that it is amoral? It is ironic that the opposition to computers appears not to come —as with the Luddites who smashed labor-saving machinery— from the people who might be replaced by them and perhaps lose their livelihoods, but rather from the people who would use and presumably benefit from them. Apart from those that are physically dangerous, machines fulfill the purposes people make up for them. Perhaps the fear of the computer is that it will, itself, overtake its planners—a fantasy the proponents of "artificial intelligence" could lead some to believe. Earlier I discussed the curious status of rationality of decision making in economic and legal theory. Decisions are socially influenced, both about money and about morals. *What is frightening about the computer is that it will actually produce rational decisions.* It will be grandly unmoved by the enmities and enthusiasms of the heart. It will scorn the meaning and rhythms of custom and lore. Perhaps that is why it is advertised by a sweet and harmless tramp who thinks that, with his Royal Garden Party costume and bowler hat, he's more than he really is.

The essence of the problem is that the relatively responsive computer emphasizes the troublesome impersonality of modern system. A smart machine representing an impersonal system can give a sort-of personal answer, or fill in your own name on a form letter, or make a decision tailored specifically to a person—Leviathan become sensitive and astute. What a confusion! A kind of indirect rule, again, this time here, of us, at home. We are colonizing ourselves! Which takes us right back to the original concern of this chapter: How did the system move from man to management? Are we moving back from management to man, but via a machine and based on the norms and needs of management?

Technological innovations expanded the distance between people who still retained their ability to pay attention to each other, cooperate with each other, maintain the idea they were very connected to each other. They permitted distance without the grimness of exile or ostracism. In fact, the tools of distance acquired a mystique and glamour of their own. Do you remember those movies in which privileged people had steamer trunks boastfully decorated with many labels from distant hotels and luxurious shipping lines? Despite the frequent inconvenience and discomfort of travel, to say nothing of funds expended and time used, usually the farther the better. This by and large remains the case, and it also remains the case that telegrams and overseas phone calls generate a sense of emotional priority; people still say, "I'll call you back, I'm talking long-distance." Of course there is a sense of drama in overcoming great distance—in talking to China or Jerusalem and in welcoming someone from Lima—obviously no one can ignore distance. Even when travel is convenient and people possess their own vehicles, distance remains important, and people try to conquer it. The Grand Tour can never be so modest again. It is ironic that the most enthusiastic warriors of air travel, for example, will schedule themselves mercilessly, compensating for the ease of travel with the difficulty of the schedule they assign themselves. Significantly, it was not the busy North American travelers who first factored jet lag into their habits. Evidently a clue was gathered from Russian diplomats who arrived for U.N. meetings and were sequestered for several days before pronouncing on mighty issues. At first this was considered mere typical Russian secretiveness and somewhat punitive. But eventually the simple psychology of it became clear: prudent travelers anticipated a respite after crossing time zones. However, individual variation is presumably enormous. Once there was a taxi shortage one evening at Kennedy Airport and people were sharing cars, which as it happened I did with former Secretary of State Cyrus Vance, who had just arrived from Tokyo. He was bright and chipper, but not I, though I had only trekked from California. When I asked about the impact of travel, he said he had gotten used to it.

Inventing Management

Management has obviously existed in any group of more than one person. The Chinese bureaucracy was operative as early as 1000 B.C. The temples of Mesopotamia in 3000 B.C. had a management system with a division of function between a ceremonial and religious high priest, and an administrative high priest who attended to the secular requirements of their communities. Military structures required some class of decision makers, some approach to the organization of human energy. The empires of Rome and the Holy Romans demanded administration. So did any other large agricultural, governmental, or mercantile endeavor. Before the Industrial Revolution was in full swing, some people concerned themselves with the nature of organization, the rights and responsibilities of leaders and led, and with the relationship of social groups to each other and their gods.

Once the impact of the factory way began to be felt, some individuals thought deeply and clearly about what was happening and how it could be controlled and improved. Charles Babbage, who originated the idea of the computer, was concerned with how human factors interacted with production techniques—though it was the latter that most intrigued and preoccupied him. Robert Owen, the visionary practitioner, was directly involved with alleviating the impact of industrialization on workers in particular. He adopted the Utopian scheme, New Lanark, to explore the limits of his remedy. It failed in practice though it was a moral and to some extent political beacon. Others such as Henry Varnum Poor were provoked by the human issues of modern technology but focused rather specifically on industrial organization and process —in the case of Poor, with the railroads. One of his major initiatives developed accounting procedures to protect consumers' interests. (Chandler, 1977, p. 111)

Perhaps the reason for the relative slowness of the development of theories of management was "that the nature of the market was more important than the methods of production in determining the size and defining the activities of the modern industrial corporation." (*ibid.*, p. 363) Nevertheless the sheer scale of activities began to demand a more tutored approach to the business of business and of production. It is commonly accepted that the catalytic or most forceful figure in the emergence of "scientific management" was the American Frederick Taylor. Taylor trained as an engineer and made a number of important contributions to broad engineering work. But he is best remembered for his effort to assess the specific nature of industrial work, break it down into bits; to relate tools, people, and work in a punctiliously planned manner which would in turn yield the greatest productivity per worker and machine.

Several elements beyond professional avocation helped Taylor along. He arrived on the scene in timely style: "The year in which Fred started his career in industry is almost squarely in the middle of the period of very rapid industrial expansion that, by the end of the century, would make the United States the greatest industrial power in the world. . . . Aided by revolutionary improvements in technology, vast natural resources, and a flood tide of immigrants (in 1882 alone, 789,000 were admitted) who provided the labor and increased size of the internal market, the United States became an industrial state of the first rank. . . ." (Kakar, 1970, pp. 29–30) In addition, it has been argued that Taylor's approach to his work was located in the dynamics of his family life. Taylor opted out of the legal career to which his father had pointed him and tried to attach himself to strongly authoritarian people who would offer him rigor and challenge. Abraham Zalesnik of the Harvard Business School writes, "Taylor had indeed tried to control his instinctual life by mechanistic means, by activity and attention to external detail. He was very ambivalent toward authority, and his own potential as an authority figure, and he tried to solve this problem by looking for the loved and hated father in his relationships at work." (cited in *ibid.,* p. x)

This recalls the colonial officer discussed earlier. The themes recur of disappointing family experience and personal issues externalized into work and other impersonal activity. Be that as it may, it is presumably significant that Taylor chose not law as he was supposed to, but engineering. Thus he could delve into the impersonal world of things and their processes, rather than the spider web of social network and personal interaction lawyers are caught in. Indeed, he went further. He did his best to reduce even the social world of work into relatively mechanical components.

Taylor had a strong sense of justification for his activities. At a meeting of British and American mechanical engineers held in Birmingham, England, in 1910, he remarked: "I say without hesitation that in the average establishment in America . . . it is possible to double the output of the men and the machines just as they stand now, and I believe the same is true throughout this country. It gives us the opportunity at the same time to give the men what they want most—higher wages, shorter working hours, better working conditions, and on the other hand, to give the companies what they most need—a lower labor cost, so that they might be able more successfully to compete at home and abroad." (cited in *ibid.,* pp. 104–105)

Taylor's managerial work began with menial activities. In 1878, he became a laborer at the Midvale Steel Works in Philadelphia and progressed upward through the ranks. He saw his associates in the factory produce perhaps as little as a third of their possible output: "We who were workmen of that shop had the quantity output carefully agreed upon for everything that was turned out in the shop. We limited the output, to about . . . one third of what we could very well have done. We felt justified in doing this, owing to the . . . necessity for soldiering under the piecework system." (*ibid.,* pp. 55–56) Workers had calculated that if they produced more pieces, they would receive less money for each of them. Since there was no certainty they would benefit from their employer's greater profits in any way whatsoever, their strategy protected the demand for their product and allowed relative ease on the job.

Taylor's response was an independent assessment of how much time the work required and how best to do it. In cruel excellence, the optimum performance determined the subsequent performance. The motivation of the worker and the ambience within which he or she worked were irrelevant. Taylor introduced something dramatically new into the mix of elements in the workplace: a persuasive independent scheme to which men and materials had to be bent. An absolute value could be obtained. On its terms, messy and recalcitrant human groups should and could be judged. Obviously this would be profitable for employers. But in the long run, he claimed, it would be to the general benefit of all. The impersonal scheme would reward everyone because of its self-evident value in enhancing the return on capital and the reward for time and effort.

Taylor introduced the Cubist's "third eye" into the world of work. Suddenly, an absolutism subtler and more provident than the overseer's whip was possible in economic analysis and planning. The "efficiency expert" emerged from the chrysalis of confusion and aggressive exploitation that had marked the beginning of the industrial system. Imprecision and exploitation were obsolete, at least in theory. Now efficiency could be the byword, not exploitation, not even pragmatism. Its great virtue was that it was founded on science, not greed. To stand in the way of efficiency was to challenge the whole basis of the forceful life of modern community.

Efficiency as a concept offered an independent, externalized means of deciding the right and wrong ways of doing things. It began to constitute the ethical method at the heart of the industrial way. We are not dealing here with an external force such as a God, or a supervening ethic such as the great chain of being, but rather with a specific and local situation. What was efficient in one plant and locale might not be so in another. The skill of the manager and his engineers was to apply the general principle to the local case. This was not a judge wielding an ethical principle or a priest determining the sinfulness or sanctity of an act. It was a process applied in what was to be a neutral way, with neither fear nor favor nor subtext nor prejudice about any group of the population. Perhaps efficiency benefited the owners at first. But this was merely an incident in the inevitable progress of things. The benefits in general would trickle down in what was to become a chronic assumption of elites about the broad ultimate advantages to the poor of the prosperity of the rich.

Was there not an inconsistency here, an awkwardness of argument? Well, yes. It could seem all-too crassly self-serving for workers to be informed that those immediate and obvious benefits of their greater productivity which flowed to the already privileged *ménages* of the owners would in due course redound to their own humble benefit. Nevertheless, there was the larger systematic picture to keep in view—that sense of an ever-improving control of economic and technical events which would, like that provident good tide, lift all boats. If employees did not immediately share this perception, it was mainly only a question of time and information before they did. Then the different classes would productively cooperate in implicit harmony.

But even if workers lacked a generous spirit of motivation, fortunately all was not lost because grimmer incentives worked too. No less influential a thinker than Adam Smith was convinced of the almost wholesome importance of envy as a principle of social organization: "Our obsequiousness to our superiors more frequently arises from our admiration of the advantages of their situation, than from any private expectations of benefit from their good will." (Smith, 1966, p. 73) If this enviousness alone did not suffice to maintain the social contract, the harder discipline of the laws of property could be invoked: "The poor man must neither defraud nor steal from the rich, though the acquisition might be much more beneficial to one than the loss could be hurtful to the other." (p. 195)

And finally the *coup de grâce* to any activism: "The never-failing certainty with which all men, sooner or later, accommodate themselves to what becomes their permanent situation may, perhaps, induce us to think that the Stoics were . . . very nearly in the right; that between one permanent situation and another there was, with regard to real happiness, no essential difference." (p. 209) Should a few cranky poor still feel irked by their circumstances, the blame is wholly and pathetically theirs: "The great source of both the miseries and disorders of human life seems to arise from overrating the difference between one permanent situation and another." (p. 210)

With such attitudinal preparation, small wonder the idea of efficiency assumed an independent value all its own. Not that Adam Smith or any other thinker was quintessentially responsible for the economic Zeitgeist. But the reigning belief in virtuous hard work and diligent postponement or avoidance altogether of pleasures and indolence surely prejudiced the matter. If hard work is valuable, surely efficient work is too. Perhaps more so, even, since efficiency was achieved by the use of that high-order quality, reason, together with that empirical, forthright method, science. Together, these had become the preeminent form of gathering and articulating knowledge of the real world. If work was virtuous, then the efficiency expert became a form of moralist and censor, able to apply self-evident values to human conduct. Suddenly the managers and the experts and their subject became more salient than ever. But where did they come from? I have noted that the first full-time, relatively self-conscious managers in America probably were civil engineers. (Chandler, *op. cit.,* p. 132) Many of these had evidently gone through West Point, which until the 1860s produced the best civil engineering training in the United States. (*ibid.,* p. 95) The connection between engineering and management was hardly casual. It was very likely intrinsic to a ready translation of skills from the management of things and processes to the management of people.

We are at the center of our problem. The independent authority arising from successfully arranging technical matters becomes integrated with managing virtually everything, including people. Decades later the basic conception has not changed fundamentally. Once I was at a dinner with the dean of an immensely important school of business who complained he faced difficulty

In inducing students and faculty alike to assume a generous and responsive attitude to social science. After a long struggle, he finally succeeded in introducing a course to the curriculum to deal with the issue. I asked the name of the course. "Human Resource Management" was the answer. He had lost his struggle to begin with.

The technobabble title would reveal and determine that students learn to treat people as just another element in the process, amenable to rules governing the management of any other resource. Or as a U.S. admiral admitted after U.S. forces had invaded Grenada to discover, because of poor intelligence about the place (they were using gas-station maps), that they faced military surprise after surprise: "We were not micromanaging Grenada intelligence-wise until about that time frame." (Taubman, 1983) The words have it. Blame is attributed to faulty technique. Human contortion and complexity are smoothed out. The United States of America invades a community the size of New Rochelle and any problems it confronts result from a failure of "micromanagement." Harkening back to the early association of management, engineering, and West Point.

I am not sketching a crude picture of villainous people setting about either consciously or with thoughtless confidence to dispossess or humiliate or, yes, mismanage, the lives of their fellow citizens. My point is, the system itself gained autonomy over everyone's individual perceptions and decisions. Remember Robert Owen, whose effort to solve the problems he perceived in the system he had already created and mastered required him to leave his home, travel to the New World, and concoct an experiment this time involving people, which failed. When Frederick Taylor delivered his first paper in 1895 on what he called "scientific management," he was formally summarizing two important forces which predated him and his talk: the function of science in assessing reality; and the search for distance between people and between people's actions and their emotions which appears to have been intrinsic to the emergence of the industrial system in the first place. Scientific management was a quantum leap in this direction. The people who adopted it were presumably the most alert and acute in their community, not necessarily the meanest and most greedy. They were at once children and fathers of their time.

Of course they might want to make a choice about the system, one such as Robert Owen took, or the workers and their trade union representatives who scorned the emergent arrangements, fighting them often bloodily and usually bitterly.

Nevertheless, like Everest, scientific management was "there." Within the pivotal period of time when the industrial apparatus was installed, it is hard to see what would have deflected an apparently ineluctable train of events. Remember that the prevailing view of human nature then was that it was malleable and relative anyhow. As we see even as early as in Adam Smith, people were expected to adjust to situations presented them. Therefore the notion of management as a skill predicated on free-floating optionality is hardly out of place. This was not a trivial matter. It had true magnitude. An indication of how seminal early decisions were about the role of management in modern business, and how massive the forces involved in establishing it, is suggested by the striking fact that when George Baker—who made a vast fortune in insurance—had to decide what to endow with his money, his final choices were either the Harvard Business School or the George Washington Bridge in New York! He chose minds over movement. Can any mere school have the vast impact of a structure so substantial and intrinsic as the George Washington Bridge? Yes, is my answer, and his.

Of course there had to be something to have a theoretical approach about. As Fernand Braudel (1977, p. 61) has shown, not until the nineteenth century did manufacture account for more than a very small part of total production, compared with the cottage and artisanship systems. These patterns of production were by definition decentralized. They depended to a considerable extent on factors out of entrepreneurial control, such as where artisans chose to live and how the cottage system related to the availability of agricultural land.

But the productivity of industry changed that. As Braudel notes, this finally supported a consistently lucrative capitalism of banking, trading, and so on. "The extensiveness of any capitalism is in direct proportion to the strength of the underlying economy." (ibid., p. 62) The system not only produced things, it produced information about itself, although science also avidly sought information about the world outside and latterly about our inner worlds too. Now it is widely acknowledged that this information has itself become part of the world of work. For example, because of the importance of information, Daniel Bell, in a most influential book, has announced the arrival of the postindustrial society. Hence, "Industrial society is the coordination of machines and men for the production of goods. Post-industrial society is organized around knowledge, for the purpose of social control and the directing of innovation and change. . . ." (Bell, 1976, p. 20) Industry produces information, information produces theory: "What is distinctive about post-industrial society . . . is the *centrality* of theoretical knowledge—the primacy of theory over empiricism and the codification of knowledge into abstract systems of symbols that . . . can be used to illuminate many different and varied areas of experience." (p. 21)

This almost seems a dream come true. The work is organizing itself! The golden calf is a dutiful machine. Furthermore, it is challenging and even fun to shepherd. It demands from us not muscle nor even dexterity but, more characteristically, a seminar. What arises is an "intellectual technology," the effort of which is "to define rational action and to identify the means of achieving it." (*ibid.,* p. 30)

Now management is totally in its element. Not only can it avoid dealing directly with the productive process—will the nut fit easily on the flange, or do the biscuits look nice as they roll off the conveyor belt and are swept into containers? But even that small direct connection with material events can be subsumed into categories of data which the productive processes themselves will generate about their own activities, printout after printout. One simple reason for the success of Japanese quality-control schemes now legendary in any book on modern management is that they took for granted that humans and systems were in fact integrated. It is hands-on, not brain only. Work is conducted with a practical empiricism to which employees are invited to respond. This can be distinguished from a style of a priori planning that plots out in theory the nature of work in practice. It is hardly believable but true that much of the effectiveness of Japanese management has to do with such simple matters as asking employees what they think of how their work is done, and how it can be improved. This is not the sole reason or perhaps major one for the broad effectiveness of Japanese industry. But it reflects a point of departure which sturdily affects a destination. The Japanese built a practical structure atop the pioneering theory of Western industry and surpassed it.

Broad assumptions of industrial behavior produced the system in the first place and sustained it during its long, triumphant, and supervening residence in Europe and North America. A formidable passion for a style of systems theory analysis, founded on confidence in the effectiveness of moving from a priori assumption to practical consequence, influenced the conduct of virtually all major sectors of the social world. From organizational evaluations to forming defense policies to creating marketing flow charts, a belief in the power of reason married to optionality buoyed the confidence of the managers of the whole mighty scheme. They had mastered it. They became Masters of Business Administration. "Hugh Briss" had come to town and settled in.

Let me reemphasize the main theme of this chapter with succinctness. The human race has been swept off its feet by the industrial way. A notion of management as an autonomous process has been developed. This is both symptom and stimulus of what is in effect a loss of linkage between the human past and the human present. The result is a social theory oddly but decisively committed to the individual as "the hard, ultimate kernel," to repeat Gellner's phrase, and a related belief that people should and can adjust to the demands of the economy and the organization embedded in that economy. This makes it very difficult for individuals to sustain clear notions of what is right and wrong. So the problem of "situational ethics" emerges—of cutting your moral cloth to suit the current fashion. Perhaps this implies that the graduate of a seminary would find it as odd to do business in a modern organization as that a manager would find it odd to dwell in Holy Orders for a career. Is this an overdramatized contrast? On the face of it, so it seems. Yet on closer inspection I think not. Should the seminary belligerently disequip a person for the burlyhurly of organizational life? Why should a project engineer find the Benedictine pose and repose so foreign to his style and goals? Do the increasing emphases on ethics in professional schools reflect just the unease represented by this question, or have they only to do with malpractice suits?

My obvious reply is that there is seen to be a dramatic discontinuity between the moral quality of serving God and of serving Mammon. In academic and theological cadres the belief remains, rightly or wrongly, that modern businesses and similar organizations do not characteristically boast the highest standards of probity. And the belief inhabits the other side of the divide that "meeting a payroll" and other practicalities violate the virgin ethics of the theorists of rectitude. One major reason for this (if it is true, which I question) is that the standards have been passed down from shepherds and small farmers who seem to have mostly lived on rocky soil with little luxury, who had little help from their friends and much grief from their enemies. Intensely communal though they were, their juridical legacy was a forceful endorsement of individual, not group, responsibility as a general principle. Hand for a hand, eye for an eye, and all that.

Perhaps the extreme outcome of a group-based legality is genocide, which is not acceptable to most communities, though some zealots would applaud it as an adequate basis of national conduct. One eerie afternoon when I was in Israel for a research project, I was toured around the northern perimeter of Israeli held territory and saw the signpost to Beaufort Castle, built in 1215 by those megademented Crusaders. At that time it was the PLO stronghold, in turn later attacked and captured by the most recent tenants, Israeli troops. Seeing that sign was rather like peering at a fossil. Had hatred such a long, vivid, and up-to-date history? And what a mean moonrocky landscape to fight over! Who so urgently needed it, and for what purpose?

Managers Maketh the Man

If war is group-based legal theory, better have an individualist theory instead. Which we have. Nevertheless, it becomes difficult to reconcile aspects of this individualism with other, real elements of the membrane of society to which all individuals are attached. In fact, when people who commit crimes are considered really crazy and therefore immune to social influence, they may be exempted from guilt. They are given medical not juridical remedy to their actions. By and large, however, the law acknowledges the reality of social linkages, so cumbersome devices must be invoked such as quota systems or affirmative action, and "Brandeis briefs" which permit the introduction of somewhat extraneous and in effect circumstantial social data into the assessment of people's legal propriety. In essence, these are efforts to recognize the fact that humans are gregarious animals. That they are subject to the strengths and weaknesses of gregariousness. But that they are confronted with a legal system which seeks to abstract them as individuals from the stream of social conditions of normal human life. Of course there are legal categories which are specifically about gregariousness, the charge of conspiracy, for example, or the matter of being an accessory before or after the fact. In homicide cases, the reduced charges of manslaughter or third-degree murder are available for people charged with crimes but who committed these as part of a social endeavor or group that realistically limited their full autonomy.

Even though individuals are supposed to be judged as morally autonomous, rational people, the matter is not cut and dried. There remains confusion. Courts must confront social animals who performed social actions but who are being judged as pristine individuals. It creates unease. Let me return to the solitary monk who has been morally admirable in his stony austere cell and in his pious devotions. Now he moves to the firmly luxurious corner office in the tall headquarters building of the complex multinational. Is it inevitable that he will founder? Is his soul in danger? Would he make his new colleagues uncomfortable? Why do people who become priests or rabbis or whatever have to swear they will abjure the worldly life? Is life Outside inevitably corrupting?

By contrast, how comfortably and deftly will the chief financial officer of a global oil company adapt to the austere monk's cell, to the disciplined search for understanding God, good and evil, truth and equity, and the value of eternal values? Will his new colleagues assume he is the moral equivalent of the monk with whom he has made this life-switch?

Why are people who are supposed to specialize in right and wrong essentially forbidden to devote their lives to gaining power in the real world? After all, if they did, they could directly affect those same potentates whose confessors and counsellors they become. Does this reveal a deep conviction or fear that power or even mere contact with power corrupts? That therefore those whose trade is in good and evil should turn their faces away from the arena where decisions about good and evil behavior are made? On the other hand, where ethical decisions must be taken nonstop, ethically trained people are virtually nonexistent. What does it mean that those who must make such decisions are by definition *not* the people best taught by their community to do so? It seems almost aggressively unfair to put a person into a situation requiring clear and often complex ethical choices, but without equipping that person with those skills which by contrast religious officers are supposed to have. A talented pilot, but with no course in navigation. Or is it assumed that the two ways of life are unassimilably different?

I have approached this problem in a deliberately simple-minded way to dramatize the peculiarity of the situation in which we find ourselves. It is exemplified in the fact that most people do not attend religious congregation on workdays—they are quarantined by time. Of course lawyers are on hand to explicate the law. But often they are hired to suggest how to challenge or finesse it, not to follow its principles at their most noble, heartfelt and elemental. They are lawyers, not ethicists.

Broadly speaking, powerful people are required to make significant decisions with only a limited amount of preparation to decide what should be done in the name of ethics, compared with their presumably ample competence in their own techniques. Obviously organizations such as the Aspen Institute and the Hastings Institute for the Study of Ethics try to overcome the imbalance with carefully designed but relatively brief (usually two weeks at most) courses for senior decision makers. I have been involved in a number of these at the Aspen Institute. The fact was that often very powerful people could find themselves confronting ethical issues in the seminar room for the first time in decades, issues likely to be equally hot in both board and seminar rooms.

I emphasize the point that the person must make a decision himself or herself or in conjunction with others. Nevertheless, most people most of the time may be unable to achieve full analytical dispassion and moral autonomy. We see once more—in the extreme case—from the transcript of Eichmann, how organizational fear and craven obedience produce the petty certainty of a poisonous functionary self-defined as a helpless lackey:

> Commands were given, and because they were commands, we obeyed. If I receive an order, I'm not expected to interpret it, and if I give an order, I'm forbidden to justify it. I receive an order and I'm expected to obey.... This government was ... elected by a majority of the German people ... every civilized country ... on earth had its diplomatic mission, and so on. Who is a little man to trouble his head about it? I get orders from my superior and I look neither right nor left. That's not my job.... My men ... knew I hadn't killed five million Jews. I have to say these things, because as head of Bureau IV B4 I wasn't responsible for everything, only for a rather narrowly circumscribed field.... I wasn't free to do as I pleased. (cited in Von Lang, op.cit., pp. 158–65)

This is gruesomely evasive, but it is a microcosm of the broad problem:

Where does a hierarchical primate take his stand?

And against whom?

*   *   *

Let me summarize my immodest proposal.

The development of the managerial or organizational weapon may have been in the order of significance of understanding flight or atomic physics or electricity. Within a relatively brief period, ten generations at most, the idea of what constituted human social possibility was drastically leveraged by widespread adoption of the bureaucratic separation of person from office. This permitted people—and forced people—to suspend or abridge the operation of moral patterns evolved in small groups. The evolved capacities could be held at bay by the opportunity, and even obligation, officials had to resist "emotion." So the most skillfully gregarious of mammals were emancipated from powerful guiding sentiments. Then this freedom was married to the energy of technology and new energy systems. The offspring was very nearly a whole new world.

Meanwhile, during the Adult Education Classes on board the *Titanic,* the social sciences, sociology especially, analyzed and chronicled these developments. They vividly portrayed an ideal world of rationality and legality in which no primordial and parochial stimuli should intervene. When occasionally they did, educational rescue squads armed with manuals about modernization and development or education in the scientific tradition stepped in. "Scientific management" as a force facilitated detribalization of the species. Modernization of physical plant was accompanied by modernization of relationships by turning them into functional and manipulable near-artifacts, as in "We're working on our relationship."

Do I exaggerate all this? Do I not? But is not the world so different now from what it was? Is not what is called "modernization" real? Is there not a hunger for the fruits of the industrial way in places where three generations ago a visitor would have seen a way of life hardly different from what it had been three hundred generations back? Is it not significant that encounters between, for example, "North" and "South" are not about God or the Devil or any other primary quality, but rather about the distribution of goods and services—about participation with equity in the web of modern production and consumption? Even the ruinously expensive contest—for what?—between capitalist and Communist countries has in a central way to do with how things are made, who has power over the productive process, and over the political one which depends upon money for comfort and option. No doubt there is a strong element of permeating morality among the combatants in all this—phrases such as "evil empire," "rapacious exploiters," and so on are tossed around quite freely. Nevertheless, the pride of Soviet ideologists in a great factory, created where none existed before the Revolution, is real. It reflects a successful commitment to a way of economic life. Similarly the quintessential free-enterprise capitalist applauding the American way of life is legitimately reflecting a long-standing set of social values that are quite specific and particular. They are at the heart of a tribal ethic surrounding wealth and its uses, privileges, and obligations.

The emergence of management theory and conceptions of business organization has exaggerated the differences in self-consciousness between members of the capitalist and Communist systems, even if the technical processes of getting things made and transported are rather common to both. Technology is relatively common between the two systems. Even if by and large Communist countries must buy or steal the most advanced products (a distinguished professor of medicine in New York once asked rhetorically: "When did a Communist country ever develop a good new drug?") from the capitalist West and Japanese East, the systems of belief of, say, Americans and Russians seem to fail to converge in the same way. Ideological friction appears to increase and wane unpredictably, depending on the political forms and forces of the moment, even though the underlying uniform commitment of both systems is to comparable styles and outcomes of production.

Is a reason for this precisely the sense of liberation from tradition and concreteness which scientific management provided? Paradoxically, the notion that any social system is possible, once the appropriate planning and training are in place, underscores the differences that do exist between systems and emphasizes their possible political meaning. At an historical moment at which dazzling, potentially congenial technological skill is displayed by, say, both capitalist and Communist military engineers and scientists, the real world is divided by profound acrimonies of an internationally pervasive and economically depleting kind, and on a vast scale. The common characteristics of American humans and Soviet humans have been submerged by the putatively different schemes of American and Soviet management. At no level does easy connection take place, not even among the scientific, technical, and professional groups where the most obvious similarities of interest and focus exist. Visitors to one bloc or the other, even philosophers and anthropologists, are presumed to have politically or militarily useful potential. I know for a fact that even the most seemingly innocent academic tour may be suspected of ulterior intent. Indeed, the fewer the foreign visitors, the more likely—so goes the assumption—that those who do visit the enemy country are seeking a double reward for their travels, one obvious, the other familiar to any reader of spy novels and screaming headline news stories about defecting scientists armed with blueprints of a dangerous future.

I labor the point for dual reasons of my own. The first is to lead the way to the next chapter, which deals with the science of psychology that underlies the industrial world of which I write. I want to show that the concept of psyche-as-product is essential to the industrial way, and that members of industrial societies are presumed in large part to begin life with a form of original psychic sin or imperfection that can be remedied by industrious self-management and self-improvement.

The second reason is that the lability or manipulability of the psychological self is accompanied by strong ideologies which manage the collective selves of the community. If selves are products and can be made, then who is to make them, and along what lines? What's the style to be? The point and the goal? This provides ample work for ideologists. Megadoses of the vitamin of conviction become routine. Ideology becomes to politics what management theory is to work. Events and facts of life may only achieve significance and meaning after interpretation in the context of whatever ideology overrides the truisms, pleasantries, and ruckuses of daily life. Of course daily life may and usually will finally overwhelm any ideology. But this is precisely the reason for even sterner, more vigilant ideology. The dilemmas of life can be regularly and confidently turned over to the experts for solution. The bureaucratization of intimacy and privacy. So the optionality of matters is seemingly much enhanced, and surely it is. Hence the vigilance and clamorousness of those who claim to know the right and the true may become ever more salient—even if belief in their rectitude is necessarily spiced with the general incredulity of a secular age.

Secularism expands the power of the idea of optionality If God is not ordering everything decisively and if man is deciding at least most things, the amount of option in the world increases. There is even more latitude if people are also optional. That is, if human nature is broadly unfixed and the human program broadly open. Recall the Indian case, in which reincarnation—fixity over vast time—is added to the predestination of beings in current life. And compare this with the contemporary notion of protean personal reformation—of the possibility of self-extension and self-enhancement.

Enter Frankenstein's opposite. The dream human, self-made, self-correcting, chronically self-improving, the flesh-and-blood partner to the endlessly progressive universe of machines. Perhaps in the past people could seek salvation and vindication in the religious sphere and then in the economic. With brilliantly admirable succinctness, Calvinism united the two for its fortunate adherents. But in the present, people can seek and do find such salvation in the personal psychological sphere. They can energetically travel the private stations of the cross of unfulfilled potential.

My opinion is that when the world turned from man to management, it helped redefine man so that in effect we could rid ourselves of the concept altogether. Managers could triumph fully. There were real managers, with corporations and cash flows and products and strategies and machine tools and definable things to do and make. But there were other managers, too, perhaps subtler yet as pervasive: the managers of symbol and consciousness, experts and commentators who helped generate a social science and a social conviction which efficiently reinforced the great industrial process making everyone money.

That social science was, principally, psychology. If sociology is the implicit science of industrial management, then psychology is the implicit science of industrial man. As an intellectual force sociology has faded, perhaps because it has already effectively made its core point about the triumph of Society. On the other hand, psychology remains a useful force to people. It provides a buffer between the primordial heart of Community, and the rigors of the industrial mode. It has become the therapist to the workers, at all levels, to all of us. It is the Company Doctor.

4. The Psycho-Industrial Complex

The United States and the Soviet Union share the vast military apparatus they have separately created to protect themselves and threaten each other. They also share an historical commitment to the science of psychology and to its origins in the work of Pavlov, who trained some dogs to salivate when they heard bells that had been formerly associated with food. In both formidable countries, a deep belief in man's ability to create and refine his reality has been centrally fed by an approach to human nature which emphasizes the environment and which affirms the openness of human option. This is a prime characteristic of the industrial way. It is no accident that the social science which is at the heart of its working assumptions about human behavior should so broadly suit the system overall. Suit in the sense that a productive system which involves the most complex and expensive tools in history for its work also boasts a belief that it is desirable, and—more interestingly—possible, through social science to help people adapt to the requirements of their work. Furthermore, they are expected to approve of this and indeed enjoy it, too.

In this chapter I want to show how the psyche has itself become a product. I describe how the experience of personal and interpersonal life has been affected by the idea of productivity as a value. I suggest that even social life is viewed as a product, that an important theme of contemporary popular writing and adult education has to do with equipping people to better manage their social activity, to maximize its effectiveness—as if an individual life were a business enterprise. Then I turn to how all this is evaluated—to the process of "human quality control" reflected by the psychological testing industry. And I describe how sophisticated statistics have affected the government of human organizations so that the notion of behavior-as-product can be smoothly integrated with the management of people.

The story begins with babies. John Locke thought he had the key, but he was wrong. He developed the idea of the *tabula rasa,* the infant blank slate on which all of life's tutorial experiences are written. But because there was no good science about it then, he could not know that infants are not a blank slate. He could not appreciate the avidity and indigenous skill infants receive as part of their legacy from the gene pool.

Nevertheless, the model of the human being as an unformed consumer of instruction was the dominating one for nearly two centuries. The child began as a creature in deep deficit. Even the astonishing complexity of language was, it was held, the result of environmental input alone, not as was finally and persuasively shown by Chomsky and others, the result of a complex interaction between the outside world of speech and the child's inner world of indigenous capacity to listen intelligently and speak effectively. Now we know that speech involves active contribution by young children. Infants even a few days old can distinguish the voices and faces of their mothers and others close to them, can mimic their facial expressions, and can orient their heads to interesting things in their world. To be coy about it, children are not passivists but activists.

The principal crusade of "progressive education" was to treat children as activists and to reduce educators' traditional dependence on rote learning and low-order analysis. Centuries and countries of children had had—where education existed at all—to endure the peculiar challenge of memorizing everything from tables of multiplication to catechisms to Bible verses. (Why have adults such an odd belief in the virtues of memorization? Because they forget so much?) The traditional model was that the child had to be constrained by the forces of society and instructed about its requirements. Otherwise forms of chaos and insubordination would ensue. In the absence of a sequence of Pavlovian training, the child would lack the equipment and demeanor for effective economic conduct as an adult. It is no accident that one of the most effective educational communities was the Scottish, which not only schooled its young rigorously and with a sense of industry but also exported its products, many of whom took influential positions in other English-speaking countries such as the United States and Canada in particular, where persons of Scottish origin dominated the college system as well as the banks (again no accident). Nor was the relationship accidental between that educational pattern and the Colonial Service, which managed the British Empire with parsimonious effectiveness.

It is no surprise that there is close connection between theories of human nature and the style and form of education. An avowed intention of educators is to improve the competence of students. Thus there must be a fairly explicit working model of what has to be improved. The John Locke theory fit neatly with the Pavlovian to support a system committed to significant change and to optimizing human capacities. Another version of Adam Smith's conception of economic rationality, this one with the idea of maximizing human capital or resources rather than economic, but nevertheless based on a similar view of life-as-enterprise. The dominance of economic individualism has been accompanied by a seemingly inexorable movement toward psychological individualism. This is not restricted to the education of the young. The principle is lately extended throughout the life cycle. The "human potential movement" celebrates the self-enhancing value of miserable and punishing situations—even for those who die, if one is to treat seriously Elisabeth Kübler-Ross's extreme perspective. Pangloss psychobabbling in California.

The idea of the individual as a psychological entity is in close accord with the requirements of an emerging industrial system that needed people to be mobile both physically and emotionally, and that could benefit as a community from both increased consumption and production by people. One supported the other. And the individual supported himself or herself.

Not that there was necessarily a plan to accomplish this. It was not the work of a group of commissars or managers arranging the inner lives of citizens. But cultures almost by definition are integrated entities. And the needs of large industrializing countries marked by regional diversity and ambitious national conceptions —the USSR and the USA—were readily served by the style of psychological analysis already in place in science. Psychologizing and nation-building abetted each other. A traditional way in which historians and political scientists described the state was that it was the family writ large. But no longer. Now it was the individual writ large. The family became less and less significant. National-ism and individualism triumphed in unexpected concert, in harmony with the new mode of economic production. The change was so pervasive. It hardly seemed like change at all. It became as ambient as climate. I want to examine this some more.

The Production of Self in Everyday Life

The "self-help book" neatly exemplifies what happened. It is a tangible symptom of a widespread value of personal improvement. Once upon a time such books focused principally on the religious realm, but later on they dealt with an array of subjects, ranging from securing money and enduring diets to various styles of social intercourse rumored to offer practitioners greater depth or autonomy or health or control over others or erotic option or competence in handicrafts or car repair. At the center of every program is a striving individual, navigating between the strong self-confidence a good student needs and the sense of deficit implied by the obligation to self-improve in the first place.

Of course the first major self-help book was *Self Help,* by the enthusiastic Victorian Samuel Smiles. With honesty equal to its title, this confronted the issue of self-improvement in the larger context of an increasingly mobile English social system. (Briggs, 1972, p. 118) Smiles was an executive with an English railway company during the early heyday of that industry and that country. From this vantage point he understood in detail the shortcomings of the system he was part of—the "skimped work, gambling, fraud, intemperance, dishonest advertisement, and sharp practices. . . ." (*ibid.,* p. 124), and he concluded that high personal standards must be the essential props of the good society. "National progress is the sum of individual industry, energy, and uprightness as national decay is of individual idleness, selfishness, and vice. What we are accustomed to decry as great social evils will, for the most part, be found to be but the outgrowth of man's own perverted life." (p. 125) While Smiles was no Pollyanna about the economic system, he was certain that the basic unit of social action was the aware and striving individual. The success of his books, and those more sentimental ones later in the United States of Horatio Alger, plainly appealed to that "hard kernel" of individualism to which Ernest Gellner linked the industrial system.

Later critics might well accuse Smiles of some complacency and capitalist apologia; after all, the clarity of his message was tarnished by the depredations of the Depression, if not earlier by the convulsive war of 1914–18. But the mechanism of individualism remains, the mechanism of a questing creature seeking more and better experience, not content with the great chain of being, not intimidated by the possible hubris of challenging the self and its limits and options. This is colorful and surely often fun, and may indeed yield real increments of competence and enriched existence. It results in a quite striking, perhaps novel form of society, in which there is hardly a full-throated society at all but rather what I called in *Optimism* a "psychiety." This is a system of life in which the principal unit of action is the individual, not the social group itself—the final atomization of *Gesellschaft*. And not only the economic system was committed to an Adam Smithian model of individual rational decision making. Now even the social system, too, has been predicated on individual endeavor.

Not only endeavor. In an analogue of capital investment, the individual is seen as a *sui generis* enterprise, the value of which is improvable by investments of money and time as education, or therapy, or the books I mentioned—which are frequently tax-deductible as business costs.

Everyman is an independent contractor.

The educational system is central to all this. Once principally an agent for mobility up the social ladder for the poor and maintaining the status of the affluent, now the schooling system is partially adapted to a form of inner mobility.

Self-help literature depends upon literate people who read, almost always alone. The basic mode of literate communication, lonely reading, became the predominant pattern.

How would another ape deal with these matters? We are a gregarious species, unlike the more solitary gibbons or orangs. But look. Members of society whom we are expected to respect invite us to privately consider a written text advising how to change and improve one's life. This is an innovation indeed. Radical. A person is being told, in private, how to leave the very social group within which he or she seeks privacy in which to read. And it could be subversive. Was it not even supposed to be, in a complicated but perceptible way—for example, when millions of immigrants to America educated their children in the ways and wiles of their adopted country, only to find them lost forever to their original tribal synthesis. The marginal man of sociological legend and real life.

Not that reading alone accomplished this; but also the simply formal nature of it as a communication mode. *The whole point of reading is that it is dynamically effective and can induce change.* We understand this well when we observe how enthusiastically dictatorial governments restrict reading by censoring existing texts and compelling writers to avoid creating questionable materials. The photocopier is a staple of modern education (I am convinced that some students confuse copying and reading, and in a magical manner believe that possession of a copy of a journal article, for example, is nine tenths of reading and understanding it). It is sobering to recall that access to photocopiers and other duplicating machines is forbidden in the USSR except to people with security clearance. Words written down and distributed can make a major difference to the serenity of a dictator's sleep.

Then, when reading became common, how could words not make a difference? It is always amusing to discover television apologists who explain that violence and gratuitous carnage on television have no impact whatsoever on viewers while, elsewhere in midtown, network salesmen are charging advertisers tens of thousands of dollars per minute to be gratified by TV's effectiveness as a sales force. A force for what to buy but not how to live? Highly improbable and an insult to the intelligence. Same with reading. It had a volatile impact which facilitated the individualization of community—to create a further déracinée scheme. Perhaps members were linked by the private experience of reading the same public text, best sellers, word of mouth, and all that. But nevertheless the private medium was in good part the public message.

The movement to literacy for *Homo sapiens* was the beginning of a major trauma because it forcefully stimulated a decisive individualism. In turn, literacy has been essential in the emergence of planet-wide systems of management and armament, and of course of ideologies, those theories of abstract certainty. If reading was associated with impersonal formality for organizational purposes—as in the bureaucrat's memos—it exaggerated the personal for psychological ones. There emerges the notion of the psyche at work. It becomes a production center. And the psyche is as manageable as any other product. In this psychiety, therapy is the back-up for failure or unhappiness similar to how religion and confronting one's Maker were in the Post-Reformation past. This therapy takes many forms, from real doctors to personnel officers

of insurance companies to social workers to guidance counselors
—the array of persons committed to helping others through intervention, all with the needs of the patient or client in mind. Back
to that "hard kernel."

The new focus is not the parish as a whole but the psyche in
particular. There are various complexities and ambiguities of great
meaning in all this: does the company doctor try to get the patient
back on the job or back on his feet when there might be at least
temporary incompatibility between these two goals? Army doctors
confront the issue most directly, or Soviet psychiatrists dealing
with political dissidents. Nevertheless the therapy model is struc-
turally different from the parish model. While there are great varia
tions in how it works, there is a new historically radical focus on
the individual person.

How does a psychiety work and what has it to do with industrialism? I have already noted that in both the major industrializing
and politically expansive societies, the USSR and the USA, a similar approach was taken to the matter of psychological theory and
hence social planning and projection. The individual was *tabula
rasa* and therefore malleable. To motivate and guide people,
strong civic ideologies were needed to fill the gap left by nature.
In both cases regional variations were to be subsumed under the
modus vivendi of the dominant group. In one sense the U.S. Civil
War was just such an assault on regional variation, while the
USSR still confronts, and increasingly, the impact of its large
Asiatic population on military and economic activities that are
based upon culturally Russo-European social values and practices.
In the USSR, perhaps one can say that the difficulty of the fit
between the demands of the system and the indigenous habits and
desires of the population is dealt with by the rigid political au-
thoritarianism of the system, by alcoholism—until the Gorbachev
regime—and by the relatively simple strategy of tolerating a very
high level of economic inefficiency—the people just don't do what
they should, given the machines and processes at their disposal.

In the United States, the issue is resolved differently if more
benignly. The social sciences have sought to find ways of bridging
what gap there is between people and economy—through industrial psychology as far as employment is concerned, market research as far as sales are concerned, and organization theorizing
as far as management is concerned. There remains a considerable
amount of individual choice and flexibility so that how people

spend their lives may seem to them very much of their own choosing or doing. It is the essence of the therapeutic mode that patients and clients choose it; this is part of its energy.

Thus the consumer of therapy assumes he can choose the means to help produce the most effective and suitable self. Therapy becomes an important concept of mature industrial communities because large sections of the population are seen as benefiting from some form of professional remedy. Economic individualism and psychological individualism—a similar result is achieved in both sectors—yield a suitable well-made product. The self as both producer and product. Perfect.

Well-known professionally but less so to the public, the sociologist Erving Goffman most effectively and profoundly represented this analysis of life. His most influential book was *The Presentation of Self in Everyday Life*, published in 1959. In it he proposed the metaphor of life-as-a-play. He asserted there was a consistent element of willed performance even in routine events of daily existence. Such Goffmanesque concepts as "backstage," "The Arts of Impression Management," "The Management of Spoiled Identity" became for his readers categories that not only described but in effect subtly or directly determined how people lived. He was a pathologist who redefined normal tissue. He saw social life as rich in facade, poor in authenticity, and crawling with manipulation. He wrote: "Regardless of the . . . objective . . . the individual has in mind . . . it will be in his interests to control the conduct of others. . . . This control is achieved largely by influencing the definition of the situations which the others come to formulate, and he can influence this definition by expressing himself in such a way as to give them the kind of impression that will lead them to act voluntarily in accordance with his plan." (Goffman, 1959, pp. 3–4)

Here is a Machiavelli without a country or a century, a classical recipe for passionlessness in public. Because people are deprived of fullness, "individuals often find themselves with the dilemma of expression *versus* action. Those who have the time and talent to perform a task well may not, because of this, have the time or talent to make it apparent that they are performing it well." (p. 33)

Furthermore, people are duped by their own pretensions to integrity: "there are many individuals who sincerely believe that the definition of the situation they habitually project is the real reality. I do not mean to question their proportion in the popula-tion, but rather the structural relation of their sincerity to the per-formances they offer. If a performance is to come off, the witnesses by and large must be able to believe that the performers are sin-cere. This is the structural place of sincerity in the drama of events." (p. 71)

So mendacity and sincerity unite in common cause to main-tain "the drama of events"! The show must go on. That is all there is. The cagey diplomatic communiques are passed, even across the breakfast table, like toast and bitter marmalade. "The implication here is that an honest, sincere, serious performance is less firmly connected with the solid world than one might first assume." (*ibid.*)

We are told that two people enjoying a charmed breakfast suffer from false consciousness. They are unaware of their pathetic social frailty. The more honest and sincere an individual may think he is being, the more likely he is to fool himself and others because his sincerity is but the tool of a false system. How is it possible that, in Goffman's perspective, the most complex and skilled social animal should also turn out to be the most chronically menda-cious? Perhaps, very simply, because like everything else behavior is just a product in a supermarket of possibility, another manipula-tion, another arbitrary confection. But this perception is ill-served by its shallow theory of human motivation, its wan understanding of the sources of human love and acrimony.

If this is not the occasion for an extended essay on Goffman, nevertheless the style and impact of his work usefully suggest that he reflects two central weaknesses of the sociological science he so eloquently mastered: sociology's commitment to the industrial system, and its concomitant rejection of biology as a source of insight into and analysis of the scheme of modern life, even human social life. Like most of his colleagues, he did not treat the body as a cellular reality but principally as a sign or signal. Thus in his large theoretical work *Frame Analysis* (1974), there are five refer-ences to the Goon Show, eight to Abbie Hoffman, none to hor-mones or depression, eight to San Francisco columnist Herb Caen, two to Merleau-Ponty, but hardly any to child rearing and preg-nancy. His *Gender Advertisements* (1978) is mainly about Madi-son Avenue's ideas on sex and gender, not about the formidable reality of physicality as described for example by Edward Shorter in his *History of Women's Bodies* (1983), or the intense social implications of female sexuality described in widely known work, later analyzed by Sarah Hrdy in *The Woman Who Never Evolved* (1981).

It is difficult to enter the fray of another science. If one is unwilling, then it is essential that the scope of what one accounts for be appropriately limited. But Goffman claimed to account for virtually the whole thing. Nothing less than the presentation of self in everyday life. An everyday self in full blossom as part of the psycho-industrial complex. Indeed, in the very first line of *Presentation of Self* he states that his analysis is useful for studying, "especially the kind of social life that is organized within the physical confines of a building or plant." Isn't Goffman implying: this is what *we* got landed with, so let's say that it's true for everybody, every day? He offered members of a culture in love with management a way of transforming notions of management and control that were appropriate to the industrial public sphere —in buildings and plants—to the intimate sphere as well. Hence no one need feel the chill of inauthenticity in moving from home to plant. The reason is, *they are both equally inauthentic.* They feature the same actors, merely in different roles. Just as the factory system produces interchangeable products, so the people of it are interchangeable, too. Anywhere one is, one's social being is still just an artifact.

But if humans are characters in a play, there is an author, nature, even if it was rejected by Goffman and his followers. His consciousness was explicit and new but sharply, almost cruelly, cut off from that other consciousness—of mammalian activity and ruckus, of the sentience of animals encountering each other in real time and a real place. Instead, we are left in a world of actors and interactors, in which the illusion of sincerity is just a better form of management, a better act. But this sociological work is itself a deception. It hides the fossil fury, the ancient color of inner states, and the calm certainty of familiar affections. We are forced to consider the possibility that Goffman's view of his own society reflected more his despair and disillusion with the industrial version of life than a balanced cross-specific analysis of human beings. Having had the privilege of knowing him personally over a dozen years, I have reason to suspect this is so, both from his lingering interest in biological science (which was not however a significant part of his work) and even more so from his particular passion about injustice and the violence of his eye when it spied human shabbiness.

So what can be seen as Goffman's tacit misanthropy is really anti-industrialism. His criticism is not of social man but of the social world modern man has made. A subtle but important difference. The psycho-industrial complex has produced a conception of social life as bizarre as the paranoid planet yielded by the military-industrial complex. And perhaps for the same reason—that they're coats of a few special colors, cut from the same cloth. And this brings directly to mind the hypothesis of the Washington, D.C., psychiatrist Fuller Torrey, who has claimed that schizophrenia, which is the most common and baffling of mental illnesses, is in fact a recent disease, of industrial civilization. A controversial assertion, to be sure. But perhaps the elusiveness of a cure for the disease is related to the fact that its broad cause is the society searching for the cure itself—that it is a disease which expresses the poor fit between the human species and contemporary industrial society. Which is perhaps why sufferers of this multifaceted malaise occupy a quarter of all American hospital beds and no less than one half those used by people ill of mind. (Boffey, 1986)

Perhaps these sufferers under the care of psychiatrists are rejects, either permanent or episodic, from a style of society which is particularly rewarding but particularly demanding as well. But even those of their fellow citizens who more effortlessly respond to the claims on them are not exempt from attention—the attention of psychologists wielding tests.

The Trial of Testing

If the individual person is the unit of capital and investment, what is that person worth? What is the person likely to be able to do with his or her "capital"? To human stereoscopic vision, Cubism added a third eye, the eye of relativity, of objectivity—not the eye of a god, minotaur, or cyclops, but of a person. And it was not at first the harsh eye of the political cop or even Big Brother, but the more apparently benign eye of the psychologist-tester, the impartial exponent of human quality control.

Objective testing of individual skill and characteristics is an obvious good thing. People find out where they stand. The organizations which educate and employ them can choose fairly who they want or not based on information that relates individuals to the wider community. In huge countries with regional diversities, class differences, religious variation, ethnic pluralism, and political heterogeneity, it seems inescapable that the decisions the community makes about itself should be determined on as impersonal or objective grounds as possible. Decision makers should be held accountable for their decisions, and the basis for them revealed. With exquisite conscientiousness, children in particular should be stimulated, judged, and rewarded in ways unrelated to their origins in life. Otherwise the rancor of envy and the reality of inequity will blight the lives of the unlucky and distort the pleasure of life of those overfavored by family history. It is a major intellectual and political challenge to find independent measures of private characteristics, to judge individual capacity without prejudice. Just as the electron microscope can see into matter without fear or favor, surely it is possible to probe the mysterious subtleties of human characters without bias or caprice.

In principle, of course. Because it is a useful point of view, I am fond of telling students considering the biological bases of human behavior that "the shortest analytical distance between two points is a normal curve." Variation is predictable and usually discernible. Because of what Darwin taught us about the link between variation and genetics, we can appreciate the role of variation in the social life of species, presumably including our own. So it is interesting and important to know the form and extent of this variation. But this raises a problem about testing and exposes a paradox. I've stressed that the psychology of the industrial world depends on the premise that human behavior is basically the result of environmental circumstances. If that is so, then what on earth is the validity of tests designed to uncover the real essence of a person—as IQ is supposed to be a measure of a person's intrinsic intellectual power in relation to age? It can't work both ways: in the extreme cases, either a person has a fine environment and therefore is helped to become accomplished, or a person is intrinsically, genetically skilled or stupid and no environment will make much difference. Of course there is a broad interaction of both and other factors—it is not an either-or matter. Nevertheless, the paradox exists in practice. Because of it there have been bitter and stupid arguments about the relationship between IQ and race, for example, and more recently about the claims, evidently substantiated, of commercial tutors who undertake to raise students' scores on various entrance and achievement tests. Remember the tests were in principle designed to reveal native ability rather than the wherewithal to afford or take courses of a remedial kind.

Let us see what is involved here, as simply as we can. A human being is asked to sit at a desk and answer questions on a piece of paper. The answers are entered on a sheet. A machine reads the answer. It assigns a grade.

The number is then made available to the person and others interested in knowing something about him or her. The results will be critical to some selection agencies, such as schools committed to national objective tests, and only advisory to others who prefer interviews, written recommendations, and student papers to the formal tests as bases for decision. Other schools will neither require test scores nor pay them much mind if they are submitted. Nevertheless, virtually all students take some of the various achievement tests marketed for this purpose. Other tests are given for personality style, occupational aptitude, emotionality, for conscious knowledge or putatively unconscious qualities, as in the Rorschach test. Some 400 to 500 million standardized tests a year are evidently administered in the United States alone, about twice a year per citizen, a challenge endured on average twice as often as completing a tax return (which at least children are spared). When one considers how many people will take no tests at all, the frequency of testing for the population at risk for them is provocatively high.

"Quality control," I called the testing industry. Quality control it surely is. But with the important difference that by and large the standards of quality are not absolute but statistical: results are given frequently in percentile terms. Your score reveals how many people were better at the test and how many worse. The competition is with a vast crowd, virtually all of whom are unknown and always will be. Your most private attributes and frailties are being scrutinized in a mob scene and being calculated by a machine. Since the student (in this case) is by definition already an insecure supplicant to the system at large, even the setting in which his supplication is heard could not be more daunting and less likely to reassure just the emotionally or economically deprived individual for whom the objective style of the test is supposed to reveal inner gifts. How else explain the pernicious correlation between economic status and test results? Andrew Strenio shows the clear relationship between the family income of students taking the

Scholastic Aptitude Test and their scores. (Strenio, 1981, p. 38) It has long been known that the best predictor of a college student's freshman performance is parental social class. Not just for vanity or reputation or simple subservience to the national dream do parents struggle for money with which to educate and benefit their children. Money cannot buy everything but it can buy much. Certainly some confidence must accompany cash flow and the status usually associated with it. Why in turn should this not affect how young persons respond to questions explicitly designed to test their speed, confidence, ability to read the official language, and their sense of familiarity with their culture? But it is not clear that the tests measure the skills and enthusiasms with which we have been endowed by evolution; they test a limited, special band of capacity.

There is an ethnographic reality to this, which one can appreciate after a visit of even a half hour to the headquarters of the Educational Testing Service (ETS) in Princeton. The overwhelming force of the industry, ETS is a nonprofit organization which according to Strenio in 1981 grossed $94 million. It designs and grades tests for over 350 different groups a year, including commercial insecticide appliers. ETS is principally located in one of the wealthiest and most prestigious communities in the United States; through its location, it is implicitly associated with one of the most esteemed and well-endowed private universities in the world. It has a groomed semi-rural ambience. According to Allen Nairns's rather dyspeptic study, ETS claims to be a farm even though it makes hay to the tune of $500 a year—thus enabling it to pay property tax in the otherwise expensive Princeton area at the farm rate. (Nairns, et al., 1980)

The grounds are spacious, the buildings elegant. ETS boasts a Visitors and Conference Center which more resembles a luxury hotel in Big Sur than a precinct of austere academic parliament. Anti-elitist tests made in a country club? By people who live in and around a community with more millionaires than any other of comparable size and which is hardly an "objective" reflection of the broad scale of American life? I recall that the principal early version of the IQ test was in fact the Stanford-Binet, partly a product of another extensively privileged community, Stanford. It makes one wonder. Do they protest too much who protest that environment doesn't matter but who themselves choose choice and lovely environments?

The Psycho-Industrial Complex

I do not want to conduct an intellectually uninteresting campaign against institutions equivalent to "ad hominem" criticism here. However, it seems that the predictable inequities of class-based experience are not fundamentally overwhelmed by supposedly objective tests. Furthermore, and this is serious indeed, the scientistic, mathematic, impersonal character of the whole testing procedure will have the effect of unduly reinforcing and legitimizing the impact of results which are claimed honestly to reveal the very quality of the candidate's cells. Thus they will seem more implacably accurate than they are. On balance they will provide scientific justification for the inability of poor kids to navigate among upper-middle-based problems and solve them. Cruelly, tests given to poor youngsters will reveal to them that not only are they poor but they are also stupid. After all, they have just been so informed by a long, thin envelope containing a number summarizing what an impersonal scientific machine attended by experts found out about them, all of this deriving from the Educational Testing Service, Princeton. A set-up, as they say in crime.

I am not denying that there is variation in human ability—I spend a good deal of my time teaching students, challenging them to show me what they've learned, and how well, and what it means to them and the world around them. Then I evaluate them, often with as crude a measure as a letter, such as A or B or C or D or F. However, they know who I am, what interests me, what I expect from them, and that they can without question claim directly that they have been unfairly treated. I am pleased to learn that anesthesiologists and surgeons are obliged to endure highly demanding training and testing, just as it is reassuring to discover that not all applicants for the work of commercial airline pilot make the cut. There can be no substitute for judgment and evaluation of human activity. What is the impact of testing on how people view their own lives?

For contrast, let's inspect a portrait of one of the prototypical and earliest systems of impartial examination, the Chinese. As far back as the Sui dynasty around the year A.D. 600, a pattern of centrally administered examinations was instituted to recruit functionaries for the Chinese Empire. Evidently its objective was to "strike a blow against government by hereditary aristocracy, which had prevailed until then, and establish in its place an imperial autocracy." (Miyazaki, 1981, p. 111) The system was theoretically open to everyone. But the examinations demanded rigorous

147

preparation which consumed time, funds for personal support, and the ministrations of tutors who often were people who had themselves failed the exams so frequently as to be unlikely ever to achieve a desirable post. There was also a rather explicit ban on persons whose parents had "base occupations"; with some of these, such as brothel owner (but presumably not client), the prohibition extended for three generations. At first there were more jobs than successful people who passed the exams for them; but toward the end of the last, Ch'ing, dynasty, between 1644 and 1911, when the whole system was abolished, there were more applicants than available jobs. In consequence, highly trained but frustrated unemployed people took enthusiastic part in anti-governmental rebellion when this was possible. This brings to mind similar situations in developing countries such as India, where the obvious value of education was supported by government funds, whereas the more complex problem of providing dignified economic employment was left to the economy at large, with the result of massive un- and underemployment of educated people.

Only boys in China were permitted to sit for the exams. They began preparation at the age of seven. While the exams were theoretically open to everyone with the base exceptions I mentioned, in practice the wealthier students received better tutoring under more agreeable conditions. And how important these must have been, when we learn from Miyazaki (*ibid.,* p. 16) that during the eight years of training, a boy was required to learn 431,286 characters. There were some seven levels of examination, and the occasion for them was matter of considerable public intensity; at three in the morning a cannon would sound in the town to wake up the candidates, and two subsequent ones would beckon the boys to the exam hall and then into it. Clearly, the exams reflected and reinforced official values of equality and were the reward for demonstrated merit. Subsequent levels of examination were conducted with equal ceremony and a constant attention to the possibility of corruption and cheating. An interesting shift evidently occurred in the examinations, from genuine inquiries into a candidate's knowledge of the classics and ability to write (these were the original projects in the Sui dynasty) to, finally, their outcome as specific stepping stones to the civil service examinations. Competition was meanly severe; usually between fifty-four to eighty-eight times the number of expected passing students were admitted to the exams.

It is hardly surprising that there was tension between the ideal values of an imperial operation, and the nepotism and corruption of real quotidian life. Was not the dynastic idea itself an affirmation of kinship, and was not family life absolutely central to Chinese social organization? But at least the Chinese tried to imbue their national carryings-on with a real ethic of effective equality, in sharp contrast to the avowedly elitist procedures of the hereditary aristocracies of Europe, for example. Not that the problem was solved for the Chinese, even by the wrenching and remarkable revolution of 1949: as recently as January 2, 1984, "China's Communist Party issued a new directive today calling for punishment of Party functionaries who have used their power to advance themselves and their relatives. . . . It called on Party organization . . . to enforce these rules: Leading Party functionaries may not meddle in the employment and job assignments of their children or other relatives. Officials have often reserved the better jobs for members of their own families. Leading Party officials are not permitted to make personal decisions about the distribution of housing which is still scarce. . . ." (Wren, 1984) Etc., etc. Hundreds of years after the Sung dynasty similar issues arise, even after thirty-five dramatically tough and often thoughtful years of energetically frank revolution. No doubt whatever currently functions as the barrier and permission for entry to desirable jobs will remain subject to many of the same tensions and forces which engaged the concern of the Sung dynasty in the year 1000. The human organisms involved are still the same. Mammals first, and officials only second.

Graded and Degraded: Tested and Detested

Tests have to do with information and skill. They also have to do with the power system of the community, its values about itself, how it doles out access to its good jobs, how families interact with economies, and perhaps most interestingly, how all this connects to the belief in the pristine science of quality control. It reveals a commitment to the systematic impersonal mode as an acceptable, even desirable way to evaluate—literally—the hearts and minds of young people.

The style of evaluation is significant. It reveals a world reliant on the primacy of mechanism and also belief in the innocence of the test situation. To my knowledge the first major joke about the problem of familiarity with competence tests was the picaresque novel *Turvey* by Earl Birney (1949), about a hopelessly stupid and rowdy Canadian Army private whose file was persistently lost, in part because his original score was so low as to constitute a challenge to the Army's system of classification: "the captain ... would give him a little test, an interesting new one that he was sure Turvey hadn't had before. So Turvey plowed through the Canadian Army Classification Appraisal Number Two. It was the same puzzle he had been treated to in hospital but he didn't like to disappoint the captain by saying so. He got quite a little further in it this time. . . ." (p. 85) By the war's end Turvey had achieved the stratospheric score of 202 out of a possible 218 and gained the respect of the officer who supervised his discharge from the military. Before *Catch-22,* or *Being There,* Birney had appreciated the caprice in the system. I had occasion to do the same myself, because I had several cousins training to be psychologists, as was the leader of a youth group to which I belonged, and all three improved their skills by administering the IQ test to me, hence also improving my own, on that test at least. When I at last took it for real, there is no question that I had an advantage over other kids less discriminating in their choice of cousins and counsellors.

I cannot remember what my IQ score was. I presume it was reasonably high, both because of my unusual amount of practice for it, and because—to judge from my ability to hold down a reasonably demanding academic job, write books, stand up and talk in public, and so on—I must have a useful level of ability to do those things about which the tests are centrally concerned. Nevertheless, I don't doubt they had a positive impact on my self-conception. I am equally confident they continue to have a direct impact on other people's self-conceptions and possibly on their ability to function in the system thereafter.

And it can cross generations, this complacency. Unpleasant though it is to reveal, I can attest to my own surge of pleasure and pride when my son received from the machine owned by the experts in Princeton news that he had been awarded a very high score in the SSAT examination he had taken while considering whether to change schools. The score was sufficiently high so that I knew it had almost the meaning of a trust fund—it was cashable at virtually any institution of education he wanted to apply to. I grant that the score was also consistent with most of his school performance, though of course that is roughly what one would expect from a test designed to predict school performance. What bothered me was the frankly unsavory sense of superiority I was enabled to feel from the result. I also knew that the opposite feel-ing, of a sense of certified ineptitude, would be the lot of kids and their parents who, *by definition given the statistical nature of test scores, had to occupy the opposite spot on the normal curve.* Were not the children at the low end of the statistical tree defeated before they got going, given the test's claim to reveal innate intel-lectual worth? Percentile-graded tests guarantee that there will be losers. Does this precise system then determine how to overcome the impediments, both practical and psychological, which the stigma of a low score will enshrine? What does it feel like to be in the 10th percentile? What is the effect of such an expert judg-ment on a child?

Psychologists are far more politically influential than they think. The testing industry is an aspect of the political structure of the community, and in this industrial age has become unexpect-edly, almost globally influential.

Let's begin at the beginning. For industrial societies to func-tion, people must acquire particular skills—literacy at the very least. They must be emotionally and technically willing and able to deploy these skills in service to the community. Their behavior is monitored from birth with the tests which evaluate their basic responses. In infancy, they are encouraged to acquire skills as quickly as possible. Toys sold to ambitious parents are held to be educational and creative. Throughout childhood the effort is to speed up the processes of learning, knowing, speaking, writing. Life is a race, getting to adulthood faster rather than slower the common goal. As Adrienne Harris of the Rutgers-Newark psychol-ogy faculty has pointed out, infancy itself has been rationalized under the "impact of technological or instrumental rationality, considered as a worldview. Instrumental rationality penetrates earlier and earlier into human life." (Harris, n.d.) She asserts that psychology functions as "ideology . . . in its promotion as a legiti-mating tool." This is directly related to the industrial mode.

> Schools, technical training and educational experience at all levels include in their objectives the production of a worker-thinker-social participant for whom abstract, alienated and technological work seems "natural." . . . Centralized day-care *and* its particular pro-grams, geared to the production of children skilled at analysis, self-

control, conceptualizing, and abstract reasoning are but two levels of this rationalizing process. At issue is whether the last two decades of research and theory in infancy and language acquisitions have been voyages of discovery or acts of social architecture serving the development of bureaucratized man, now seen as rational, goal-oriented, and technocratic from birth?

She concludes that psychology of infancy has been an act of "social architecture." So do I. Harris's point can be extended backward in time. The process she describes has been intensified over the past two decades, but its basic shape has been the same for far longer. Harris associates this with the development of capitalism—fair and accurate enough since capitalism and industrialism are historically so closely associated. But the more general connection is to the industrial mode rather than the capitalist one per se. The system of ownership is less important than the nature of the productive resources employed. The Russians too have seen day care as prelude to productivity. Who owns the means of production is less significant than their form and meaning.

Again, the self has become the product. The small child is already a productive worker in the industrial system. For a while his or her only negotiable product is behavior, particularly on tests. Its "value" is calculated by the psychological quality controllers. Calculated not on the old terms—learning the catechism, the Koran, the Torah—but rather in the modern numerical mode, relatively, competitively. Graded by the curve. It has all become almost endlessly self-fulfilling and self-supporting. For example, a comparatively new service of the testing agencies is to evaluate a student's chances of securing entry to the schools he or she wants. If you get a score of 680 lah-de-dahs and you want to apply to Emory or Wisconsin or Columbia, you report this to the system. A computer informs you that on the prior record, people with 680 lah-de-dahs stand a 45 percent chance of receiving admission either based on the lah-de-dahs themselves or in combination with other factors. There is a seamless merger of past, present, and future based on the interaction of relative numbers with other relative numbers. The individual's private destiny is submerged in a seemingly benign contest of decimalized karmas. Such statistical realities are like driving through a rear-view mirror.

Remarkably, a highly skilled gregarious primate, man, has consented to abdicate much of an array of insights, sensitivities, intelligence, and judgment to a cadre of professional test givers who claim psychological science as their legitimacy and objectivity as their gift. But where does this presumed objectivity derive from? All the pertinent tests emerge from testing procedures that are supposed to be "culture-free," that is, uncontaminated by any of the social conditions in which test takers live. Social class, region, ethnic background, religion, certainly race and sex, are all laundered out of the final tests by statistical manipulations designed to produce impartial instruments. In much test construction, questions which sharply distinguish between male and female responses are largely removed. To leave them in would allow a supposed "culture-bound" bias to corrupt the result. The same applies to questions answered differently by Catholics and Protestants, Armenians and Asians, blacks and whites.

But these categories are relatively unimportant. They refer to nothing cellular, no fundamental distinction in nature. Whereas gender is a profound and pervasive matter. While there are chronic controversies, the evidence accumulates that males and females process some information in some different ways, may be cognitively interested in some things in different ways and intensities, and may focus in different ways on different forms of solution to problems and dilemmas. This is fully understandable. As the Canadian psychologist Sandra Witelson has said, "the brain is the principal sex organ." Yet the broad intention of the test makers is to remove sexually differentiating questions—precisely those ones which might most sharply reveal the skills and vulnerabilities it is presumably the function of the tests to uncover! Even so, many tests continue to show some differences in how males and females respond, despite the best sanitizing efforts of their doctrinaire makers. Life continues to confound theory.

A stunning anecdote. I attended a meeting on the relations between biology and the social sciences in Bad Homburg, sponsored by a West German foundation, the Werner-Reimers Stiftung. Among the participants was Professor Albert Bandura of Stanford, a highly respected psychologist who had conducted a series of widely cited and influential experiments involving children who had watched varying amounts of film of other children physically beating various objects and each other. On the monkey-see monkey-do principle, those children who saw the most lengthy and violent episodes were most likely after the viewing to beat a large plastic model doll most strenuously. The obvious implication was that violence was stimulated by the social act of watching other people on film. (Bandura, 1979) Bandura discussed the results, noting there were no significant differences between males and females in the intensity and duration of responses. After the formal session was over, I remarked on how curious this was, since so many other data suggested that males and females do differ in their displays of physical bellicosity. Bandura said something roughly like: "That's during the experiment. You should see them afterwards. The girls stop the violence immediately and go on to something else, while the males continue"—here he feistily put up his dukes—"to act that way. It is almost as if they inhabit different universes, that the boys and girls have different eyes which see and attend to different things as far as this violence is concerned."

But this was not in his formal paper! The made-up test did not reveal the genuine reality. Yet Bandura's results stood unchallenged, even by his own data. This scandalous situation can be found elsewhere. The notion of behavior as product overwhelms the reality of behavior as event.

Studying human behavior is scientifically difficult if one wants to replicate the precise control of variables and responses that is the rule in the experimental method. Many experiments succeed in reproducing realistic social circumstances. The results of the experiments may be legitimately taken as representative of real life and possibly of the real social nature of people. Yet having had the fascinating experience of analyzing and evaluating applications for research support which came to the Harry Frank Guggenheim Foundation over a twelve-year period, I became convinced that even otherwise thoughtful and accurate researchers all too frequently confuse excellent operation of the scientific method with really finding out things about people. Mastery and even enjoyment of the research technique overwhelm what it is being used for. The display of scientific finesse and integrity seems in itself such a self-evident mark of social and professional responsibility, that the overarching question: what is this experiment about and can it really tell us something about people? becomes lost in the flurry of technique. A similar misplaced confidence and confusion of realms of endeavor also affect the professionals in the testing world.

The lure of the industrial method of acting and thinking about behavior and its nature simply overwhelms simpler and more accurate ways of understanding human behavior. Exaggerated and inappropriate use of a scientific method, which derives principally from the physical sciences, has had a significant impact on the way in which medical drugs are evaluated for impact and consequences, a way which makes it far more likely than it should be for important sociobehavioral effects of drugs to be totally ignored or at best obscured by the kinds of studies that are frequently conducted in these matters. However highly sophisticated and careful these studies may be, they are far from adequate in tracing the results of drug use, which may be subtle and diffuse but are still necessary in any assessment of the effect of widespread use of the substance in question. The overall issue is another case of the mistranslation of methods from one sphere of research into another.

Let me describe two personal experiences as examples. The first has to do with the psychoactive drug Valium, and the second with Depo-Provera, which is used worldwide as a long-acting contraceptive preparation, though it is not licensed for this in the United States.

In 1969 I suggested in an article published in *The Observer* (London) that one impact of the birth control pill, then still relatively new, might be on males. My reasoning was that insofar as the chemical simulated the hormonal conditions of pregnancy in a woman's body—and therefore she could not become pregnant—it could have some impact on her own sexual behavior and on how males responded to her. Given the economy of nature, on principle and on balance there was a case for saying that there should be less enthusiasm for sex with and by pregnant women. It seemed reasonable to try to test this, if only because the contraceptive medication was the only drug given on a daily basis to healthy people. It affected the process of sexual selection and reproductive effort Darwin showed at the core of animal life. So it had an unusually broad potential impact.

Five or six years later with colleagues in my department and at the Rutgers Medical School, and with funds from the Harry Frank Guggenheim Foundation, I was able to take part in an experiment designed to observe how the contraceptive agent affected the social and sexual behavior of monkeys in a relatively natural setting. We secured access to a tiny island off Bermuda where we were able to house a group of eighteen macaque monkeys, observe their behavior over a settling-in period of some three months, and then implant half the adult females with a three-month dose of

Depo-Provera (progesterone) to observe its impact on their behavior and the dominant male with whom they copulated. Then we administered the drug to the other group of nine females, then administered the drug to all of them, and then to none.

This species is an harem species, and the politically dominant male controls access to the available females. The male in question had demonstrated during the initial nonmedicated period that he had three favorite partners among the nine. When any of these three were medicated, he ceased copulating with them and replaced them with other nonmedicated females. When we allowed the medication to wash out of the system, and after nine months of perturbation, he returned—to his original three loves! The point was clear. The drug had a behavioral effect, most likely mediated by smell, but an effect nonetheless, and a total one at that. (Steklis, et al., 1983)

Even our relatively modest study was unique in the literature. The great body of research on this and similar substances was not on the broad social behavior of the individuals affected but on their individual circumstances, and in particular on perceivable and dangerous physiological impacts of the drug. And often even these studies were conducted in cages, in effect in jails, where enthusiastic reproductive élan was likely to be severely affected by the emotional ecology of the environment. In general, research had focused on the physiological individual as a receiver of medication, far less on the broad social impact of the drug. Of course this was far easier to control and so satisfy the scientific experimental method, narrowly conceived.

A rough-and-ready, and quick, exhibition of the consequences of such an approach to the social impacts of medication was given me when I received a call from a senior medical research supervisor of the company which produced Valium. They had heard of my research on the social effects of progesterone and wondered if they could discuss the possibility of supporting me in a study of, and I quote, "the social benefits of Valium and Librium."

I suggested this was rather editorial but could we talk about it over lunch, which we did. I asked what data they had available on the broad social impact of the drugs and how using the medication affected the patient's relationships, for example, with spouses, employers, children, friends, and so on. What they reported to me was scanty and scientifically negligible, almost unbelievably so. I told them they would have to expect two years or so of research, which would involve interviewing not only patients and doctors but also the people surrounding the patients for whom this psychoactive drug could have some importance. Whether we would find "social benefits" was an open question.

The lunch ended rather grimly, and so did my relationship with those people and that company. About a year later serious medical and Congressional inquiries began about these particular drugs—then the most widely used in the world. It seems that I was supposed to produce a preemptive research strike against a series of negative criticisms that may have been in part responsible for the general decline in use of these preparations. In my view, such drugs designed to affect users' social behavior should not have been on the market without prior testing of precisely those social networks which the scientific method finds more awkward to assess and quantify than individualistic accounts of relatively captive behavior. Respectable techniques of responsible research in one field may be used in inappropriate ways in quite different fields. The result in this case was a lamentable poverty of understanding of the complexity of the drugs' impact. In the same way that the impact of the contraceptive pill on the behavior of men was not even researched in a preliminary manner. Perhaps in both cases the impact of the drugs was wholesome and benign. But could we be sure? And shouldn't we?

Safety in Numbers

Problems of evaluating people and skills must be approached and solved by contemporary communities. Earlier on, I described the normal curve of variation as a recurrent feature of living systems. This obviously applies also to human capacities. Though it is controversial, the various forms of the IQ test are useful in predicting academic success, in part because both challenges, the test and the school system, are concerned with similar problems and procedures. Other factors such as family support, persistence, and further outside conditions may come into play. Other things being equal, some individuals will be more likely to achieve certain goals than others, and inherited factors may be involved, though the estimates of how much of inheritance is integral to performance vary from zero to 50 percent. It is unquestionably possible that some tests will with reasonable accuracy indicate to students, teachers, or occupational advisers something about what

157

a person is like, what they might like to do, and how they might do at it.

A fierce and often unforgiving orthodoxy abjures any possible association between test performance and ethnic, racial, and any other general category. Richard Herrnstein of Harvard University has bitterly described his own rather particular experiences on the subject and also warmly argues the case for the egalitarian value of testing; "selection without . . . tests which means reliance on grades, conduct, or family connection—is likely to be more biased than selection with them." (Herrnstein, 1982, p. 74) As an executive vice-president of the Educational Testing Service wrote in a mock test on the Op-Ed page of *The New York Times* (Solomon, 1981):

> If the opponents of standardized college admissions tests are suc-
> cessful, what factors does history suggest will probably become
> more important in deciding whom to admit?
>
> (a)   the wealth, influence, and social position of the applicant's
>   parents and friends
> (b)   the reputation of the applicant's high school or prep school
> (c)   the whiteness and/or maleness of the applicant
> (d)   all of the above.

Solomon suggests that the last answer is correct. He is probably right, given the rigidity and thoughtless technicism of much of the school system in North America—neatly exemplified recently in the decision of the Dallas School System to "award bonuses to teachers on the basis of students' scores on standardized achieve-ment tests. . . . We use this measure because it is cheap, easy and convenient. It seems to be objective. It is a nice tidy variable . . . it is more simple than spending the time and energy to make complicated human judgments about what students are learning and teachers are teaching." (Hammond, 1984)

The overall situation has become almost tragic, contrary to everyone's intention and interest. The tests themselves stimulate precisely the situation they purport to try to overcome because they so deeply enshrine those very values of industrial pseudo-manageability that appeal to overburdened administrators of edu-cational institutions. The Educational Testing Service has itself renounced such use as Dallas makes for its competency tests. (Fiske, 1983)

But ETS is charging Dallas with a form of excessive technicism that it has itself enforced and even celebrated for decades. Its wounded claim that its tests are being misused in a specific and quite petty manner must be seen in the broad scope of the overwhelming situation it has itself created. In fitting symmetry, the College Board which supervises the tests ETS produces joined commercial publishers in 1983 in offering books containing past tests, as well as advice on how to prepare and take these tests, which were (remember) claimed to reveal innate competence unaffected by specific training and cramming. As a spokesman for the board rather lamely described their change of heart: "We try to provide the services our members want or need, and people want to see the tests. But the Board's position is that we don't believe in short-term coaching or cramming." (Sherman, 1984)

Indeed. Trying "to provide the services our members want or need" is precisely the problem. A bunch of lazy or demoralized or brainwashed primates trying to run a community on the cheap and with the easiest of technofix solutions. Perhaps that's what they want, but is that what they need? Recall that the point of ETS is that it is all about machines, and that answer sheets of the students "click in and out of the machine at the rate of one sheet every 0.2 seconds, 300 every hour, 100 million every year." (Fiske, 1979) And realize that the machines are improving their characteristic skills faster than the managers of them, and the buyers, are improving theirs. Machines are also becoming less expensive, a mixed blessing in some areas evidently because they can be employed by more people who are not necessarily skilled enough to do this well, if anyone can.

A daunting example: an editorial in *Science* comments that the typical computer test subject is usually left alone. The subject reads the usual list of written instructions, then punches in replies to the battery of queries. Seconds later, the tending psychologist receives "a computer printout of up to 50 pages of valid-sounding narrative statements describing the subject's behavioral traits, personality disposition, temperament, vocational interest, intellectual abilities, potential for suicide or drug addiction, medical-legal-psychological details, and a host of other personal details." (Matarazzo, 1983) Meanwhile, "To date there is no evidence published in peer-reviewed journals that one full page of the narrative descriptions is valid." (*ibid.*)

Surely this is madness of a sort, unmitigated by the smooth impartial hum of the efficient machine. I am prepared to say that the indignity and eeriness of the testing event in this case so far overwhelms whatever predictive or other humane value the test may have that it should be forbidden. The method of the test—with all its idolatry of impersonality and numbers—and its controversial accuracy, far overwhelms what might be equalizing effects of the results when used by the educational system. Not that I had then or have now any easy solution to the vast problem of replacing such instruments. But for the reasons I have outlined, it may well be that the current easy solution is no solution at all but really part of the problem.

Let me summarize. We face a paradox. The community which supports tests accepts as an official value that human lives and careers are overwhelmingly the result of environmental influences and that human biology is not a vital factor in explaining the situations of individual people or groups of them. Yet the implicit assumption behind "culture-free" tests is that they reflect an individual's inner potential or basic quality, which merely awaits revelation by the correct instrument. *This idea, of a basic inner quality or potential, is a profoundly biological one.* It implies that we are born with particular traits which can be identified in the absence of their social expression. But in a gregarious species such as ourselves, nothing can exist independent of social meaning and history.

Culture-free? Value-free? These must mean "human-free." This major muddle has yielded an altogether bizarre social double bind; a system founded on the environmentalism of classical psychology has produced a highly coercive social technology committed to culture-free tests. But this is the most broadly innatist, geneticistic concept it is possible to have about human abilities. It denies or tries to ignore the validity, power, and predictive implication of personal and social experience. What a mess! Small wonder there is confusion when there is such a discontinuity between a community's assumptions and its practices.

The problem flows from the well-meaning endeavors of decent people trying to organize a decent society. As the biologist Richard Lewontin has said: "The reification of intelligence by mental testers may be an error, but it is an error that is deeply built into the atomistic system of Cartesian explanation that characterizes all of our natural science. It is not easy . . . to replace the clockwork mind with something less silly. Updating the metaphor by changing clocks into computers has got us nowhere . . . we do not know how to think about thinking." (Lewontin, 1982, p. 16) We are a community with particular values and history. What we do is an outgrowth of that. However, the history is exotic and the values equally so.

Nevertheless the use of tests remains remarkably widespread. Various forms of testing have rather successfully replaced the difficult moral problems posed by human connection and the exercise of face-to-face judgment with a technically elegant if questionably founded theory of social ranking and human ability. From innocent beginnings, and with benign activism and energy, a powerfully alienating force has had surprisingly influential success in inducing members of the society to suspend belief in their own perceptions, their own certainties, and their own estimates. These we have replaced with the formal authority of stranger-experts.

We have also become constrained by formal ideas of how students in groups should behave. I recall that when I first began teaching at the University of British Columbia, I was responsible for an introductory course of about three hundred students. After my first semester's grades were submitted to the administration, I was called in for a chat, to be told that my grades were too high. I had gone above the normal curve of expectation. Brashly, with the enthusiasm and aggressive energy of a newly minted Ph.D. trying to make a mark, I informed my superiors I was simply doing an unusually diligent job of teaching in a large class where the kind of detailed individual tutoring, essay reading, and so on I provided would not normally exist. Then I was told I had not failed enough students. But I replied that the poor ones were precisely the ones I was concerned about and paid special attention to them so that they wouldn't fail, and most hadn't. Anyway, why had the university let them in in the first place, if they expected, or even seemingly wanted, a certain percentage to fail?

Presumably in the end I was assumed to be some form of well-meaning simpleton. But the lesson was not lost on me: high standards meant low grades; not necessarily eager teaching and motivated, effective students, hence high grades. All classes and all instructors were basically the same. Any variation was suspicious. This was implicitly a kind of tautology, what we can call statologic, which I will discuss a few pages on from here. My antipathy to it had been stimulated by McGill University math instructor Donald Kingsbury's intriguing campaign, who had essentially decided that a pass grade was 75 percent or so, because if a student got 50 percent in a course it meant he knew 50 percent correct mathematics, but also 50 percent wrong, which was too much, and so Kingsbury provided additional tutoring to raise the standard. Peculiar and expensive, perhaps. But since reducing ignorance is the job of teachers and teaching is required to do this, it was hardly aberrant.

And this does raise some seemingly naive but not uneventful questions, such as: when a neurosurgery student gets a passing grade of say 50 percent, what *about* the wrong neurosurgery?

The testing interaction represents a basic element of the psycho-industrial complex. The strange belief in the ability of machines to reach into a person and instantly pull out a truth is of course at the root of the widespread use of lie detectors—machines supposed to determine in one thrash a person's fundamental ethical reality. Not only criminals or other malefactors are induced to submit to these highly unreliable tests, but, "in 1981, well over one million employment-related polygraph tests were administered, representing at least a fivefold increase over the number in 1975." (Samuels and Rollins, 1982) Not just the masses must endure this, but among the carefully chosen elite of the U.S. government, the Reagan administration proposed requiring its responsible officials to confront the machine ethicist to inhibit leaks of government information. Tens of thousands of people, presumably among the most socially committed and formally qualified in the community, were to be treated as potential common liars and subjected to a spurious symptom of psycho-industrialization. Apart from its inefficiency, the indignity is striking, with negative impact on the motivation of people harassed by those to whom they are expected to show complex and mature loyalty.

The process proceeds. Tests graded by machine will soon be obsolete. The candidate will interact with the machine directly, at a computer terminal. "Adaptive testing" will permit the machine to respond to the candidate's level of skill and eliminate questions too easy or too hard; as a U.S. Navy scientist explained, "Our goal is to reduce the length of the exam by half." To achieve this, "The armed forces are working toward converting to computers, starting in 1984, the test that is used to qualify and classify recruits. It will be one of the first uses of a technique known as adaptive testing." (Pollack, 1982),

What is most striking about all this is that it represents a fundamental abdication of management. A mechanical procedure, while superficially efficient, will spawn poor outcomes and lazy supervision of the personnel system. The ninety-year-old Lincoln Electric Company is famous to social scientists and some business commentators because it has a highly personal form of management and outstanding success in virtually controlling the arc-welding business—in 1981 it did more than half a billion dollars worth of business. The company is prosperous and employees are rewarded with high bonuses and stay for a lifetime; labor turnover is less than 3 percent a year. The company has never used employment tests during the hiring procedure. Instead, applicants are interviewed by personnel officers of the company, and if it appears an individual will fit in with the company, he or she is then interviewed "by a committee of Lincoln vice presidents and plant superintendants whose approval must be unanimous. 'It's pretty much a gut reaction type of thing.' " (Serrin, 1984)

One outcome of such careful attention to employees before they are hired is that afterwards they require drastically less supervision than employees evidently do elsewhere—the Lincoln Electric ratio of supervisors to workers is 1 to 100. Where do economies lie, then? In the hiring phase, when a cheapjack machine test made by psychologists in Princeton or California will try to determine important information about a complex mammal and how that person will work and work out over a period of years? Or in the expensive hiring process of Lincoln Electric, where the time of costly personnel is absorbed in the matter of learning as much as possible about another human being and how that person's life will integrate with an organization intimately well known to everyone concerned?

I am asserting that using inexpensive mass-produced tests is foolish because it leads to expensive mistakes. It provides the illusion of expertise and knowledge where little or none exists. It is remarkable that people in organizations accept using fundamentally different means of judging people in organizations than they do in their personal lives. Of course in part they are required to demonstrate impartiality for legal and moral reasons. The Mickey Mouse test is seemingly more impartial than a searching two-hour or twenty-minute interview by a real person with his or her own views of life and work. Nevertheless, the very existence of the difference between personal and official decision suggests the immensity of the problem and how difficult it is to change to a less mechanically precise system, but one that is finally more accurate and pertinent to the task at hand.

The technofix solution to the problems of equity and scale, the mass test, itself produces a new situation that exacerbates the problem it is meant to solve. It permits managers not to manage, teachers not to evaluate, politicians not to lead and inspire but instead to tinker with lie detectors. It may encourage members of the community to treat their own skills and enthusiasms with the same impersonal heartlessness that the machine tests do. Meanwhile the U.S. Navy, which hopes to hire people for a lifetime to live twenty-four hours a day on its ships, looks forward to the great time when "adaptive tests" can cut the time of trial by half. Clearly it is difficult to think through to different ways of organizing large communities so that the prosaic pathology of machine judgment looms less heavily over lives than it now does. But as always, if the problem is difficult and large, then it is best to confront it sooner rather than later.

The New Deuteronomy: No Statistic Is Ever Without a Friend

The challenge of responding to large numbers of people with some semblance of attention to their individuality has yielded the reliance on psychological tests I have just discussed. A community committed to general, nondiscriminatory laws will inspect reality and people with as much generality and lack of idiosyncrasy as possible. But anthropologists know that how a culture solves the problems it faces inevitably affects other elements of its life—ones on the face of it with little to do with the original issue.

So solving problems about successive waves of conquest and immigration and the impact of this on elaborate marriage laws led to the remarkable caste system of India. This involves far more than laws about who one could and could not or should not marry. Similarly, psychological tests have an impact beyond their finite function; they represent a particular moral attitude to people. They depend for their integration into the community's life on the sense made of them by the statistical measures with which they are so directly associated. Now I want to suggest how the use of various statistics that claim to describe social life come in fact to define it, with rather striking and singular unexpectedness. I am suggesting again that "the medium is the message," that there is an implicit *ordering* of life's experience by a system of notation that is supposed simply to *describe* this experience.

In a letter to *Science,* Wassily Leontief charged that modern economics is characterized by an excessive reliance on statistical models often independent of empirical data, or models which used data about the real world in an indirect and finally unreliable and uninformative way. "Nothing reveals the aversion of the great majority of the present-day academic economists for systematic empirical inquiry more than the methodological devices that they employ to avoid or cut short the use of concrete factual information." (Leontief, 1982, pp. 104–07) In an analysis of the contents of the *American Economic Review*—"the flagship of academic economic periodicals over the last ten years"—Leontief shows that at least half of all articles which appeared there involved "mathematical models without any data," while only about *1 percent* reflected "economic analysis based on data generated by the author's initiative." (Truly extraordinary when one considers that in the journals of most sciences, the great majority of publications involve the description and analysis of data which the author has gathered—this is frequently almost the only kind of article that will see print, for example, in the "Research Reports" section of *Science* itself, which published Leontief's letter.) As Leontief concludes, "Year after year economic theorists continue to produce scores of mathematical models and to explore in great detail their formal properties; and the econometricians fit algebraic functions of all possible shapes to essentially the same sets of data without being able to advance, in any perceptible way, a systematic understanding of the structure and the operations of a real economic system."

This is particularly interesting, coming as it does from an economist who won a Nobel Prize for Economics because of the mathematical sophistication of his input-output model of economies. On the other hand, I had quite extensive discussion with Leontief about this model, precisely because he felt it lacked a solid component of empirical information about the behavior of people in households and wanted to involve anthropology in gathering some. The household is an important element in any economic analysis, but in Leontief's view there was little substantial knowledge about how economic transactions were affected by the structure and events of kinship. The research project which would have been necessary to begin to gather this information turned out to be too expensive to finance from the sources we had available at the time, so the initiative was dropped. But what was impressive was Leontief's practical commitment to empirical work as an essential basis for more theoretical analysis.

His letter refers to a more general situation than the bizarre one in economics. A characteristic of the psycho-industrial complex is that it is comfortable with the statistical technique employed to summarize data which may themselves be already conjectural—about attitudes, say, or the theory of rational expectations (Adam Smith's wrong assumption) to which Leontief referred in his original complaint. Then these shaky descriptions of reality will be turned into even shakier generalizations, expressed in numbers. Not that I am hostile to statistics in general—recall my affection for the normal bell-shaped curve as a useful description of the characteristics of living systems. But my concern is with the ease with which technical descriptions, through numbers, of often extremely complex and perhaps fugitive social and psychological circumstances, have come to be taken seriously as realities of life, not as notations of it. The pleasing logic of counting is combined with the reassuring formality of bureaucratic classification and procedure to produce ways of describing reality more rigid and mechanical than warranted by particular cases.

Statistics are Arabic numerals wearing a white coat. They depend on the authority of the scientific method, which in turn depends on them. As Leontief complained, certainly in economics the rituals of graduate training rigorously impose highly mathematical approaches to social phenomena. While economics is more blighted by this problem than other disciplines, nevertheless there is widespread enthusiasm for statistical and mathematical formulations in the sciences. There seems little question that scientists who are adept with numbers are regarded as "harder" than those adept with words. Justifications for scientific research projects are also regarded as "harder" if they contain strong statistical supports as opposed to logical or allusive demonstrations. There is no question that such statistics are often, if not usually, essential to the successful completion of the work at hand. However, work which does not require statistical endeavor is less likely to be proposed in the first place than the currently conventional kind. The "halo effect" of the statistical measures may carry over to other realms in which the precision and mechanism they reflect are unnecessary or perhaps inappropriate.

I want to emphasize how much of the nature of the social system is derived from industry, and its impact on people's lives and feelings about them. It is first of all necessary to understand the link between the growth of governments and governmental control of "local and private activity." (Alonso and Starr, 1982, p.34) "The growth of statistics is surely tied to the growth and evolution of the modern state. . . . A modern statistical system needs an institutional structure, technology and ideas. Without them, neither statistics nor the modern state could have developed as they have." (*ibid.*) In a tangle of interdependency, the technique of using numbers to represent reality has permitted the growth of that abstract reality, government, because it is on the basis of numbers that governments can creditably and comfortably generate policies to achieve particular results. So population movements, unemployment rates, reading scores of children in a school district, the number of infant mortalities, all become critical levers of policies to act, or of that more complex policy, not to act.

More intimately, taxation policies have stimulated a quite drastic intervention of governments into people's lives—not for the conventional Tory reason that the least government is the best government, but precisely because of the myriad arrangements made by particularly capitalist governments to permit capitalists to function. Such devices as tax deductions for business entertainment, tax shelters, and so on, all produce real impacts on private lives and have broad consequences for the nature of civility hardly understood so far. Almost all citizens swim in a soup of numbers. The precision and memory of the computer has expanded the soupbowl immensely. The tax system has turned everyone into an accountant endlessly on duty. The upshot is a society living with that third eye which with increasing frequency and effectiveness glares at numbers about life rather than at life itself; numbers are in danger of becoming highly specific rumors about the facts of life. But because they are numbers, they are more believable than word-rumors.

Of course, operating a large organization requires numbers. Financial and other controls depend upon numerical statements. But the numbers appropriate to financial control have expanded their importance. Now they pertain not to matters as precise as how many dollars or lira are spent, but to issues as impossibly diffuse as how many hours a scientist spends doing one thing such as teaching or another such as research or consulting or loitering in committees. Having been required by my own university to complete questionnaires involving just such information, I know how lyrically fictional it can be. Once I discovered what kind of information would satisfy the administrators of the university responsible for that particular government program, which was the reason for the request, that was the information I provided.

Perhaps this is dishonest. But like any member of an organization confronted with a modest request for civilized behavior, I am happy and eager to please. The fact is that an academic's schedule is a stew of things, and it is difficult if not impossible to clarify which bits contribute how much of the overall result, particularly over the span of a whole year. Perhaps other members of faculty are more knowledgeable than I about their daily round, and less mendacious in reporting to their employers. So perhaps a statistic is generated which means something about the real work of the university. If it is, well and good, though I am uncertain about the use to which the information is put and do not recall being told. But if the numbers that emerge are inaccurate or only general rumors about behavior, then not only have people had to spend time mugging up their story, but the end product may be a misplaced certainty about the life of the university which its managers may have.

Perhaps my position on this matter is ethically weak, for which I am apologetic. Nevertheless, I have tried to provide a personal example of a larger procedure that has some real influence. (The legitimacy of my small mendacity was somewhat supported by a much-applauded 1986 decision to abandon the practice.) The Syracuse University sociologists Robert Bogdan and Margaret Ksander have written with considerable impact of what they call "enumerology": "Enumerology is the study of the social processes by which numbers are generated and the effect of these processes on behavior and thought." (Bogdan and Ksander, 1980, p. 302) Their broad point is neither to dismiss the possible veracity of statistics and what they represent, nor to claim that numbers are invariably the wrong instruments to use. Rather, they are concerned with the process itself of using them, with the impact of the business of collecting, reporting, and evaluating them. Their conclusion is that "We relate to our environment through quantification, and it intervenes in the relationship between our minds and bodies. Enumeration is not only a measure of behavior and our environment; it is central to how we experience it." (p. 304)

They show how the obligation to report particular numbers creates social outcomes. For example, when directors of the Head Start program were required to enroll 10 percent of handicapped children in their classes, their perceptions of handicap changed. Rather rapidly the number of handicapped children rose to meet the quota, though of course the children were the same as before, just counted differently. Only now they were handicapped by definition as well as deprived! In another case involving children, they argue that the concern about mounting rates of child abuse is misplaced. Children are being abused no more or less than ever, but the standards for what kind of behavior is acceptable have changed considerably. What was once "healthy discipline" is now unmistakable abuse, but the new numbers do not reflect a new situation. This does not excuse maltreatment of children or underestimate the misery and cruelty of what is happening. But it suggests how the use of numbers may decisively affect how a society views the trends in its behavior and how therefore it may prepare to meet them if it is so inclined. (p. 304)

Professional groups may try to expand the public demand for their services by defining otherwise adequate members of the population as potential clients in deficit. Thus, "Some learning disability specialists report that up to 40% of all children are afflicted" (p. 306), a clear impossibility once it is recognized that if disability refers to a marked difference from normal capacity, then there is no way 40 percent of any natural population can be that far from the norm, because of course they would constitute a great deal of the norm themselves. Moreover, organizations may bend their activities to produce numbers reflecting good results rather than real results, which may yield poorer reporting statistics. Hence, people training "hard-core unemployed" for jobs may encourage them to take dead-end jobs rather than better ones that take longer to qualify for or are more difficult to get. The training agencies are rewarded for job placements, not necessarily for the better lives of their clients over the long run. Similarly, some medical organizations will be reluctant to accept patients with grave illnesses which are difficult to treat because the high risk of patient death may lead to unfavorable numbers in any evaluation of the institution's success rate as a curing force.

Much of this is unpleasantly banal. "What else do you expect?" But this is the point. When people come to distrust and disrespect organizations specifically established to help them, then it is important to know how and why they are failing to achieve what they could. One reason may be precisely those statistical and reporting controls established to make sure that the organizations work well. This is hardly surprising in itself. While it is sad and often tragic that such failure occurs, it is not terribly interesting from a social scientific point of view.

However, the phenomenon can be seen as part of a much larger and more formidable pattern of industrialized experience. Life is forced by an assumption from a real state to a reified one. Now the seriousness of the situation becomes clearer. The underlying reason for the depersonalizing and distorting impact of statistics—of the new belief in numbers—is precisely that the bureaucratic mode has been dependent upon the separation of person and office. Therefore the numbers produced by officers have independent authority and are thought to be uncontaminated by the whims and wiles of possibly fickle or unsuited people. Accordingly it becomes possible and indeed highly valued to use the rigmaroles of "statologic" to describe the events of life. The assumption is that the numbers refer to the genuine reality, which a sensible administration should regard as its challenge to confront. Of course the quality of numbers and statologic will vary substantially. Their use may well produce a good insight into the real results of what people do. Inventory statistics, for example, are usually accurate and helpful to managers and planners. The reality of buys and sells of products, commodities, and services is reflected in the real numbers of dollars or whatever currency that flow from spender to receiver. Certainly demographic statistics possess a relatively high level of accuracy and predictive value, even if their meaning may be ignored by people who should know better. Comes to mind the report by the then president of New York University, Allen Carter, who in the early 1960s warned his colleagues in education against pell-mell expansion of the university system on the patent basis that the baby boomers stimulating the expansion of that time would not be followed by an equally large group of offspring of the years after the unusually fecund postwar ones. Needless to say, his admonition was hardly followed; so in the late seventies and eighties the higher educational industry had to beat the bushes for clientele, and—a harsh blow to the illusions—endless growth came abruptly to an end.

Presumably just as well, too. One cynic estimated that for Canada, had the rate of expansion of universities and colleges continued at its 1960s pace, by the end of the eighties, every second Canadian would be enrolled in higher education.

The Fantasy of the Long-Distance Number

The central issue is only in part the accuracy of numbers. Also at stake is their uses, and the bias or expectation in the context in which they are interpreted. I recall Aristotle's Nichomachean ethic that it is inappropriate to render things more explicit than they need be. This ethic is violated routinely by those who buttress whatever position they wish to defend with the precise authority of numbers, which however bear only imaginative relationship to what they purport to describe. This must surely have been what so infuriated and gleefully interested readers of William Greider's famous interview in *The Atlantic Monthly* with U.S. Budget Director David Stockman, who as much as admitted the various budgetary projections which he had—with his reputation as an omniscient, punctilious number cruncher—created rather fancifully, almost poetically, to satisfy the requirements of financial duty and political exigency. And three years later on the occasion of presentation of another budget, *The New York Times* columnist Leonard Silk wrote that "This year's budget is a political document that ought to be labeled 'let the buyer beware.' It consists of projections that the projectors themselves disown, based on dubious economic assumptions that are in turn based on faulty assumptions about future budget deficits, offering solutions that are unspecified and in that sense unassailable." (Silk, 1984)

Silk accurately reflects a general anger at the misuse of numbers. Powerful figures who abuse their almost pious meaning are scorned as if they had committed sacrilege. Obviously people know that numbers can be manipulated for self-serving purposes. Nevertheless there is presumably some point in a science-based society at which it is no laughing matter to be cavalier about their meaning to the people who attend to them. In vast societies with millions of people performing billions of acts for countless purposes, those numbers which purport to draw the apparent randomness together should be more than fictions. They become the tissue of communal self-consciousness. They vouchsafe the integrity of those who claim to know how to find the right road ahead.

With a frivolous compass? Never. Have numbers become the entrails of a new style of soothsayer? To an extent, yes. The art of politics depends upon a smooth segue from the formality of enumerology to the complex busy-ness of people's lives and communal action. And there are consequences, also, which are formidably real. Of that same budget seen as a strategically organized conjecture by Leonard Silk, a colleague on the *Times,* Robert Pear, points out that the net effect of the need to pay interest on the bills caused by the projected deficit will more than overcome the savings induced by often severe cuts in health, education, welfare, and social service programs. "Under Mr. Reagan's 1985 budget ... the Government would pay $116.1 billion in interest on the debt, or $47.4 billion more than the amount spent for the same purpose in 1981." (Pear, 1984) What in effect was supposed to happen was that government expenditure to people who theoretically need the money more—the poor, students, the ill, and so on—would go in the form of interest to those affluent enough to be able to set money aside from current accounts in the form of savings or investments. Rates of interest are in essence rates of "salary" for the already wealthy. The fact that the sums of money involved are enormous, almost fantastically so, does not mean that the impact of their expenditure on the real and private lives of people is also a fantasy. To the contrary, for people seeking the basic accommodations of shelter, transport, and education, the impact of interest rates affects quite patently the quality and extent of what is affordable. The same applies to entrepreneurs large and small who must borrow to invest in new productive facilities. Interest rates signify how much the future costs and thus are numbers of immediate significance. The pertinent element here is that they are the result of decisions made at various levels of activity, not the least of which is the governmental, where judgments may be founded on enumerological processes of scanty reliability and realism.

A person I know quite well and respect very much has been involved in a highly responsible position in the organization that prepares the U.S. budget. His description of the process involved in deciding on budgetary proposals suggests the rigor and energy deployed in making them, to say nothing of a willingness to take political decisions on fairly explicit grounds of ethical judgment

172

and social commitment. A genuine concern appears to exist about the relationship of policy and moral and ideological belief, clearly reflected in various policies. Nevertheless, the technical rendition of such policies depends upon the numerical information available at any time, and on the quality of assumptions about behavior. As I have already argued, the "rational investor" model of behavior is inadequate as a broad guide to predicting behavior. Yet almost by definition—how do you formalize nonrationality in a rational, politically explicable manner?—it is difficult to replace it with a more accurate model.

Hence it is easy for projections to founder and for economic activity to occur in the shadow of distorted policies. Perhaps the most serious impact of government on private economy is the impact of wrong ideas, not particular ideologies. The issue is intrinsic to managing industrial society: the belief that human processes are knowable in numerical terms, and that their management can depend on managing the numerical processes.

A significant characteristic of such numbers is that almost more than their absolute values, their tendencies or directions are defined as important. So newspapers report that steel production is down 4 percent, unemployment up 2.1 percent, housing starts down by 68,520, the balance of payment deficits up by 6 percent. The tails of the graph seem to loom more dramatically in view than the middle part, which after all represents most of whatever life or process the numbers refer to. On the basis of these slight movements, people inspecting them are happy or sad, optimistic or the opposite. Obviously harder-headed inspectors will know the small limits within which small changes have meaning. Yet the self-feeding movements of the stock market, for example, suggest the power of small changes to produce large changes in the feelings people have about the future of stock prices. Volatile movements in stock prices, and hence changes in the putative wealth shareholders enjoy, may occur with very little reference to actual productivity and profitability of specific companies, or of entire groups of stocks. No question there are real declines and increases in the worthwhileness of particular shares or bonds as investment vehicles for various purposes. My point is quite simply that the impact of numbers is strangely unlinked to the real life which they're about.

One other facet of this: the official definition of a recession is that there has been no growth for two consecutive quarters. Of depression, that there is negative growth. So the numbers which emerge from governmental statistic bureaus obviously will have real impact on economic decisions because of what they cumulatively reveal about the particular state of grace of an economy at a particular moment.

But note. The assumption is that growth is stable and its absence is an interruption. Recall my earlier comment about the decisive shift to high leverage in the industrial mode, so that more could derive from less, almost as if the law of gravity had been repealed. With recession-depression statistics, we have a clear case in which assumptions about the pace of production and the way it is recorded unite to produce a quite firm and demanding bias about how it should perform in general. This is not a steady-state universe. It characterizes the scheme of life I am talking about—one with a sharp definition about controlling the future and making it productively benign for everybody.

Nothing wrong with this. But a decently affluent community can come to regard itself as a depressed economic failure because it declines slightly in income for a relatively short period of time. This attests to the power of the combination of numbers with industry. Suddenly even massive communities are united by a web of numbers and share a psychological approach to the present and the future which may have little directly to do with people's quotidian experience of their lives. And because human emotion is such a potent determinant of behavior—emotion is a behavior too, after all—then the announcement that there is recession or depression will stimulate healthy prudence, expenditures and investments will be more cautiously made. Lo and behold a small effect becomes larger, a ripple a current. Where capital is able to flow freely, wealth will actually be removed from one country and sent to another, there, not here, to do its productive work.

There is another kind of number which is interesting, the one that is not reported, the number that seems to unite Manhattan in the first years of the 1980s and Italy for almost a generation, the number which is the invisible cipher describing the so-called underground economy. The off-the-books, pre-numeraliterate economy, in which nothing is written down and certainly nothing accurate is reported to the authorities, a tax evader's preindustrialism. What united Manhattan and Italy was not just the Italian genes they share, or the tourists or the restaurants or the olive oil and

panforte they savor in common, but the fact that, according to the
overt official numbers, both communities were in severe money
peril despite the fact that the evident public lives of their populations betrayed a gleam of affluence. While the published statistics
for both places revealed gloom and escalating depression—which
indeed blighted the lives of countless citizens—nevertheless the
facts of life seemed different, in the shops, restaurants, rents,
dwelling prices, and from the winter suntans of large legions of
more fortunate inhabitants.

As many as 20 percent of transactions have been estimated as
the underground share in Manhattan, and almost a third in Italy.
Be those numbers fantasy or fact, no question there is that not until
1983 did the U.S. Internal Revenue Service assume that waiters in
restaurants earned tips of at least 8 percent of their employers'
gross—an underestimate, probably. It appears to remain the case
that the major auto makers in Italy still bring piles of bits and
pieces to machinist families in the Italian hill towns, to receive
transmissions or gearshifts in return. No questions asked. No statistics recorded.

*   *   *

I have explored some psychological and sociological characteristics of societies based on the industrial mode. How the
sciences which attempt to describe and explain this behavior have
been affected by the recent history of industrial communities. How
the society in turn has come to incorporate its own explanations
of itself into its very modus vivendi—a case of life imitating sociology. This is not surprising, since anthropologists know that cultures are elaborately integrated near-mechanisms, and that exotic
though a society may be, there are few surprises in its own terms
which should perplex the careful scholar.

Ethical implications follow from the codes of behavior derived
from the phenomena I described, such as psychological testing and
statistical descriptions of individual people's activity. The particular effects of these social patterns may constitute a form of evil-
doing against the lives and sensibilities of people who may not
fully appreciate how they are being treated by their own society,
by people who though powerful themselves do not know the extent
to which they are prisoners of their community's assumptions and
ways of doing things. So in a peculiar way, no one is directly

responsible for what is happening. There is a genuinely structural cause of social patterns which—if freshly reconsidered—might come to seem unnecessarily bizarre. Such as having machine graders and stranger-experts help importantly determine the destinies of young people. Yet this seems like a communal Eichmann defense: we are all just doing our job, it's not our fault, nothing's our fault. This may indeed be the case, a theme to which we will have to return again and again.

But first I want to explore yet another feature of the industrial mode, its literate mode of communication. This can become articulated in the form of ideologies. Ideologies are passions which marry the ability to read and the hunger for community.

5. Exiles from the Heart

The Jewish Cemetery outside the main old synagogue in the old town of Prague is a famous jumble of tombstones planted with crazy intensity and density in the crowded land: a ghetto in death as full as the one for the living must have been. It is tree-covered and rather shadowy and dark, or so it seemed the day I saw it. Its unkempt chaos and fierceness summarized in silence the lives of those whose final act was to use a little more of the limited garden of the dead. Then you pass by the cemetery to the synagogue to enter with astonishing pleasure the virtually empty holy room, white-walled except for a lovely gold embroidery extending over the walls and ceiling—an enchanting yellow space, airy and light, almost stunning in contrast to the ancient grimness outside of stones and tired earth. The sun shone in and danced off the gold. It was all suddenly a beautiful waltz for the eyes.

What happens in the central nervous system to create the sensation that you have been struck on the back of the neck with a log? I approached the walls and realized that the gold was writing, the writing of names. Each name was of a Jew killed by whomever in the Second World War. The handwriting on the wall was as powerful as a moving object. The intensity was phenomenal. Somehow the name of each murdered person was more striking written down than the physical graves of people outside. Passionately fitting that this was the concentrated memorial to those violated people of the Book.

Wars later, in Washington, D.C., the Vietnam Memorial shortly after its opening became the most visited monument after Lincoln's—by more than 10,000 people a day, who come to do nothing more nor less than see the names of the 57,939 Americans whose deaths are recorded by the words of their names engraved in the shiny black marble that forms a V-shape entrenched in a slash in the earth. Many rub their fingers on the words. Some rub a pencil across paper to take a record of the record. The memorial stuns with its simple, unalloyed impact. No single name loses force for its inclusion in a mass of names.

In both cases, the simplicity of denotation works.

Writing has power because it is so unnatural. Writing is a human innovation of perhaps six thousand years standing. Still, more people grow up illiterate than literate. Children must be taught to read, but they do not have to learn how to watch television. When they are old enough to be able to stumble to the set, they turn it on, and watch it for seventy-five years. As much as seven hours a day per family, or so it was announced about the United States in 1984. But reading is a different matter. Teachers, pop-up books, bedtime stories, even special television shows extolling the craft and use of reading, and the years-long suasion of eager adults, are all mobilized to get children to read.

Some read voraciously and as much as possible; some even enjoy writing. But the contrast between what is easy to learn, such as TV and tunes, and reading, is patent and revealing. What is revealed is that reading is an unnatural act and writing a kind of unspeakable practice—writers as a group endlessly complain about their job and its difficulty and loneliness, with excellent reason, in my view. The idea that it is a good thing that everyone read is rather new and associated with the Industrial Revolution, in England in particular. Perhaps a salient feature of the malaise I am trying to identify is its principal and characteristic mode of communication, which unites the people in the system and permits them to carry on as they—we—do.

The wide diffusion of reading and writing has made it possible for people to become exiled from the elaborate community of face-to-face contact which has always been the location of important human action. The existence of writing has made possible a wholly new form of privacy and private witness, one that before writing only shamans, priests, and prophets could claim to have. This chapter is about literacy and ideology. Literacy drives us apart. Ideologies arise to try to draw us together.

I am posing a crudely large kind of question, such as: What would happen between chimpanzees if they could send love letters to each other or diplomatic notes, or between two aggressive dogs who didn't like each other if they were able to write nasty editorials about each other or reviews in *The New York Review of Books* which their common friends could read? "The medium is the message." The mode of written communication made possible and stimulated the emergence of new forms of social organization, in which positions can be taken in private, expressed in private, made known to others without necessary physical contact, and the consequences managed also solely by exchange of script. There need be no intervention of the potential primate confusions of sound, sight, smell, and speed of movement. Writing is a form of communication that enables people to keep apart while nevertheless accomplishing something together.

Glue, barrier, ambience, stiletto—words can act in many ways and serve a variety of masters. For people such as you and I who clearly employ words for at least work, and presumably fun, in their written form and always in their spoken, it may seem bizarre that anyone should suggest that writing is unusual. But it is. It is relatively new. It is very consequential. It is one of those taken-for-granted phenomena to which anthrocommentators should be alert. For me to have to use writing to say all these skeptical things about writing emphasizes the inevitable forcefulness of literacy. It literally changes the world and makes nonliterate communication difficult to accomplish. Because writing makes such a difference, we have to examine why and how.

There is much scholarly attention to the nature and content of literature and writing in general. New work on semantics, semiotics, the evolution of language and its neurophysiology is quite elaborate. But there has been surprisingly little attention paid to the broad social and organizational functions of language. The scholar who has most effectively and skillfully described this situation, and proceeded to remedy it with elegant and wonderful erudition and good sense, is Walter Ong, S.J., of the St. Louis University in Missouri. His latest work on the subject, *Orality and Literacy: The Technologizing of the Word* (1982), is a state-of-the-art statement, as was his earlier work on the subject when it appeared (1977). It is difficult to understand why his remarkable oeuvre has not received greater attention, given the seriousness of his subject, the radicalism of his vision, and the striking meaning of what he concludes.

Ong shows how overwhelmingly human beings prefer spoken

rather than written communication: ". . . of the . . . possibly tens of thousands . . . [of languages] . . . spoken in the course of human history, only around 106 have ever been committed to writing to a degree sufficient to have a literature, and most have never been written at all. Of the some 3000 languages spoken . . . today only some 78 have a literature. . . . The basic orality of language is permanent." (Ong, 1982, p.7)

A naturalistic perception must conclude: (1) speaking is easy to learn; (2) writing relatively difficult; and (3) this is a measure of the biological priorities of the species. The resistance to writing is not only at the level of easy access but also philosophical. As Ong notes (*ibid.,* p. 80), Plato in *The Phaedrus* has Socrates complain that writing is inhuman, that it will cause people's memories to fail, that they will rely on what is in front of them rather than on what is within—a not-unfamiliar modern argument against computers and calculators. Yet of course Plato must use writing to make his argument, the embarrassing problem I am having to endure here too.

This is surprising because it appears to challenge the consistency and gray dignity of a major philosopher, and indeed a whole intellectual lineage. Perhaps we can reduce its oddity in our minds if we recognize that writing has always been associated with power and the management of elite communication. It was not designed as a means of self-expression. The creative writing course is a brand-new invention. Ong carefully and persuasively informs us that the major thrust toward written language was first in such systems as written Latin, which were used exclusively by males—the only people allowed in school. It had to do with managing power structures, not with achieving individual pleasures. "Learned Latin has not been inherited from within the family and has normally been used exclusively to deal with tribal and public affairs rather than with domestic affairs . . . it has been used for more or less abstract, academic, philosophical, scientific subjects, or for forensic or administrative or liturgical matters." (Ong, 1977, p. 25) "This form of separation of 'official' or 'administrative' language from the languages of people at home was not confined to Latin alone; the same dichotomy emerged around Sanskrit, Classical Chinese, Classical Arabic, and Rabbinic Hebrew." (*ibid.,* p. 28)

This is fascinating and striking. Also puzzling. As Ong notes, "The fact that at a crucial stage in its development the most advanced thought of mankind in widely separated parts of the globe has been worked out in linguistic economies far removed from the hearth and from the entire world of infancy would seem to deserve far more attention than it has received, if only because it has received almost no attention whatsoever." *(ibid.)*

My interest is in the relationship between writing in general and the industrial system in particular. Ong suggests a plausible if somewhat sweeping connection between written communication and the particular history to which I refer: "An affinity seems to exist between early modern science, in its need to hold at arm's length the human lifeworld with its passionate, rhetorical, practical concerns, and Learned Latin as a tongue which had been isolated from infant development and from the physiological and psychosomatic roots of consciousness and which had been given instead an artificial base in writing." *(ibid.,* p. 35) There is a specific connection, he decides, between the modern scientific mode and the abstract nature of a language not learned in infancy. The word "infant" itself derives from the Latin *infans,* which translates as nonspeaking! Ong accurately sees the importance of the connection between how a mammal learns its first pattern of communication with the world and how in turn that connection may become abstract and independent of those feelings, some of them infantile-adult in the way modern psychiatry knows them. I have already suggested the route to industry through the family. Here we see another kind of link, even if a negative one. The implications of this are far-reaching and unclear at the same time. To cite Ong's pithy remark, "The fact that the entire academic enterprise out of which modern science emerged had been conducted in an international no man's language would appear on the surface of it to have implications which would be at the very least bizarre and possibly profound." *(ibid.,* p. 38)

"An international no man's language"! We confront the possibility that the large social forms we use to conduct our communal lives depend in coercive ways on an exotic communicative scheme. It permits and even encourages a formal separation between the individual, the individual's writing, and the action such writing may stimulate or permit. In one sense this is a fully outrageous proposal. It seems to assume that the scratches on paper we call writing can have vast impact on what kinds of factories, armies, shops, governments, sports, and so on are available for contemporary use. If not, why then the emphasis in industrial communities on teaching reading as early as possible? We do know for certain how important verbal training is to developing what is considered intelligence. Insofar as IQ is an artifact of skill in relation to age, the effort to speed up children's development to create a competitive advantage is hardly likely to produce merely casual results. Furthermore, if reading is not a decisive change from illiteracy, then why is it regarded as such an important feature of modern equitable existence? I do not want to beg this question altogether but think it should be addressed: If literacy is not consequential for countless people, then why is it thought to be so politically, morally, and economically important? And if it is important, then why? What are its effects?

Whether or not it's an effect, there is a strong association between the world map of illiteracy and the world map of poverty. (Oxenham, 1980, p. 2) A similar association exists between literacy and urban life as compared with rural. During the beginning days of the Industrial Revolution, "Literacy and schooling were seen as technologies, which by their very use were to transform their users. Moreover they were regarded as technologies indispensable to rapid socio-economic growth." (*ibid.,* p. 17) In political terms, Lenin specifically sought Russian literacy because "an illiterate man is non-political; first he must be taught to read." (cited in *ibid.,* p. 12) Lenin believed in the autonomous protean character of the literate person—an individual able to weigh evidence and make personal decisions about how to act.

Please note how significant this is. A crystal-clear assumption became worldwide. Literacy was associated with progress, modernization, democracy, economic development. It was necessary for acceptable conduct of contemporary social and political affairs. Virtually nowhere was the opposite assumption entertained at all—that illiteracy was the key to social, economic, and personal progress. Such an idea was unthinkable, is unthinkable. It is wholly out of keeping with the regnant view that learning to read and write is central to contemporary experience.

Literacy is supposed to produce the verbal equivalent of Adam Smith's economic decision maker. After the Second World War when the world became decolonized, it was crucial to the modernizing impulse that people become literate, both to make Lenin's kind of political choices and of course to take part in economic activity. Following Ong's analysis, we can now see that one of the implicit intentions or at least outcomes of the literalizing process was a breakdown of tribal orality. The traditional structure had no clear place for the private ratiocinating individual operating according to his own lights. The individualization of action which the Protestant Reformation began now we see provided the dowry for the literary reformation. It is also pertinent that so much effort has gone into producing literates able to read the Bible, that book uniquely left in the hotel rooms of the temporarily homeless. A very symbolic donation.

But this affirms the particular political influence of things written down. It reflects the origins of broad literacy itself—that when human beings moved to pastoral and agricultural economies, when our groups became larger, our conditions more crowded, and our social systems more stratified, then there was a burgeoning of religious and ethical systems. The codes supporting these were written down. This was new. They had to be managed and interpreted by priests who could read. This was relatively new, too. The priests had to be supported, on the tithe, the first leisured organisms in history, the first agents. This was new. In a number of important cases such as the Bible and Koran, the texts were declared to be divine and the books themselves became sacred objects. *Written words supposed to specify reality became the carriers of magic.* And the priests who presumably understood both the reality and the magic translated the force of the books into social solidarity, into theocratic social structure. Convulsion after convulsion.

What happened after the Protestant Reformation and then in the secular age, when priests became less necessary and by and large less influential over people's personal salvation and ethical decisions? Just as, increasingly, people became individual contractors as far as the economy was concerned, so too did they become more independent managers of their own moral accounts.

What happened when the account was the individual's? When the individual was on her or his own? What or who made the society's ethical connections then? Was there a moral equivalent of "the unseen hand" Adam Smith saw subtly guiding the world of wealth?

Whatever the origin of all this, the historical evidence is unmistakable. People who can read enjoy greater opportunity to earn money than illiterates. It is a ticket to modernity. On a worldwide basis both nationally and individually, literacy and economic power are closely associated. Does literacy make it possible to become affluent? Or can you only become affluent in a literate

THE MANUFACTURE OF EVIL

society if you are literate? The second answer seems more obviously correct. But among others, Oxenham has asked whether or not "a major effect of literacy lies not in the use of the skills *after* they are acquired, but actually in the process of acquiring them." (Oxenham, *op. cit.,* p. 45) This is critical. Perhaps there is more than just an ordinary skill involved in learning to read. A reader's experience of life is categorically different from an illiterate's. The kind of argument raised by Ong suggests the seriousness of the process of being literate. Perhaps it is not as clear-cut a change as, say, losing one's virginity, or becoming a parent. Nonetheless, reading causes "technological transformations of the word [which] also alienates man from the real word, the living spoken word, and hence from himself." (Ong, 1977, p. 47)

Isn't this a burden? Sustaining the literate's discipline, a style of déracinée private decision making, may simply be very dry and difficult for most people. So when they are offered a choice of reading or watching television, for example, they will watch television for seven hours a day but read for hardly a fraction of that. Even in a highly structured and sophisticated educational system such as the French, there appears to be a cumulative decline in the amount of reading people do, and in the quality of the writing and spelling of all levels of the population: "L'Orthographie en Ruine" announces the magazine *Le Point.* (Richard and Stehli, 1983) The wealthiest country on earth, the United States of America, has had universal education for decades. But reading skills have evidently fallen off so noticeably that the U.S. military is rewriting training and operating manuals from the tenth-grade level to the sixth. This is trying for military planners because while the levels of skill have generally declined, the requirements for skill become greater and greater. However, there has not yet been, evidently, any forthright or aggressive effort to confront the fact that reading may be generically "difficult to learn."

This reveals how the military hierarchy thinks about its work. At the highest managerial levels, enthusiasm for literacy prevails. When commanders and politicians alike were offered the opportunity to evaluate new weapons systems or other proposals, not through the usual copious paper documentation but rather with film cassettes giving visual displays of what was involved, the upper hierarchy refused. It preferred the paper to the film. This is not surprising, if it is true as I have argued that literacy and management are closely linked in structural terms. I suspect this is particularly true of American management style. How many North American readers have engaged in a detailed and seemingly successful conversation about solving a particular problem only to have one's interlocutor conclude the talk with something like "Will you send me a memo on that, please?" The paper is more important than the reality. Or, put another more drastic way, the paper is almost the reality itself. Of course part of the function of committing an agreement to paper is to permit it to be described and monitored. The paper fixes the flow of social reality and holds it up to potentially dispassionate scrutiny. This is essential in the socioeconomic system with which we are concerned. This is the point. The essence of social order depends on a relatively abstract and impersonal form of communication very different from the characteristically robust and grainy forms of human relations.

Another reflection of this same dichotomous process is in the increasing contrast between written and spoken language. An emeritus professor of Romance language and literature of Harvard, Dwight Bollinger, has commented: "It is not hard to imagine a 'diglossic split' like that of the vernacular vs. church Latin in the past, or classical vs. spoken Arabic today. We shall have a church English understood by writers and understood more or less by those schooled at greater and greater expense to read it.... Universities will offer training in English as a classical language." (Bollinger, 1981, p. 8) I am occasionally inclined to make the exaggerated observation that the only sizable group in North American life which reads and writes a great deal and carefully is lawyers, who demand up to $300 an hour for subjecting themselves to this. In fact, one common complaint against lawyers is for their "legalese," their jargonic insistence on using language truly as a technology, with few if any referents to known normal language. Hence it is baffling and soulless to those who confront it. The same accusation is also frequently made about bureaucrats, particularly ones in large governments, who with equal zeal turn spoken language into an arcane mechanism seemingly designed to suppress common responses and betraying no vernacular verve.

The problem is not that the users of such language are snobs or incompetent. They are creating the equivalent of learned Latin, or trying to. They do this because it is easier to conduct large-scale impersonal modern structures by communicating in the manner which allows people to become bureaucratic officers in good conscience. They are the fluent users of the dialects of *Gesellschaft*.

Dozens of anthropologists and biologists have struggled to teach other primates to talk. By and large they have not succeeded, even with a generous definition of speech. Their often hilariously misplaced enthusiasm to extend the empire of talk and backtalk in nature seems even stranger placed alongside the inventively grotesque ways in which people can talk and, more bizarrely, write. While much effort has gone into inducing a chimpanzee to express "Please let me poke at that broken-down water pump," surprisingly little is understood about the specific processes by which human-primatological talk is translated into officialese.

My proposition may be nothing more complicated than a simple rule, which would go something like: "The bigger and more abstract the activities an organization has to perform, and the less real human contact is necessary to maintain a steady state, the more its form of written communication will depart from vernacular speech." You can probably also add: "And the more the written communication will incorporate modes and phraseology from the natural sciences and from economics in an effort to add prestige and borrowed forcefulness, for example, in the memos of Regional School Supervisors."

Why does mean-spirited and clumsy jargon get created?

Perhaps as machines become more powerful and less direct human activity is necessary to accomplish things, then more opaque and confusingly complicated language becomes possible, because it matters less.

Perhaps the stimulus is the very nature of the system itself—the industrial mode which permits and indeed requires large-scale organization and the administrative jargon to maintain it. Whether it works or not is not for me to say. But consumers of this kind of language don't really like it and don't use it at home. If people don't like the language they have to use, this must mean something. After all, people usually find speaking their own languages an agreeable matter—a way to exercise skill and have a bit of fun and impact on the world. When communicating becomes a pain in the neck, then the form it takes must somehow be interfering with the plainly considerable linguistic skill human beings have. So it is appropriate to blame the form, not the people using it. Can't even blame the makers of the form. They are just as much victims of a way of life which stimulates their silly jargon as the clients with whom they communicate as if through woolly fiber. Another kind of communal Eichmann defense, this time linguistic. This is not unreasonable. A language finally reflects the lives of its users. If many important users of language in a community are constrained to produce an awkward lingo, then that is an issue to be addressed at its source, which may be sociopolitical more than linguistic.

The problem may be most irritating when subgroups want to communicate with each other, when there is inappropriate adoption of one style of language to the challenges of another. Part of the reason for this must be that workers in both the arts and sciences and the administrators in both have, as Northrop Frye has said, "for all their obvious differences ... a common origin in social concern." (Frye, 1981) They think they should be able to communicate pleasantly with each other. But they may not be able to. So it is common for technically oriented business people and others to hire expert word users to write speeches and communications for them which will be understandable by plain, nontechnological people.

This is curious. Why should people active and effective in their own field feel that their linguistic styles are inadequate for the communicative work they have in mind? Do they lack confidence in themselves? In the quality of their thought or speech or writing? Or do they know how poorly they contact the world?

Whatever the answer, the fact is different parts of the social system experience difficulty in communication with others. This is one reason surely for the growth of the public relations and advertising industries. Another part of the problem must be attributable to the development of specialized sublanguages, which appear almost foreign to nonspecialists and hence in need of translation.

The Columbia University sociologist Robert Merton said, "No scientific virtue inheres in bad writing." His quip may well have had a larger point than on the face of it: that the inability to render in usual language what is going on in a subsystem of the wider community symptomizes more general alienation. Why, when virtually all humans learn to talk quite well, do some become gibberers when they have to talk about what is presumably very close to their hearts, their work? Does the Devil catch their tongue? Since these are people who talk readily to children, dinner companions, bookies, and cobblers, the problem must lie in the style or nature of their work, and not in them.

The sentimental legend is that Eskimos have dozens of words for snow, which is central to their lives. Perhaps it is not surprising that cultures coping with the mix of bureaucracy and technology have dozens of equivalents. The bureaucratese of organizations such as the Pentagon, and governments in general, may be kin to all those words for snow.

As William Whyte wrote in *The Organization Man* (1956), "The more exquisite distinctions are, the more important they become." My suspicion is that a similar principle affects behavior. To the in-group, the distinctions may seem eventful, but to an outsider trying to read the language, for example, when a layman tries to read a full-regalia legal document, first ocular glaze and then sleep may interfere with the process of communication, even if the aspiring reader is a client to whose interests the document is addressed. Then he will probably turn the reading over to a lawyer. When I lived in West Africa and walked in the marketplaces, there were scribes who set themselves up in business writing letters for illiterates. In a real sense, lawyers are scribes of industrial society, employing the skills they have patiently learned in order to be able to address higher authorities and translate what higher authorities write in return.

Talkin' Too Little, Writin' Too Much

The story is that when Mahatma Gandhi governed India, he wanted one workday a week set aside in which civil servants were silent and went about their activities on their own. An interesting idea, similar to others which have been proposed such as having one workday a week in which meetings are forbidden or in which there may be no telephone conversations, or one week a month during which no official may travel away from his home office. One strategy that has not been tried to my knowledge would involve a ban on writing over a particular period, say a day or a week, as part of a systematic bias against producing written materials in an organization. This depends on the notion that written communication involves a very particular kind of information. In some circumstances it may permit the most pertinent and indeed only pertinent information to see the light of day. Nevertheless, the specialness and partiality of writing and reading may mean that organizations which depend heavily on these modes lose a substantial proportion of the skills and motivation of their employees. Literate communication may evoke a relatively narrow range. Most people write with difficulty, often badly and in jargon. But they talk and meet easily, with all the luxurious skill to be expected from a highly gregarious mammal nurtured in extensive and complex societies.

So, hiring an expensive manager and having that person spend much of his time writing is just a waste.

It is like renting a car and using it as a sofa.

When I was attending a meeting in Brazil several years ago, I met and became very friendly with a remarkable Brazilian engineer who invited me to visit with him the dam he was building. It was the one at Itiapu, the largest structure ever built by human beings, and it was under construction by a Brazilian consortium of which Gabriel was the chairman. This was a project begun in 1966, which was coming to completion within six months of its schedule and within 6 percent of its estimated cost, in a community where such close and refined management control was supposed to be difficult to achieve. It was an accomplishment dazzling in any context. How was this success achieved?

Gabriel asked me to meet him at the airport in Rio at about seven one morning, and from then on I observed how at every step of his journey he engaged in friendly, warm, and informed communication with everybody he met—baggage handlers, airline personnel, drivers, policemen, and so on. When we were on the final leg of our flight to Foz de Iguacu, near the dam site, dinner was served in neat plastic containers that folded up like lunchboxes. Even though airlines in Brazil provided what I thought was an unusually high standard of flying fish and fowl, I supposed we would dine in our hotel. But I was told by Gabriel to ask for the dinner and take it with me. He would give it to his driver, who in turn would give it to his child for school the next day—an attractive prospect for the child, and the source of some additional solidarity in the organization Gabriel was responsible for. Throughout the entire time I was in the town near the dam, and on the site itself and in our hotel, Gabriel was engaged in nonstop talk with an array of people, some of whom had specific questions about the work, and others with whom he chatted about general issues or personal ones involving families, friends, and so on.

I was reminded of the intense conviviality of a primate troop, in which the work of maintaining the social structure goes on all the time. Successful animals must display a variety of social skills in a manner appreciable to their fellows. Everywhere Gabriel went, he was surrounded by a hubbub of social activity. It was almost possible to begin to see the connection between the flurry of conviviality and talk and the astonishingly immense structure being made. On the one hand there was the dam, five miles long at its crest, eighty-three stories high where the lake was to be deepest, with the largest generators ever built in a structure simply unbelievably large. Everything was vastly larger than life. Yet the person finally responsible for building it conducted his work with firm modesty. He shared his office with three other people, he talked to everybody and stood on no ceremony. When I asked him about his way of managing, he said, "I write about five business letters a year."

Of course legal documents had to be written and sent, but as Gabriel said about managing issues involving people or engineering problems: "When there's a problem, I go." He wouldn't even discuss with me how useless it was to write letters; there was no point. Gabriel had rented a car and was driving it, full of passengers, for all it was worth. We were not using it as a sofa.

I do not want to exaggerate the meaning of this particular case, even though the drama and success of the accomplishment are real events in the human record, and the dam and turbines are now at work. Gabriel is (at least in my experience) an unusually gifted leader—warm, precise, available, with humor, and demanding. The particular circumstance was obviously special and stimulating—of building such an immense thing, involving two governments, a town newly carved out of the forest, and requiring new ways of introducing the indigenous people of the forest to the ways of hydroelectric grandeur. Nevertheless, no time was wasted following up meetings with memos describing what happened at the meetings. People knew where they stood, where they were going. There was a directness about management.

Now this is the standard kind of example routinely retailed by admonitory commentators on business practice. "Hands-on" management has become the corporate equivalent of the theological laying on of hands. Clearly there is a sober and significant practicality to this, and the case of the angel Gabriel reflects the importance of direct contact in even the largest of organizations. That's the positive. Perhaps there is less clear understanding of the negative that what is involved in "hands-on" management is not only personal force and earnest interaction but also the absence or deemphasis of written communication. The medium of management is the message, too. The memo is not only the symptom of a style of ineffective management. It may be its cause as well.

I recall by way of oblique contrast some time I spent at UNESCO headquarters in Paris trying to accomplish something there that proved impossible because the Director-General's Annual Report was being prepared and it seemed literally the entire organization was doing nothing else. It reminded me of some unexpected giant insect which fed itself on itself, spent its energy digesting itself, and emerged from all this unchanged.

Building a dam is a categorically different matter than maintaining an organization, part of the full-throated function of which is precisely the exchange of written and other information about the extraordinary variety of human experience and culture. Nonetheless it seems that in such an organization it is easy for the torrent of writing for internal purposes to reduce the organization overall to silence and inaction. The organization proceeds to solve issues created out of its own peristalsic process.

Writing permits human beings to conduct organizations beyond the capacity of individual people to encompass. Then bureaucratization becomes essential. It becomes possible for people to take actions as officers or members of organizations which they would be unwilling to tolerate in their personal lives, or which they would at least question rigorously—were not the salient issues blurred and muffled by the fog of precedent and divided responsibility. It is possible large groups of people will undertake actions no individual singly would advocate on his or her own.

Consider the memo circulated to fifteen people. All who receive it and who do not protest its contents or somehow comment will be assumed to be in tacit approval. A genteel form of gang action; all are involved, none is specifically responsible. Of course there is little alternative, given the industrial system and the large political and economic groupings it appears to require. Nevertheless the existence of written records, of which the interoffice memo is perhaps the most characteristic, provides a real amount of safety in numbers. The web of activity is expanded, responsibility for it diluted. Even though one goal in maintaining close records is to achieve accountability, the process by which the record is created and sustained permits diminution of clear-cut individual responsibility. The memo becomes a defensive weapon, a formal garment covering your ass, a partial commitment to a wider conspiracy or shared avoidance of a particular issue. The lengthening and widening of the paper trail may permit an initially minor and inadvertent error, trivial malfunction, or malefaction to gain force and authority through unopposed precedent and the cumulative justification which time can provide.

My case here is that it is historical synergy, not accident, that the rise of the industrial system occurred at the time literacy was broadly gaining legitimacy, when reading and writing became essential tickets to entering the halls of commerce, industry, and the accompanying governments. This also coincided with rapid population expansion, the growth of national and international markets, and a general burgeoning of density and size in social institutions.

My proposition is obvious: without literacy, this would have been impossible. But the particular character of literate communication not only enabled this world to form and prosper. It also shaped it because of the special difference between literacy and orality. The most ambitious and effective members of this particular primate species had to learn a new language. They emigrated from orality. In so doing, they also produced a new form of society which they supervised and even owned. One in which we could communicate in code. In which we could store experience, and wholesale it, and retail it over controllable intervals. In which we could accept comfortably a distance between proposing an action, taking it, then accounting for it. In which the routines of socioeconomic and even private life could be affected by what were in effect manuals of procedure, comparable to the elaborate religious menus such as the Tanakh and the Koran. The self-help book, the Horatio Alger story, the incandescent industrial ethnographies of Charles Dickens, the eruption of newspapers. Under the circumstances, it seems no accident that the language of the industrial system was initially preeminently English—and it has become overwhelmingly so. Because literacy and industry went together, and go together, and first did so in England. Made in England. Small wonder the place of origin of industrial products must be described in English no matter what the producers really speak.

The industrial community assumes reading and writing are both desirable and necessary for full membership in the system. Literacy is so much a part of the industrial way of life that it is unthinkable that it produces no significant or major effect on the character of that way of life. As the blind or deaf or speechless will testify, how one communicates is of moment and usually also momentous. Still, the broad basic taken-for-granted of the industrial tribe, literacy, is not understood with a confidence and imagination appropriate to its significance. I've noted it also appears to be a mode of human communication difficult to learn, compared for example with televiewing, which is so easy to learn it seems to require no learning at all. It was also not surprising when the Library of Congress announced in 1986 that in fifteen years the circulation of Braille books had increased 19 percent while that of audiocassettes increased over 450 percent. Easier to learn to listen, easier to listen, easier to do, more attractive, evidently more fun.

It appears that the industrial system has elected to send messages to itself in a manner which it itself finds trying and perhaps even irritating for some to master. Therefore it is no surprise that in communities, even such as the USA, there may be a decreasing reliance on effective literacy over time, rather than the inexorable increase which the self-evident importance of the skill should provoke. And in a country such as Colombia where rural people once had to learn to read to join the web of information of the wider society, evidently the knack declines in significance as people become wired into their country by the growing electronic media. They forget how to read.

It may seem as if I am trying to say two paradoxical or contradictory things here. The first is that reading and writing are very important and deeply affect how things happen. The second is that when people get a chance to, many often return to preliterality. I think both are true. I have tried to argue the first point already—that literacy involves a wrenching shift of a categorical kind for human beings. That when they learn to read, they learn a novel set of ways of communicating with others, evaluating their experience, and assuming responsibility for what they do and what happens to them. Recall for a moment the person described by McLuhan who does not accept that the experience of going to a game or concert is complete until he reads the review of it the next day in the newspaper. I have done that myself. I fully understand that impetus. It is the beginning of the curse of the pure pedant. But it also has to do with the power of words to define and concretize experience. Especially written words. In the beginning was the word. Libel remains more serious than slander. Written contracts are different from spoken ones.

In the switchover to the *Gesellschaft* pattern from *Gemeinschaft,* writing became far more important. With a shift "from status to contract," the contracts must be written. Thus the impersonal document became essential for people. So did literacy. It could no longer be the preserve of priests keeping order and merchants keeping score. It had to be extended widely. Even in that most intimate and hopeful of flurries, courtship, what may happen just before marriage is that a legal agreement is created to outline what happens to property in the event that the spirit flags. Does such heavy formality threaten to depress the soufflé of romance and true love? Perhaps the words are usefully sobering. But once the words are entered on paper, they are of a different character than the free-flowing tides of courtship's season.

The steady march of lawyers bearing documents gathers strength. More and more formerly private behavior becomes subject to the impersonal record of litigious encounter. There was the stunning case of the child who sued his parents for bringing him up badly. He may well have been justified. There could hardly be better proof than his miserable lawsuit. It was a relief that the case was rejected by the court. The prospect was horrendous that there could be costly legal invasion of yet another heretofore inexpensive arena of fuss and human acrimony.

The implication is that writing made it possible for communities to atomize and for individuals to become more distinct from each other. To go a step further, the entry of lawyers and comparable experts into the mix made possible an additional barrier or at least "space" between people. Indeed, "my own space" is the psychobabble translation of an embrace of private values eagerly sought and carefully defended. *The Fall of Public Man,* as Richard Sennett (1978), has put it in his illuminating book on the subject.

I would not be so absurd as to lay the cause of all this on literacy alone. But the manner of communication reflects and forms who is communicating and what is being exchanged. Literacy reflects what individuals think. The impartial implacable existence of authoritative words, which continue to answer back without change, without responsiveness, is obviously what infuriates despots and other censors. This is a vivid clue to the power of literacy. The latest dictator dons his tin-pot hat and lashes out at whoever annoys him. You can get good odds that the first van of new prisoners en route to the secret service prison will be full of writers. And again that is why in the USSR access to copying machines requires high-security clearance. This affirms the volatile nature of things written down.

The various forms of new electronic technology are so swift and elusive that it is easy to understand why they may discomfit ruling groups. As well, the new technology has not been without its own ethical provocation in Western societies; computer criminals, the invasion of privacy, finagled access to someone else's machines and hence economy and decision making, the impact of loss of memory—these are all significant issues, and there are others, which arise from the new machinery.

But so far not a single bit of product of this machinery has been, like the Bible or the Koran, declared divine. None has become an independent forceful determinant of how people should behave. This is no accident. It raises another question. The Bibles and Korans were holy and overwhelming, complicated and long. What they said had to be authoritatively interpreted by priests, who helped bring people together. What happened, first after the Protestant Reformation, then in the secular age, when priests became less necessary to personal salvation and ethical decision? What happened to the morality of the independent contractor? What or who made the society's connections then?

Ideology as Brain Damage

Reading and writing permitted human beings to develop distance from each other and to live their lives with greater than ever sense of privacy and independence. Ideologies are social forms designed to draw people together. What literacy tears asunder, ideology seeks to put back together again. It relies in good measure on literacy for this purpose. This is directly connected to basic biosocial processes. It reveals something to us about the nature of thought itself in our species.

From the beginning. We proudly call ourselves *Homo sapiens*. This implies that the function of our great brain is to be sapient, to think a lot. But the brain could only evolve to its present size and prominence if it led to action. Like any other organ, the brain was designed to be a part of the system in which it exists. It is designed to act. As Darwin told us, it had to act in direct context of the process of sexual and natural selection. So ideologies and other kinds of coded belief such as religions are directly related to social action and basic social affiliation. In turn this has to be firmly linked to reproduction. Perhaps this is why so often monks, nuns, priests, are obligated to be celibate.

Ideological ideas have to be seen not as truths but as reflections of gregariousness.

Ideological constructions may assert that they are objectively and logically independent of particular social circumstances. They may claim to be intellectually and historically perfect; for example, Scientific Marxism has. But they are not necessarily designed to stimulate dispassionate, clear-minded, passionless perception of moral and social reality. They are forms of affiliation. The brain is designed to act. Action is affiliative. Ideologies are special forms of codified affiliation.

An immense philosophical literature exists on the nature of belief and the sources of certainty about the world, people, and what they do. I neither want to account for this nor enter the discussion at a level of detail and brilliant sophisticated historicism such as Gellner's *Legitimation of Belief* (1974). I am not concerned with the complex history of ideas about right and wrong and the correct political state. I *am* interested in the emotional penumbra surrounding ideological productions and their use, not in their internal coherence or general appropriateness. Let me cite an extreme example of a contemporary ideologist who inhabits the dictator's chair in Libya, thus possessing a platform for broadcasting the virtues of his views of social matters. Those views are gathered in his *Green Book,* about which in a famous interview Oriana Fallaci recorded Qaddafi as saying, among other things, "The day of the revolution has inevitably arrived, thanks to the *Green Book.* In the whole world. And the masses will seize power, and the guide will be the *Green Book* . . . I can resist the attacks of the entire world and . . . the *Green Book* has resolved the problems of humanity and society. . . . In your gospels it's written, 'In the beginning was the word.' The *Green Book* is the word." (Fallaci, 1980)

This is peculiar. What are the sources of certainty in such a statement? Yet the Colonel's views do inspire some confidence in some of his followers, notwithstanding the fierce measures needed in Libya to ensure the longevity of the government against people who would rather march to a different drummer or not march at all. Certainly the Iranian revolution led by Khomeini to which Qaddafi referred in the Fallaci interview has had extraordinary success in stimulating strong and widespread commitment to the ideas of Khomeini's social movement, even to the extent of inducing young Iranian men to undertake suicidal missions to locate unexploded mines in disputed areas or accomplish other exceptionally dangerous military objectives, often with no training and with useless equipment. The willingness to risk one's life for an ideal or at the request of a leader is clearly an extreme, if grotesque form of affiliation. A connection so unquestioning and vital as to threaten life itself.

Contrast this with the extraordinarily precise and nonpersonal form of affiliation scientists have with each other through the scientific method they share. The number of working scientists in any community is relatively small, if one counts not those concerned with technological development or applied matters, but only the individuals working to find out things about physical and social nature. Their commitment is to making discoveries which are true, not necessarily those which may reflect their political or moral views, improve their living standards, or whatever. While science is a highly affiliative activity—the approval of one's peers is enormously important in science—scientists are obligated never to lie to protect others or in producing and reporting their findings. They may have to report results which would in other contexts produce disaffiliation. They may challenge or show inadequate the results or theoretical propositions of their colleagues. What in politics would be betrayal—for example, when a junior scientist demonstrates the inaccuracy of a famous senior scientist's measurements or conclusions—is scientific work as it should be done.

Of course there are highly defined protections that persons in this trade have, such as academic tenure and the careful manner in which appointments, promotions, and disappointments are made. Of course there are often subtle or serious distortions of the system, the result of favoritism, incompetence, greed, mendacity, and so on. But as human systems go, the academic scientific one is rather far removed from the ideological, at least in those institutions defined as of high quality—often defined this way for the very reason that they carefully respect the venerable traditions of a protected pursuit. A demonstration of the exoticism of this small world is that it emerges as a real force very rarely in societies. There are only a handful of effective scientific communities. Even where science is well established, it remains fragile and can be decisively affected by its ambient environment, as in the USSR where biology was decimated in that powerful and sophisticated country until 1964, because of the ideological commitment of its politicians to the theories of Lysenko, which in turn became the only acceptable scientific orthodoxy.

Science is about the empirical world, whereas ideology is a

self-sustaining social message to both individual and community. While ideological thinking may be truly a product of the intellect, at base it is really an act of affiliation. We know from interest-group theory in political science that when political groups have ideological disputes, these may result not from dispassionate analysis of the facts of the issue but from group divisions bred by economic, regional, ethnic, religious, or similar factors. These patterns may seem like ideologies, but in effect they are rooted in the ongoing nature of social grouping. There are important exceptions, and many of them—such as for example the difference of opinion among French-speaking Quebecers about the virtues of Quebec's legal separation from the rest of Canada. Here differences of opinion may reflect genuine differences of philosophical and moral attitude to such matters as ethnic diversity, centralization and regionalism, the role of the clergy in political life, and so on. But the general pattern of political affiliation has to do with social commitment, for instance in the way children tend to vote like their parents, spouses like each other, and so on. There are variations on these themes. But politics is a social process first and a cognitive one second.

There are broad and basic reasons for this. I have already referred to Robin Fox's paper on the relationship of kinship and reproductive categories. (Fox, 1979) His summary point is that kinship categories in human communities are, not surprisingly, related to real genetic linkages, and that the evolution of the human brain had to do with cognitive development involving sexual selection and kinship classification. I am adding here that what we now call ideology—who we are with and who we are against —used to be called kinship. The beginning of codification and therefore the essence of the evolution of thought had to be articulated through kinship terminology. This is one reason why the study of kinship in anthropology still matters so. It is the bread and butter and chocolate of the discipline because it is a central concern of the anthropologist's subject matter: people. This also helps explain why family terminology finds its way so readily into ideological politics—talk of brothers, sisterhood, and so on. Similar passions incite the use of similar words.

Let me further associate ideology and reproduction. Do you remember those political fires of adolescence and youth, when the world burned with conviction, with the absolute knowledge that the world had to change, that there was a way out and a way in, that if only that correct scheme were followed, all would be well and everything would be better? I think the emotionality that attaches to the politics of youth has to do with the fact that this youthful period, from about sixteen until twenty-four, is a prime reproductive time of people. It is also a period of life in which it appears that thought is indeed difficult to sustain—namely, late adolescence and early adulthood. Extraordinarily expensive, elaborate, and often beguiling structures known as secondary schools and universities are required to produce in students even the modicum of distance from their own tempestuous concerns to permit them to "think." Much of their time and energy goes otherwise into the reproductive fray itself, or into a series of ancillary behaviors which may promise to improve reproductive success—getting on the football team, playing the lead in the Shakespeare play, being "popular" in general. Is the prime time for reproduction the non-prime time for ratiocination, and that is why schools have to be skillful in inducing it? Whereas with reproduction they must do the opposite? That is, to try to inhibit its impact, as for example in the past by rules and regulations about sociosexual behavior and currently by the more subtle lures and invocations. That they have to reward thinking and suppress reproduction? There are many eager and skilled students who need no urging to approach their academic work at a high level of accomplishment. Nevertheless the broader pattern, as reflected say in dropout and other failure rates, is that, it seems, philosophy is harder to learn than the latest dance or team cheers or even the latest political sloganeering when this is in the air. And the reason philosophy is harder to learn is that it is an older person's game, requiring careful emotional distance between person and idea, precisely what is called the "academic" approach.

This differs from strong commitment, that ardent connection the squire has for the knight, the apprentice for the master, the full loyalty to the gang or club or secret society or Tong or Triad society or whatever agency for uncritical identification is available to a young person. Or of course the political group—Tupamaros, Parti Québecois, the IRA—particularly a group committed to the achievement of strongly defined political objectives linked to a benign and radical shift in the status quo. In the political sphere, the meaning of such connection is obvious. It may be less so in religious orders. Nevertheless, the importance of commitment is clear, particularly in those religious groups such as the contemporary Catholic or some Buddhist groups which insist that religious devotion and reproduction be separated. Celibacy confirms the reproductive sacrifice the priest or priestess makes in order to affiliate to the wider spiritual world. (Even police may have the problem; in the old days the Canadian Mounties could not marry for their first seven years of service.)

Such a choice might seem curious on the face of it. Why not encourage the most devoted and skilled members of the faith to propagate it literally as well as symbolically? It is less curious once the connection between ideology and reproduction is taken into account, even in its reverse form. It is also pertinent that priestly celibacy and literacy are historically and I suggest psychologically linked. The Columbia University classicist Henry Steele Commager suggested in a curious apercu which is as haunting as its subject matter that there is a clear etymological connection between grammar and glamour as words and forces, and in turn between literacy and power: "Because literacy was rare, it was mysterious, and because mysterious, it was deemed powerful. (Just how powerful is suggested by the archaic word 'dominie' or 'teacher' which derives from the Latin word for 'lord' or 'master,' 'dominus.') So impressive were the powers of the learned that in time 'grammar' became associated with magic. . . . 'Glamour' was a late Scottish variant of 'grammar' and at first it had exclusively the sense of a magic charm." (Commager, 1984) Weird, this, yet somehow sensible in the context of human groups, which insist on uniting belief with learning and with anti-reproductivity. It is also sensible in the wider context of the romance and sexual attractiveness of poems, poets, writing, and writers, and of the modern form of troubadour, the musician-singers of the electronic age.

To carry the argument forward, let us go backward once more, to those Paleolithic societies of our formative period. We can see from the scale and probable composition of those communities that they were organized on the basis of kinship. Indeed, it was the ability to transcend kinship by "marrying out," or exogamy—marrying someone specifically of another group—which, according to those such as Lévi-Strauss and Fox who have considered the issue, made it possible for *Homo sapiens* to prosper demographically. Exogamy let us expand our alliances with otherwise threatening groups by the exchange of our grown children. Who were held in sweet hostage in the marriage bed. Their children in turn would additionally cross-connect groups that may have started off apart and hostile. In essence, kinship was an organizing principle by belief or choice. To this day people are named according to their families—why should this be?—though a few individuals change their names either for political reasons, as with American black people who take on Muslim names, or others with "ethnic" names who adapt or anglicize these to the dominant group of the country to which they or their parents have moved.

The core argument is: the force of kinship as an organizing principle of people's lives has been reduced under the impact of modern conditions. But people still appear to relish or even require some intellectual and moral principle or identification. This is because social codification and thinking are closely associated. As kinship has declined in centrality, the role of ideology has become enlarged. It is no accident that ideologists from Christ to Mao have seen the usefulness and force of turning children against their parents in the name of ideology. It almost seems as if there is only a certain amount of commitment people can have and it must be focused: the secretion of the commitment gland should not be random, otherwise its strength is too dilute to make a difference. The connection between ideology and families is through the process of making social codes and deciding which is one's own group. In the children's classic chronic game, which are the bad guys and which the good?

"Guys" is right, because the trade of ideology-making has been mainly followed by males. Of course most dominating public jobs have in the past been male preserves, so it is not surprising that so is the production of social codes by which communities define themselves and determine how to make choices about communal action. Since ideology is intrinsically involved with writing, and since only recently have women and girls been able to learn to read and write, and use written words for self-conscious effect, then it has been all the more likely that ideologizing has been a disproportionately male endeavor.

But there is another reason beyond literacy, to which I have already alluded in my earlier discussion of the essay by Shirley Strum and Jonah Western on the evolution of the difference in how males and females deal with kinship. They considered how males deal with their uncertainty about who specifically their offspring are. Females are absolutely certain, Strum and Western argue that therefore males will more likely interest themselves in general social groups and matters, whereas females will devote themselves more assiduously to the kinship group, of which they are certified markers. This differentiation also accords with Carol Gilligan's hypothesis about sex differences in the development of moral thinking, a view shared by other psychologists also. (Goleman, 1984)

So an overall picture emerges which begins to provide a context for the fact that overwhelmingly, to date, Utopias—those ideologies gone perfect—are male products. As we saw in the Israeli kibbutz, the ideology was finally unsympathetic to the kinship orientation reflected in kibbutz women's decision to remove their young children from the children's houses to have them live at home—despite the cost and affront to the anti-familial ideology of the idealists who founded the system. There was enormous variation between how kibbutz males and females operated their lives in that communal setting. The firm and finally successful demand by females to revise child-rearing patterns made by male ideologists suggested that the whole proposal was originally a male plan—even a male fantasy, as far as females were ultimately concerned. There is now of course a considerable literature about women's responses to conventional Utopias and ideologies. As Ehrenreich (1983), Greer (1984), and others have asserted, even feminist ideologies have failed to consider female interests in the reproductive system. An overestimated emphasis on politics and employment has in an odd but profound sense been to the erotic, if not broader advantage of men.

Ideologies have come to replace kinship as a defining principle of social organization in these modern times. This process has gathered speed as the emphasis in most men's and now women's lives has had to be on the productive system first and the reproductive later. The situation has been exacerbated by a forceful male commitment to ideology, possibly because men's already shaky confidence in kinship arrangements has been eroded even further by the overall decline of kinship as a vigorously operating scheme in industrial life. So perhaps for dual reasons, the salience of ideological productions has increased; the so-called Cold War—that male paranoid fantasy become reality—is so vast we may forget its male ideological origins. Various Books, Green, Red, or whatever color, litter the moral landscape with sharply etched injunctions and instructions about how to behave and which (almost invariably dominant male) person to listen to, even from his grave.

Thus can literacy extend a man's reach beyond all primatological grasp.

As ideologies have replaced kinship, the development of relatively widespread literacy has made the impact of this quite enormous. Qaddafi's and Mao's coloring books, the Bible, the Koran, and sundry other artifacts of the literary persuasion have been destabilizing and in a real sense dangerous contributions because they have produced in an otherwise small-scale primate community the possibility to exaggerate whatever tendencies might be around in any community at a particular time. They rather readily appear to provide an instrument of control by small elite cadres over the wider mass of populations. You can see the bare bones of the business in the seminaries of the Greek Orthodox quarter of Jerusalem, perhaps the most beautiful and certainly the most placid part of that remarkable City of the Books. Or in the Jewish or Christian sections too, as platoons of young boys and men in whatever robes are their proper garb slide to their proper schools: Onward, O literate soldiers. Only an understanding of the power of ideology and literacy can make that mad improbable city at all comprehensible.

Jerusalem is strange enough, even on the small scale of village life. But now the enthusiasm for reading and studying Belief is planetary. Young fellows from Zaire are flown to Friendship University in Moscow or Georgetown University in Washington, to take back with them from the metropolitan country not only a taste for the artifacts and styles of industry but also the ideologies appropriate to the various sects of the economic church. Literacy provides the leverage for an unprecedented intrusion into societies which may have formerly operated with integrated, intimate systems of belief broadly insulated from the larger ideological structures of the world.

Such isolation is no longer possible. In El Salvador as in Afghanistan, what books have started, the electronic missionaries of radio, television, movies, and music carry on. The marketing of ideology is as easy as switching the transistors from "off" to "on" in a world of ever easier certainty, hope, and thus finally disillusion.

In 1983, the psychiatrist David Hamburg was appointed president of the Carnegie Foundation and indicated that he saw a major responsibility to try to accelerate understanding of the grim fact of aggression in the human species. Twenty years earlier in a paper which did much to clarify the scientific issues necessarily part of such understanding, he indicated that the important question to ask about an animal's behavior was not, is it instinctive or is it learned, but rather, what's easy for the animal to learn? (Hamburg, 1963) I am claiming here that cool, dispassionate thought is hard to learn, while ideology, which is hot thought, is far easier to learn. The implication is not that we are dealing with an evil or stupid species, but one which has never really become adapted to learning anything else than committing itself to strong beliefs. At first these beliefs were focused on families, and the Montagues and Capulets, the Hatfields and McCoys, are the modern versions of that ardor. Intermediate structures of commitment were and are possible too—to the town, the neighborhood, the province, the county, the company, the union, or the college, or even, as in contemporary Japan, the massive corporation, which nevertheless permits and invites a warm identification of person with group.

But ideologies may be destabilizing when they permit pure affiliation, without real quotidian connection. By contrast, families and the emotions which surge in and surround them are formed and generated by the challenge of getting through the day, getting through the life cycle. The affections and antipathies of real kinship-ideology have an empirical origin and also resolution. Ideologies are purer than this. They motivate a person because the ideas are attractive or self-evidently efficacious or fair or colorful, not necessarily because they may easily or successfully correspond to the real life of real people. We saw one case, of the kibbutz women. We know for a grim historical fact how the backlash of disappointed zealotry is a source of danger to the body politic and social. Precisely because ideology is too theoretical, it shares the promise of both power and peril. Recall Hollywood movies during the Depression—so elaborate and perfect and rich while people's lives in the industrial countries that adored these films were mean, displeasing, and of minimal hope. Ideologies can have the same artificial and extravagant connection to real lives and real options of people as the movies did to those who gathered in darkened palaces-of-the-people to watch the lords and ladies of the screen.

Like literacy, ideology is another potential source of exile of the heart. It can render life so theoretical and hence perfect and perfectible that people find it possible in their hearts to commit things which may be literally unspeakable, and which are in any event hostile to their real purposes. The quest for ideological purity is one of the miserable odysseys of modern life. I have already alluded to the harshness of views such as Khomeini's or Hitler's or Stalin's, or of less spectacular devotees of the marriage of certainty and the sword. Even on the more self-consciously benign liberal side of the political spectrum, Robert Sherrill (1983) has commented on "The Zany Sport of Liberal Fratricide: Firing on Our Own Troops," complaining of internecine struggles among relatively like-minded public figures who give "ammunition to those who [are] criticizing us liberals as unrealistic kamikaze purists and Rube Goldberg strategists." Having myself been the baffled victim of some feminist ideologues who focused on minor issues which may have divided us while our basic positions and broad intentions were politically and morally similar, I am well aware that often the bitterest struggles may be between those who are really closest to each other and have in fact most to gain from compromise and alliance. But there exists in opinion-making circles precisely that heady certainty which makes compromise seem like a vital sell-out and moral blight. Ideological blood is thicker than the wine of congeniality.

And the sanctimony, good lord, the sanctimony of this ideological tribalism! With old-fashioned ethnic prejudice there are clear markers which are the highlights of the despised group—the black skin, the almond eyes, the chinless face. For ideological racists, subtler and equally irrelevant but as real markers may become identified with one group as opposed to another—tofu, pasta with vegetables, white wine for the liberal diners; shrimp cocktail, steak with potatoes, mixed drinks for the table on the right. The quest for purity stains and strains all segments of the political spectrum —just as it always has in the arrangements of marriages and families. Perhaps in some circles the marriage of a son to a Democrat or Tory is more irritating than those old-fashioned antipathies to Catholics, Jews, Gentiles, or whomever. Of course there is a difference in permanence between being a member of an ethnic or even religious group, and an ideological one. Ideological antipathies may be less grave than ones based on unchangeable givens of people's lives. Nevertheless, they seem to be as stimulating as kinship and ethnicity as far as violence and mayhem are concerned. It is an open question as to which particular source of commitment to a power structure—belief in family or belief in belief—has yielded more trouble for innocent bystanders or those unfortunate enough to have been defined as of the wrong group on whatever ground. The reason they are similar is that they come from the same emotional/cognitive source—kinship, and the boundaries that surround it.

Is it hopeless, then, this transition from kinship to ideology as a source of group affiliation? We know that a critical human innovation was exogamy. You married out of your immediate family group and became hostage to the good fortunes of the group which you left and the one to which you went. Once the connection with the formerly dangerous or loathsome or uninteresting group was made through marriage, there existed a larger community of purpose than before. More people had a real interest in real compromise should there be divisive matters to confront.

Is there an ideological equivalent to exogamy? Can there be? The answer is vital because what are defined as ideological conflicts have destroyed and are destroying so many people, so much social order and social and material wealth. Obviously the first step is understanding the profundity of the passion—that the ideological urge is related to the basic reproductive and affiliative one, and that therefore it must be treated with great caution and respect.

No more citizenship classes, then? Or Young Communist League meetings on The Thoughts of Chairman Whomever? Perhaps. After all, high schools do not try to stimulate students to more and more arduous reproductive activity because it is obviously an unsettling or at least volatile business. Why then advertise the virtues of ideology when it may share an equally unpredictable or potentially unwanted outcome because it taps into the same reservoir of enthusiasms and forces? This is of course an old assertion and an old dream—World Citizenship and all that. Once children are taught that all people are equal and equally good, the sectarian war of group with group will be impossible; no one will believe the leaders' jingoistic mumbo-jumbo. To some extent, in the United States at any rate, this did happen during the time of the Vietnam War, but then that was a truly remote and theoretical war in the real context of American lives.

Perhaps the role of ideology in the United States is rather special because it is such a powerful country with enemies so far away that American ideologists have had to develop a particularly exotic form of true belief. As a result, the Cold War has a purity of theory and an immensity of scope almost mathematical in its ordered and general quality. The stakes are so high that they are almost theoretical, a perfect field against which to play the ideology game. Is it not fittingly inexorable within this logic—both biologic and technologic—that the operators of this system should seek a place for combat in perfect space? The new war will be fought in the vast remoteness of planetary space, but with finely calibrated ways of keeping score; at least that is the plan, which may well not work. Nevertheless, such "Star Wars" successfully express the translation of ideologic into technologic. The ancient passions about cousins and kin and the strangers across the river achieve new articulation with laser swiftness through computer programs of astonishing scope and precision.

Just as weapons encircle the world and sensors monitor the movements of people and missiles over countless square miles on land and under sea, the same force, electricity, creates links between communities newly tied by propaganda about ideologies. Perhaps there is a global village as McLuhan envisaged it, but it is a very divided village. Rivalries are often identified and stimulated by the particular mixture of defense treaties, political connections, ideological beliefs, and working arrangements about such matters as the use and supply of weapons, credit, and trade in materials. There has been a transition from the parochial concerns of families trying to make do to extended systems eventually requiring treaties and officials who write things down. The things written down assume more and more importance. Eventually ideologies develop which more people can embrace more fully when they can read. The other more accessible media based on electricity increase the leverage of leaders over people even further. So self-justifying is the overall system that few if any locations in the world are exempt from affiliating to a far larger ideological scheme than they would produce on their own. The United Nations as an organization both accelerates this process and then helps mitigate problems it produces.

A soft-skinned primate, intensely skilled at communication, has created several methods of contact which are beguilingly controllable, or seemingly so, but which have had the consequence of turning the act of communication itself into a form of distance from the correspondent. Writing and reading permit people a distance from their social groups which yields them autonomy and a sense of conspectus. But they may also become alienating. So ideologies are written to join people in political camaraderie when their familial affections become inadequate. If we are to judge from the effort of ideologue leaders from Christ to Lenin to Mao, who selfishly claimed their followers away from their childish pasts. Who almost literally demanded that their followers become exiled from their previous homes and thus also from a crucial part of life's changeless familial heartland.

Well, not so changeless, actually. Turn the page.

6. The Body and the Body Economic

I saw the film *The Right Stuff* about the United States' astronauts and space program at a movie house in Times Square in New York City. At one point in the action the astronauts were being shown by proud scientists the capsule in which they would flip into space. The astronauts complained that there was no window in the capsule. They wanted one. They were pilots, not monkeys. They wanted to see where they were going. The scientists protested that the window was unnecessary. It would be a nuisance to create one. By threatening to Tell All to the journalists milling in the distance, the astronauts got their way. The audience cheered for this victory of man over machine. One episode in a chronic dialogue about the relationship between human beings and the industrial system—about how man can humanize a mechanical system which he has himself made. A system which evidently often feels hostile to human purposes. So when its scientific protagonists lose a struggle over it, Everyman cheers.

On one hand, audiences cheering opponents of the system. On the other hand, cheering celebrated astronauts who have become weightless in space, thus achieving a dream of emancipation from the earth's forces, finally becoming like gods, at least as far as gravity is concerned.

Hovering somewhere between the stubborn insistence on a window and the joy of cellular independence from real worlds lies the daily life of *Homo industrialis*. Remember that the astronauts who had to learn to maneuver weightlessly in the world had also to learn to urinate and defecate within their clothes, into systems designed to accommodate their body wastes to be sure, but nonetheless on their own bodies. From the sublime to the ridiculous, you might say.

Yet a reality all the same, even if the glamour of weightlessness received far more press attention than the irreducible requirements of elimination. Now I turn to the broad matter of industrial bodies and the impact of bodies on production and reproduction. I found it exhilarating to sit in the pilot's seat of a Boeing 747 (on the ground please note) because of the astonishing disproportion between the vast and complicated object and the small, familiar human who commanded it miles from the ground. Whenever there is an accident with one of these giants, the legal arguments that follow are almost invariably over whether or not the machine misperformed or the person. Did a valve stick or a gyroscope get lazy or a man tired or careless? The issues are always ardently joined, both because of the important equity and amounts of money involved, and because of the metaphorical implication of the truth of what happened. Did Icarus' wings melt, or his heart, or his nerve?

In this chapter, I want to talk first about the broadest behavior of *Homo sapiens,* our reproductive activity, in the context of the emergent system of productive life that increasingly dominates the planet. Then I turn to how the world outside the skin affects what goes on inside it, and also vice versa. Then I want to see how the ideas we have about our bodies affect our policies about the social world, and how they have an impact on everything from college admission to the tax system. You can never tell how seemingly innocent assumptions about social behavior produce outcomes of inflexibility and unexpected oddity. Finally, I want to locate all this in an integrated picture of the role of modern bodies.

Production Si, Reproduction Non: The Score at Half-Time Is Marx 3, Darwin 2

By now the bowerbird is as famous a performer on educational television and school movies as Leonard Bernstein, because the creature exquisitely and with unexpected assiduity exemplifies a principle of nature. The male bowerbird collects any style of junk or treasure to make the most elaborate possible nest with which to attract a strategically minded mate. For example, the satin bowerbird of eastern Australia creates a dancing carpet at

his nest and collects colorful objects for its decoration. His preferences run to dark blue and yellow-green colors. He will also add
to berries, feathers, and flora of nature the bric-à-brac of man
where available, such as beads, strands of wool, and, triumphantly, tinsel. He even paints the inside of his structure with
blueberry juice he squeezes in his beak. A bowerbird's housework
is never done. He continues to replace old flowers and berries with
fresh ones. He may steal shamelessly from competitor bachelor-
applicants. When a female comes a-calling, the male engages in
energetic song and dance, and also plucks out choice bits of his
interior decoration for her close inspection. In the heat of this
display he is evidently able to change the colors of his irises to
match his plumage. This enthusiast of color coordination persists
in his ardor until the female either accepts his courting and mates
with him, or scorns him and moves on so that he must redecorate
his bachelor pad for another prospect. (Von Frisch, 1974)

Perhaps the bowerbird is extreme in linking mating to property, almost as much a caricature as an aspirant Victorian pater-
familias boasting of his lineage and country estate and urban clubs
and national regiment. Yet there is in the systems of selection that
nature employs a real connection between resources and reproductive opportunity. One important model involves males establishing some pattern of competition amongst themselves, for position in the social group, or for resources, or territory. Then females
judge for themselves which candidates suit them best and select
accordingly. There are among humans a vast number of complicat-
ing factors such as kinship arrangements made by parents, caste
barriers and ones of religion and ethnicity, and the powerful ones
of personal taste and cultural preference. Nevertheless, even without dowries and marriage contracts, there is an extensive and
noticeable pattern in which females tend to marry males who are
higher rather than lower than they in whatever hierarchical structure pertains. The opposite obviously applies among the males.
The bowerbird principle at work, to stretch the point, but not too
much.

I refer principally to human societies in which reliable contraception does not exist, or before it existed. Then a female's choice
of partner also implied her opinion about her partner's suitability
as a possible parent. There was (and for many people still is) a
rather clear connection between sexual selection and reproduction—a picture fascinatingly drawn by Heather Remoff in her *Fe-*

male Choice (1984), a study, by extensive interview, of the mate selections of sixty females of various socioeconomic and occupational type. Despite the stereotyped view of "the poor"—that they have many children—there is a consistent relationship between increasing income and childbearing within occupational groups. The social theory of relativity applies, so that the couples who have the fewest children in any socioeconomic group are those at its bottom. The poorest plumbers have fewer children than rich plumbers, the poor doctors have fewer children than wealthy doctors. There is a "very high rate of childlessness among wives of college-educated husbands in the lowest income category" (Kunz, Brinkerhoff, and Hundley, 1973). The same pattern of association between relative wealth and fecundity applies in other sectors of society. It appears people determine their child rearing by comparing themselves with their peers, their immediate reference group. Productive prosperity—at whatever level of activity the individual defines prosperity—may translate itself into reproductive prosperity.

It should surprise no one with even cursory understanding of evolutionary biology that there is a connection between resources and offspring. Animals assess this connection in ways often hard to fathom, for example, reducing births when there is drought or in response to social or environmental perturbation. We know what some of these mechanisms are, stress for one, and spontaneous abortion is another. But there remains an interesting link between what is available to support offspring, and how many of them are born.

Among humans, the situation is very different, because a vast array of varying patterns marks our behavior. I am concerned with a rather consistent association between high industrial productivity and low reproductivity. In a striking way it contradicts a natural principle of linkage between prosperity and reproduction at the core of the persistence of other species. The richest organisms on earth, industrial humans, have in the mature industrial countries reduced their fecundity. This is now a pattern of some two hundred years standing, which slowly became defined. With the introduction of good contraception controlled by women, the decline in birth rates has been unusually persistent, rapid, and substantial.

A paradox: while the more prosperous members of particular class and occupational groups seem to grow more children than their less affluent colleagues, overall there is a downward trend in the system as a whole. For example, in the nineteenth century, the birth rate of American whites dropped from roughly 50 per 1,000 around 1800 to 28 per 1,000 at the century's end. (Reed, 1979) Various reasons for this trend have been advanced, from the obvious awkwardness of the high cost of raising children who, unlike kids of farmhouse yore, would be unlikely to earn their weight in work, to the more skeptical idea that some of the change in American fertility at any rate could be attributed to the efforts of corporate philanthropy to study and then affect birth control. So James Reed of Rutgers has suggested that research on reproductive behavior was dominated by corporate philanthropy, in particular that of the Rockefeller family and also of the Carnegie, Harriman, Milbank, and Gamble families. (*ibid.,* p. 6) And Donna Harraway of Johns Hopkins University extended this apercu by claiming that the direction which primate research took, particularly in the experimental laboratory work epitomized by Robert Yerkes, functioned as showplace pilot plants for "interpreting the place of human beings in scientifically managed, corporate capitalism—called 'nature.' " (Harraway, 1979, p. 11)

A substantial case can be made for the reality of the relationship between the corporate capitalist system, controlling reproduction, and its bedmate sensuality. Was this not what formal Victorianism was about? Or the fact that boys in North American culture would have no way of learning at school until the 1960s that, for example, females menstruated and that their own sexuality was volatile and often problematic. Or that girls could not appreciate the hectically importuning sexual bravado of their adolescent male coscholastics for the inept perilous rehearsal that it was? Or that censorship made it impossible for movies to depict men and women sharing the same bed? Or that in the United States widely used words could only be printed with the consent of the Supreme Court?

But the same story can be told about Communist countries, which may if anything be more diligent in their commitment to public Victorianism. So the explanation for all this must rest elsewhere than in the sexual Cold War. Certainly one common factor is the industrial pattern, which may yield efforts in both indigenously capitalist societies such as England or Belgium and Communist ones who Care Enough to establish elaborate schemes of sociosexual control in the name of a large public good.

How does the common factor operate? Pressures on urban

space have consistently increased with time for even well-off people. More generous notions of what is minimally acceptable housing for poor people have increased demands on housing supply in the industrial countries. Perhaps this is clearest in the centrally planned economies of Eastern Europe, where the discrepancy between acceptable housing and available housing is the source of much government apologia and private manipulation of the system to secure space. There may be empirically superior and more ample housing stock available per capita than, say, in the parental generation of the current cohort of potential baby producers. Nevertheless, the public perception of what is available is that it is inadequate. The relative assessment will be more of an influence on couples' reproductive decision than any physical limit on the space needed to house a child or children. If an apartment feels too small for another child, then willy-nilly it is too small. For virtually everybody there will be an evident contrast between housing available to the bulk of the citizenry and what is awarded to the elite. Low birth rates may reveal that a sense of inequity is an effective contraceptive. Among other animals there is often a relationship between the low morale which accompanies low status, and low fecundity. It is reasonable to consider that for humans who concern themselves so much with symbolic matters, symbolic low status may as much depress a pair of observant people as any direct loss of resources or access to fun and conviviality.

Recall that I am considering the puzzle: why do the richest humans in the world have the fewest offspring, when in nature there is a clear connection between space, resources, and reproduction?

Is there something intrinsically contraceptive in the social arrangements of the industrial system?

Does the birth rate reflect the fact that children are not only an economic liability to their parents but perceived as drains on an already strained planetary ecology? If the current low birth rate persists or declines further, what if any political, economic, and socio-psychological impacts will there be? What has all this to do with controversies about gender? Was Marx's proposal about the alienating character of capitalism also applicable to industrial communism? Was Darwin's implication wrong—that health and prosperous reproduction were linked and so well-off species would burgeon in numbers?

Of course human beings differ from other animals. It is in the nature of species to differ from each other. In any case, the human species as a whole is enormously and dangerously reproductive. But it is deeply interesting that the industrial world has arrived at this point. Knowing more about that world may reveal something useful about both production and reproduction in their lopsided relationship. The unproductive countries have too many children and the productive ones perhaps too few. Leave the military implications of this aside (is this one reason for the endless alliance-making of the industrial powers?) and consider the economic. Who will buy the products of rich countries if there are relatively few of their own people with wads of bills in their hands? Where will the poor countries get ever more food for ever more people, particularly when increasing their food supply may require the expensive seeds, fertilizer, and often machines made by the expensive countries? Will there be an equitable distribution of knowledge and expertise in the world, when one year at a good American college could cost an Indian village its savings for a decade?

I am not saying that there are any interesting or significant biological differences between different human groups and that there will be genetic improvement or decline because there turn out to be relatively more of one group than another. Such eugenics talk is basically nonsense. My only concern is with the fact that masses of people in poor countries will be hungry and feel bad, and that they will suffer without relent or meaningful explanation and justice. Everyone's world will feel more rotten and be more rotten. So the impact and meaning of all this is totally social, economic, and political. But insofar as some of the causation must be linked to the biological matter of reproduction, then there—and only there—have we to consider the broader biosocial issues. But please, I am talking about the quality of life, not the quality of genes.

When zookeepers compare the quality of zoos and the care they provide their animal tenants, how successfully the animals reproduce is one important diagnostic. A robust birth rate implies the zoo's environment is appropriate to the species's evolved pattern of response. There is not too much stress, the food and exercise facilities are adequate. The creatures are able to produce enough of a range of their "natural" behavior to include the frequently complex and delicate ones that are a part of fruitful courtship and mating. Of course some species seem equally reluctant suitors in urban zoos and in the wild—the Giant Panda is now world famous for its sexual obtuseness. If its overall reproductivity is any indication, its extraordinary finickyness in zoos is similar to its behavior in its Chinese home range. Among other more fecund animals, it appears that the strong trend among zoos over the past three decades to house animals not in formal cages but rather in enclosures as far as possible like their indigenous habitats may well be a factor in the improved breeding experience. So must, also, the greater knowledge about animal social and sexual behavior which followed the sophisticated animal behavior studies of the 1950s.

If we have learned so well to help other animals reproduce under artificial conditions, have we created artificial conditions for ourselves which hinder our own reproduction? Is the situation we're in the one we want? Is this our zoo of choice?

Or to put it one more way: if production yields things and services, and reproduction yields people and obligations to them, are we witnessing a shift to relatively private consumption of goods from the relatively social production of behavior? A shift from interaction to action? A shift from the uncontrollable longevity of parenthood to the individually direct management of time?

We know that when contemporary young women in North America are asked how many children they would like to have and think they will have, they provide estimates which are lower than ever in history, usually two or three, rarely the four common in the early postwar years. In fact, the actual birth rate is closer to 1.7 children per female. At least 2.1 are necessary for the population to remain stable—leaving the nontrivial factor of immigration aside for a moment. Overall, the international picture is confused and paradoxical. The Chinese government has instituted a severely restrictive population policy in which an array of controls are merged with economic sanctions to prevent families from having more than one child each: "If each couple were allowed to have three children . . . the country's current total of one billion people would, within 100 years, grow to more than four billion, about the size of the population of the whole world today." (Bennett, 1983) Nevertheless, the injunctions seem principally successful in urban areas. In rural regions there is much violation of the policy, if only in part paradoxically because children are increasingly useful in the family-based farming system being introduced by the same Chinese authorities also trying to reduce the birth rate. (Erik, 1982) In the USSR, abortions slightly exceed births each year, despite evident efforts by authorities to "talk the women out of it, but in the end it's their decision." (UPI, 1984) In the United States, the abortion level is considerably below the Soviet's; roughly one of four pregnancies ends in abortion. (*New York Times*, 1982) In India, where the aggressive sterilization campaign of Indira Gandhi's government was widely regarded as a significant factor in her defeat in a previous election, population growth has continued unchecked over a decade, by roughly 25 percent over ten years. (*New York Times*, 1981) And in France, where government policy has been strongly pronatal for decades, the Mitterrand government introduced a campaign on television advising French women to take advantage of publicly supported contraceptive clinics; "according to a 1978 survey, 'Only 30% of French women between the ages of 15 and 50 use any form of birth control.' " (Prial, 1981) The intention is not to reduce births but permit women better choice of when and under what circumstances they would have them.

In the United States, the annual number of illegitimate births has multiplied five times between 1940 and 1975, despite the extensively greater availability of contraceptive options. It is not clear that even well-publicized options are adopted, particularly by teenagers who may be both unmarried and relatively poor, but nonetheless carry pregnancies to term. For example, in 1980 in New York City, one third of births were to unmarried women, 14 percent to teenagers, with a strongly ominous association between such births and the mothers' economic poverty. (Sulzberger, 1981) A bioproletariat in the process of creation. This is a major matter in the black community. An estimated 55 percent of black children born in 1979 were to unmarried women. Among white women also there was a 24 percent increase in the birth rate of unmarried individuals. (Auletta, 1981) In a brilliant paper tracing economic factors in this, Bernstam and Swan (1986) describe the "State As the Marriage Partner of Last Resort." At the same time, there is an apparent trend of increasing infertility among young women usually able to conceive easily without medical intervention. Based on a 1976 survey, the National Center for Health Statistics concluded that 45 percent of the nation's nearly 27.5 million couples have experienced difficulty or been unable to conceive; 19 percent of these have been sterilized for contraceptive reasons, 10 percent for medical, while 16.3 percent failed to conceive for other reasons. (UPI, 1983)

The Darwinian urgency for reproduction has been clearly mitigated by the varieties of socioeconomic schemes newly possible in human communities. Reproduction is now a clear option, not obligation. It is a focus of government as well as theological policy. Raising children may appear to both individuals and many governments as prejudicial to economic well-being.

The extent of reproductive option would not exist without reliable contraception. In particular when conception is controlled by females, who after all are the principal activists in pregnancy and who for better or worse end up sustaining more than men of the quotidian and often financial responsibilities of parenthood. For example, in the sizable population of divorced American mothers, fewer than half who have custody of their children receive child-support payments from their ex-husbands. (Fuchs, 1983) Unmarried mothers also must, much more than their children's fathers, respond to the needs of their offspring. Many working mothers—which is most mothers—in Eastern European countries must assume a disproportionate share compared to their husbands of household duties, including the bizarrely time-consuming process of shopping, particularly in the Soviet Union. The high abortion rate in the USSR must surely reflect the physical difficulty of coping with the exigencies of domestic life in that society, as well as its traditional function as a "contraceptive." Just as surely, if a surprising number of American teenagers become pregnant, this must be because, particularly in the black community, they dimly but effectively perceive that the opportunities for work for the young man with whom they consort are limited. As many as half of young black men will not find work in urban areas. So the young women are not confident about male partnership in the cycle of child rearing and will try to manage on their own.

In my opinion, these are important elements but nonetheless subordinate to the larger circumstance. This is that effective contraception has introduced the factor of consciousness into the reproductive process more pervasively and precisely than ever possible before. For perhaps the first time in the history of the mammalian arrangement, it is possible for one sex, the female, to determine with relative unilateralism the reproductive outcome of a courtship. If a woman can now decide to have sexual relations with less risk of unwanted pregnancy than ever in history, she can also affirmatively elect a time and person for reproduction with far greater deliberation, skepticism, and enthusiasm than has been possible in nature before. The cortex which was the result of sexual selection is now much more than ever a cause of that selection. And in a different manner because of the amalgam of foresight and control which contraceptive technology makes possible. Once again the industrial knack has made a decisive difference. This time it has actually gone into the body. The body has become industrialized. Just as children become their own products when they assess themselves in the marketplace of test scores and national comparison, even before they are born, before they become children, babies are products too, of a decision to "return to nature," to enter into sexual relations without restrictions about its outcome.

Industrialized bodies? A study by the Alan Guttmacher Institute found that of the 36.5 million fertile women in the United States, one third, or 11.6 million, rely on sterilization for contraception. Another 10 million use the birth control pill, and 2.3 million the intrauterine device. Nearly half the 10 million remaining women rely on their partner's condom, 1.9 million employ diaphragms, while 1.5 use spermicidal chemicals. Of this group overall, 26 million have in one way or another become subject to a varyingly significant intervention in the body's process. This is what I describe as industrialization of the body. It is relatively new. And it is all the more significant because it is voluntary.

Consider the lengths to which particular religious groups have had to go to achieve functional sterility of their priesthood—lifetime food and shelter, prestigious clothing, the promise of salvation, life-enhancing work. It is by contrast all the more remarkable that so many people choose to be sterilized. Particularly given the relatively high divorce rate. When one partner is sterilized, both are affected, even if the new partner of remarriage is not the one with whom the original decision was taken.

Perhaps this is more mysterious to me than to those who elect this form of emancipation from life's process. Their choice becomes clearer when it is recognized that more than half the women who choose sterilization are over thirty-five and earn under $6,000 per year. However, the latter fact implies they may be married and supported by a male or the state, while the former fact places them at risk of divorce and abandonment in effect. Where do they turn if they connect anew with a new man and want a child? And are the men who choose this operation fully committed to its implication? I know of too many cases of both males and females who regret their surgical sterilization—because their lives turned good and loving again. It is reasonable to ask why on earth such a drastic contraceptive choice is made by people who have other options even if they are more demanding and recurrent. How subtle and provident are physicians who participate in an irreversible procedure in an unpredictable period of sexual history? What are the broad effects on people of such a decisive operation? Psychiatry and Literature describe the subconscious relationship of sexuality and overt life. They suggest that a substantial disenfranchisement, even by choice, may have a subtle but real impact on the lives of people. While the situations are not comparable, enough information exists about the impact of enforced barrenness and sterility on people that we may suspect that the medically created version of the situation may also have an impact. As for impotence—a problem of rather different quality—while there is no comparison functionally between sterility and impotence, nevertheless the disturbance which impotence may cause in a man's life may find some echo in the circumstances which even voluntary sterility may produce.

I doubt a massive medical intervention can be neutral in impact where the reproductive system is concerned, even if it is an intervention welcomed and liberating. I am suggesting that the faith patients have in surgical sterilization is undue, and that the medical profession has corporately acceded to a procedure that is mostly unnecessary and a "cure" more drastic than the "disease." I will later suggest that using the contraceptive pill is also an unnecessary overkill with implications for health and behavior too cavalierly dismissed by those who should know and do better. The IUD too appears to involve a nontrivial risk of infection and subsequent sterility. It is perhaps significant that women in the higher income brackets, presumably the ones most educated and relatively well informed, choose the diaphragm method—the female contraceptive with the minimal risk. Of course the condom is equally risk-free, and carries the additional advantage of restricting venereal disease transmission, a virtue of greater importance than ever since what is in effect a form of sexual crowding (crowding in time, not space) has produced large numbers of carriers of afflictions such as gonorrhea, herpes, and AIDS.

Thus a large population of women has adopted contraceptive tactics that reflect strong rather than mild medical intervention. This typifies a reliance on hard rather than soft methods to solve a problem that can be softly solved. Other reasons than belief in the efficacy of technology help account for the choices I've described. The methods which involve the most drastic medical intervention require the least personal intervention at the time of use, unlike the condom, diaphragm, and similar methods. Given the delicacy of sexual decision making, particularly among unmarried couples, the setting aside of the contraceptive issue in the heat of the moment may be desirable, as a pleasure or a strategy. Given the overall esteem of the medical profession, it is to be expected that the medically most direct and definitive solutions to what are perceived as problems will be favored by the public at large. We know that the medical profession is committed to its own technological finesse, often at the expense of the emotional needs that accompany frailty and treatment. So it is no surprise that patients will be offered technoremedies.

Still, sterilization!

Modern medicine turns the human body into an arena for displaying the power of the industrial system. Only a fool or a believer in immortality would quibble with the value of the accomplishments of medical science and curative impact on the lives of people. As technical triumph and human contribution, there is little to equal modern medicine. Yet there is a "but" about the social implications of technical events, precisely the overall issue in this book. The industrialization of contraception has far-reaching impacts to consider.

There is power for men and women who know they can control the reproductive system, permanently, or at least without considering it on a day-to-day basis. What a change from the past, what a new freedom! And what a burden removed for people, women in particular, who don't wish any children, or any more, but who nonetheless relish the sweet convulsions of sex. But remember that I noted that this was the first occasion in nature in which among complicated mammals one sex could control the reproductive future. Females. One salient consequence is that males have either lost confidence in who their children are or lost concern to help care for them. When females control contraception, males may concern themselves less with the matter. When women do get pregnant, the pregnancy like the contraception remains their responsibility. Not the man's, who no longer may feel the need to "do the right thing" and marry the woman. This it is estimated used to happen in perhaps a third of marriages before modern contraception. And so what is a woman to do, with a possible child, no possible mate, lots of difficulty down the road? She seeks an abortion.

This is why the pressure for liberal and safe abortion emerged in the industrial world *after* good female-controlled contraception existed.

A paradox? Yes, but not such a strange one once it is realized that the ways of the reproductive heart are logical not in the usual fashion but in a biologic. As Kristin Luker (1975) has shown, women decide not to use contraception in part because they are interested in what their partners will do, should they become pregnant or even otherwise. Or they don't want to use contraception lest their partner think they have other partners. Or they have had more than one partner and are unable or unwilling to attribute the pregnancy to a particular man. What do they do? End up in the Berkeley abortion clinic where Luker studied them. Often twice, sometimes more often, even after counselling. What do their men do? Hardly anything. Only 10 percent were willing to pay even half the cost of an abortion. The rest assumed the whole matter was women's business. Men have been cads before, the subjects of novels and family crises forever. Nevertheless, the new circumstances provided by medical science have evidently made the cad's career markedly more trouble-free.

So what medical science has in a real sense created—females' reproductive autonomy but also to some extent loneliness—medical science must solve. Hence the abortion clinic for those betrayed by a man or their own bodies, in an environment of medical control they have been given but have not taken.

Is this situation so thoroughly different from others in history, in which men and women employed various contraceptive techniques, such as certain Indian tribes of Nevada who employ the plant *Lithospermum ruderale,* which has been found to inhibit the activity of rats' ovaries, if not of human? (Gregerson, 1983) Consistent and effective contraceptives apart from coitus interruptus and similar behavioral procedures have been relatively rare, particularly ones which require mechanical or chemical intervention. As Charles Westoff and Norman Ryder have noted in their detailed report (1977), the basic innovations in contraception have been the pill and the IUD. Sterilization is less significant, given the availability of these two methods; that is, it adds less new contraceptive effectiveness to the overall system. So in effect the title of their book *The Contraceptive Revolution* indeed reflects a reality. Something new has occurred. As they note, "Our analysis suggests . . . the decline of marital fertility during the decade of the 1960's was due almost entirely to the reduction of unplanned fertility. This . . . is . . . attributable in large measure to the advent and wide diffusion of a new, highly effective birth control technology, particularly the pill and the intrauterine device. Later in the decade there was also a significant increase in reliance on both male and female sterilization. . . . It appears . . . planned fertility has probably declined and . . . unplanned . . . much more. We are coming closer and closer to the perfect contraceptive population." (pp. 300–09)

It is important to appreciate the enormity of this change and its meaning for the lives of people. The human interaction most precisely and significantly related to natural selection—the gatekeeper experience of this and any other species—has been finally brought under firm control. Forethought and technology unite not only to change the rules but to make many old ones obsolete. There is a new balance of emphasis on the present and the future, the former enjoyed, the latter controlled. Time and the body are in a new relation. Short of repealing the law of mortality, it is difficult to think of a more serious shift in human arrangements.

I have little enthusiasm for the dingy anti-intellectualism revealed by God's decision to exile Adam and Eve from Eden because they bit into the fruit of enlightenment. The most visible symptom of their new knowledge was their anti-nudist gesture, which suggests how eager Management was to control sexuality. Adam and Eve were being told that sexuality was not trivial. It had literally to be kept under wraps. For *their* benefit, since apart from the Serpent there were no prurient bystanders leering at their nudity. A little knowledge evidently drove them a long way.

What if Management had known Adam and Eve would so skillfully study the body that they banished innocence from its inside as well as out? Not only could they enjoy the visual preliminaries of the sex connection but the event itself, all without consequence. What has happened to Adam and Eve since 1960 has been at least as pivotal as their light lunch of fruit in Eden. Their consciousness and control, by Eden's simple standards, are off the scale. *At last our ancient body has itself become modern.* There *is* something new under the sun and under the moon. The engine of evolution—passions that may suspend or narcotize thought—is now controllable by thought. Lose your head or your maidenhead. It doesn't really matter.

Earlier, I described the effectiveness of the industrial pattern in providing leverage. It multiplied the impact of human skill and desire in an unprecedented way. It allowed people to float free without much of the ballast of life's traditional requirements. Now with unprecedented specificity, the force of reproductive urgency can be molded, mitigated, or ignored once the products of industry are in use. In a stunningly short time, the complex and mysteriously persistent forces which Darwin and Freud helped uncover and appreciate have been tamed by that other more overt force, industrialization, which Marx so often despairingly described. In this scheme, every man and woman can be Management, every child a product smilingly awaited, every lover a curtailable episode in a far-reaching and quite risk-free drama. The grand pleasure of sexuality, which presumably reveals its portentousness in the scheme of things, can be enjoyed without the heretofore inevitable throw of the reproductive dice.

Geneticists use the concept of "funnel effect" to describe what happens when a particular population finds itself in a defined area in which an appreciable amount of genetic change may occur. Then the population moves out into a wider area. An observer may assume that the traits the population carries are related to the area it now inhabits. But in fact they may disproportionately reflect its special concentrated time in the "funnel." Metaphorically sexual intercourse has heretofore been a behavioral funnel, and decisions made about it may have been exaggerated in their impact. But sexual relations need no longer be such a funnel for people or the species. They can engage in sexual relations with no greater sense of moment than in any other relatively intimate connection. Of course for many if not most individuals, sexual intimacy remains an unusually privileged form of conviviality. For only a handful of people and under very particular circumstances are sexual choices made in a seemingly random or promiscuous manner. Nevertheless, as with other kinds of consumption, industrialism has widened people's range of sexual choice. The consequence of a single encounter with a particular person need not result in a possible pregnancy that will inexorably require one response or another. A remarkable freedom, which need never be licensed, has been obtained. It is difficult to overestimate its significance.

Look, Ma, Rosie the Riveter Isn't Pregnant

A dominating image of early American industrialization was the mill towns of New England, such as Lowell, Massachusetts, and Manchester, New Hampshire. The solemnly rooted brick buildings now begin to form the core structures of "Historic Areas." They have become part of the pastoral image of society past. Another image intrinsic to these structures is the procession of "Mill girls," who lived often in dormitories provided by the mill for a period of a year or two after working in their parents' homes and before marrying. Much of what they earned, they remitted to their families; this pattern persisted until the mid-nineteenth century, when these native women were replaced in the mills by cheaper immigrant laborers from Ireland, French-Canada, Portugal, and Eastern Europe. (Hareven, 1982)

The phasing of the young women's work away from home well suited the patterns of the time and the expectations of men and women about their lives. Not that when women married they ceased all effortful activity and simply luxuriated in domestic leisure. To the contrary. Many of the goods and services now purchased on the open market were part of family life. There was no doubt in anybody's mind that what women did was as important to life as what men did. As time went on families became increasingly involved with employment choices of their members. The work of women and children was seen as necessary for a family's survival and economic progress. "Because interdependence and collective effort was the key to survival, family economic strategies took precedence over individual choices and priorities." (*ibid.*, p. 89)

Of course there were immense differences between the experiences of wealthy and poor women. Because of the pattern of women marrying men rather wealthier or of higher status than they, wealthy women might see fewer options for acceptable marriages. There were only several careers for them, such as teaching at the elite women's colleges. But the overall pattern for women was one in which working life was a prelude to family life. Even when that did not happen, family life remained the preeminent value and expectation of the wider culture.

While the change has been in process for a long time indeed, the current preeminent pattern is different. No sensible young woman will assume that working is mere prelude to a reliably lengthy and exclusive life of familial sequestration. For one thing, as we have seen from American data, with a rate of roughly 45 percent of marriages ending in divorce, it would be foolhardy for either a woman or man to depend on the economic support of a marriage for their lifetimes. If only because of rather substantial change in public expectations about the employment of females, women in the courts of most jurisdictions cannot expect to receive substantial and enduring alimony arrangements. They may at best receive a period of support for a few years to enable them to acquire or restore skills lapsed during absence from the labor force. Such funds may be inadequate. Writing about California's innovation of "no-fault" divorce, Lenore Weitzman has character- ized the situation as "an expectation of self-sufficiency for most divorced women—and for virtually all of those married for less than fifteen years—and second, a significant gap between the real- ity of support awards and the law's stated intent to provide transi- tional support and support for women with impaired learning ca- pacities." (Weitzman, 1981) In general, the California experience has been that women have been awarded about two years of support for retraining, a period Weitzman considers likely to be too brief, while only one fifth receive any alimony payment at all, and that for a limited period. While more conservative states pro- duce more "traditional" court decisions, nevertheless the trend is to the California style. Widespread noncompliance by men with whatever decisions the courts do make in effect obligates women to go it alone.

Therefore it is hardly surprising that expanded and improved employment opportunities for women have been high on the agenda both of politically active groups and of individuals them- selves. And not only women have been involved. Every woman has a father and many men wives, daughters, and companions. The overall force of circumstances has strongly influenced a change in attitude and behavior which—even by comparison with a generation ago—may have to be characterized as fundamental. For what an attitude poll is worth, *The New York Times* reported on a survey taken at the end of 1983 which showed significant differences with 1970 in women's attitudes to work and family: "More than ever American women think their place is on the job. ... They generally regard work and independence as elements of life that are as satisfying as husbands, homes, and children. ...

Thirteen years ago, 53% of the women surveyed cited motherhood as one of the best parts of being a woman . . . and in the latest poll just 26% did." (Dowd, 1983) There is a virtually seamless increase in the extent of women's commitment to the labor force, of wanting interesting, well-rewarded work, of understanding the balancing act that may be necessary should they wish to sustain both effective working lives and motherhood and, to a lesser extent, marriage. There is awareness that women must make their own decisions about their own lives. Perhaps they will enjoy the affectionate and helpful cooperation of others. But, finally, they are on their own to balance needs, resources, and desires.

The net impact in the United States is a strong and seemingly inexorable trend toward emphasis of the productive as opposed to the reproductive systems now for both men and women. The economy of impersonal contribution, of monetarily calculable endeavor, has expanded in a decisive manner. It now encompasses the last large group of people— women—who had been able to conduct their lives in terms of schedules, routines, settings, and priorities broadly determined by their own and their intimates' lives, not by economic entities willing to buy time for money. Of course the trade is far more elaborate than that. It involves satisfaction, the sense of contribution to a wider community, the enhancement of professional skill, mixing with a wider world, communication with adults rather than children, etc., etc. But the basic fact is that men and women alike are asked by interested strangers at parties, "What do you do?" The answer ideally includes an occupation. *That* query provides the hot critical information, not the old-style "Who is your husband and what is his status?" Is it going too far to say that when a woman answers, "I am a housewife," her answer is read as "I am now partly unemployed and potentially fully without work. I am not a self-sustaining force. Treat me accordingly."

Where this is so, it is unfair, unnecessary, inappropriate, and so on. But intimate experience has been devalued. Public monetary life has been identified as the principal source of individual authenticity. I take this to represent the victory of one system over another. It is the predictable conclusion of a long historical trend toward the bureaucratization of intimacy and monetarization of experience. A trend almost inevitable once every person becomes a full-fledged enterprise—the individual contractor—separated

227

from family and peer group for economic purposes, beholden only to himself or herself and to the wider economy which is the sustaining force of everyone.

Is it not alarmist to talk of "the victory of one system over another," to overdramatize the meaning of changes in the behavior of men and women? Perhaps it is only a temporary shift—though that seems unlikely—in the level of fertility and in the emphases of men and women in how and where they conduct their lives. Perhaps all that has happened is that, as Marxists have been urging for years, the economic basis of the family has at last been revealed for what it is, with the result that women will have little or no part of a pattern that exploits their time and energy in the name of domestic effectiveness and bliss. Or perhaps the increased participation of women in the labor force is a response to inflation, so that two incomes are necessary to sustain whatever level of consumption a couple has in mind. And without question the increased pressure on the world's resources because it supports more and more people has raised the ante once again. There is less wood, oil, food, space, even fresh air and water, per person. Whosoever wants a comfortable share of these goods has simply got to work for them, and perhaps more and more.

These are reasonable explanations and certainly part of the story. But the reproductive part of the story obviously is influential, too. We must assume that since the means for reproductive control are now available more effectively than ever, people are choosing to do what they want to do, or at least what they have decided they should do or have to do. For women in particular not only in capitalist but Communist society, managing work and household is hardly easy. In 1983 *Redbook* magazine in the United States ran an advertisement for itself picturing a business-suited woman of perhaps thirty-two throwing three balls in the air: one a picture of a smiling infant, another of a smiling husband, and another of the woman herself at work. The headline for this display was: *"Redbook* goes for the Juggler." The woman who wants to or has to and possibly can manage the myriad demands on her time in carrying off three challenging roles in three different settings. In 1950, each of these would have been regarded as a full-time challenge in itself.

As they used to say on the Left Bank, "The problem is structural." Broadly speaking, the working day was originally organized around the cycle of availability of light. It assumed the individual would abstract himself from personal concerns for a period of eight to ten hours or so. It assumed separation of home and workplace both spatially and in time, a separation certainly easier to contrive for men, but only of course if women stay put to deal with children and domestic tasks, or if men have no children and have only themselves to care for.

The issue of how to define the workday and the workplace is hardly new. In the earliest days of the earliest large-scale manufacture, of cloth, the issue was already lively. During the fourteenth century, there was widespread controversy over the *Werkglocke*, the workbell, which was a form of factory bell except that it was a very public one, perhaps even installed in the belfry of the church. It summoned workers to the mill; it signaled them to return home. (Le Goff, 1980) Perhaps this involved an excessive stimulus. But people didn't have watches then, the general reason for church bells in the first place, and the towns in which the *Werkglocke* operated were often principally "company towns"—the cloth industry being the main if not the only one. Where it was not, in Paris, for example, there was no *Werkglocke*.

Big ringing bells tolled now for Mammon not for God. This marks a significant shift to sliced-up time, divided loyalties, and bureaucratized behavior. The minute is to time what the right angle is to nature. Neither occurs in nature. Both are constructs of the systematizing human. Both have been essential for the spread and superiority of the industrial way, both permit careful measurement and management of time and space in an effective sequential way. Both the minute and the right angle are building blocks. They enjoy the luxury of predictable intervals. They permit the future and the way ahead to be defined in an easily describable and negotiable manner.

Neither minutes nor right angles have anything to do with babies. Right angles, you try to keep babies away from, because the joins may be sharp and hurt the soft creature as yet uninformed about the possible painfulness of matter. As to minutes, infants and babies cry, gurgle, eliminate, eat, whatever, according to their own inner plans. A friend had a rather robust and lusty baby being fed on a bottle. Three ounces every four hours was the recipe from the pediatrician. The inexperienced parents dutifully monitored the child's input from the world according to this neat scientific program. But the child cried a lot. The usual grave speculations about "colic" and other afflictions were earnestly discussed until someone suggested that the child was hungry and that the doctor's menu was not enough for this particular creature. Only then did the mother realize that had she been breastfeeding the child, there would be no way to weigh its intake punctiliously. The meal would be over when the child was good and ready. So what was this specificity about, this three every four, or four every three? She fed the child more. It stopped crying. It had just been very hungry, because it was being fed by a kind of chemist. The value of scientific calibration was lost on the infant.

This same nonspecificity of infantile life in part accounts for the difficulty of the Juggler's balancing act. It always takes twice as long as the feet need to walk a little child to school because it wants to stop and look. Trivial though it might seem in the larger scheme of industrial things, the recalcitrant idiosyncrasy of baby schedules is the source of much real and problematic discrepancy. Babies are atonal with respect to time, whereas the industrial system has perfect pitch. Virtually everyone carries the system with them on their wrist. Usually mothers are the buffer zone between baby time and modern time. This is significant in itself. It also represents a larger set of mediating responsibilities. A parent is a child's translator and diplomat to the wider system, and vice versa. Specific encounters of two distinct ways of using time have to be handled.

Perhaps hired people can do this. But they have to be paid with money acquired somewhere. Or an institution can do it, such as a day-care center, but there appear never to be enough of these. Or relatives and neighbors can take a hand, and the grandmother is particularly important. In a variety of circumstances the informal arrangements of neighbors and kin may well serve temporarily and episodically to reduce the strain on the Juggler. Nevertheless, the problem of integrating quite different spheres of experience remains the underlying feature of parenthood in the industrial world.

Therefore it is hardly a mystery why when most women work, fewer babies are born than otherwise. Perhaps it is understandable that a woman will bear one child, if only for the sheer adventure, experiment, and joy of it, or for whatever reason of her own and her partner's. But with the knowledge of what is involved, giving birth to another requires a clear commitment. It is therefore no surprise also that many families will be limited to one child, even though there remains a perhaps largely sentimental and lagging attitude that it is desirable to have two at least rather than one child; the canard lingers that only children are "spoiled" (I hope not since I am one).

The strenuousness of the new reproductive arrangements arises not out of attitudinal matters such as consciousness or role models, nor out of fear of success, or chauvinism, or whatever, but out of life's equivalent of the stream of consciousness. The way the events of time emerge and become salient and interesting or fearful and then ebb, to be supplanted by others. How events occur. With what pace and meaning. With what kind of obligation to people to respond.

The routines of the young are different from the routines of the mature. This is a trivial observation describing a situation of formidable practicality. The very young are a different tribe, foreign to the carefully sculpted procedures of industrial work. However earnestly communities may want sexual similarity in child rearing, the stubborn mammalian scenario remains the starting point for the drama. From this point of departure, men and women and their increasingly few children must arrange how to be immersed in childhood, which is reckoned in years. But performance in work may be reckoned in months or quarter years or weeks or, in Shoshana Zuboff's pulp mills, four times a second. And that mammalian scenario perforce begins with a woman carrying a baby for rather a long time and then perhaps wanting to nurse it for a while in the old-fashioned way which, when it is possible, by all accounts remains the best way. (Short, 1984) We go from there.

The most drastic version of this are those countless cases in which women are abandoned to raise their offspring on their own, or with the help of the matrilineage. Half of all U.S. families living below the poverty line fall into this category. (Sheppard, 1982) The median income of families headed by females is slightly less than half that of families headed by males. Unfair this is, heartless for the children, a comment on the system overall which stimulates it.

Not that the problem is restricted to poor women, at the bottom of the occupational pyramid. Among the well-off and highly qualified too there is a gap between women and men. A cover story of *Fortune* is called "Why Qualified Women Aren't Getting to the Top." (Fraker, 1984) *"No* women are on the fast track to the chief executive's job at any Fortune 500 corporation. That's incongruous, given the number of years women have been working in management. The reasons are elusive and difficult for management to deal with." (p. 40) "A woman on the fast track is under intense pressure. . . . The pressures increase geometrically if she has small children at home. Perhaps as a result, thousands of women have careers rather than husbands and children. In the UCLA Korn/ Ferry study of executive women, 52% had never married, were divorced, or were widowed, and 61% had no children. A similar study of male executives done in 1979 found that only 5% of the men had never married and even fewer—3%—had no children." Furthermore, "Motherhood clearly slows the progress of women who decide to take long maternity leaves or who choose to work part-time." (p. 44)

These latter data if anything increase the severity of a comment I made in 1969 in *Men in Groups,* to the grim effect that women who took part in the heretofore male occupational system would in the short and long run reproduce less than their more traditional sisters. Despite assertive efforts to change public attitudes, to induce legal remedy, revise stereotyped school texts, and so on, the overall structure of reward and reproduction has little changed during a turbulent generation, except insofar as both men and women have fewer children. According to House subcommittee testimony on April 30, 1984, by Judy Goldsmith, then president of the National Organization for Women, "Women's economic status has already worsened over the past three decades. . . . Fewer than four percent of all women make more than $30,000 per year, while more than 25 percent of all men are paid that salary." And when I attended a conference of rather well known and accomplished scientists in 1984 at the Kinsey Institute at Indiana University, on Masculinity/Femininity, a member of the staff with whom I discussed some of these issues ironically remarked, "If you look around the table of conferees, consider the personal lives of the women compared to the men and consider what it took to get to that table." In science, as among the executives described in *Fortune,* the same situation applied: they had fewer children if not also less income. Even among people who are some of the most knowledgeable in the world about the beginnings, ends, and means of gender.

Does something arcane and mysterious underlie all this? At first glance there are obvious causes which appear to be remediable. For example, certainly in large urban centers day-care facilities that are acceptable to high-demand people are tightly limited. As one provider of facilities said: "We have children signed up who are not yet born. Mothers are anxious to further their careers, but they cannot find care givers who can create the kind of stimulating environment in which they want their children cared for. They really need help." Since, in 1982, 42.7 percent of children under one year old had mothers in the labor force, the enormity of the issue is clear. (Brozan, 1983) Interestingly, on a national scale in the United States, churches and church-related organizations provide the majority of day-care places currently available. Nevertheless the shortage remains, a difficulty not eased by recurring concerns about the quality of care in existing centers, the health dangers to children whose immunities may not have evolved to cope with large numbers of children the same age, and even fears about child abuse, possibly sexual, in centers run for profit. These are all real concerns with practical bases and perhaps practical solutions. Yet the reality remains that the disparate schedules of parents and children are difficult to reconcile. As well, emotional recalcitrance persists about the considerable separation that is necessary if parents are to work.

Ultimately this may not be a severe difficulty, nor certainly is it a novelty for men, who have traditionally been separated from their children for a substantial part of the workday. Commuters with long treks may hardly see their offspring at all until the weekend. The impact of mothers working as well as fathers may be no sharper than of one parent alone. Certainly there is no strong evidence that children growing up in female-headed households suffer particular deprivation as a result of the absence of a male, though there is clear evidence that they are disadvantaged by the absence of a male income. (Hacker, 1982) However, having been through the remarkable turbulence of leaving a household in which a child lived, I find it difficult to accept that there are no or even few implications of the parental absence. No doubt it is endurable. Where an awful, unreliable person abuses his housemates, it is presumably preferable. Nevertheless, it is as erroneous to assume there is no impact of such disruptions as it is to uphold the traditional position that the only adequate family is the intact conventional one.

What has this to do with the industrial system, with lathe machines, computers, airplanes, right angles, and tight schedules? Again, the factor of time is illuminated. I know a highly regarded federal judge in a U.S. jurisdiction who works such long hours she must hire two maids to work two shifts to attend to her children and domestic establishment. Apart from the fact that she had calculated that the costs of all this essentially consumed the take-home income she received from her $59,000 salary (a curiosity, since her husband's income was perhaps three or four times that; why was his income not responsible for the domestic help?), she was also fully aware that her children enjoyed a particular kind of relationship with her servants which they did not and could not with her. Juggling emotions and affections may well be more diffi-cult than the already trying enough factors of day-to-day coping. The tempo and duration of the work of elite members of the legal and indeed other occupations constitute an almost revolutionary demand on the human system—if not also on adults, certainly on children. *That* may be the new industrial revolution.

The system works day and night. Telephones and now in-teractive computers knit people across space and in different time zones into a web of mutual availability and obligation, which blurs the distinction between work and private life in a formidable way. Perhaps this is how things should be; after all, I am evidently lamenting the separation between work and domesticity. But by and large the game of work/life is played more by the rules of the workplace than the hearth. There are relatively few protections— certainly informal, but informed decency is one—in place to pro-tect the frail, ragtag structure of the house of domesticity from the mighty demands of the world's most effective system of organized endeavor. Perhaps doctors don't make house calls anymore. How-ever, many professionals do—they work at home after work.

Articulating the disparate schedules of adults and babies is one challenge to the industrial system which it has only haltingly approached. Another is the issue of pregnancy and its conse-quences. Birth rates are low. Women appear to anticipate fewer pregnancies than ever. Yet the majority of women will have chil-dren. Therefore one would expect a thoughtful or at least practical community to make appropriate arrangements for this. Some in-dustrial communities do, particularly in those European countries such as France and Sweden concerned with their birth rates. For example, France provides four months of benefits for mothers of newborns, while Canada provides nearly as much. In both cases, employers are obligated to restore jobs to women who leave them for this purpose. The Swedish arrangement is the most substantial; up to 90 percent of a parent's salary is paid for up to nine months, by the state. Either father or mother can avail him- or herself of these benefits, in sequence, on a half and half or similar basis. There were broad reasons for including fathers in the plan: "The goal was to encourage fathers to share the responsibilities of parenthood with their wives. Despite an intensive campaign . . . fathers were slow to respond. The proportion of eligible fathers taking at least one month of paid leave has increased slowly over the years, but now seems to have stabilized at 5%; about 2% of those eligible take two months or more." (Lamb, 1982, p. 72)

The American situation is considerably more difficult for pregnant women. Less than 40 percent of women are legally entitled to six or more weeks of leave around the time they give birth. With almost spectacular crudity, where benefits are provided, they are reckoned as "disability payments." They should be "ability payments." Federal laws define pregnancy and the period following childbirth as disabilities. Obviously this is an effort to narrow the legal availability of benefits, to align maternity provisions with others under the health benefits umbrella. But the net impact of the description of a profoundly positive phenomenon as a disability cannot be nil.

In practical terms, pregnancy is treated as a disability because as a behavioral performance it does indeed interfere with the smooth operation of a relentlessly ongoing system. The operating assumption of the system is that all participants in it must be available at all times during the regular periods of work; this seems appropriate if simplistic. The problem arises when one healthy regularity, of work, encounters another healthy regularity, of pregnancy. If there is a disability, it is of course not of the mother, who is performing her function efficiently and productively, but of the system of employment which appears to react awkwardly to a plainly predictable reality. For example, an article in *The Wall Street Journal* complains: "Maternity Leave: Firms Are Disrupted by Wave of Pregnancy at the Manager Level: After-30 Motherhood Snags Debenture Offer, Clouds Rating of TV Show: Careers Put on Slower Track." (Gottschalk, 1981)

It is tempting to accuse the operators of the system of being recalcitrant and insensitive to the reproductive vivacity of the living system. This is without question partly so. But the situation is fundamentally designed for collision between system and people. Since the larger and wealthier prevailing force is the system, people must make do however they can. There seems little doubt that as feminist writers have complained, if an activity routinely and healthfully undertaken by men occurred, such as pregnancy, the system would have by now accommodated to it. Normality would not be a disability. However, the whole pattern of work was designed in terms of the schedules and habits of first men and now machines; the daily clock, the yearly, and even the life-cycle clock are all subsumed by the requirements of efficient production of machines or office space, or the amortization of training, and so on. The system is very productive, but what makes it productive is a high investment in goods and people. This investment must be protected. At least, such is the perspective of the individual employer considering a pregnant female's relationship with the machinery and people with whom she works. The individual may as a citizen and a family member applaud the generous impact of pregnancy. As an employer, a different calculus may well apply, to judge from the marketplace. Under open circumstances, when they can, employers do less rather than more for pregnant employees. They appear to assume they needn't bear a burden or a cost their competitors may be avoiding. While the situation may improve for women (and of course their husbands) as more women become essential members of work groups, the compromises so far in place suggest that incompatibility between the systems will not be easily reduced. Even the experience of countries with more generous approaches to pregnancy suggests the difficulty of facilitating births under current circumstances.

The majority of women using contraception in the United States have essentially ingested the industrial system within the body. The industrial system within which they must live and work appears also to produce a contraceptive impact on their behavior. They are enabled to forego having children by what they choose to take into their bodies. They are constrained from having children by how they choose to or must live in society.

Two momentous changes are occurring at the same time. In the reproductive system, with contraception; and in the productive system, with lifetime female employment in the money economy. These processes are elaborately related. They have probably irretrievably changed the nature and prospects of intimate life in ways not yet clear but nonetheless tangible and apprehensible. Already substantially larger-than-ever numbers of people live in small households, many in the smallest possible household, of one. For example, in one decade some seven million Americans were added to the ranks of the living-alone (Hacker, *op. cit.*, p. 37), an extraordinary increase of 64 percent. In Manhattan, it has been estimated that 50 percent of the population in rental housing lives alone. (Daniels, 1982) In the United States as a whole in 1980, some 23 percent of all households were composed of one person—involving some 20 million people of whom 11 million are female. (UPI, 1981) These are quite unprecedented developments, exotic to the planet, that have arisen swiftly. While it is unlikely that the pace of change will continue, there are reasons to assume that the direction of the changes will not be radically altered. For example, it has been found that women who earn more than $25,000 per year are four times as likely to divorce their spouses as men who earn this amount. With their increasing salaries, we may therefore expect greater female independence from the family unit. On the reverse side of the same token, there is decreased obligation for men to continue contributing any support to women, or for that matter, to begin doing so in the first place.

An unmistakable result of these processes is that it becomes possible for men and women to live in greater independence of each other, whether they live together or apart. Reproduction and production can be independent of family life. Thus there is reduced reason for marriages of convenience, coercion, or economic necessity.

There are additional consequences, in turn. Since females control contraception, males can enjoy less "paternity certainty," as the biologists call it. This is presumably as it should be, since as we have seen females inevitably must assume more of the burden of raising children both in and out of families. But the broad effect of reduced paternity certainty is I believe a reduced male commitment to females. As a group, females have more reproductive autonomy. Fewer claims can be made on them—to seek to have a child, to bear it, to avoid abortion, and so on. At the same time they can make fewer claims on men, as a group. We see this reflected in the generally declining level of responsibility to unmarried pregnant women, which in turn has made it essential throughout the industrial world to have reasonably available abortion facilities at least for unmarried women whose circumstances favor neither marriage nor single motherhood as a possibility. Less anxiety about sexuality may have reduced the importance of connection on one hand. On the other, the increased economic independence of women has reduced the likelihood that men will be essential or at least very desirable—if only as economic partners.

So for two fundamental reasons, the "sexual-economic relation," as Charlotte Perkins Gilman described marriage in the nineteenth century, is less necessary both sexually and economically.
Compare the current situation with Gilman's pungent and bare-
bones description of what she saw around her: "The working
power of the mother has always been a prominent factor in human
life . . . but her work is not such as to affect her economic strata.
[This] . . . bears relation only to the man she marries, the man she
depends on—to how much he has and how much he is willing to
give her. The women whose splendid extravagance dazzles the
world . . . are . . . the women who hold most power over the men
who have the most money. . . . The female of the genus homo is
economically dependent on the male. He is her food supply." (cited
in Degler, ed., 1966, pp. 21–22)

Though this remains a fact for countless people, the number
is declining. It is certainly not the ideal pattern for women, and
seemingly not for more and more men either. The influential feminist writer Barbara Ehrenreich has documented what she describes as "the flight from commitment" of American men. She
asserts that the cultural changes are of major consequence: "by the
end of the 1970's and the beginning of the 1980's, adult manhood
was no longer burdened with the automatic expectation of marriage and breadwinning. The man who postpones marriage even
into middle age, who avoids women who are likely to become
financial dependents, who is dedicated to his own pleasures, is
likely to be found not suspiciously deviant, but 'healthy.' " (Ehrenreich, 1983, p. 12) Ehrenreich emphasizes economic and psychological issues, and is evidently less concerned with or aware of the
alterations in the sexual bond produced by the new contraception.
But her argument seems a sturdy one, particularly in her descriptions of male independence, even if she pays too little attention to
the essence of the reproductive interaction with which she is in
fact concerned. However, let there be no doubt that if there has
been any of the vaunted "liberation" that is the focus of such a
journalistic industry, it has been as much of men from the needs
of women as of women from those of men.

Put it another way. The sexes are giving and getting less from
each other. And they are reproducing less in this new bargain.

In this scheme, independence is a desirable characteristic.
Both men and women must see it as a desirable goal. More than
that, even. In the olden days, men would save money or work hard

to advance themselves and then propose marriage when they were economically able to do so. Their job was in effect a form of dowry. It suggested their strength of character and their capacity to command the economic system. Now women must do the same, to assure themselves that they are capable of surviving on their own. They too have to demonstrate adequate skills as independent contractors. They must reassure their potential mates that they will be contributors to the exchequer, not simply users of it, and that two will be able to live as lavishly if not more so than one.

Look, look! Two keen bowerbirds, not one, building the nest, both arranging the bits of straw and blue glass just that attractive way.

Strategists in the Dark

Biologists describe animals as having "reproductive strategies." These are organizing principles designed to permit them as much reproduction as possible, as safely as possible, while using resources as efficiently as possible. In the sexually reproducing species, males and females may operate in terms of different strategies. It is not necessary that the animals "know" what their strategy is. It is enough that their behavior is sufficiently patterned and predictable so we can develop a sensible explanation of what the animals are about. As George Gallup and Susan Suarez have succinctly and clearly put it: "Evolution is not represented by the survival of genes. . . . Fitness can be defined only in terms of reproductive success. Sex is the final common path for all evolutionary change.

"Evolution can be thought of as an unconscious existential game . . . played according to cost/benefit ratios. . . . In terms of playing this game, the best interests of human males and females are strikingly different. . . ." (Gallup and Suarez, 1983, pp. 314–15) They base their conclusion about differential strategies on three broad biological differences. The first is that females know for sure who their offspring are and may therefore more wholeheartedly and confidently engage in the reproductive process. The second is the converse of this, which is that females also bear more of the burden of reproduction and must make a greater investment of time, energy, and attention to the process. Finally, the "vastly different" reproductive potential of males and females—the comparison between the limited number of ova a female has at her disposal and the millions of sperm available to males—places a premium on careful female choice of partner and yet rewards relatively profligate male enthusiasm for sexual congress.

It can be argued that the sexual emotions and performances of both sexes are somehow in accord with these different relationships to sexual activity. Motivations and satisfactions still reflect a system of courtship and choice evolved in one set of conditions but having now to operate in a different one. As I have tried to show, changes in the productive system have been particularly marked and indeed momentous for women. Even had there been no substantial change in contraception, the economic shifts would have likely produced socio-psychological ones of corresponding import. But since there have also been fundamental alterations in contraception, at the very core of the sexual interplay, the general impact on how men and women estimate and conduct their reproductive strategies has got to be substantial. So it appears from the statistical record of recent years.

Perhaps the new economic opportunities for women will permit them also enhanced options for childbearing. The anthropologist Caroline Bledsoe studied the Kpelle people of Liberia and among other things noted that women in that society may prefer not to marry if they are able to find other ways of ensuring security for themselves and their children. (Bledsoe, 1980) In a wide variety of human societies, women who bear children are supported not only through their own efforts but by their natal families—father, uncle, aunt, mother—rather than, as in the Euro-American tradition, by the father of the child. Nevertheless it is clear that within at least the North American context, female-headed families suffer plain and large disadvantages. Following on the controversial Moynihan proposal about the relationship between welfare and family structure, even more controversially George Gilder has asserted that welfare payment to unwed or otherwise unsupported mothers with young effectively disenfranchises males. It has in the long run contributed to a deterioration of living conditions in the black community, compared for example with more recently arrived immigrants with strong family groups and evidently an emerging record of economic stability and success within the system. (Gilder, 1982, 1986)

Certainly there are considerable variations in the response of communities to working mothers, ranging from the relatively laissez-faire, "it's her choice," attitude in the United States to the carefully planned arrangements in Scandinavia and somewhat less so in the Communist countries. Still, as her 1979 survey of nine nations shows, Alice Cook describes the problems of working mothers as reiterated, common, and nowhere simple to solve: "Married women represent the largest single additional increment to the work force over the past five to ten years and . . . the outstanding element of structural change in the labor market." (Cook, 1979, p. 1) Even the predictable, common, and in some circumstances essential pattern of shiftwork, a particular burden for working mothers, has been confronted ineptly and inadequately as far as women are concerned. (*ibid.*, p. 34)

Part-time work, a frequent choice of women, remains less well paid, although part-time workers frequently produce better than full-time ones. Unions resist them, and so may managers who prefer the fixed clarity of firm arrangements day in, day out. (*ibid.*, pp. 38–39) On the obvious issue of maternity leave, "it is doubtful that the philosophy underlying maternity and child care even where it does exist springs from consideration . . . of the mother as of the child. If the mother were a major object of concern her need for income during leave would have to be considered." (p. 53) It appears that people turn away from facts which stare them in the face.

Why? I want to conclude this particular section with a discussion of the wistful problem of why people don't act on real information about real circumstances. Why does some information stick in the craw? What is the cognitive character defect in this smart primate which presumably explains why obviously good and useful information is ignored?

The question becomes especially important in a society with pride in its cognitive knack, and in which, when headlines such as "Information Explosion Hits Agriculture" appear in the newspapers, everyone understands.

This is particularly interesting where sexuality is concerned. Earlier on, I cited Robin Fox's assertion that the brain evolved to act, not to think. If the genetically productive acts also involved thinking, which in turn involved the addition of brain tissue, fine. But acting was necessarily still the goal of thinking. Like the metaphorical centipede suddenly flummoxed by the question, "Just how is it you work your feet when you walk?", the man anxiously contemplating his possible impotence is doomed to failure, just as any performer who is too obviously self-conscious will violate a performance.

A haunting aperçu about the possible relationship of mind and birth was published in *The American Naturalist* by the biologist Nancy Burley of McGill University in Montreal; a later and fuller analysis along the same lines is by Denise Daniels of the University of Colorado. (Daniels, 1983) Haunting but also stunning, because Burley wants nothing more than to explain why ovulation in humans is concealed. Why there is not, in humans as there is in other primates, that pronounced estrus period, "a sharp peak of interest in sexual activity that typically occurs at or near ovulation." (Burley, 1979, p. 835) As anyone who has observed the social life of primates knows, the visual and behavioral forcefulness of the ovulatory cycle is formidable indeed. While the fact that most humans wear clothes may be an additional dampener of periodic enthusiasm, no evident clear and present sexual reality, except for menstruation itself, marks the difference between the fertile and infertile phases of a woman's cycle. As Burley notes, the timing of the cycle itself was not fully understood until 1930. Unbelievably enough, the variability of the cycle was not appreciated until Treloar's publication in 1973 of the results of a study of 40,000 woman/year cycles. She cites his conclusion that " 'perfect regularity in menstrual rhythm is a myth; regularity within three or four days is a rarity; irregularity is normal.' " (*ibid.,* p. 837) Whether because of its unpredictability or because of its subtle character, it appears women do not clearly or often know when they are ovulating, except for a small percentage who have pain at ovulation, the so-called Mittelschmerz. So while other animals' cycles are regular and they may well be aware of them, human cycles are irregular, and females and certainly males appear to be unaware of them.

Why? If nothing else, the large thinking organ, the brain, should enable us to understand something so basic and predictable. But it does not, for which Burley describes various explanations advanced by other scientists. One is that the estrus cycle declined markedly in behavioral importance so that men and women could remain in permanent sexual connection, without the flurry of enthusiasm and then disinterest stimulated by the cycle. That is, the "pair bond" at the heart of the Euro-American system would not have to withstand the threat of the sexually tranquil part of the cycle—which could well be a time of ovulation of another female in the group whose endocrinological blandishment could unduly tempt an otherwise happily pair-bonded male. But while this may explain why ovulation could have evolved as concealed from males, it fails totally to explain why ovulation is concealed from females as well. As Burley recreates the possible evolutionary scenario, concealment from males very likely was evolved first as a mechanism. The interesting question is, why did humans evolve a pattern of ovulation that was concealed from the female herself?

Burley concludes that in the cold eye of nature, it would be to the disadvantage of the species were women able to control their fecundity with specificity and foresight. She distinguishes between egocentric birth control, which is helpful to the individual, and biologically adaptive birth control, which is helpful to the group and the species. For example, a woman may not want the restriction and pain of a pregnancy and childbirth at a particular time and decide to forego pregnancy. From the point of view of the species, however, her decision is unwarranted because it will reduce fertility for no reason other than that of the individual female's comfort or specific program. Let me cite Burley's clear statement of the matter: "Biologically adaptive birth control includes those forms of contraception and abortion that enhance reproductive success. An example is increased spacing of offspring (which may also be effected by infanticide) that allows older children to receive sufficient food, nutrients, and attention. . . . Other adaptive measures include the prevention of childbirth when the mother's health or life is endangered. . . . Egocentrically adaptive reasons include pain avoidance and rejection of parental responsibility." (*ibid.*, p. 844)

She concludes that concealing ovulation from the cycling female herself is "nature's way" of decreasing the role of egocentrically adaptive restriction of childbirth. For example, that is why there are more natural clues to women that they are approaching menstruation than ovulation. Why should this be so, when it is clearly more significant and useful to women to know that they are going to be fertile in a day or two than that they are going to menstruate? Burley's answer is: reproduction is too important and too connected to too many subtle matters for human foresight to operate the system. Like the centipede's gait, it is too complicated and too vital to be left to the analytical discretion of an imperfect organ of ratiocination.

In effect we are paraphrasing the common argument about the computer—that it is too simple-minded to deal with the complexity and nuance of human behavior. Now we are presented here with the possibly dispiriting proposal that human reproduction is too complicated and too subtle to be left to the conscious brain to govern.

Do we not see a graphic demonstration of how correct this natural principle is in the facts about contemporary fecundity? Once women can control their reproduction accurately and effectively, they do so. The result is that few babies are born, fewer in strict terms than are necessary to replace the population, that is, 2.2 per female. What the human mind was once prevented from accomplishing by the secretiveness of the body and the ineffectiveness of contraceptive techniques, now can be achieved.

Alienated from the Means of Reproduction

Once more the industrial system has born a surprising fruit, another apple of knowledge. Once more there are sexual consequences. Once more Adam and Eve have to reconsider where they stand. Five hundred generations ago our species began the transition to pastoralism and agriculture. We began to be able to plan what we eat and when. Just ten generations ago we moved into the industrial age. Rather suddenly we could plan an immense number of aspects of life, such as how high we would live, how fast we would go, how easy we could work, and how we could see in the dark and speak softly over long distances. Just one generation ago, we changed the nature of generation itself.

Ten thousand years. Two hundred years. Twenty years. Before that, thousands of centuries of formative human-primate life in which males and females negotiated with each other about their energy, space, and time, about their needs, affections, fears, and puzzlements. Negotiated evidently without such efficacious tools as are in the market now. Counterproductive reproductive tools in a new situation still propelled by ancient emotions. Sometimes things do change. That protective lack of foresight which permitted action when thought about it might interfere has now been replaced by the potent foresight made possible by industrial technique. So of 36 million American women employing contraception, 26 million are able to forego the possibility of pregnancy by measures taken at a remove from the time and place of sexual action itself. The outcome of sexuality need be only the pleasure, pain, ambiguity, or whatever, of physical closeness and possible intimacy. Suddenly the stakes are tiny. Therefore the strategies for playing for them are trivial.

In that continually changing delta where the river of private experience meets the oceanic world in which all the other people live, a new precision tool has been located. The mind has been industrialized, at an important point, where it meets the body. But, mind you, principally the female mind and body, because it is with females that the basic decisions about reproduction lie. It is for them that the consequences are most immediate and also extensive. Females are the gatekeeper sex of the two. How they decide to arrange their sexual lives also of course affects deeply the men with whom they are in conjunction. People seem to have an almost inexhaustible enthusiasm for sexual congress, and no doubt also (but with less single-minded clarity) for the intricately risky near-lubriciousness of courtship. Courtship being one of those odd businesses in which there is only slight penalty for not succeeding. Failure is the norm, if reproduction is the goal. The new industrialized physiology has drastically increased the likelihood and possibility of failure. Since everything matters less, there is more room for maneuver and space for experiment. More candidates can join the tryouts. Whether this is satisfying or agreeable or effective is another matter. But what can happen under current circumstances is different than before. It constitutes a new kind of limiting condition for the reproductive enterprise.

Back to the male bowerbird. What would he do if he hadn't had to fuss extensively about his nest, or if, worse, he did so as usual but found that the females who would normally respond to his mise-en-scène either had their own or gave up altogether the enterprise of laying eggs and rearing chicks? The human case is by no means the same, nor is it even analogous except in a metaphorical way. Nevertheless, the substantial structural changes in how men and women conduct their economic lives have certainly reduced the influence men can have over what women do, and reduced likewise the influence women can exert over what men do.

Insofar as women can control contraception and hence conception, to paraphrase Marx crudely, men have become alienated from the means of reproduction. Economists define a recession as the absence of growth in an economy for two quarter years, depression as decline for two quarters. By that standard, the reproductive system is in deep depression. One has to assume that the underlying changes I have been describing are to some considerable extent involved. It is almost as substantial as if a wholly new technology had been introduced, which decimated important industries with subsequent effect on the national account.

Members of industrial communities are becoming increasingly reproductively underemployed. Many will be unemployed altogether. In principle, this is neither a good nor bad thing except insofar as I have already noted—that good zoos are frequently regarded as those in which the inmates reproduce and bad ones those in which for whatever reason they cannot or do not. From the inside of the zoo, the reasons for what happens may seem self-evident and the consequences hardly severe or even interesting. But from the outside, the view is of course different. This is the view I have been taking here, to try to emphasize lines of social change which may still seem faint from inside the system.

Why focus on social change? Are not the plain facts of the matter explanation enough? The plain facts: women work. Mostly they have to. The economy makes having babies inconvenient. Good contraception enables women and men to have liberal sex and few children rather than many children and little sex. Plain enough facts, indeed. But there may be more to find out about all this.

"Alienated from the means of reproduction," I said men were. Let me be more specific. Biologists divide the endeavor of reproduction by what is involved in mating, and what is involved in raising offspring to the age at which they will themselves be able to have offspring. (Kurland and Gaulin, MS) Obviously this involves a greater problem for the male than the female, since what a male does to ensure successful mating may not result in offspring. Furthermore, a longer-term problem arises if the male is to contribute fully to the rearing of the offspring. Is it his, or has conscious or unconscious cuckoldry occurred? Kurland and Gaulin among others have offered an intriguing and persuasive case about the regularities in other species which govern this relationship. This can take bizarre form among humans—such macabre coercion as clitorectomy, chastity belts, the double standard in general. There is almost universally greater severity of punishment for women who are sexually active outside marriage than for the men with whom they are presumably consorting. This reflects a grim prejudice, of course. But the prejudice in turn may well reveal the deep process I am considering.

[A friend told me that he was once waiting to meet someone for dinner in Riyadh, capital of Saudi Arabia. His friend arrived late and shaken. En route he had stopped to see what he thought was a quaint local ceremony, which involved two strong, uniformed men striking a large leather ball that hung from a stake high off the ground. They hit it back and forth between them slowly and with some stateliness. Suddenly blood began to flow from the leather ball, and it turned out that inside was a woman accused of adultery. If she confessed to adultery, then she was allowed to be killed before being stuffed in the bag; otherwise she began this punishment in fully conscious life.]

Along the same lines but far more blandly, the scrutiny of women in traditional rural and even urban Iran is constant and strict. It is literally forbidden for a man to touch a woman other than his wife. People go to great lengths to avoid the possibility of even inadvertent physical contact. However, for all the apparent puritanism of the set-up, once a married woman is pregnant, then men may happily and legitimately clasp her pregnant belly—the barrier has been broken by the fact of conception. (Paula Ardehali, personal communication) Another side of the story is told by the permanent rejection by their husbands of Pakistani women raped during the Bangladesh war of 1971.

On one level it is quite enough to rail against such gross injustices and indecencies and to establish firm laws and civilities to forbid their occurrence. But in contending with pathology, it is well to understand as much of its causation as possible. This improves the possibility of realistic cure and prevention. Understanding the situation permits technical acumen to be added to moral assertion in coming to terms with it. Recent studies of the history of the family as it is known in Christian Western society suggest that extramarital and premarital sexuality occurred consistently and widely. Relatively good data about so-called illegitimacy suggest how frequently sexual connection occurred outside the known and obvious rules of whatever culture is under consideration. An outstanding student of illegitimacy, Peter Laslett, has written, "No student of the subject can fail to find himself amazed at the capacity for disapproval which everyone displays." Notwithstanding this censoriousness, human beings continue to function reproductively in the context of the broader strategies we share with other beings. (Laslett, Oosterveen, and Smith, 1980, p. 62; see also Hartley, 1975)

However, the situation has changed. Even if the same force and enthusiasm prevail in the chambers of courtship and seduction, the technology of contemporary life has altered the forces decisively. The situation overall is novel for both men and women. Before, men and women could defy or ignore the forces of Church and kinship, but they invited damnation and ostracism. And they still could conceive children stigmatized by the world they knew and the afterlife they might fear. Now they need not conceive. The result is that fewer babies all told are born, even if there remain high rates of out-of-marriage pregnancies for very young women in particular. What the supposed granite forcefulness of even the late medieval Church could not achieve, with its astonishing buildings and seemingly total control of man and morals, has been accomplished by chemists and manufacturers.

By the same token, centuries of double-standardized harassment of females, control over funds, restriction of movement, legal ownership of children, abuse of bodies, exile from religious equality, etc., etc., tried to ensure the knowledge and control of paternity. In a relative instant this has been overturned by technology. The rules of the sexual contract have changed suddenly. The contract is altogether less coercive. People can operate as almost independent agents—atomized individuals in the Adam Smith sense, seeking their own ends with their own means.

It will be fascinating to observe how the first generation reared under these new conditions conduct their sociosexual lives. They are the first offspring of the first truly emancipated mothers and fathers—the first products of a generation of nonpossessive reproductive individualism. In a sense there is more new equality in the sexual relationship than seems evident at first, both of opportunity and liability. Both males and females face comparable uncertainty. The male wonders, If a woman with whom I am associated has a child, will it be mine? The female wonders, Will I have a child at all? If I do, will I have to care for it alone? These are powerfully intimate matters, with extensive social impact. Meanwhile, without respite, the commitment to the productive system—the job and career—endures. Inevitably this must be a commitment sustained alone; individuals are hired, not families. Another new direction for a gregarious mammal so committed to kinship that it has even often contrived to worship dead ancestors. What will the independent sexual contractor do?

Another broad matter may affect fertility, I cited the well-known intelligence that in general the more highly placed in traditionally male occupations a woman is, the less likely than her sisters she is to be married, if she is married to have children, and if she has children, to have as many as the average. Obvious reasons of time and commitment may well account for most or all of this—certainly for decisions about marriage and parenthood.

But other factors in other species affect whether a pregnancy occurs. Some may also apply to human beings because many of the basic physiological mechanisms are similar. We begin with the striking, hardly understood fact that just about one of two human pregnancies fails sometime between the time of conception and the time of potential birth. (Wasser and Barash, 1983) The story is the same in a variety of other mammals. The obvious explanation for this—that there is something wrong with the reproductive capacities of the individuals involved—is inadequate. A study of women supposed to be high-risk childbearers for various reasons —age, past history, diabetes, drug use, and so on—showed that only 12 percent of these individuals endured complications. So other factors are involved, such as "anxiety, depression, low self-esteem, poor coping skills, negative maternal desire, and a perceived lack of social support while undergoing stressful life events. . . ." (*ibid.*, p. 514) In addition to the very effective contraceptives that are available to humans, and abortion which is frequently employed as a contraceptive, for example, in parts of the USSR, where "It is estimated that some eight million abortions are performed annually, amounting to more than double the number of live births. . . ." (Lapidus, 1978, p. 299), there may be other social variables which interrupt pregnancies. Perhaps such social influences are in part responsible for the surprisingly large number of cases of unwanted infertility.

In any event, there are formidable natural mechanisms which produce successful and unsuccessful conceptions. Wasser and Barash complain that "our ability to predict poor reproductive outcomes in humans, as well as in other mammals, remains embarrassingly low." (*op. cit.*, p. 514) Ingestion of substances such as alcohol or other drugs, to say nothing of cigarette smoking, may have clear impacts on fetal health. Among macaque monkeys, whose reproductive system is physiologically similar to humans, alcohol self-administration over a six-month period severely disrupted reproductive function, a finding also appropriate to humans. (Mello, et al., 1983) Among males, it has been reported that use of cannabis may inhibit testosterone secretion and production of sperm, while alcohol has a well-known degenerative effect on sexual performance. Apart from such dramatic innovations as "test tube babies," a host of techniques have been introduced within the past decades to facilitate conception and childbearing in couples who probably would have been stymied by one medically traceable problem or another.

I am interested in socially induced infertility—the form of population dynamics related to the "Bruce effect." Bruce discovered that pregnant rodents would abort spontaneously if they came into contact with the bodies or even the bedding of males who were not the fathers of their offspring. Other social patterns have impact on fertility. It is difficult to make firm statements about this, apart from such extreme cases as women who do not ovulate or menstruate under conditions of great hunger or extreme stress, as in concentration camps, or when men enduring major traumas such as sudden unemployment or loss of status and self-esteem turn sexually impotent, a behavioral equivalent of physiological sterility in many cases. Women athletes engaged in strenuous long-term training, for example, for running, may experience irregular and infrequent menstruation. Dancers report this, too. The ratio of body fat to body size has been implicated here, especially by the work of Rose Frisch at the Harvard School of Public Health. (Frisch, 1982) It is also possible that the stress itself of preparing for demanding activities affects inner bodily processes.

Work involving the body has obvious effect on the body. It is worth considering that strenuous effort with nonphysical tasks will also have an impact on the body. The field of psychosomatic medicine in part is a tribute to this relationship. Even a dozen years ago there was a respectable body of literature on the relationship between inner states and outer processes. (Tiger, 1975) Current research suggests a clear biochemical marker of political status in monkeys and humans. The substance involved is whole blood serotonin. Investigators at the Medical School of the University of California at Los Angeles, in the Department of Psychiatry, have shown that in groups of vervet monkeys the level of whole blood serotonin in the "leader animal" is markedly different than in the subdominant ones. (McGuire, et al., 1983) Douglas Madsen, a political scientist at the University of Iowa, has challengingly suggested that this same substance is related to power-seeking in humans, and may also correlate with the so-called Type A behavior of hard-driving individuals unusually prone to coronary damage. (Madsen, 1985) It is also known that when men are engaged in competition, winners show more elevated testosterone levels and heightened mood than losers; "no changes in hormone are seen in circumstances where victory is achieved and mood is high, but not as a result of a performance (i.e. winning a lottery)." (Gladue, 1983, p. 88)

This is fascinating. It suggests that the process—winning—is more important than the result—a win. It underscores the close connection between social and bodily systems. The significant trend of recent research in this area demonstrates that bodily events affect social ones; you get a virus, become depressed, and snap at your dog or gerbil. But social events can also affect your body; you do pleasingly well in a tennis game, your surly mood changes, and only sunniness surrounds you. McGuire, et al., assert that this "has important evolutionary implications, for if behavioral changes do precede some physiological changes, then animals should be capable of responding." (op. cit., p. 326) Certainly so should humans, since we have been capable of adapting to a huge array of environments and conditions, perhaps in part because of the kind of psychophysiological mechanism with which we are here concerned.

The bald question is, is there a connection between the movement of women into the labor force with the competition that may involve, and the inner processes of reproductivity? Is this part of the reason for the seemingly firm negative connection between industrial work and fecundity? Recall again the phenomenon that the higher placed they are in the occupational structure, the less likely women are to have marriages and children. Obviously this is partly a function of time and commitment. But I come back to the fifty/fifty split among conceptions between those that make it and those that do not. Have these challenging odds been further reduced by participation in that perturbatious system against which Marx railed and of which Darwin had no skilled sense?

All Work and No Sex

As reproductive gatekeepers, women must estimate how reliable are the males with whom they may reproduce and then decide if the risks and opportunities balance out with particular individu-als. The low birth rate implies that the cast of male characters whom women are considering is not reassuring. By marrying later and later, which women are doing, and delaying pregnancy, which they are also doing, they add time to assess their overall reproduc-tive situation. Even so, as we have seen, the odds are relatively negative, given the enormity of what is involved. Even in Japan, the industrial country perhaps still the most securely tied to traditional family values and to the monogamous sequence of courtship and reproduction, the odds against women have escalated rapidly since the mid-seventies. "For the first time divorce exceeded death of the father as the primary cause of families without fathers ... three-quarters of divorced women did not receive child support money from their ex-husbands." (AP, 1984) There has also been a 250 percent increase in ten years of women raising children born out of wedlock; a small number in absolute terms but perhaps a revealing index of the emerging pattern. It is a symptom of the general strenuousness of the male-female connection in Japan where reproductive stability and responsibility are concerned.

The seriousness of this for Japanese women is heightened by the difficulty they experience in securing good work at fair pay on which they may depend through their active working career. More than four hundred companies listed on the Tokyo Stock Exchange flatly refused to interview female job applicants from the most prestigious and demanding four-year colleges. In the experience of one candidate: "While men from her class were wooed with pro-mises of lifetime employment and steady promotions by Japan's top corporations, the same companies made Miss Bessho very different offers. In addition to her office duties, she was to serve tea and 'help make working life pleasant for male co-workers.' ... She was expected to live with her parents until she married and stop working when she became pregnant." (Trucco, 1983) This situation will obviously change. The forces I am describing in the North American case will probably take hold as one would expect. The system will adjust in a more egalitarian direction. But the reproductive options may remain limited, and become more so, again for the broad but fundamental reasons that appear to come into play in mature industrial economies in which most women work.

The empirical experience is: The industrial system in its devel-oped form produces contraceptives. It may also be contraceptive.

There are demands upon women for direct, long-term, and ample participation in two systems that remain in disarticulation. This appears to translate into a further reduction of that 50 percent of conceptions which manage to make their way past whatever screen existed before. Some of the reduction is obviously clear and conscious and depends upon the use of contraceptives. But there may be other mechanisms at work which are relatively subtle, even fugitive, but which nevertheless result in the real demography of the current period.

What might some of the mechanisms be? Back to the Bruce effect and those of its ilk. A pregnant female is exposed to a male not the father of her offspring and she spontaneously aborts. Among wild horses, Joel Berger has reported that when a new male fights to take over a harem of females and wins, already-pregnant females evidently abort, probably as a result of the stress of the situation. It has even been argued that in an extreme case of this process, in the langur, the male who replaces another as leader of a group will kill the former male's infants, perhaps so that females will stop lactating and therefore begin ovulating again. Lactation is accompanied by hormonal conditions in the body which are often effectively contraceptive. (Short, 1984, p. 35; Hrdy, 1979)

A common and growing complaint of women in the workplace is about sexual harassment. I have myself been surprised at the frequency with which friends have reported cases of outright efforts at sexual exploitation by men of subordinate women who work for particular men or are trying to sell them goods or services. In the military, sexual harassment as an issue has burgeoned in importance as the number of women in uniform and near the combat zone has increased. While in my view the explanation is superficial, it is nevertheless revealing that personnel policy analysts regard sexual harassment as a major cause of the high frequency of female resignations from the military, particularly among white females.

One way or another, sexual harassment is another contraceptive. I cannot avoid proposing that a consequence of increased female participation in the male workplace is more harassment, more stimulus of the sense of outrage, fear, and loathing which may be the human analogue of the Bruce effect. Not so severe, of course, and certainly remediable by sensible legislation; better still, avoidable by enlightened conduct. Nevertheless, the possibility exists that a reason for the immense irritation sexual harassment causes women is the unfairness, indignity, and possible danger it may create, but also that it causes some women to feel violated and internally bad in a manner sufficiently upsetting to bring about reproductive repercussions. Even in a relatively simple primate with presumably no cultural sense of rectitude and personal dignity, the squirrel monkey, Christopher Coe and his colleagues found significant hormonal responses accompanying fear and agitation. (Coe, et al., 1982)

Perhaps the inner response to an interaction involving actual physical intrusion, or the threat of it, will be tangible and unsettling. In view of the 50 percent survival rate of conceptions, it is possible the consequences can be severe and ramified. When a woman is sexually harassed at work, both her vital productive and reproductive functions are being threatened in an environment that often provides few real options for redress or self-protection without jeopardizing her job or at least drawing unsettling attention to herself. The recalcitrant behavior of some men continues to affect some women's sense of fairness and well-being. In turn this may affect their general sense of health and enthusiasm—a possible factor in the fecundity of fragile pregnant women.

In this context, it is interesting to reconsider the finding of Shepher and myself about women at work in the kibbutz movement in Israel. They were more resistant to men working in their groups than the other way around—which I had expected according to my hypothesis about male bonding contained in *Men in Groups*. Instead, we found that women's work groups were more segregated than the groups which were broadly male. When women were asked about it, they indicated they preferred this state of affairs. In turn this may be related to the relatively high birth rate among kibbutz women—about four children per woman. This may suggest that fecundity is not only related to working in the labor force as such but also to how, when, where, and with whom.

The stressfulness of a working environment may also have an impact on a mother's child. The primatologist Leonard Rosenblum and his associates at Downstate Medical Center of the State University of New York have been conducting fascinating experiments with macaque monkey mothers of small offspring. The mothers are subjected to a variety of regimes of food gathering. That is, rather than being given food as captive monkeys usually are, these individuals are obligated to perform a somewhat demanding task in order to gather their food for themselves. Of the various conditions which the experimenters visited upon their subjects, one produced the most disruption between mothers and infants—when every two weeks the difficulty of acquiring food was markedly increased or decreased without any visible cue beforehand to the mothers. (Rosenblum and Paulley, 1984) The infants of mothers in this situation "showed the most sustained clinging to mother, the lowest levels of social play and exploration, the highest level of affective disturbance, and repeated evidence of depression. . . . These findings suggest that in monkeys, as in humans, when, because of competing demands, mothers are psychologically unavailable to their infants, attachments are less secure, normal development is disrupted, and psychopathological patterns are more likely to emerge." (p. 305) The authors stress the destructive impact of unstable and seemingly uncontrollable environments on the way in which mother and infant adjust to the demands placed upon the mother for food gathering. The impact seems greater when there is an unpredictable obligation to "work" than when there is a predictable one on the one hand and none on the other. And again, if a mother has sexual stress added to economic in the workplace, it is possible there will be an impact on her maternal situation.

*   *   *

I have been trying to show how the large movements of the economy coerce the soft intimacies of people's lives, how people's emotional destinies may be affected by stern processes of which they may hardly be aware. As far as the ethical issues which are at the heart of this book are concerned, my focus has been on the reproductive rights of individuals, because I think it is as wrong to make people eunuchs or barren by behavioral means as by surgical, if they are unaware of the nature and gravity of what is happening to them. My claim is that significant reductions in people's options have occurred because of the kind of economic system we have created and even seek to make more effective. This is evil in the same way as when a smokestack spews junk into the air. Even if no one wants it, everyone smells it. It now appears that as many as 25 percent of North American women will not become mothers, which at least to me seems a high price for a mammal to pay in order to have a system of factories and phones and studio apartments. If this continues, and a lot of people have no children, then this means that their parents have no grandchildren. The flow of life is at least changed if not interrupted by a novel condition: that prosperity, not poverty or catastrophe, caused fewer babies to be born.

I am also aware of the wider issue of population growth in the world at large and the mounting frailty of the relationship between people and resources on the planet. As Lester Brown of the Worldwatch Institute has written, "In an age of slower economic growth, improvements in living standards may depend more on the skills of family planners than on those of economic planners." (Brown, 1984) Brown stresses the importance for its economic planning of China's one child per family program, though he recognizes the practical and political difficulties of sustaining it. And it is plainly useful for poorer countries if fewer babies are born in the rich ones because rich babies consume as much as twenty-five times the resources as babies from poor countries.

What is the effect of all this on the lives of well-off people? Will they focus even more on things and even less on people? Will they become unconcerned about children if they have none or few, and restrict public generosity for education and the health of children? The full impact of the demographic changes has been scarcely felt in a cumulative way. The industrial community moves to a new pace and density of family life. It is essential to bear in mind just how new this is, how different from the vast time past.

7. Queen Victoria's Revenge

Pavlov's simple and imperfect experiments have had a disproportionate influence on psychology. It is also surprising that anyone thought his dogs were doing anything unusual. Any dog owner knows that dogs respond to cues. The mere sight of a leash being lifted off its hook can turn an urban dog into a windmill of tail. Animal trainers, hunters, and pastoralists have known about the ordered relationship of animals to their environments and how they respond to social and other cues based on their breeding and training. The rediscovery of the possibility that animals are rather conscious and may even "think" is a comment on the species-centered hubris of the scientists who ever said they did not, not the lay people who enjoy animals precisely because it is possible to communicate with them, who understand how and why they operate, and who appreciate the often wacky, charming way animals interpret the world around them.

But was it not a characteristic of Victorianism in its formal manifestation that it denied the rhyme and reason of the body? Was that not a period which decided that Sigmund Freud was remarkable, probably a genius, because he concluded that human beings lived an inner life as well as an outer one, and because he related this inner life to the history of our species? Compared with much of so-called primitive thought, in which there is seamless unity of physical and social, natural and human, person and personality, the Victorian notion of the body was perhaps useful for science in its formative period, but it was also a provocatively weird and unduly corrosive social theory.

Corrosive because it emphasized the importance of an animal's environment while also permitting the onlooker to treat the animal's inner spirit of things as neutral or minor or at least manageable. Yet at the same time as inner essence was ignored or downgraded, it was somehow assumed that all animals, including humans, were sort of the same. How else can we explain why experiments done with maze learning in rodents, for example, were also supposed to generalize to humans, or salivating dogs to cadets learning military skills? Inner behavioral nature didn't matter because it was all the same. The important element to isolate, understand, and manipulate was the outside environment. The inner one would fall into place.

Environmentalism helped promote a political ethic associated with progressivism. It offered a strong helping hand to reformers and revolutionaries who longed for a political shift as fundamental as industrialization was an economic one. Now I want to turn to the matter of how bodily nature has recently been defined, to make the point that a central element of modernist feminist thought is its suitability to the industrial mode.

Along with other sociological endeavors, broadly speaking feminism has sought its major basis in the realm of consciousness and cognition. It has sought to claim from the realm of animality as much as possible of the essence of modern gender action. In so doing, it is part of that sociological denaturing reflected and stimulated by writers such as Erving Goffman. In a curiously casual manner it has maintained the general Victorian abjuration of frank procreative or recreative sex which so conspicuously marked the lives of people living where the Industrial Revolution was being waged. Particularly of course in that heartland of Victorianism itself, ruled by a queen who donated her name to a giant denial of skin and bones. Her name itself became adjectival for sexual nature's banishment from proper discourse. This was at the formal level. Peter Gay has recently underlined other undercurrents of real sensuality in the private lives of people whose public sensual ideology was prim and pale pastel. (Gay, 1983)

What? Feminism is a legatee of Victorianism? Can this be serious? I believe yes, in the sense that in both enthusiasms the role of coercive nature is assailed. In both, anatomy is overcomeable. In both, destiny is activity, in the proper public realm of noble, or good, paid work. In one mode, the home is the suitable arena for propriety. In the other, effective participation in work. In both, private passions are subject to the needs of social order. If this is

less explicit in feminism than Victorianism, the strenuous requirements for the proper mode are explicit indeed. Motherhood? Career? A bit of each? Colorful clothes or reassuring ones? Dress for
sex or success? Popular culture has only begun to reflect real and
extensive dilemmas about the body in its private and public work.
These dilemmas are no longer just about sexual congress itself, but
about a wider congeries of related matters.

Certainly there has been a renewed and feminist commitment
to the examination of female physicality—from the publication of
such eventful books as *Our Bodies, Ourselves* to relatively adventurous explorations of female sexuality in general, as in the right
to orgasmic fun, the right to initiate encounter, the right to control
reproduction and still engage in joyous intercourse. And there has
been an often tumultuous frankness too about events of private
erotic life, a frankness without prurience or snickers. But in the
new sexual meeting place—at work—Victoria rules the moves. Or
it is said by many she should. In part as a result of this, women
who work with sartorially conventional high-status males frequently adopt a conventional high-status costume themselves, the
business suit, usually dark, often with an effort at a redemptively
colorful tie or kerchief at the neck. But it is a form of transvestism.
As if a group of men seeking to merge into a world of women began
to wear dresses.

The shift is real. With a friend I watched an episode of *Wall
Street Week,* the popular and influential American television program about business. A friend and associate of my companion was
to be the featured guest on the show, an appearance of great value
to her career as a business analyst. The program began. I asked my
companion why her young friend, who was wearing a business suit
and a high-necked blouse, looked as if she were choking. It turned
out that they had discussed costume earlier in the day, when the
show was taped near Washington. The woman on camera acknowledged that the neck was too tight and harsh-looking. But
there was nothing she could do about it because she did not know
how to remove the button and sew it back on. No reason why she
should. Her business was not seamstressing. But she looked miserable and lacked friendly charm through the eyes of the tube. It was
an unexpected and trivial but graphic index of how what women
do and cannot do has changed.

At the same time as there is in the public realm an increasingly
explicit and masculine "dress code" (an inappropriate term be-

cause a code refers to something that isn't obvious, whereas this whole business is fully obvious), there is a seemingly antidotal attention to underclothes for women, evidently in the Victorian mode. Garter belts, camisoles, even the seemingly archaic bustier and bustle, are once again part of the wardrobes of women of fashionable intent; "Victoria's Secret" is the name of one of the most successful mail-order vendors of such intimate garments. Does this mean anything beyond the fashion of the moment? After all, during the period this was written, a major designer began to market women's underwear styled on the most conservative underwear of men. Yet clothes are, as we know, nonverbal forms of communication—animal behavior-marking. The interesting contrast between firm, relatively dour business suits and frivolous, delicate undergarments—evidently marketed to the same group of people—may reveal a real emotional dichotomy experienced by the women who buy them. More subtle but perhaps as important is the possibility that the men who interact with these women want or need or are at least reassured by this dichotomy, too. While by definition it is ephemeral, nonetheless fashion may reveal interesting emphases in such central matters as making work congenial and making sexuality beguiling. The connection between office uniform and the most private garments cannot be altogether random. Neither is the connection between what people will do and what they are willing to wear.

Now let's get under our skin, the skin clothes flavor in such profuse variation, and often with such surprise, but which nevertheless remains skin. The controversies surrounding feminism, gender, and sex differences have been intense, interesting, and vital from the publication of de Beauvoir's *The Second Sex* in 1953. There is no controversy about one insight from all this that has been clearly established, which is that widely and persistently women have received and still do receive fewer of the negotiable goods, services, and assets of the world, unless they inherit them. By the standards of public life, women are less salient and influential over what and how communities do what they do. There is no question that a powerful "anti-female tradition," as I called it in *Men in Groups,* has had a persistent impact on whether or not women could enter the restricted precincts where wealth and power are managed. They received little realistic information from their society encouraging them to join elite cadres. Some societies such as the Islamic did not allow them even to consider such a possibility. Of "role models" there were few. When women did enter the precincts of power, significantly often it was as widow or daughter, for example, in the U.S. Congress. Far less often did a woman become a reelectable incumbent wholly on her own. At various levels, of practice, myth, even idealism, sex segregation was strong. It could be said the general idea of reproductive destiny determined the general shape of the social structure. That there was conscious connection between a view of nature and the arrangements of society.

Some writers see this as an explicitly political decision, essentially designed to repress women and maintain the status quo. For example, Nancy Chodorow has argued that concepts of mothering and nurturance directly affect political access: "the social organization of parenting produces sexual inequality, not simply role differentiation. . . . Any strategy for change whose goal includes liberation from the constraints of an unequal social organization of gender must take account of the need for a fundamental reorganization of parenting, so that primary parenting is shared between men and women." (Chodorow, 1978, pp. 214–15) From a more general perspective, Lewontin, Rose, and Kamin see in the broad field of biosociology an explicit political assertion which is at once unscientific and anti-progressive; their position is part of a program of criticism of behavioral biology stimulated by a group truculently called Science for the People.

Morality has a biological and hence emotional basis. This is why it is so satisfying to social commentators to adopt a moralistic position. More satisfying than one which begins with empirical openness to what is happening and draws conclusions about possible intervention. I have sketched the profound changes in the dialogue and reciprocity between males and females. The warmth, color, and persistence of the feminist controversy suggest the gravity of what is going on. A lag in perceptions produces further and unnecessary perturbation. Social forms are used to cope with social problems for which they were not adapted. For example, it has become increasingly common for parents and children to live in rearranged families—a pattern I once called "Omnigamy" because it appeared that eventually nearly everyone would have some marital relationship to virtually nearly everyone. A joke, but not so funny, as I discovered from some of the correspondence that followed the article's publication. In California, evidently children rather routinely refer to "steps" and "biologicals." Where does the idea of stepchild come from? Not from the optional act of divorce, but from the implacable fact of death. The word's origin is the Anglo-Saxon *steopchild*, orphaned or bereaved child. What was once a state determined by nature is now a condition produced by culture. Yet the same social form and semantic categories are supposed to do for both conditions.

Just as California children talk about steps and biologicals, efforts persist to retain other old forms. Once I was moderating a seminar at the Aspen Institute. One Saturday afternoon a lively and happy group of local people were celebrating in one of the dining rooms in the restaurant where we all ate. I asked a member of the seminar who was in fact the School Superintendant of Aspen if she knew what these rambunctious people were enjoying so. She left to gather facts and returned saying, with a wide smile, "It's a first marriage."

Why bother to retain any of the old forms, such as weddings, Mother's and Father's Days, the elaborated rituals of kinship, even the protocols of sexual prudence, when contraception renders these technically superfluous if not also in a sense politically conservative? Why bother? Because the mammal remains much the same. Gender renews in each generation its grip on everything from the nature of bodily cells themselves, to the average size of bodies, to the tone of voices, to how the brain works, perhaps to what males and females decide is of interest to them.

This is controversial, in part because of the evidence about the deep stereotyping of men's and women's social roles. Part of the house of gender is built with stereotype and prejudice. But there is other evidence about the biology of gender suggesting that: (a) the genetic codes are not wholly random about gender; (b) the social differences we've been discussing reflect other differences already in the beast; and (c) for whole populations, the differences are recalcitrant; other things being equal, they keep reappearing in each generation.

Not, mind you, for individuals, but for the population as a whole. Some women will be taller than many men. But the average of all men will be taller than the average of all women. This is the model of the overlap that occurs with physical characters, even more so with behavioral ones. There will be overlap. The existence of biological differences does not mean they are absolute and categorical. No, they are relative and variable. This seems a rather simple concept but difficult for many people to grasp, perhaps

because Western cultural forms depend upon logical distinguisha-
ble ideas. Therefore the "ordered imprecision" of biological populations—the different bits of the bell-shaped normal curve in which
so many variable living phenomena fall—may appear to be no
order at all.

Instead, too rigid an order may be concocted, as in racism,
when people thought the differences between the races were definite, usually large, akin to appreciable chemical differences. Not
only that, races could be ranked in this analysis, since they were
so different, with the awful and endemic consequences the world
has known all too well.

The essential thing to say about this is that xenophobia existed before biology. There was racism before biology. There was
Social Darwinism before Darwin. There was ample racial murder
and hatred before a scintilla of evidence had been gathered in
favor of the modern theory of evolution.

The second essential thing about this is that it is modern
biology in particular which demonstrates the unity of the species.
It decisively and profoundly reveals the inconsequentiality of racial differences, which are mainly skin-deep and often not even
that. As to the endless, senseless furor over race and IQ, my earlier
comments on that subject will have made clear how spurious are
any serious discussions about human differences based on such
superficial and laconic forms of scrutiny of inner life.

However, this miserable episode of false identification of racism with biology has made it difficult to conduct serious discussion
about sexual differences because it is feared by many, not without
some reason, that discussions of difference in nature will promote
differences in society. That as usual the already subordinate will
lose out even more, thus closing the door more tightly—which is
anyway only relatively ajar for women who seek entry into the
parlors of power and a fair chance at a fair deal in economic and
public life. There is an incontestable case that notions of the privileges and impediments of nature have been used to restrict the
options and even physical movements of women. This explains if
not excuses the opposition of some feminist politicians to any
formal distinction used for public purposes, for example, the legislation in New York State which compels bar owners to post notices
advising pregnant women that drinking may affect their babies.
The objection was that the notice was discriminatory and took no
notice of the depredations of alcohol on the lives of men and

possibly on their reproductivity. Any discussion, even one seemingly justified by plain facts and good wishes for the health of babies, was deemed detrimental to the feminist cause and women's rights.

This is part of a feminist case that law and social practice should be gender-blind, should assume that being male or female does not matter. It is not clear that this works in practice. Indeed, the common complaint is that the efforts have not been successful. Economic and political statistics underline the severe conservatism of the system in this regard. My point for twenty years has been that the inequities are likely to continue so long as women are obligated to enter a man's world and act just like the men already established in place there. The system was established with lines of separation between work and home which characterize the industrial pattern. The dominating individuals in this system were and are still men. It has been shaped to their convenience, whether they planned it consciously or not. So it is unlikely that more of the same will produce something different.

Paradoxical? In the old days, women were assumed to be different from men and thus unable to do or to want to do certain things. As a result, they lost out in the search for fun, reward, and efficacy in the public world. But now, in the new days, it is assumed that they are the same as men. Now for *that* reason they are losing out in the search for fun, reward, and efficacy. How can this be? Simple. Once the systems of public life were set up in the male mold, men obviously benefited from them, compared to women. So long as the overall system does not change to accommodate the realities of women's lives, men will continue to benefit. Not necessarily because they want to be unfair. Men have wives and daughters and friends who want to work, and men are often committed citizens just as women are. But that is how the worlds of work and power are organized.

At least the public worlds. I am leaving aside considering such issues as the close and subtle connection between family ties, marriage, land trading, and formal political power. My focus is on the businesses, services, and administrative agencies in industrial settings to which men and women are recruited and where societies bestow challenges and rewards. It is here that commentators locate the principal difficulties women face in management (Farley, 1983) and in general employment throughout the labor force (Silverstein and Srb, 1979).

Are men and women sufficiently different as groups of people that there is a reasonable expectation individual men and women will approach and do work differently? That as groups they can be expected to produce differing profiles of action and enthusiasm? Even where money as payment is not an issue, in the kibbutz settlements Shepher and I studied, the differences between male and female work were marked and persistent. There was some bias in this because the individuals who assigned work (they were elected, but rotated according to the desires of the General Assembly of each community) may have had stereotypical prejudices about male and female work. Nevertheless, the clear message of our data was that women and men not only wanted to do different things in the labor and administrative cadres, but also specialized in different kinds of work and government. Small-scale societies such as the kibbutzim, mainly rural and broadly dependent on agriculture, may not represent an adequate model for industrial community. But even kibbutzim with extensive industrial establishments from which they derived their main revenue showed much the same division of labor as agricultural ones.

In good measure this resulted from women's preferences for work that kept them near their children at work and play. For example, a pattern first informal and then institutionalized involved visits by women to their young children for an hour or somewhat less during the workday. This made in-camp work far simpler than tasks in the extended reaches of a community's agricultural or industrial installations. But even when this factor was hardly relevant, for example, in political and administrative activity which took place at night when children slept, there was still a substantial difference, by general choice it seemed of both women and men. As I noted earlier, this pattern may be most efficiently understood in relation to the high reproductive rate of kibbutzim—about four children per woman. At the same time, women in the kibbutz set-up have determined many of the conditions of their lives by voting for them.

Why did kibbutz women choose to change their way of life? There have been a variety of explanations, ranging from the most obvious one, which is that kibbutz women are just the modern reflection of traditional Jewish patriarchy, to Bruno Bettelheim's tortuous, even ludicrous neo-psychoanalytical proposal—that somehow kibbutz women are highly "feminine" and traditional because they are reacting against their mothers' more robust

265

egalitarianism. (Bettelheim, 1969) All things considered, and bearing in mind the political and educational sophistication of kibbutz women and men, it seemed to Shepher and me the most sensible explanation for what happened was that kibbutz women and men wanted it to happen. The women more than the men, as a matter of fact, because men by and large thought the changes to a more family-oriented system violated the founding ideology of the kibbutz movement and were expensive to boot. But the women prevailed at General Assembly after General Assembly. The best index of the change in the underlying pattern is the large growth in the number of communities in which kibbutz children now live with their parents and not in the children's house.

This is not a surprising action for a complex and aggressive mammal. But in the context of the strong ideology and extreme restructuring of social life in the kibbutz, the outcome over time is interesting and significant. We see here the result of a set of decisions by thoughtful people. The decisions happen to form a pattern of behavior appropriate to the human primate whose evolutionary consistency has been broadly established.

Ideologies may depend upon a view of the human species incomplete or at variance from the range of our probable behaviors. Almost by definition, ideologies are formulations designed to differ from the reality around us. So it is no surprise when these ideologies make impractical assumptions about people and therefore weird demands on our behavior. My assertion is that a full-throated environmentalist approach to the study of behavior is the ideological reflex or product of the industrial system itself. Perhaps the most profound symptom of this is how gender is treated and what people decide to do about maleness and femaleness.

This remains pop-controversial but is banal because the serious scientific discussions are over. Few responsible students of the interaction of biology and behavior will claim that genes fully determine behavior. Some tediously reiterate the old positions, such as Lewontin, Rose, and Kamin, who allege that behavioral biology is essentially the product of bourgeois capitalism—that it is an ideology. However, by some unexplained causal alchemy, Lewontin, Rose, and Kamin and their ilk regard themselves as exempt from whatever process causes this; *their* assessment of the facts is independent and true. They enjoy a sense of moral superiority so automatic as to equal the sanctimony of missionaries in a hostile country. But they are dupes of the industrial system the capitalist version of which only they hold responsible for human woe. The environmentalist theory is the house theory of the industrial company. These characters are Playing Doctor—company doctor.

The Class Slipper

In analyzing gender, it is possible to end up with the same model of real behavior beginning from seemingly opposed positions. For example, Jean Bethke Elshtain has pointed out that Steven Goldberg's position about the inevitability of patriarchy, that the sex hormones determine different ways of dealing with power (Goldberg, 1974), and Kate Millett's assertion that everything to do with sexuality is political and that men rule the roost and shouldn't (Millett, 1970), both share commitment to a full-fledged biology of male dominance. (Elshtain, 1981, pp. 212–13) They view the sexes as deeply opposed to each other in an almost irretrievable way—a position also taken at about the same time by Susan Brownmiller, who with flamboyant acrimony decided that rape was finally the model within which all sexual encounter took place (Brownmiller, 1975), or by Shulamith Firestone, who asserts that the distinction between the sexes is a form of biological tyranny leading quickly to extensive disadvantage for women, including what she calls the "barbarism" of pregnancy. (Firestone, 1972)

A more subtle complaint comes once again from Barbara Ehrenreich, who discovers in men shaped by feminism a greater sensitivity but also a greater self-involvement and apparent reluctance to form commitments to women on an enduring and equitable basis. Ehrenreich locates this change in technical facilities available to men which make bachelor existence relatively simple, such as frozen food and drip-dry clothing, and also to an enhanced concern about the problem of establishing social class. (Ehrenreich, 1984) While her approach is fair-minded, it continues to suffer from the Buddhist feminism of many of her colleagues insofar as she excludes the more bodily reciprocities I tried to identify in the last chapter, and which—invoking the law of parsimony—seem far more significant than frozen lasagne in determining the broad changes she is undoubtedly correct in identifying.

The changes have been rapid and substantial. Between 1970 and 1982, the number of women remaining single (12%) and men

(17%) has doubled. "A similar trend is evident among people in their mid- to late-twenties; 23% of women and more than a third of men in that age group were still single in 1982, compared with 11% of women and 19% of men in 1970." (UPI, 1984) It appears that creating and sustaining domestic connections has become more difficult, while avoiding them is easier and perhaps more tolerable. More than ever, the system of possessive individualism extends its reign over private lives. Less than ever do members of a gregarious species share their caves in durable bonds with their fellows. A new habitat based on private cells is in formation.

The Birth of the Bioproletariat

Marx and Engels were convinced that history was the story of class struggle, and class revolved around property. But the implacable impact of the system of production on the system of reproduction has created new conditions of class formation based on biology, not property. A male and female are required to conceive a child. But the emerging pattern increasingly emphasizes what the mother does. The father's long-term contribution, if any, is often difficult to track. In the United States the number of two-parent families with children has declined drastically. There has been a doubling of one-parent families—mainly of a woman and her children—who made up almost half the families living below the poverty line in 1981.

For more and more people, reproductive status determines economic circumstance. We witness the birth of a *bioproletariat*. A class locked into poverty and demoralization as firmly as the rules of inheritance sustain the elegant and glad good fortune of lucky offspring of landed or monied gentry.

The bioproletariat secures one major inheritance—an economic deficit. Called "the culture of poverty," the system proceeds with relentless consistency often over generations. In North America the situation is most parlous in the black community, if only because of the cumulative impact of racism and discrimination. It is particularly difficult for black men to maintain consistent rewarding employment. One result is a "steady attrition" in black males able to support a wife and children. In 1984, the National Urban League reported that in 1982, "29% of black men between the ages of 20 and 60 were unemployed or not seeking work." The report estimates that "black couples separate at five times the rate for whites. This creates special economic pressures for black men. . . ." (Barron, 1984) The folklore is that there are five black professional females for every black male of equivalent status and income. The match-up is even more difficult because most women marry at least slightly "up" in the economic structure.

The most severe impact is on women and children. The effects of poverty on children are clear-cut and enduring, and can show up years later, when they take academic tests, for example. Unsupported families are out of synch with the wider culture both economically and socially, and are grievously punished for not conforming to the ideal normative scheme. But the ideal model is false. In the United States it has been estimated that only among 7 percent of people does the "ideal" lifetime pattern still apply: Daddy fully at work, Mommy fully at home, children at school—an intact family. Individuals and families are punished for deviance from this illusory ideal. Yet there is nothing intrinsically wrong with wanting to become a parent and rear a child. This is robust, vital. It can be seen as a vigorous act of pro-social commitment. The problem is how the community responds when childbirth occurs outside the ideal pattern. Badly. The matter is not handled well. The system works poorly. The result we know.

It is fascinating that even the irreducibly sovereign episode of pregnancy can be treated in a confused and reluctant fashion in such a sophisticated community as the United States. This betrays a profound ignorance and trepidation about biological process, about our own nature. A new version of Victorianism, this time grounded in law, not morality. Animated by juridical paranoia, not emotional coldness.

I noted that pregnancy benefits are considered part of a disability package. This is principally because of fears about the possible impact of prejudice against women should they receive any benefits unavailable to men. The American Civil Liberties Union and the National Organization for Women (though not its California Chapter) take the position that any positive discrimination will quickly turn to negative; once again women will be the losers. Others advocate positive help for pregnant women and mothers. The controversy is fierce. Both sides have firmly sketched positions and strong arguments for their views. Both claim the justification of history for their approach to the future.

Wasn't the belief that women were biologically different from men the basis for decades of discrimination against women in the workplace—preventing them from working much overtime, from lifting large objects, from being trained as fighter pilots, even from being able to vote in Switzerland? But isn't it desirable that women nearing childbirth should avoid the tribulations of the labor force and then enjoy peace and quiet with their new infants for as long as possible? But isn't there good evidence that when women are permitted to claim benefits for maternity and mothering, employers will be loathe to hire them because of the possible disruption and potentially greater cost? But isn't the history discouraging of unsupported women and children—people with no claim on the time and resources of the male who fathered the child? But do not all efforts to create desirable legal differences seem to lead inexorably to undesirable inequities; "separate but equal" is an unrealizable myth? But don't children need extensive, intimate, custom-tailored care, which in a mammalian species it seems most realistic for the mother to provide at first?

But but but. A clear choice exists. The broad picture reveals that women are bearing fewer babies and sustaining more jobs. Is there a causal connection? Would women have more babies if jobs were better adapted to motherhood? Would fewer women receive suitable jobs if they carried with them particular obligations for employers? Or does the problem result from a labor pattern wholly defined by the male life cycle as it existed at the turn of the century?

Certainly there are major changes in the texture of contemporary industrial life. Two women on my street were strolling along talking, and one said to the other, "Does your husband know you're coming home for dinner?"

Efforts to approach this issue will have to be more imaginative, yet also more rooted in biosocial reality adequately to protect people from suffering as buffers between an outmoded system and a biology that would be familiar to an Upper Paleolithic visitor. Meanwhile a woman is expected to work as well as usual, with as much focus, whether or not her child is ill or perhaps in hospital. A child is supposed to return as warmly to an empty home and television set as to a welcoming person with a cookie snack, a reassuring hug, and a question about the day. Meanwhile, bewildered parents consume compromising seminars about "quality time," as if some of a child's hours could turn to jewels, others to sawdust.

The Big Red Telephone

Once Robin Fox and I spoke at a seminar of government administrators, business executives, and officials of the University of Los Andes in Bogotá, Colombia. We addressed the theme I am following here. A man who owned a large ceramics industry asked for an example of one thing that could be done to mitigate the asymmetries and tensions of which we spoke. Often a clear sign of working-class status is that it is difficult or inconvenient to call home or receive personal calls, even important ones. So I suggested that he install a conspicuous telephone, perhaps big and red, right in the middle of the factory floor. The understanding would be that it was for important calls involving children or other relatives. At the very least, knowing the facility was there should be a comfort and an honest embrace of the reality that family crises do not arrange themselves before 8:00 a.m. or after 5:00 p.m. —an important matter particularly in a community such as Bogotá in which kinship is so central an organizing principle.

I haven't heard that the phone has been installed. I still think it could have been as important a symbol of the company as its logo. Telephone companies spend much money advertising the pleasures and usefulness of calling home. Could organizations improve employees' peace of mind by creating facilities for calling home, with all that this implies?

It is banal to make a comment such as this. Nevertheless, millions of people spend their workdays in circumstances which assume they can hold in abeyance the impacts of the social worlds they inhabit. In general it is acknowledged that their physical needs must be attended to, as far as health and safety are concerned at least. But the matter of social needs is far more controversial and variable. This reflects general inattention to the range and intensity of the wider social networks within which people live.

Is this by default? I've suggested that work groups increasingly represent the major form of kinship many modern people have. Being deprived of the community of work may, money aside, be as serious as exiling them from their families. Like everyone else's, my city block is richly full of social event and meaning. For a four-month period a man wearing one of the three three-piece suits he evidently owned would come to a street corner near a busy bus stop, and sit there on his upturned attaché case. He did this day in, day out, whatever the temperature. When it was sunny on his side of the street and as hot as New York becomes in summer, he would sweat copiously, still sitting on his attaché case and talking nonstop, to no one, throughout this bizarre performance. Had he been fired and like other people known to history simply carried on his daily routine without informing his family or neighbors? Was he avoiding confronting the fact of his unemployment himself? I have no idea. He seemed crazy. Yet what he was doing was a caricature of the needy person maintaining the facade of a productive life.

Buddhist Feminism

How coercive is the body? We are with violent implacability constrained by our bodies, by death. Are we constrained by our bodies in life? I used the phrase "Buddhist feminism" to refer with obvious censoriousness to an effort to shrink the enormity of physicality by locating its source in the mind, thus adding an immense amount of optionality to the whole matter. We know the capacity of the human mind for adventurous novelty seems limited only by the number of hours of a day and night.

Ponce de León and his fruitcake voyage notwithstanding, is there such optionality? Human beings may resolutely believe. To some extent the placebo effect operates; belief can be effective. I am altogether aware of how hungry for optimistic scenarios people are. While the principle of *caveat emptor* appears to apply for example as far as religion and government-sponsored lotteries are concerned, in general responsible governments restrict the right of charlatans to abuse the credulity of sick people. The authorities exercise reasonably stringent controls on what can be claimed by medicines and doctors, and by prohibiting sundry quacks from victimizing people whose ill-health makes them particularly vulnerable.

Social theorists who base political and psychological Utopias or more modest plans on a strategic disavowal of the impact of the body are dangerous to the body social. They are trying to establish conditions for social life which cannot possibly exist—as if Ponce de León were allowed to set actuarial tables for a life insurance company! Few people other than specialized religious cultists firmly disavow the reality of the physical body. However, about its active manifestation, its behavior, a different story prevails. The broad force of feminist interpretation holds that males and females behave the same except where interfered with by coercive or biased cultures. Contemporary behavioral differences are seen as stark and simple proof of this. If there are some behavioral differences between males and females, these are considered either trivial or impossible to track with any accuracy. For scientific and policy purposes, it is appropriate to ignore their existence. Overall, they balance each other out. Their net impact is decisively less significant than the cumulative power of the traditions, privileges, and inequities which divide men and women. Such is the claim.

For example, the psychologist Sandra Bem of Cornell University has generated a psychological measure of androgyny, the BEM Scale. This is to reveal how sharply individuals hold to stereotyped notions of maleness and femaleness. The animating idea is that androgyny, a kind of amalgamated middle ground between the sexes, is the broad norm of human life. Individuals who deviate from the androgynous group are in some sad sense the unfortunate victims of endless pervasive stereotype.

But there *are* two sexes. There is no androgynous population. Most individuals whose physical makeup is truly indeterminate or variable usually end up, by their own choice, in some form of medical treatment. They seek professional assistance for what is perceived as an anomaly, not the norm. It is possible to argue, as Michel Foucault has with great compassion and skill about the French hermaphrodite Hercule Barbin, that there is an arbitrariness to sexual categories which could be changed. And there is no reason to punish or censure individuals who want to dress or act in a manner not customary for their sex in their society. Or groups who wish to pursue their own gender-aesthetic. For example, Esther Newton has described the albeit rather grim world of female impersonators who carry to formal extremes the effort to produce a distinction between physical sex and social image. (Newton, 1972)

Perhaps it is of interest here to recall an experience I had during the taping of a television program for the BBC in London. Robin Fox and I were asked to appear as the protagonists on one of a series of programs called *Controversies*, which involved a particular book singled out for lively challenge by a group of four or five experts and the studio audience, all ranged either for or against the work and whoever was speaking for it, usually its author. The show was taped in the main lecture hall of the Royal

273

Institution in Mayfair. The chief speakers stood behind the desk at which Michael Faraday had performed his fundamental experiments about the nature of electricity. The proceedings were moderated by Professor Sir George Porter, president of the Royal Institution. The BBC distributed tickets to interested groups, and advertised the shows in pertinent quarters—seeking the controversy the title promised.

I had an inkling it was to be a bumpy flight when I saw a rather stiff guard in the marble halls of the Institution do a severe double take outside the men's room, which had just been entered by someone in a dress and flowery hat. It seemed that among the representative sample of the British population the BBC had managed to invite for the taping was a group of Trotskyite tranvestites, conducting a bitter row with a group of Lesbians, who were in turn at odds with a rather puritanical group of Marxists who saw this gender fuss as a diversion from the real issue of class conflict.

The taping began amid the ceremonial architecture and evidently went relatively well until the question period, when the questions and comments from the floor appeared to have more to do with the ongoing stream of antagonism between the groups mentioned than with Fox's and my book. At one point the diatribes became markedly more severe. Suddenly perhaps a dozen gaily dressed women, in flowered dresses and garden party hats, swept down the aisles and out the doors, muttering complaints all the while, and all on national television.

But the women were men. Since I happened to be in mid-response to some question or other, I was able to make a comment on the dramatic departure of these men-women which suggested the point I am making here—about the persistent interest in conventional categories of gender and how even violating the norms underscores them. I thought at the time I had been rather sensitive to the turbulence the self-exiled men reflected in what they had done and how. I thought I had turned the event into a positive contribution to the program and to understanding the bases of what we were all concerned with. And I thought it was "good television," about real things.

Then I went to Europe for a holiday and missed the transmission of the program but did see a review in an English paper which commented on the boycott of our remarks by a group of women. I did not fully understand this, since it hadn't of course happened. Upon returning to London, I asked for a screening of the show at the BBC television headquarters in Shepherd's Bush and was surprised to see that my comments dealing with the demonstration and exit had been edited out of the program. When I asked the producer why he had chosen to do this, he said: "The British public would never have accepted that those were men, not women, and so we couldn't leave your comments in." Thus, I thought, missing the whole point about the need people have to know, is it a boy or a girl? And not incidentally making Fox and me seem the unresponsive enemy of well-dressed women interested enough in science to come to the Royal Institution but enough irritated by us to perform the un-English gesture of walking out. In fact we had several letters from viewers apologizing for the unmannerly behavior of contemporary English women.

Have for centuries and over many cultures people been brainwashed to expect definition of gender because they are afraid not to know? Or do they have to know because the requirements of primatological society obligate members to know about gender? In a famous if gnomic sentence in his *Philosophical Investigations*, Ludwig Wittgenstein wrote: "The human body is the best picture of the human soul." While every such overpoweringly pithy statement can be subject to endlessly different interpretations, one sensible one is that how people see the nature of bodies allows us to see into the nature of minds. My simple point is that the universal human division of bodies into male and female may not so much reveal the real quality of physical gender as more directly show how the principal sex organ, the brain, deals with the whole issue. It is almost as if the brain operates on the same principle of binary off-on that computers use.

Like computers, the brain deals with an immense amount of information. It comes to decisions and judgments of vast subtlety and complexity—unlike computers. But, surprisingly, not about gender, where the outcome of its calculations is almost inevitably as simple as possible. It is either one thing or another. Gender has been an absolutely fundamental building block in the animal world. If unambiguous certainty would be needed in any major matter in nature, it was this. The burden of proof is on those who call the dichotomy between the sexes an imposed unnaturalness, not on those who treat it as an elemental bedrock feature of the procedures of species. Particularly, the differentiation between human males and females is enhanced by the symbolic and interpretative processes of the brain. Precisely that organ supposed to emancipate us from nature! It is also essential to understand that even if the differences which do exist are relatively slight, they may nevertheless be influential—perhaps particularly influential —because they are brought to bear relatively decisively in an otherwise similar universe. The few differences that exist may loom like Alps in a prairie.

How to relate public policy to scientific understanding? One favorite convention is to associate biology with conservative capitalism. So Stephen Jay Gould announces that "Theories of biological determinism gain attention in conservative climates, our own included." Certainly societies with an apparently progressive political ideology, such as Eastern Europe, have explicitly based social policies on an environmentalist belief in the similarity of men and women. But this has resulted in a situation of major disadvantage to women. As Gail Lapidus reports, there has at last been "a growing recognition that present arrangements fail to provide optimal conditions for the harmonious combination of women's dual roles. . . . This failure . . . places such enormous burdens on women as to compromise their ability to function adequately in both work and family roles." (Lapidus, 1978, p. 286) As we would have expected, "Among the serious problems that have compelled a fundamental reconsideration of previous assumptions and institutional arrangements, the declining birthrate is unquestionably of prime importance." (*ibid.*) But the declining birth rate is also a feature of capitalist society. So are the burdens of working women. So perhaps explaining the situation of women lies not along the conservative-radical axis—the one embraced enthusiastically by politically committed commentators—but rather along the inaccurate-accurate science axis.

Back to my general point about biological Fabianism. If you want to change a system, it is best to understand it first. The more fundamental the process to be encountered, the more basic should be the information brought to bear on analysis and judgment of the situation. Attitudes, social roles, employment opportunities, political emancipation, etc., etc., are critical elements of a changing situation. Nevertheless, there remain to be answered significant questions about the point of analytical departure. Is it to be assumed that men and women who join a place of employment will at some point become parents? Are women more likely to than men? Will parenthood have a different impact on women than men? Will the adjustment of the employer be different to women than men? Is it appropriate or even legal for employers to consider this issue? Is the workplace likely to be seen as interesting to people concerned with finding mates? Will life be difficult or easy for someone who does find a partner on the job? And will general concerns about sexual harassment restrict people's courtship options where these exist perhaps most generously, at work?

Interesting questions. But just hypothetical?

Another instructive personal experience. Through an Army officer I met at a seminar, I was invited to provide a talk to a group of relatively senior people in the Pentagon, including the highest-ranking woman in the General Staff and a male three-star general, all of whom were concerned with efforts then under way to attract and retain qualified women in the service. For every good reason, not the least being that the U.S. Congress had demanded good performance on this issue, there was great concern about how eagerly men and women stayed on after their initial recruitment. It turned out that men, both black and white, stayed in much the same percentages. But white women left very early, while black women stayed on much longer than their white sisters. It was explained to me that the reason for this was that sexual harassment was a principal concern of the women in the Army, as it indeed was of the senior staff of the Army itself. Their hypothesis was that white women were less skilled at or willing to endure sexual harassment. But black women coped with greater fortitude, overcame it, and stayed on.

What did I think of this explanation? I was somewhat incredulous. I knew the harassment issue was serious and justifiably received much attention. Perhaps a more positive reason was more salient in the long run. For reasons I have already discussed in this chapter, it is relatively difficult for black men to find stable and good employment, which the military has traditionally offered them, at least since the Korean War. This meant for black women that they were in close, decent, and interesting contact with a large group of potentially reliable mates, who at least shared the cultural experience of service life as well as the factor of race—still virtually all-decisive in American mate selection. This would have applied much less influentially to the white women. Hence the different willingness of the two groups to stay on in the Army.

This kind of interpretation had hardly been considered, though it seemed both plausible and relatively wholesome. An informed and sensitive response to it could redound to the benefit

277

of the Army and its members. But those responsible for the issue were rooted in a relatively narrow kind of interpretation, an unintentionally mean-minded one at that. They paid no sympathetic official attention to the broad reproductive lives of their employees. Only to their productive, of which sexual encounter was clearly disruptive. No doubt these individuals were personally concerned with the personal lives of those with whom they worked and for whom they were responsible. The official manual of procedure told a different story. It seemed to require a different ending. In effect, they were using a disease model of the whole matter rather than one which saw people's behavior as healthily attuned to their own productive *and* reproductive needs and concerns.

Involved were the lives, futures, and energies of tens of thousands of people, millions upon millions of public dollars. At stake too was the overall sense of morale in the organization—that it was competent at meeting its goals rather than chronically failing because of the vexatiously selfish, inappropriate, and inconsiderate behavior of its members. The whole situation was even more silly. In the Army young men and women at the prime reproductive and sexual age find themselves living together in summer camp! How could the reproductive system not become salient? Some years earlier the Army had become very alarmed when the newly enlarged group of female officers occasionally had sexual or neosexual liaisons with enlisted men—a violation of traditional hierarchy were there ever one. To solve the problem, it issued an order that there was to be no further "fraternization" between female officers and enlisted men. No Nobel Peace Prize for that fatuous nonsolution.

As employer and indeed hometown, the Army is a cross section of the society at large. I assume that the same misunderstanding of sexual politics occurs elsewhere in the society of which the Army is a sample. Though the officers I met struck me as well intentioned and well informed, their information was about more superficial systems than those they were in fact having to confront. Of course the military must operate in a situation much more complex than civilian employers because it not only provides jobs for people, it also provides them their homes, their daily routines, their clothes, and much of their recreation. It has to consider a range of events much beyond what is pertinent to the corner shop with three employees or the urban factory or the suburban corporate headquarters. Nevertheless, despite the military's very encompassing responsibilities, it seems to have failed to confront issues which so clearly stare everyone in the face. Another version of the Victorianism I referred to, which inhibits people from understanding the reproductive process? In view of the tradition of raunchy military argot, of sailors hitting shore, and so on, the powers that be cannot be unaware of the issue. But as we have seen, legal and informational as well as attitudinal barriers appear to prevent an organization from understanding the hearts and minds of its personnel.

An ideology about nature finds its most consequential expression here in the approach to gender. A new synthesis is required to help those creating and administering the social groups to engage with equal weight the various factors which go to make a life. In the Israeli kibbutz, an ideology produced principally by men and informed by male concerns about production and the public sphere began to unravel because of pressures from women about reproduction and the private sphere. The extreme male scheme failed.

In the kibbutz, people can get together and talk things out. Massive industrial societies haven't the system for such dialogue. There is not the political leadership to respond appropriately to women as voters, as politicians, and as the largest of interest groups. Perhaps a fear similar to what people have about mortality itself surrounds any discussion of reproductive issues. Perhaps we cannot bear too much reality. But individuals suffer when communities are not capable of realistic analysis of the broad conditions of social life. Some help is on the way from within the feminist community itself in response to the evident unreality of the first wave of theorizing. For example, Germaine Greer's most recent book is a highly assertive variant of parts of my own argument here, though I think it is significant that there has been markedly less enthusiastic response to *Sex and Destiny* (1984) than to her first, more traditional feminist essay, *The Female Eunuch* (1971). A similar result followed the publication of Betty Friedan's *The Second Stage* (1981), in which among other things she affirms the value of family life both for members of families and for the community at large. As Friedan replied in an interview published in the *Smith College Quarterly* after she received an honorary degree there, "In the second stage we must come to new terms with the family. We cannot turn our backs on women's needs for family: to nurture and be nurtured. . . . The choices we have now make life more complex. . . . I see women today coming up against the biological clock faced with impossible, bad, bad choices. . . . I am not saying that a woman has to have a child to fulfill herself—it is legitimate to be generative in other ways." (Haddad, 1981) But as Ellen Willis wrote in *The Nation,* the book was a "step backward," while Jean Bethke Elshtain thought that "The movement must part company with Friedan and unite with those forces of social change and political renewal that are resisting the increasing power of unaccountable bureaucrats animated by a technocratic ethos." (Elshtain, 1981) And it was Elshtain herself who with persuasive and learned cogency argued that the crusade of feminists against the family was "a rather bleak Hobbesianism rejuvenated in feminist guise." (Elshtain, 1979)

Nevertheless, the theoretical dilemma about what to do with families has been solved only as partially and finally unsatisfactorily as it has in practice, and for a similar reason: the failure to understand and respond to what happened when an ancient hunting-gathering primate with big ideas found itself living in our brand-new system. And so priests, politicians, philosophers, pollsters, and just people struggle ceaselessly with the issue of "the family."

The struggle appears to have made mincemeat of our confidence. It is hardly surprising that having failed to produce a pattern of social roles that can be smoothly integrated with the animal that must effectively assume and enjoy them, the next-best solution has been adopted: change the roles, change the rules, change the people, scramble everything up.

Among the self-styled sexual progressives, the androgyny tribe is one colorful lure to immigrants from tradition. Another is the homosexual tribe. Perhaps not the broad population of homosexual people themselves, who proceed with their lives as citizens, not crusaders. But at least the professional enthusiasts for a "life style," who proclaim the virtues of the deliberate indeterminacy of their community. Hence Jan once James Morris, the consummate travel writer who described with brilliant skill the places he had been, and then in the ultimate voyage, where he, James, had been and where now she, Jan, is: "So there, perhaps we are all on the road to intersex; perhaps the world of today, by some inexplicable perception, sees characters like Boy George and me as examples of its own sexual future, and so greets us diplomatically. . . . The sexes are recognizably becoming more like each other. We have perhaps a million years to go . . . men and women of all kinds seem to be converging upon some physical median." (Morris, 1984, p. 11)

Morris's placidly bold evolutionary biologizing is of course rather thin. The stark, memorable essence of the voyage she describes remains: it was taken at the edge of a surgeon's knife. Her point is interesting, that she personally has encountered a surprisingly sympathetic response from the public at large. Other assertions by other experimenters with gender suggest that their road, newly traveled, is bumpy. Not only in their contacts with others but also in their own lives, at least for some recipients of sex-change therapy. Leslie Lothstein of the University Hospitals of Cleveland followed studies of those operated upon and reports serious controversy about the long-run success of the operations in the wider context of patients' lives. The closing of the Johns Hopkins University Clinic, a main contributor to the field, has raised questions about the professional value of the treatment. While Lothstein concludes that for some few patients the surgical treatment appears to succeed, less drastic alternatives are available to their doctors. The ambiguous results of follow-up research suggest that milder remedies should be the treatment of preference in the absence of strong evidence to the contrary. (Lothstein, 1982) So Morris's enthusiasm may not be fully shared by precisely those medical personnel who would have to be her partners in this odd adventure.

I happened to meet a physician who was leaving New York to become head of a department at the Hopkins Medical School who expressed one very elemental consternation about the sex reassignment clinic: "They're cutting guys' cocks off down there." And indeed raised questions about the good sense of the whole program, which was subsequently closed. It was an extreme example of the effort to alter nature with advanced industrial technique. Even gender had become a product which could be produced and purchased. With hindsight, the endeavor seems more breathtakingly intrepid than even it did at the time. It is appropriate that one of the world's finest travel writers, Morris, should have been its notable chronicler because a genuinely new journey had to be described. But the question remains, was the trip necessary?

Why am I concerned with such problems in a book about the industrial system and its relationship to ethics? For two main reasons. The first is that because of the declining reproductivity of the industrial world, the whole issue of gender becomes more, not less salient. As it becomes evidently more and more difficult to bear

281

and rear children without a sense of harassment or at least conspicuous challenge and cost, the option of homosexuality becomes the more salient too.

The second main reason is to assert that homosexuality is not a flavor or a fashion. It is not just a "life style" or an option such as of occupation or political party. The trivialization of its meaning into a subculture is another version of a belief in life as product and of a disbelief in life as nature.

On a contentious issue, it is necessary and fair for pertinent personal points of departure to enjoy the light of print. Here are some. I am not a homosexual person and have not been inclined to become one. I find it difficult to understand the motivation toward homosexuality but can understand very well the pleasures of community, culture, identity, and security which defined membership in a defined group can offer. Though homosexual people may experience more than their share of psychological anguish and sense of personal defeat—in part perhaps because of hostility toward them—I think the American Psychiatric Association was correct to remove homosexuality by itself as a category of illness; it shouldn't have been there in the first place. I see no grounds for discrimination for or against homosexual people in politics, business, education, medicine, and so on, or for assuming that homosexual people may exempt themselves from conventional standards of public decorum, or be subject to harsher-than-usual requirements to conceal their emotional, erotic, and personal choices. Some of my best friends . . . etc.

I do not see homosexuality as either a crusade or a curse, though my obvious pro-natal position (for individuals, not societies) in this book will suggest that I think that homosexual people who do not have children (like heterosexuals too) are missing out on much rich fun, even if there may well be other satisfactions resulting from their choices which I cannot compare with mine. In general I think homosexual people like anybody else should be left alone if they want to be, as they should leave other people alone if they want to be. How one does sex and the gender dance should stimulate neither persecution by others nor sanctimony about oneself.

My simple, basic point is that homosexuality is not a life style. It is not gay. It is sober. It is more meaningful than style, more important than taste. However mysterious its origin and however ramified or not its impact, it is a phenomenon which fundamentally affects nearly the whole lives of many people and also the lives of those around them. It cannot be seen solely in medical, political, aesthetic, or any other special terms, but rather as the result of a congeries of forces and realities which produce that inflexible fact, a human being's history. In urban areas, sizable homosexual communities have gathered, who, perhaps because of their relatively reduced child-rearing responsibilities or greater commitment to public life, enjoy considerable amounts of disposable income and hence have become an important market for advertisers and others concerned with selling products and employing people. (An authoritatively successful force in the fashion industry told me that a complex merchandising problem for New York City department stores was treading a fine line between attracting the affluent homosexual male customers they wanted and retaining the heterosexual ones they already had.) But this does not therefore mean that the money or the style maketh the man or the woman. There must remain a passionate center to what may be a distinctive form and attitude of life. The mortal coil does not unwind that easily.

An anecdote introduces some dimensions of the story. I was invited to attend an organizational meeting of a group of New Yorkers in and out of public life who were trying to find ways of reducing the obstacles homosexual people faced in going about their public and private lives. The meeting was at the home of a man who has since died of cancer. He was relatively young, about thirty-five, the son of an affluent and well-known designer of clothes. She had publicly and fiercely disowned him because of his sexual choice. A dramatic case of what the meeting was about.

At some point in the evening I entered into conversation with Dr. Harold Brown, then the Chief Medical Officer of New York City, who some time later resigned with the announcement, front-page news in the *Times* that day, that he was homosexual. He could no longer live the deceptive pinched life he felt he had been forced to lead till then. It too was a dramatic case, described in his autobiography which appeared some time later. (Brown, 1975) We talked about the host of the meeting and his mother, and after a bit I asked:

Does Mrs. X have any other children?

No.

Well, then, that is the end of Mrs. X.

Dr. Brown was baffled by my concern about this matter. After a few words about parents, grandparents, reproduction, et al., the conversation came to an end. The intricate mechanism of cocktail party folderol carried on.

For my part, I was baffled by his failure to understand that just as Mrs. X's history of conceiving and raising a child might reveal her commitment to reproduction, her son's decision to opt out of the process could be a fundamental blow to her own sense of her life's continuing vivacity. So she disowned him from the productive system because he had in effect disowned her from the reproductive one. A miserable and small-minded exchange, perhaps, but the animating energies of it are hardly obscure. A similar cause must underlie much of the difficulty the celibate Church experiences in attracting nuns and priests. The large Catholic families of yore, with two, four, six, eight children, might quite equably agree to see one of them in the Church since their overall long-term fecundity was assured. But since families are small and becoming smaller, the decision becomes far more portentous— "In 1790, the average American household had 5.8 members; by 1975 this number had fallen uninterruptedly to 2.9." (Cohen, 1981, p. 48) The same force will presumably be brought to bear on the nonreproductive homosexual children of small families. So at the same time as there is an evident and relative relaxation of the public pressures against homosexual lives, there may well be countervailing private ones, from families, of a presumably coercive even if well-meaning kind.

Another anecdote, with an opposite result to the plight of Mrs. X and her dead son. A young American man was an active and self-acknowledged homosexual. His family owned a nationally distributed line of clothing. The man was told by his parents he would not inherit the business, either to own or to manage, unless he produced two children. He found a wife, complied with the conditions. All parties were elegantly satisfied, on the surface at least.

This is hardly strange, complex, or unexpected. In his work of remarkable erudition and scope, John Boswell has noted: "Only in societies like modern industrial nations which insist that erotic energy be focused exclusively on one's permanent legal spouse would most gay people be expected to marry and produce offspring less often than their nongay counterparts, and it appears that even in these cultures a significant proportion of gay people —possibly a majority—do marry and have children." (Boswell, 1980, p. 10) Exactly the issue. Since the pair-bond procedure is the way children are largely produced in industrial society, and the way in which, as we have seen, it seems to be generally easiest, people who cannot or will not engage in heterosexual bonds are by definition taking a very special and portentous position that can hardly go unnoticed and to which there will inevitably be some response. This can range from the private chagrin of a woman who discovers or concludes that a man who interests her is unavailable to her or indeed to any other women, to the irritation of a man who realizes a colleague wants his body not his business, to the destructive hatred of individuals and mobs who may try literally physically to destroy people whose sexuality they so detest. In between, there is the bitter complaint of a materfamilias that the summer-house enclave on Fire Island she shared with other heterosexual families and a large number of homosexuals became forcefully and in her view obstreperously bigoted sexually and proselytizing to boot. "Having been defined, or defined themselves, as political victims, they must turn their way of living into an ideology and stand four-square behind it . . . thanks to Gay Lib, what was once a strategy of flight, tricky and absorbing, has been transformed into a tactic of frontal assault." (Decter, 1980, p. 48)

Why is this relevant to the argument here? Because I am asserting that the issue of sexual preference cannot adequately be explained by a marketplace model of consumer preference. The homosexual world is not describable principally by mise-en-scène and style. There must be substantial underlying causes which go beyond the obvious. The law of parsimony must be obeyed; the wellsprings of a significant arrangement of life must surely depend on more than the salience of Bloomingdale's department store and the fashion in mustaches. Does any basic thing happen in the lives of homosexual people different than in the lives of other people? Or is randomness what is going on?

A substantial literature explores broad-ranged theories about the origins of homosexuality. Some writers focus on the psychological or psychoanalytical factors which emerge predominantly from the interaction of the individual and his or her parents. Such factors undoubtedly play a role in the origin of any and all major orientations of people, including the sexual. It does not seem possible or even worthwhile to separate out the various elements of familial life that would be part of both the real experience of homosexual people and the psychological theories that claim to account for homosexual behavior. The absence of a father, or too strong a father, or a weak father, or an overwhelming mother, or an unconcerned mother, or an incestuous seduction, or seduction between schoolteacher or other adult or older child—these must all be taken into broad account. I feel neither qualified nor inclined to emphasize any particular element of the mixture. Some of the explanations cancel each other out. Many seem self-evidently valid in more or less degree and fit well within the relatively conventional explanations in the social sciences. I want to focus briefly on two others which may appear contradictory or opposed to each other, though both are directly linked to a view of homosexuality related to broad and basic evolutionary forces. The first is an account of one fascinating study of possibly portentous and disturbing impact. The second, a general theory of differences between male and female homosexual behavior, which analyzes how homosexual people adapt conventional evolutionary strategies to their own needs and wants. Potentially, both hypotheses can explain a lot. In terms of this book they suggest how contemporary homosexual behavior may depend on the industrial system, within which it has achieved such recent importance.

June Reinisch is a feisty and sensitive psychologist who had been a colleague of mine at Rutgers University and is now the director of the Alfred C. Kinsey Institute for Research at Indiana University in Bloomington. She has long been interested in the impact of hormones on behavior. She made her reputation with some extremely careful studies of the effect of maladministration of even tiny amounts of hormone on the offspring of pregnant females. She has also investigated the effect of fetal hormones on human sex differences in the brain and cognition, and maintains a lively commitment to understanding both the cellular bases of behavior and the social milieu within which it takes place. (Reinisch, 1976, pp. 69–94) She is concerned, too, with how substances ingested in the body, particularly during the fetal stage, affect the social and sexual behavior of youngsters and adults.

One of her most interesting recent studies is of a commonplace phenomenon with possibly drastic results—the administration of barbiturates to pregnant women. Drugs containing barbiturates enjoy a vast distribution in the United States and Europe, prescribed both on their own and as components of other preparations. It is estimated that as many as 25 percent of pregnant women are prescribed these drugs during pregnancy for a variety of problems, ranging from lower back pain to migraine to insomnia to morning sickness to duodenitis to dry cough. Not only are these substances widely used, they are also the most widely abused of drugs. The number of women ingesting them during pregnancy is likely to be higher than one quarter. But barbiturates cross the placental barrier. They affect not only the mother's malady but also the fetus's development.

With what results?

It is difficult to know because, alarmingly, Reinisch and her coworker S. Sanders of Rutgers state that "there exist little if any data on longterm consequences of prenatal exposure to barbiturates in humans." (Reinisch and Sanders, 1982, p. 311) So they began with the results of experiments performed on other animals who share some similar reproductive systems with humans, the inevitable laboratory mice.

One effect is on brain growth: "during the era of its most rapid increase in size [it] consistently . . . [produces] reductions in weight." (ibid.) Significant deficits occur in the hippocampus and cerebellum, which are both fundamental managers of the flow of information and behavior that constitutes social life. Not only was size of brain affected, but also efficiency of function. Most interesting from our point of view here is the impact on sex-linked characteristics: " . . . differences between male and female rodents, which seem to be dependent on exposure to androgens during early development involve those same structures which have been shown to be affected by barbiturates—the cerebellum, hippocampus, and cerebral cortex." (p. 314)

It has been shown that areas of the central nervous system are marked by differences between males and females, so this finding takes on added significance. The upshot is that there are "striking and permanent" effects in animals on reproductive function after the use of barbiturates. Furthermore, "exposure to barbiturates during the period identified as critical to the development of sexually dimorphic behavior interfered with masculinization, resulting in males that behaved in ways which are more characteristic of the female of their species." (p. 317)

The significance of this becomes clear when it is recalled that in the mammalian world, the "basic model" of organisms is the female. The development of maleness requires additional secretions precisely and appropriately timed during the period of gestation. To produce a male child, the mother must generate from her own body substances which are the signature of males. She must do so within relatively narrow limits of variation in order to achieve the normal result. When a pregnant female is sedated, drugged, the delicate mechanism appears to be directly affected. This makes intuitive sense because, being sedated, she is able to do less and create less than were she in full use of all her physiology. Being less competent, she produces less of what is needed to cook a male. The result is an offspring less "normal" than had she been allowed to manage her pregnancy without industrial interference of a consequential kind.

No one would prescribe sedation to an airline pilot going to work. Why then to a pregnant mother?

I understand how explosive this material is, but there seems no alternative to exploring it and what it means as carefully as possible. We must know about the impact of the industrialization of the body.

Randy's Dream

Reinisch and Sanders suggest how drugs taken in pregnancy may produce an unexpected sexual orientation. Another view of the matter emerges from a rather cryptically speculative essay in *Perspectives in Biology and Medicine,* published by the University of Chicago Press. George Gallup and Susan Suarez look to evolutionary strategies for a clue about the origin of homosexual behavior. In seeming paradox, they see it as an adaptation of robust heterosexual enthusiasms. That is, homosexual people do what they do for the same reason as heterosexuals. The important difference is in their object of desire.

Their reasoning is based on three principles current in evolutionary biology. The first is that females possess the advantage over males of knowing who their offspring are. This conduces to an altogether different level of equanimity about the whole process. Males cannot possess what biologists call "paternity certainty." This is held in part to account for greater male ferocity about sexual possession, not only in species famous for this such as the terrestrial baboons but also in the human case. For us it may take less physical but equally irritating forms such as the double standard, chastity belts, deflowering rituals, virginity values, and other admonitions of the night.

The second principle is that females are more directly obligated in raising offspring than the male. For the female, the choice ot mate is far more consequential. Gallup and Suarez conclude, as have others, that females are likely to be much more careful before entering into a sexual relationship because they have more to lose by recklessness and more to gain should offspring result from their liaison.

The third principle is that female ova are very limited while male sperm are by comparison virtually unlimited. A male can father many children whereas females are far more circumscribed. Therefore the sexes will display different behavior as a result of this principle and the others too.

Gallup and Suarez want to explain why the sexual behavior of male homosexuals is more like that of males, while female homosexuals act more like heterosexual females than like male homosexuals. Many homosexual people don't have children and so can arrange their lives as they wish, without obeying the antediluvian law of infants' exuberant chronic neediness. Also, gay men and women have both taken a comparably idiosyncratic position in relation to the wider community. Then why don't their common circumstances yield common attitudes to sexual partnership? Gallup and Suarez report that while men have dozens and even hundreds of partners—a thousand in a lifetime is not uncommon—the study of Lesbian women reveals that the large majority had between one and eleven partners, with three being the median number. They suggest that women interested in long-term faithful relationships become fundamentally disenchanted with fast-moving males who want only one thing, and turn to other women for the enduring commitment and companionship they seek.

But gay men are able to conduct themselves in hectically "polygamous" ways. As the expert chronicler of homosexual society Edmund White has written in a brilliant essay, "Of course, gay men behave as all men would were they free of the strictures of female tastes, needs, prohibitions, and expectations." (White, 1983) Once I was on a panel convened by *Harper's* magazine to discuss masculinity. Among the participants were George Gilder, the economist, with strong views about the value of the traditional family, and Martin Duberman, the historian, who among other subjects has written about homosexuality. In an exchange between them, Duberman claimed that irresponsible critics such as Gilder accused homosexuals of having a thousand partners a year. No, said Gilder, a lifetime. Oh, said Duberman, that's not much.

Gallup and Suarez take the formulae of the typical form of reproductive life and as it were change the signs from male to female. Too simple? Perhaps. But the approach helps account for the energy and form of the communities in question. Is it true that all men would like as much sexual variety as homosexual men may, and as White claims? Certainly men seem at the very least less resistant to the call of variety. There appears to be little comparable in the female homosexual community to the "quickie" bars which have been widely described, perhaps best by Edmund White himself. (White, 1981) Whereas a heterosexual woman once told me proudly that "I have only had sex with a man once, once."

Gallup and Suarez try to understand the motivation of the homosexual way of life. They find it principally in the same forces which stimulate everybody else but with a different focus. The strength of their assertion is to help explain why sex differences persist among homosexual people whose orientation should in theory produce common practices. It is however likely that various medical menaces will reduce these behavioral differences, AIDS in particular. It may also put AIDS into historical perspective, to see it as a modern form of crowding disease, like tuberculosis, but this time crowding in time not space. Too much intimate behavior in too little time for the body's defenses to absorb.

Reinisch and Sanders and Gallup and Suarez have offered two apparently divergent views of homosexual life. One locates the situation partly in the physiology affected by drugs administered for plausible reasons. The other is an adaptation of healthy repro-ductive motives to the satisfactions of body and heart, but satisfac-tions without issue. The different directions of these explanations converge because they both deal with primary levels of behavior. They seem constructively obedient to the law of parsimony. They suggest that more than reduced inhibition, more than a change in the courage of individual homosexual men and women, more than just a greater confusion about sex roles and a disdain for tradi-tional ones has been responsible for an evidently larger and more forceful homosexual community than ever.

I have suggested a twofold way of explaining a major sexual change related to the industrial system. The first is straightforward and chemical and is based on the possibility that drugs given to mothers affect their sons. The second emerges from a dominating idea of our economic system, which is that "life-style" is essentially a composite of market choices and forces. Hence, sexual orientation is no more or less than a consumer choice. So men may decide to focus a broad male enthusiasm for sexual variety on other men, not women. The two explanations are related, because they both pertain to the deep stirrings of the human body. And it is surely easy to see how the effect of industrial chemistry can become part-cause of an empowered way of life. New chemicals affect an old chemistry, and the community is different from before.

It is unlikely that the closet in which the newly released people were supposedly confined was ever large enough for their number. Something else, at least, has also been happening. Has the decisively increased control of contraception by women meant that men have lost all paternity certainty, or nearly all? Have those confounded by this chosen a homosexual route for their affections and private ambitions? Do both men and women fear they will find it difficult and costly to become parents of children, children which they may need but the world doesn't? Is sex over?

Not likely. The controversial nature of sex depends on its importance. It is old but newly emerges in each person's life. Unexpectedly, for anyone, another person can come to constitute the answer to life's banality, the encircling arms the locale of confirmed passion, the buzz in the brain the latest chapter in an ancient plan. Ensuring celibacy is a major operation which literally requires eternal vigilance. The flesh is not weak but the opposite —insistent. Do not forget the vaunted head and brain are also organic matter.

What is to be done about this persistent pattern during times that admire change, times of a protean sense of new beginnings? In looking to biology for answers there is an immediate danger, one pointed out by among others Edward O. Wilson: "The trap is the naturalistic fallacy of ethics, which uncritically concludes that what is, should be. The 'what is' in human nature is to a large extent the heritage of a Pleistocene hunter-gatherer existence. When any genetic bias is demonstrated, it cannot be used to justify a continuing practice in present and future environments. Since most of us live in a radically new environment of our own making, the pursuit of such a practice would be bad biology. . . ." (Wilson, in Caplan, ed., 1978, p. 274)

I noted earlier that this leads to confusion between diagnosis and moral recommendation. People concerned with gender policy must not confuse the inheritance of some characteristics of social life with guarantees of their persistence or desirability. New data about the significant archeological record will change its interpretation. Different societies will interpret such materials in the lights of their own traditions and goals.

However, I have tried to argue that there is a major ideological commitment in the industrial communities to the effort to reduce the nature and impact of any sex differences, for the dual reasons of equity and apparent efficiency. If that commitment is based on broadly erroneous assumptions and is therefore likely to fail or be difficult to implement, how does the "communal mind" get changed, if that is possible?

In a small community such as the kibbutz, it is possible for everyone to convene and discuss the issue, weigh the elements of the matter, and arrange for different policies to try for different outcomes. But in huge industrial societies, that town meeting can hardly take place. Changes must originate with or be assisted by the scholarly opinion-leaders with access to the information and some expertise over its interpretation. But people do not often say they are wrong, in particular about issues close to the moral bone, ones about which there is a general ideology.

Occasionally it does happen, with encouraging effect. A case in point. The anthropologist Melford Spiro of the University of California, San Diego, contributed a number of distinguished studies of the kibbutz pattern, using the style of analysis characteristic of the Euro-American social-scientific consensus. Then he returned to review his earlier findings. These, in his words,

> forced upon me a kind of Copernican revolution in my own thinking. ... As a cultural determinist, my aim ... in 1951 was to observe the influence of culture on human nature.... In 1975 I found (against my own intentions) that I was observing the influence of human nature on culture; alternatively, I was observing the resurgence of the old culture (in modern garb) as a function of those elements in human nature that the new culture was unable to change.... For if, as these data suggest, many of the motivational differences between the sexes are precultural, and if, moreover, these differences are more or less accurately reflected in the system of sex-role differentiation presently found in the kibbutz (and in almost every other human

society), then the challenge for scientific inquiry presented by the kibbutz experience is not why . . . (those born in the kibbutz movement) in their system of sex-role differentiation, conform to "human nature" but why the kibbutz pioneers had attempted to undo it. (Spiro, 1979, p. 106)

*   *   *

I have tried to review and account for material suggesting the endurance and significance of differences between males and females, often in major areas of social behavior. These may affect social policy, how individual people decide to run their own lives, and influence people around them. They may directly affect the art form of lives and the economic form of lives. But they may not. One option about sex differences is to work with them to avoid their unwanted consequences. For example, by using the judo principle of turning the aggressive energy of the opponent into the source of one's own control of the battle. "Going with the flow." But, also, knowing where it is likely to go, how fast, and for how long.

In the broad context, what is important is "getting it right." Not in terms of prejudices, affections, fears, inertia, or thoughtless tradition, but in the clear light of the information available.

To do less is in the argument of this book an evil act. As usual not motivated by plain and hot malevolence, but instead by a combination of well-meaning inattention and self-satisfied coercive ideology. The new challenge presented by the fact that so many mothers of young children work, for example, is far more demanding and complex to solve than many of the fairly straightforward technological problems of modern communities. There the answers can be worked out within the technological context in which the problems are produced in the first place. But where people are concerned, children especially, the subtlety and range of variables with which to form a social policy requires the scrutiny and matured decisiveness of the best of town meetings.

Yet, for whatever reason, important evidence about the subject matter has been deliberately withheld from the town meeting. Those participating in the discussion are at a disadvantage. This is an evil result of an effort to change a situation by coercing the discussion of it rather than approaching it realistically. The broad science of psychology, misled from the beginning by Pavlov and his moist-mouthed dogs, provided an implicit service to the economic system that supported it by claiming that nature, even our nature, could be produced, molded, created. The company doctor came through—for the company, not the patient.

As with most forms of denial, this is not sustainable over the long run. The recurrent urgencies and routines of sexual existence continue to affect men and women, their children, and their parents, no matter what magazines say. It is as unlikely that the facts of gender will be altered by attitude-mongering as that male and female bodies can be luxuriously altered as to sex by the surgeon's knife. In effect the whole community has been attending a sex reassignment clinic about its behavior. Now the clinic has been shut down and the former patients are at a loss. It may have been malpractice in the first place to have opened the clinic for business. The facts of flesh were fictionalized, but that story is almost over. The town meeting awaits a full and fair report.

8. Makin' It and Breakin' It

Our Architecture, Our Arms

The mollusk is known by its shell, the ray by its sting, the beaver by its damhouse, the boa by its remorseless grip. What a creature builds, what it destroys, how it destroys, mark it like its face or smell. It is impossible to stroll in the perfect Piazza in Siena, on the street to the main wall in Dubrovnik, or past the graveyards of the Great War in Flanders without a stunning sense of the contrasting forces of human creativity and destructiveness. Or to read about the firebombing of Dresden or Hamburg or listen to careful generals who expect pensions talking about new weapons which can destroy people without disturbing property. Yet there is an apparent discontinuity between the general banality of modern building and design and the remarkable effectiveness of the industries of destruction. What does it say about *Homo industrialis* that his skill at building is generally depressing while his skill at killing is totally terrifying?

How a society shapes nature into material form speaks for it as candidly as its language. What it strives to protect and studies to obliterate are calling cards as well. Sometimes the dual passions of destroying and creating are linked: for example, in atmospheric walled towns such as Carcassonne, or the luxuriously tooled armor of dead kings which stands silently in Les Invalides, that stone-cold museum to war and Napoleon's fury in downtown Paris. There seems to be a walnut of interaction between making and breaking in the scheme of natural things and also in the schemes of people.

I link these two performances because at their extremes they constitute a modern paradox. Banal or thoughtless contemporary architecture is a demoralizing reminder of what well-meaning incompetence can inflict. Contemporary arms manufacture involves processes that are virtually pure technopoetry—perhaps the endpoint of human mastery of the forces of speed and gravity and of the swoop of objects around the world and heavens. The precision of the weapons is almost domestic. A missile can be targeted for a particular building ten thousand miles away. By contrast, a radar survey plane such as the Grumman Hawkeye can inspect over 126,000 square miles of the planet as it makes its watchman's rounds. The development of modern weaponry has been driven by a relentlessly accumulated technique and technologic.

From the viewpoint of individual countries, there is a fierce arms race. But from the perspective of the species, this is the collective work of a group of like-minded people in different centers of action but sharing a common commitment to the improvement of technology they have created. They depend for the pursuit of their art as much on the ingenious threats of their enemy as on the tax dollars collected by their own governments. They are less in a race than an ongoing tournament. Winners and losers need each other to practice their art. An almost farcical symbol of this is Werner von Braun, who managed rocketry research for Hitler and who when their war was coming to an end maneuvered himself in position to be captured by American troops, since he had calculated (correctly, it turned out) that in the United States was he most likely to be able to continue to build sleek objects that went whoosh in the night. Just a hired rocket available to any aggressive Croesus, any Croesus with enough cash for his expensive game of brilliant, beautiful war.

Now I examine the industrial system as it builds things and destroys them. What assumptions of mind and concepts of life does it bring to this? What the system builds seems to boast endless and almost universal attractiveness. Individuals as well as governments go into debt to possess now the objects they can pay for only later. Many of these objects are for explicitly public use —bridges, roads, monuments to ethnic heroes. Such objects concern me little in contrast to those which are for private employment, such as sofas, houses, spoons, and fishtanks.

Why do we build the kind of structures we do? Houses are the largest and costliest objects most people ever own. Then why is there such a paucity of imagination and research-based innovation in housing products? Why are the industrial designers—the folk artists of our system—virtually unknown to the mass of the population which craves their products? Why does the system educating students so poorly and listlessly inform the young about the industrial arts of the old?

Inevitable personal note. Why is a social scientist with no expertise or responsibility in the visual world proposing to segue from the reproductive and kinship systems, his stock in trade, to the built environment, theories about architecture, the impact of things on people?

A bag of reasons. All people have eyes and feelings. The impact of their surroundings is as palpable as the taste and quality of the food they eat and the social relationships they have. Concern about the world of built things is neither confined to museums nor to some special group of *cognoscenti*. Pick up any newspaper and scan the advertisements. Enter any department store to see how much people care about the objects with which they surround themselves, how seriously they treat the issue of what particular style and impact they wish to achieve with their mise-en-scène. A social scientist exploring the forms of social life must also consider the form of the material environment. Another version of a new scholarly concern with "semiotics"—the study of nonverbal, nonliterate forms of human communication.

Consider your own situation. You are surrounded by design. You sit in a chair each contour and surface of which was chosen for its function and its appearance. You reach for a glass. It is a container but also a form someone fashioned. What you are wearing does not just keep you warm and covered. It makes you colorful, austere, it defines you. You switch on your radio or stereo to animate an object whose form has been carefully planned. Perhaps your eyeglasses boast some designer's name on them; they have been affected by someone's idea of what looks good. They are to be seen, as well as to see through. Perhaps that is why you chose them.

You are surrounded by objects created by human beings, yet this environment of yours is as forceful and as aesthetically vigorous as a flowery meadow or a looming rain forest. The industrial world teems with shapes we've made, shapes with not only color and texture but meanings. Seemingly cold and impersonal, it is in truth highly charged. You are surrounded by design, surrounded by significance. If you don't know this, you might as well be blind in an art gallery or reading Braille with giant sheepskin gloves. Many people suffer illiteracy in the three dimensions, they are foreigners in their own sensual city.

A legacy of the Puritan passion for austerity and chronic self-denial? The result of a sense that attractiveness is not only morally destabilizing but also expensive, even though it may well cost as much to make an ugly object as a handsome one? The result of a view that it is morally superior to endure spartan aesthetic conditions rather than lush ones which may be called "decadent"?

What caused the loss of the lust of the eye?

The behavior of children and other primates affirms that a basic predisposition and capacity for visual pleasure exist in an almost cellular sense. The way some things smell good, others look good. Many years ago when Desmond Morris was Curator of Mammals at the London Zoo, he introduced a local chimpanzee, Congo, to the craft of painting. The animal relished the task, produced works which were successfully put on sale, made decisions about color and form which it could be argued were categorically similar to those made by human nonfigurative child-artists. He became more annoyed when interrupted from painting than from any other activity of his daily round, including eating.

This was controversial in the art world. Enemies of abstract painting saw confirmed their worst prejudices about the quality and value of a style of work they detested. However, Joan Miró evidently offered Morris one of his works in exchange for an original Congo. Pablo Picasso was asked by a journalist whether he saw any interesting value in the experiment with chimpanzee art. Picasso turned. Left the room. Reentered it swinging his arms low to the ground the way chimps do. Bit the interviewer on the shoulder. And left. End of interview.

Animal stories are not necessary to claim that human beings enjoy visual stimuli and are capable of sophisticated views on the quality and interest of what they see, even if they have not been formally trained. What is often called "primitive art" is essentially the work of members of communities which may not be literate, with no scholastic tradition of stimulating and evaluating artwork. The work is done because people have always done it or it is fun to do. Probably both. It sizzles without benefit of academic support or adjudication. What pain is to medicine, ugliness is to the design professions. Agreeable design—natural design—can achieve the force and insight of "primitive art" in contemporary design. And reduce the pain of the eye.

This becomes particularly important in industrial communities where on the face of it there is easy reason to assume that the machine which makes things must also be the model of what is made. The industrial mode of production should determine the aesthetic nature of what is consumed. This was the Bauhaus in its extreme form—a group which sought aesthetic purity in the linear formality of art and architecture married to the machine and the rational ideas nourishing it. Or the Socialist thinkers who saw in industry a way to democratize standards of taste and make the products of socially responsible design available cheaply and without folderol to the masses.

There are a miscellany of approaches to the relationship between art and the machine. But what about the people in the thick of the relationship—the industrial designers who stand between, or link, the user and the industrial product? Let us assume that industrial designers somehow represent similar energies and social functions as folk artists do. They occupy themselves with the events, objects, and processes of daily life, and strive to make these more interesting, amusing, or memorable as well as useful for people. Their basic aim is, somehow, to take what is ordinary and necessary and add an element of luxury and art. This needn't be expensive. Ideally, it shouldn't be. The design should reflect commitment to the well-being of the communal eye, and a sense of the healthy and even entertaining value of the object to the user.

I took an opportunity afforded me by a publication to visit and talk with a number of influential and effective industrial designers in North America and Europe. Conversation with some eleven individuals hardly qualifies as even the beginning of a sample of the profession of industrial designer. Nevertheless, the people were all vivid and assertive. They conveyed a strong flavor of the world in which they worked.

It is a world in which all the designers felt beleaguered and underappreciated. Yet these were people with substantial and in some cases dramatic accomplishment—designers such as Dieter Rams of Braun in Germany; Ettore Sottsass of Milan, who had worked on the Olivetti line of office machines and more recently the Memphis Group of home furnishings; Sir Terence Conran of the shops which bear his name; Allen Fletcher of Pentagram, the busy design consultancy; Michael Lax of New York, who has designed products for Salton and Copco among many other clients; Robert Gersin, whose firm has designed overall programs for companies such as A & P and Sears; Massimo Vignelli, whose firm has worked worldwide and who has been president of the International Design Council; and Takenobu Igarishi, a major contributor to Japanese design and graphic art.

What had they to say? They were unanimous in complaining that their professions lacked autonomy. They were hard-pressed to produce work which met their own high standards. The Europeans complained that because of the relatively small—perhaps 50,000—production runs of what they designed, they could not engage in adventurous design; the Americans had all the luck in this respect. However, the Americans claimed that because their production runs were so large, manufacturers were reluctant to commit to two or three million copies of an object without extensive market research and other skeptical controls that inhibited lively and creative design.

Which position is correct? Or are both? Or perhaps neither— the interpretation to which I lean. It seems the reason for the tension designers generally feel about their work lies in the gulf between themselves and their clients, and the relative design illiteracy of the community for which they work. I was told by Lou Dorfsman, who as Director of Design for CBS was one of the most effective designers at the higher reaches of U.S. corporate industry, that for the most part people who managed companies were unable to understand the importance of design beyond its surface implication. Vignelli said they hardly appreciated the economic value of good design. In part this was because they were untrained in the area. Only at the Business School of the University of Hartford did Dorfsman know (in 1983) of an American business program which dealt with all elements of design and architecture as an intrinsic feature of the whole management process. Elsewhere, design was part of a separate, discrete course of study. Allen Fletcher, a senior partner of Pentagram, which is located mainly in London but also New York, informed me: "I am compelled to describe my work to a client as cheap, efficient, easy to manufacture, simple to repair, anything but beautiful. You never say the product looks good. You're dealing with people whose design age is twelve. The last thing you talk about is design to people who've hired you as a designer. So we talk vigorously to each other. We're an international fraternity, like the original Freemasons who made churches. They'd recognize each other anywhere. We're rather like that and are amongst ourselves rather forceful. You can't be a quiet bloody designer."

My miniature survey of designers bore that out. This was a group of boldly formed and assertive people. Even Dieter Rams fit the pattern, Rams who had been the design force behind the Braun Company whose products have been internationally celebrated for their crisp, lucid, and confident form. As Rams himself said in a public lecture: "We are not simply a company like many others. We are *the* Company which—in 1955—dared the sensational breakthrough into a new dimension in design. . . . In 1955 Braun had sales of 50.5 million DM and today . . . sales totalling more than 700 million DM." Yet Rams claims that he wants his objects to fade into the background when they are not in use, to perform their work with the least possible disruption of the universe. Rams himself lives in a Bauhausian world of punctiliously completed fine lines and inhabits a dwelling colored only by white, shades of gray, and black, except for plants. Nevertheless, as Ettore Sottsass said about him, "He is really a poet though he will deny it." Despite his carefully tailored subtle clothing, his precise office and highly organized demeanor, the sense of explosiveness in the man begins to be felt once he slides behind the wheel of his Porsche and with a practiced eye for where speedtraps lurk, races into Frankfurt. Our appointment, which had been made for two in the afternoon, spun on for twelve hours, through talk in the factory, in the design studio, in the car, then in the shop in Frankfurt which sells the furniture Rams designs, then through dinner at nearby Restaurant Adloff (perhaps Frankfurt's premier table), and then back to the furniture showroom, the whiskey bottle, the always probing talk. At 2:00 a.m. this undergraduate-revolutionary conversation ended. No light matter, this design.

At first it seemed lighter in the scheme of things of Ettore Sottsass, who greeted me in a burly jacket of Italian workman's blue at the door of his color-strewn atelier on a Milanese street. Though his appearance is soft and his manner is Mastroianni-mild, Sottsass's line of argument is tough if curvilinear, and his perception of what designers should do firm if also paradoxical. Yes, he says, design should not be consistent because it must reflect an inconsistent society. Systematic theories are coercive because they misrepresent an unsystematic society. Hence there must be willed disorder, a celebration of the inappropriate. Only that can

301

do design justice to the social reality. There is no excuse for making all television sets look only like television sets. Some should look like little cheap nightclubs, as glitzy, chintsy, and shallowly fashionable as much of what they purvey. In the Memphis furniture and artifact line he helped inspire, a colorful garden of congenially surrealistic objects innocently explodes the process of daily life, turning a bed into a mock boxing ring, a chest of drawers into an Egyptian icon, a lamp into a florid punctuation point. Fun though all this is, it is also a highly designed comment about the philosophical irrelevance or superfluity of design. While Dieter Rams wants his designs to merge indistinguishably with the stream of life so as to deemphasize design, Sottsass shows how arbitrary it is and how colorfully unexpected industrial design potentially can be. A garden of tropical-flower form.

These two seemingly disparate designers are united by a fully thought-out dissatisfaction with their wider role in the society of which they are actually privileged and esteemed members. They are folk artists who claim to be unconvinced by both their artistry and the folk of which they are part. Henry Drexler, Curator for Architecture and Design at the Museum of Modern Art in New York, asserted in a conversation that the design field is in general disarray, with no integrating standards, no overall perspective that functions in the industrial field. He cited the example of the Japanese, who have not themselves employed any of the indigenous brilliance of their traditional design in their industrial products but have instead engaged designers following an international style. I myself bought a tapedeck made by Yamaha of Japan in good part because of its intriguing triangular shape—produced by the Italian master Mario Bellini, whose signature actually adorns the object. Later I learned from Ettore Sottsass that this was the result of a careful marketing plan by these manufacturers to distinguish their products from the competition by packaging attractive to North American enthusiasts for design. The tapedeck is pretty, and perhaps there is no traditional Japanese way of housing tape equipment. But perhaps there is. It is significant that technological objects internationally receive a relatively stereotyped treatment by designers. There seems little effort to integrate them into the traditional cultural patterns of the communities in which they are used and produced. Evidently the technical forces of modern production coerce what the eye is able to see no matter where or by whom the objects in question are produced and used. The international style may be less a style than an outgrowth. In any event, I learned from Igarishi that the Bellini tapedeck is now virtually unattainable in Japan and is regarded as a classic treasure of contemporary design. It is in fact on display at the Museum of Modern Art in New York. Few designs matter. Those that do stand out.

Why? In so-called primitive societies, objects of daily use are often invested with ritual meaning and formal importance. They communicate. They do so also in our own society, even if we are hardly aware of it. If industrial designers are the folk artists of the industrial system, they must assert themselves in as sharply etched a manner as Fletcher, Rams, Sottsass reveal.

If designers are such assertive people, perhaps it is because they must endure a compound struggle—to create the function which they must then advertise themselves as being able to perform. Sottsass describes his luck in becoming associated with the scion of the Olivetti family who was fascinated by design and who wished to work closely with him. A similar relationship existed in the Braun organization, when the son of the founder turned his talent to good design just as his father had turned to good engineering. Igarishi in Japan was significantly aided by his college connection with the son of the owner of the giant Suntory Brewing Company.

But these were lucky links. Indeed for even successful designers, without a patron the struggle remains. Allen Fletcher noted it was rare for an English designer to earn more than £25,000 to £50,000—those at the top of their profession. In France, he noted —his view was corroborated by the Parisian architect and designer Marc Held—it is virtually impossible for a free-lance industrial designer to make a living solely and full time at industrial design. Is it not puzzling that in such an elaborately sentient society as France, those who shape the very products which are at the essence of the productive system are so poorly rewarded? Compare them with cooks or designers of clothes.

The issue goes beyond France. It is pertinent to recall Marshall McLuhan's curiously generous statement in *Understanding Media* (1963) that one generation's technology is the next generation's art form. Witness the affection people newly feel for old machines, for restoring industrial buildings of the last century and turning them into chic lofts for pop singers of the present one. For bestowing cultural imprimatur on sweatshop factories of historical Paterson, New Jersey, or milltowns in France or restored centers of European cities. There is an appreciation of the mellow confidence about form their creators evidently enjoyed. Perhaps such advocacy of the past is a rebuke to the builders of the present, a vote for the old-style style.

But why care or bother about whether design is good or bad, honest or deceptive, flamboyant or seemly? To repeat: perhaps ugliness is to design and architecture as pain is to medicine. Concern for how industrial civilization looks has been an important feature of the politics of the eye since it began. An influential statement of the classical position was made by William Morris in a famous lecture on *The Beauty of Life* given at the Town Hall, Birmingham, in 1880. He spoke of the "danger that the present course of civilization will destroy the beauty of life," and that "the civilized world" will forget "that there had ever been an art *made by the people for the people as a joy to the maker and the user.*" He struck the populist note that "You cannot educate, you cannot civilize men, unless you can give them a share in art." In an early minimalist response to the proliferating production of crass and ghastly objects swamping the dwellings of England, Morris firmly abjured both poor design and *knick-knackerei:* "Have nothing in your homes that you do not know to be useful, or believe to be beautiful."

Belief in the ennobling, even redemptive value of beautiful and appropriate objects and arts is deeply rooted in this and other cultures. It is part of the animating force behind the world of museums and the educational outreach from once-elite institutions. A hundred years after Morris spoke in Birmingham, the design firm Pentagram published an account of its activities called *Living by Design.* This belief in art and artfulness is hardly casual. It is seen as having a purpose over and above the pleasure, surprise, or excitement it may provoke. It is frequently accompanied by the strong feeling that not only is good design desirable in its own right but it is also a metaphor for and a symptom of larger things to come—again the politics of the eye.

An influential manifesto about architecture produced by Team Ten in 1968 offers a clear statement of relationship between objects and large social process: "One has, for example, a perfectly clear notion of the sort of city and sort of society envisaged by Mies van der Rohe, even though he never said much about it. It is not an exaggeration to say that the Miesian city is implicit in the

Mies chair." (Smithson, ed., 1968) To paraphrase Mao Zedong, a city grows out of the mouth of a chair.

To the influential Marxist architectural critic Manfredo Tafuri, the corrupting impact of capitalism is linked to rationality itself. Architecture is a consenting accomplice in violating the rights of people in this politics of the eye: "Architecture . . . is always creation *against* nature; its history is the story of the subjection of nature to the constructive activity of the ruling classes." (Tafuri, p. 185) It is in his view hopeless to try to create in architecture or design a version of the didactic painting, literature, and drama of various assertive governments ranging from the Chinese and Stalinist Communist to Boy Scout camp songs to the strident political posters of regime after regime. He dismisses the classical view, itself caricatured by Ada Louise Huxtable: "Architects sincerely believed that health and happiness were the natural corollaries of the right way of building; they even believed that human nature could be conditioned or changed by the right physical environment. This was the century that equated art, technology, and virtue, and concluded that the better life, and the better world, were finally within our grasp." (Huxtable, 1981) A view which, as Robert Stern of Columbia University has described it, "sees architecture as built ideology and that unquestionably conflates the history of modernism in architecture with that of moral virtue in the past 100 or 150 years." (Stern, 1981, p. 22)

The disillusionment when such grandiose ambitions fail seems inevitable in retrospect, and perhaps alienation of a bitterer intensity too. As the Canadian architect and designer Norman Parker told me, after the Second World War he shared the belief in the relationship between good design and a better world. Now he concludes that much effort of his colleagues is devoted to producing attractive objects which consumers do not need, to build in obsolescence when raw resources are apparently in increasingly short supply. He seemed to regard the designer as a kind of maitre d' to the industrial factory, inviting in the client and having him order more than he needs, more expensively than he should.

By contrast, the English designer and entrepreneur Sir Terence Conran saw the problem as the result of an excess of theory. Of the French, he said, "Le Corbusier was a disaster from whom the French have not recovered." Conran's own strategy has been to take well-designed objects and make them available at relatively low prices with a convincing and "safe" presentation: "You cannot buy what is not available and too expensive." He considered solving the problem of easing buyers into the purchase of firmly designed objects a major challenge because of their timidity and lack of understanding of the impact of form. Interestingly, his major commercial success has been in France, where his enterprise perches midway between the expensive shops for the elite who purchase high-design items and the mass market which purveys objects of indeterminate aesthetic meaning. Nevertheless, even Conran's success raises some hackles in the design field, a contentiousness that corresponds to the internecine professional acrimony of architects whose evident response to the absence of a unifying sense of professional agreement is in part to develop strong sectarian positions. These may or may not connect to the lives of those who use their products. But they become strongly identified with what is something like a brand name.

It is understandable, perhaps desirable, that different voices are heard in the ongoing seminar about design. After all, the objects may be extraordinarily costly. But there is an apparent lack of congenial mutual prosperity among the practitioners of the various trades who together produce the shapes and processes that characterize the industrial way. Perhaps one reason is the relatively noncumulative, nonresearch-based nature of architecture in particular. I have always thought of any building as an experiment which could be tested and whose impact could be evaluated. However, budgets for a building rarely include funds for systematic evaluation of how it works, and what it means to the people who must use it for the purposes to which it was directed. In a discussion on the subject, the architect Moshe Safdie of the Graduate School of Design at Harvard affirmed that hardly any such provisions were taken into account in the design phase, and that it was far from the concern of any architect to consider the broad testability of the social uses of his or her work.

A curiosity of the industrial system which is founded on the scientific method is that it does not in architecture rely on that method to assess its activities. For example in the way the medical profession does, when it creates a case history on a patient and follows the course of illness and treatment to evaluate the efficacy of the medical intervention provided. I am not referring to testing of materials, forms of structure. This is a well-developed field of expertise, in which cumulative experience and the cautionary lessons of time are brought directly to bear on new projects. But more where physical materials are concerned than social patterns. Architects build considerable redundancy into their plans so that the possibility of disaster is sharply reduced by the exercise of broad human prudence. In this context, it is interesting—even striking—that the collapse of walkways in a Hyatt Hotel in Kansas City with much loss of life occurred in one of the first major structures whose architectural and engineering tolerances and safety factors were created by a computer program designed to produce a building with minimal redundancy and hence maximal economy. It turned out that the clumsy cumulativeness of the safety margins preferred by humans, with our imagination of disaster, could have made the difference between a tragedy and a sturdy, useful structure. For some reason, this reminds me of a far more benign problem raised in conversation by the concert pianist Byron Janis, who preferred pianos tuned by people operating with their ears alone rather than with newly available electronic tuners that yield a perfect result. In the deeper notes produced by three separate strings, perfect tuning of all three reduces the warmth and interest of their sound. The overall tone of the piano is flat and its artistic usefulness restrained—technical perfection is boring.

Elements of fashion and social conventions significantly affect the choices made by the designers of buildings and built things when they create our world. Even particular colors, let alone shapes and arrangements, may be determined by the dominating mode of the moment. Designing is among other things a business. Its practitioners will have to respond to the marketplace. Nevertheless, a commanding undertow in the industrial scheme takes all lesser currents with it eventually: the Modern Style. It no longer reigns without question. But it continues to reflect a mechanical conception of form, and embraces the technical advantages available to users of the modes of manufacture and planning that flow from technically precise systems of producing and building. I once had the ambivalent fortune to tour Brasilia, the new capital city of Brazil carved out of the inland jungle of a country which has historically striven to open its interior regions, often at great cost. It is a city of tall government buildings and controlled apartments of either three or six stories, all so spaciously situated that citizens say they must be born with three main body parts—their heads, their bodies, and their cars. It also appeared to me to be tryingly uninteresting, arbitrary, and almost mad in a sterile way. My point here is to recall that a Brazilian friend asked me after the tour if I had seen the most important building in the city. Which one was that, I asked. The house that the architect of all this, Oscar Niemeyer, lived in. It was a one-story, traditional Spanish villa, as different as could be from the zut-moderne epic Niemeyer concocted when he was at his drawing board. Evidently what he wanted. For himself. What he built for others is a collection of formidable buildings set among ample parkland, as if the city were an uneasy compromise between the urbanity of a great nation's capital and the jungle that surrounds it.

Among others, Jane Jacobs has argued "that the emphasis on parks displays a concealed hostility to the city and its works. The local conclusion of this hostility—the tower block rising without neighbors out of a park without streets—was embraced by Le Corbusier, and preached to the world with an inflammatory rhetoric. . . ." (cited in Scruton, 1984, p.9) The hostility is not only to the city and its work but to the inhabitants and their works—to the buzzily dense character of cities, and perhaps even more to the socially intricate conviviality of the ongoing world of *Homo sapiens.* This is a broad result of an unself-conscious rejection or avoidance of human biosocial nature, a nature foreign to the right angle, the straight line, and the repeated regularity of forms built in the aesthetic vocabulary of the machine—the machine which couldn't care less about repetition and indeed is better adapted to it than to variety.

But people are less tolerant of repetition than machines, and are in striking physical contrast with the angular, linear world of machines. We are round and soft in our bodies and variable in our movements. Our way of using time and energy is highly irregular in contrast with machines. Hence the Machine Style appears highly inappropriate as the commanding model with which to build our world. Nevertheless, it has been the supervisory conception for many long years because of the tantalizing coherence and seeming progressiveness of the industrial model. That it is ceasing to be so is without question. However, there is no evident replacement for it in the world of design. Perhaps there should not be.

Architects have designed workplaces where no natural light penetrates, where windows can be neither opened nor closed, and where inhabitants must oppose endless sameness with their own messy idiosyncrasies of high school banners and baby pictures pasted on firmly color-coordinated walls. Why expect any greater sensitivity to the broader social variation and flow of human groups? The best zoos provide settings for animals as close as possible to those in which they evolved and thrive. But the fundamental questions about human nature are not so easily answered, particularly in an era that would almost rather not have any answers. It is therefore understandable that the all-powerful machine should have so thoroughly suffused the design professions with the lesson of its logic and its sovereign impartiality.

But what about biologic? Are people ever impartial to their surroundings? Of course not. Norman Mailer has shared his personal rule, which is that if he is in one building and there is another across the street which is fifteen years older, the older one will likely be more pleasing. This may be so. The perception that it is so is vibrant and durable. Why? Does progress not extend to the eye? Is the machine a subversive influence over the normal curvilinearity of the species? Is it inevitable that a wealth of things is accompanied by poverty of their shape? Are members of the design world self-deluding collaborators with an intrinsically inhumane system, at least in aesthetics? Or has the system broadly rounded a corner, to return to a more comforting, tastier scheme, now that the prophets of machine-shape have lost their franchise on perfection and the ideologues of mise-en-scène their assertions of authority?

A sign of how strongly people feel about their artifacts is how they react when what they have made is destroyed.

The Embrace of Arms

In the fourth century B.C., armorers serving the dictator Dionysius of Syracuse in Sicily invented the catapult. The machine used counterweights, twisted rope, and stressed wood, thus literally leveraging some available materials of the time. It could throw missiles over fortified walls into towns, it could break down those walls, it could kill people at distances of hundreds of yards with impressively and devastatingly heavy objects. This was all hardly reassuring to potential enemies of Syracuse; it was fiercely irritating to people living in towns which had been hitherto relatively invulnerable because of their fortifications. Warfare has continued to be deeply conjoined with technology since.

By comparison with the catapult, a crude and definite danger, contemporary warfare has become staggeringly complex and yet also mysteriously theoretical. To the outsider, the sophistication of modern weaponry is so elaborately linked to the precise exploitation of physical principles that the complexities of warfare may appear to be analogues of some inner complexity of the natural world itself. Military operations have become super-sensitive, super-devastating, super-secret, endlessly intricate. Unless it was night, and perhaps even on many nights, a fortress guard could see a catapult moving into range, see the projectile as it flew, and easily understand the human movements necessary to throw the object and protect against it. Sometimes this is still the case, but more often the techniques are enhanced almost beyond comprehension. So the Grumman E-2C or "Hawkeye" surveillance plane is able to keep electronic watch over 126,000 square miles of water or land. Flying at an altitude of 30,000 feet, it can be programmed to track some 600 air targets, if necessary each tracking process attuned to the rhythm of a different drummer.

In a real war such as over Lebanon in 1982, this meant that the Israeli Air Force had jet fighters constantly flying to a predetermined pattern near Haifa in northern Israel. The moment any Syrian aircraft moved ten feet off the ground, a Hawkeye noted its position and began calculating its speed and route. One of the patrol jets in an appropriate location was assigned to supervise the rising aircraft while its missiles were automatically locked on to the potential intruder. Should certain predetermined critical points be reached in the flight pattern, the computer decided to fire. If all worked to plan, one life and sensibility would be destroyed and an aircraft costing millions of dollars of human resources would fall flaming into the desert. In the Lebanon battle, this happened seventy-nine times.

After the bizarre war in the Falkland Islands, there was controversy over the extent to which French technicians assisted the Argentine Air Force in launching Exocet missiles from Argentinian aircraft at British ships. Perhaps French advisers did supervise the aircraft which released the missile which skimmed the waves and then struck and sank the British destroyer *Sheffield*. Perhaps there were no French people directly involved or physically present. But the overriding reality is that they might as well have been. Designer, builder, salesman, buyer, user, and victim of the Exocet transaction were all locked in a convulsive international intimacy that began with physical principles, commercial programs, and military intentions. It ended with violated bodies, the reality of mortal combat, and a new military money-calculus in which a $250,000 device destroyed a floating community costing at least $50 million to build. And, irony of irony, because the British armaments industry was itself responsible for some 15 percent of the construction of the missile, then in part the British sailors were destroyed by their own military-industrial complex.

The disproportion had escalated between the small scope of the decision to push the blast-off button liberating the Exocet, and the human consequences of that decision. It seemed at the time to be a graphic symptom of a quantum leap in the efficacy and danger of burgeoning military technology, even of the nonnuclear variety. But as the folk commentator said, "You ain't seen nothing yet." The fiery reality is that the technical brilliance, military capacity, and economic cost of weapons systems continue to burgeon and increasingly dominate the technological forces of rich and needy societies alike. But the physical frailty of people and the vulnerability of the human social world are the same as they have always been. They have not changed in a manner or degree commensurate with the methods available to defend them. What so nutritiously feeds this vast and encompassing process is the technological system itself. The servant system has become the master builder. It is all the more prepossessing because it remains theoretically subservient to the lords of politics.

Command Takes Mechanization

Earlier I referred to Siegfried Giedion's *Mechanization Takes Command* (1969). Now I want to explore the impact of technology on military activity in the context of what appears to be the relentless expansiveness of an already overwhelmingly dangerous and expensive sector of the world community. It is a banal truism that the destructive capacity of the existing military machines of the great and moderate powers is unimaginably beyond the scope of the targets they could possibly in practice have—there is only one globe. The cost of the systems in place and those planned is acknowledged to be near or beyond the outer limit by all but a handful of particularly zealous or fearful planners and politicians. Nevertheless, the growth in cost and capacity appears almost surreal, as if the armament process received its life orders from a different quality of genetic code than the other rigmaroles of life.

There is no need here to document the force and extent of the military machine in the world's arrangements. It is more interesting intellectually and possibly more useful to explore why military expenditure is so attractive for governments, even when the security these expenditures provide is so closely tied to the expenditures of similar if opposed governments. When, in arm's length intimacy, both pro and con military forces may depend for their existence as much upon the threateningness of each other as the strategic generosity of their countrymen.

The Big Arms Race and the smaller ones are bathed in the analytical comfort which acknowledged competition provides. Not only that. The technological system creates its own rules and thus the games that are playable within them: If we possess X weapon, then obviously they must develop an X-plus weapon, to which we will inevitably find a generally adequate reply. The mutually interdependent competition is abetted by dark-colorful spies whose task is to gain an advantage over the enemy by learning something they do not want to reveal.

But the overall impact of spies, since we must assume the spies of competitive nations are competitively adept, is to both equalize and accelerate the races by spreading technological information wherever it is relevant. In addition, there are double and triple agents, neo-spies who are simply entrepreneurs selling facts as a prohibited substance, the impact of normal trade and commerce in processes and products, and the massive amount of information which life itself generates, all adding to the general if unspoken collegiality. And this unites the military technologists with their enemy/opposite numbers. Like artists whose work will be best appreciated by their fellow artists whatever their nationality, defense scientists are scientists still, members of a defined if informal freemasonry of skill and enthusiasm, presumably an unusually exciting one because of the drama and high stakes of the quest they share. "Dr. Malevich is an arms scientist's arms scientist."

Technology is not neutral in its impact on the emotions. Old-fashioned steam engines had one effect, the Olivetti Lettera 22 portable typewriter another. The physical form of the industrial world is one of its most endlessly influential and imposing features. Its landscape is right-angled, skyscrapered, neon-lit, motor-noisy. Since the industrial world took hold, the domestic artifacts of the world of armament have been among the most drab and prosaic of objects. Olive green cloth, shined but serviceable boots, the plainest decor, all deliberately austere. Weapons are drably painted, designed with function never pleasure in mind, unlike the elegant artifacts for violence of even the Upper Paleolithic tenants of Europe's caves.

Nevertheless, the dull military function can be superindustrial and super-imposing too. During a television program shown after his assassination, there was a film clip of John F. Kennedy on the deck of an aircraft carrier at a demonstration of an aircraft prototype seeking a home in the Pentagon budget. As it swooped and snarled, an utterly improbable new form of bird, the effect was drastic and phenomenally dramatic. I recall thinking at the time how persuasive was the display, and the object, and how difficult if not impossible it would be for a lively, aggressive President to avoid a surge of enthusiasm for the onrushing object and its remarkable defiance of the known laws of physical motion. Such weapons are virtually a form of technopoetry, an art form of the tough-minded. Is there evidence about the aesthetic attraction of weapons? Presumably the principal reason governments buy weapons is that they are afraid of the danger of not doing so and of being invaded or destroyed by an enemy. But practical reasons do not altogether explain the apparent bias for purchases of expensive and dramatic high-tech materiel in contrast to mundane domestic expenditures such as for replacement parts, salaries, housing, footwear, and so on.

Technopoetry seduces.

Free Trade, Expensive Product

It is understandable that communities in the full flush of aggressive technical creation, at the cutting and killing edge of military technique, will invest in products that are triumphs of their own culture. Weapons represent their best technical accomplishments. The machinery is of a piece with the lives of its makers and users, an indigenous art form. More puzzling, perhaps more revealing, of the attractiveness of weaponry is the enthusiasm of governments whose own populations are remote from the technological plateaus on which high-tech armament is made. As military equipment has become more complex and expensive, it has also evidently stimulated more governments to spend more money on it than ever. Supply appears to create demand. Imports of weapons to the Third World rose in value from $6.2 billion in 1969 to $15.5 billion in 1978 and probably by an additional 50 percent by 1984 —all this reckoned in constant dollars.

Not only has the extent of the trade changed, but so has its nature. In the past, mainly obsolete weapons were traded—the cast-offs of former wars and used surplus weapons. During the colonial period, some weapons were explicitly developed for colonial wars; for example, the French developed the "Modèle 1902" rifle for use in Indochina. The British were by 1860 sending some 100,000 to 150,000 guns a year from Birmingham to West Africa to be used by slave stealers and vendors. The stark effect of powerful weapons on the wars between American Indians and whites is also well known. Incidentally, such arms movements could backfire for their makers. Essentially, the First World War was fought with weapons developed by France, Belgium, Germany, and Britain in forty years of colonial wars—the only wars they had been fighting. Coerced by technology as well as the theory of warfare of the time, the nations tried the same techniques and strategy in the First World War as in the colonies. Going "over the top" of the hill to fire at Dervishes or Sudanese could and did succeed. But leaving the trenches in the same way in Flanders was literally suicidal. The vast deathroll of the First World War, its legacy of meadows of graves, reflect the inappropriate application of military technology and concepts from one situation to another.

Looking backward was a hazardous military pose for arms importers in the past. Looking to the future may prove as hazardous in the present and the future. Extensive lists of the dead may be the unwanted result of undue enthusiasm for the most advanced weapons in societies whose social structures and economies, to say nothing of military requirements, are broadly unsuited to them. The military technologies of governments whose strategic scope is planetary and even interplanetary will inevitably be of a complexity out of scale and disruptive to governments with military concerns such as border protection. Literally, the problem of overkill. Rather like a Burmese small farmer installing a nuclear engine in his oxcart.

It appears that even if there is no compelling reason of clear military danger, the blandishments of technology and a sense of modernity are sufficient to stimulate advanced weaponry to spread quite beyond the military requirements which a matter-of-fact military judgment should compel. Not only that. The selling of weapons is no lighthearted matter. The advertising pages of the trade publications of the arms industry as eagerly coax Ministers of Defense as cosmeticians court teenagers. There are obvious compelling reasons for independent companies to try to sell their wares abroad. But governments too may have a vital interest in spreading the development costs of weapons over as many units as possible, and ideally many of these should be sold abroad. As Thomas Friedman wrote in *The New York Times:* "As the cost of sophisticated military hardware escalates, arms manufacturers are seeking foreign orders more than ever to raise their output and thereby keep unit prices affordable. This trend . . . raises the disturbing question of whether the industrial powers will be able to afford to arm themselves in the coming decade without arming the rest of the world at the same time." (Friedman, 1982) There are undoubtedly foreign policy implications for many of these sales, and clear ideological justification for a variety of them.

President Dwight Eisenhower's prophetic warning about the military-industrial complex evidently applied well beyond the borders of the United States of America. This is not surprising given the striking intimacy between countries that technology has made possible and also inevitable.

Such macrostructural considerations may seem less important than the fact that even if a community's only enemy is the modest despotism across the river, the existence or even rumor of a brilliant missile invites a costly look at the bulging catalogue of machines of retaliation. When heads of state meet and talk shop about their store of military materiel, surely it is awkward for the one with the oldest and least exciting array. Perhaps more awkward than admitting to poor dental clinics or an undeveloped program in intermediate math courses.

The result is likely to be that a poor country's government will experience its most costly and significant contact with advanced technology through warfare. The extent to which poor countries buy expensive weapons suggests that this is so. As Ruth Sivard wrote in 1980 about a planet-wide situation: "For the eighth year in a row world military expenditures increased faster than the rate of inflation." (Sivard, 1980, p. 5) The unequal classic contest between guns and butter is played for higher stakes.

The preeminence of military technology redefines the notion of what science can do, which scientists should do it, and to what end. Inevitably, secrecy and seclusion accompany military activity. This means any educational or modernizing influence of military-scientific endeavor is lost on people at large. Nevertheless, they may experience an uneasy mixture of feelings of protection by their government and sheer terror at the destructiveness of the weaponry from which they are supposedly being shielded. The impact of the military-industrial complex will go beyond the money spent and goods and services provided. It may alter how communities perceive science and the value of independent intellect in a complicated world. World and world view are at risk.

The Mender Gap

Advanced military technology is perhaps the extreme version of a common problem: complicated machines are introduced into a community and used for a while but when they break as they inevitably will who will fix them? Someone experienced in the foreign aid world once told a seminar at the Aspen Institute the story of Peruvian anchovy fishermen who through an aid program had been given powerful and sophisticated outboard motors with which to work. However, the aid officers began to notice the new outboards lying in disuse on the docks while the old machines they were supposed to replace commanded a premium price. The simple reason was the newer machines had preprogrammed microelectronic components impossible for the local people to repair. The old-fashioned machines were simple to repair and thus more desirable. In principle this should be a manageable problem to solve, but evidently in practice it is not. As Arnold Pacey has carefully noted, the complex cultural values which surround technological approaches do not exist broadly enough in the receiving communities. (Pacey, 1984)

Where weaponry is concerned, the people facing the problem lack even the direct and material incentives fishermen have for getting boats on the water and fish into them. The challenge for the soldier is relatively theoretical. It is more abstractly linked to the official military career, the threats of superior officers, and how much the individual is fascinated with the machine. Technology can be inherently interesting and lures countless people into its orbit just as artworks do. In the military world, there is obvious practicality in learning all about machines which may help save not only the lives and welfare of their operators but of their countrymen and women too. Nevertheless, when military technology is considerably more sophisticated than the ambient local circumstances, there is an obvious discontinuity between the world at work and the world at large. Which can readily stimulate the growth of an elite and independent military cadre.

The technological gap between troops and maintenance crews and the sophistication and frailty of the best modern weapons is most pronounced when the machinery is imported to countries unfamiliar with the social and scientific assumptions on which the weapons are based. This problem is not confined to disparities caused by international differences. Within the U.S. military itself, the difficulty of instructing recruits in the whys, ways, and wherefores of weapons systems has mounted. The literacy level of incoming recruits declines while the demands of the machines they must use gather force and intensity. So while in past years, as we have seen, the training manuals of the U.S. Army assumed a tenth-grade reading level, these vital books are now being rewritten for people only able to master the sixth grade. This adjustment reflects the underlying situation produced by the uneasy mixture of average people and tightrope-poised technology. In the USSR, the growing population of citizens of Oriental origin and relatively declining numbers of Russian-born have posed an acknowledged challenge to the Russian military. It has to train recruits about complicated equipment in the dominant national language, Russian. This may well be their second language—which is comforting to neither friend nor foe. One remedy has been to restrict responsible jobs and senior posts in technologically based units to Russian-born personnel. But it is recognized that this is an unstable situation in the short run and intolerable in the long.

Here is another version of the overarching phenomenon that military technology is so complex and decisions about its use must be made so quickly that human beings can no longer act in the heat of the moment. The broad decisions must be made before the fact, by writing computer programs which will determine what still other machines will do. No person can calculate the forces, speeds, trajectories, winds, and so on that affect what happens in warfare. In a multitude of situations, even highly trained personnel are obligated to wait on the deliberations of computers. As if people had made gods and stipulated the rules the gods were to apply. But then they came to lose their autonomy. They had to subserve a process of their own creation. With their new colleague General Frankenstein, Ph.D.

It is remarkable that governments put out so much tax money on military expenditures producing relatively little visible impact on the lives of taxpayers. They may never or rarely see the guns, particularly if they are secret. They may enjoy very little butter. Nevertheless, the spending races proceed. Politicians who crave schools and hospitals for their constituents will somehow vote for wealth to be fired off into space and hidden in unbelievably complicated and expensive installations performing military functions far from obvious to the lay observer.

There is no question that fear of enemies known and unknown is an important stimulus for this politically odd behavior. However, as Sir Solly Zuckerman has argued,

> A new and anxious future was shaped by technologists, not because they were concerned with any visionary picture of how the world should evolve, but because they were merely doing what they saw to be their jobs. . . . The main reason for the irrationality of the whole process is that ideas for a new weapon system derive, in the first place, not from the military, but from different groups of scientists and technologists concerned with the replacement or improvement of old weapons systems . . . the momentum of the arms race is undoubtedly fueled by the technicians in government laboratories and in the industries that produce the armaments. (Zuckerman, 1982)

As someone who was himself chief scientific adviser to British prime ministers and the Ministry of Defence from the Second World War on, Zuckerman knows well the relationship between scientific expertise and political and military judgment. His conclusion about the matter is authoritative, at least for the United Kingdom, if not also inferentially for other defense establishments with which his own was in constant and interdependent contact. My own sense of the seemingly autonomous process of growth of weapons supply and complexity is heightened when I recall that five years before Reagan's "Star Wars" speech, a senior Pentagon official told me firmly if matter-of-factly that developments in military technology would take virtually the same form as the President unexpectedly announced a long time later.

This is not surprising when we recall Mary Kaldor's estimate that approximately 40 percent of the nations of the world's expenditure on research and development is focused on weapons, as well as the efforts of 25 percent of its scientists. (Kaldor, 1983, p.

420) By comparison with the other major industrial societies, Japan spends a negligible amount of its technological energy and money on weaponry; this fact, it is reasonable to conclude, has had substantial impact on the quality and imaginativeness of its nonmilitary productivity and on Japan's international trade in turn. Obviously the nature of armaments production is not solely determined by numbers of people involved and amounts of resources committed. Nevertheless, they have had a cumulative and massive effect on the world's military and political circles and inevitably on the level of potential military danger contained in the world's collective armory.

The relationship between people who think systematically and research nature, and the militaries of the world is hardly new. Archimedes the mathematician designed fortifications and the catapult. Leonardo da Vinci was a celebrated military scientist of his day. Michelangelo not only painted angels on the crown of the Sistine Chapel but was at one point in his life the engineer in charge of fortifying Florence. Any ethnographic museum or collection contains enough objects reflecting care and skill lavished on instruments of war to confirm that weaponry can be an art form as well as a practical necessity—that it stimulates effort and often brilliance among those responsible for creating it. The cold fact of where the money and talent go in countries rich and poor suggests that more than policy is involved but a form of affection, enthusiasm, ardor, all energized by the belief in enemies real or feared.

In this context, let me refer briefly to the work of Robert Ardrey and the controversy it stirred. Ardrey was an American dramatist turned accountant-of-science who in *African Genesis* (1961) argued that a major impetus in human evolution was an emotional and procedural commitment to aggression, the violent protection of self and kin, and the decisive world of the weapon. Ardrey's book was the subject of relatively casual and relatively fierce antipathy. He was accused of being a popularizer on one hand and a partisan and creator of an unpopular view on the other. Yet the range of material he arrayed in one book is in retrospect quite remarkable to re-encounter. Furthermore, his implicit prediction about the course of human events was unfortunately far more accurate than his antagonists', for example Ashley Montagu and Marshall Sahlins, anthropologists who considered Ardrey's gloomy diagnosis part of an avoidable disease. That is, a pathology and nothing normal, nothing to be dignified with historical ancestry in our formative past and our emotional present.

Be blunt about it. Whose view of the aggressive arms-bulging world more realistically predicted what has happened, Ardrey's or Montagu's? Ardrey's, whether either of them liked it or not. I claim some diffident evenhandedness about this judgment, since a book I co-authored was probably the first and last to receive favorable blurbs from both these men, whom I also had the pleasure and honor of knowing and enjoying, Ashley Montagu to this day.

Ardrey sought to account for the people's enthusiasm for warfare, the excitement of combat, the fascination of weapons, and the overall emotional impact and aesthetics of the bellicose spasm. At the time he wrote, in the late fifties, warfare had its own controls —it was, with the exception of bombing, a relatively hand-to-hand matter. Killing was a custom-made artisan's endeavor. Ardrey had not yet been able to see the extraordinary extension of military endeavor by electronically guided and managed weapons systems. He could not foresee the details of the synergetic interaction of primal aggressiveness with science and fascinating pure technology. He could not foresee that the most technically skilled people of the most sophisticated societies would devote themselves to the pursuit of the arts of war through the art of science.

Few people anticipated what has happened—futurist *naifs* such as H. G. Wells thought peace lay just ahead. But it appears that a new alloy has been formed, perhaps the costliest and most dangerous ever. Commanders have taken to mechanization just as mechanization itself in Giedion's phrase "took command." Improbable weapons become routine issue. The forms of real warfare become inextricably linked to the forms of imaginative science. Technopoetry with vast impact on a fearful new world. A phenomenal majestic extension of human power, which is at the same time a quotidian reminder of the frail weakness of flesh and the confusion between motives and actions that has been the suspenseful subject of playwrights and novelists forever. The result of this frailty, the catapult, hovers in the middle background. Through the miracle of modern science, it really hovers. Where will it glide next?

It's Structural

Physical things matter, coming and going. The industrial way of life has had its most vivid and obvious impact on the planet in the objects and processes it makes and how it plans to destroy both artifacts and people. To stand before the great Pyramid of the Sun at Teotihuacán near Mexico City is to be compelled to consider the nature, the passionate nature, of the society which produced it. What of the nature, the passionate nature, of the industrial plan? What does the swirl of a freeway interchange mean about the control and precision of the lives of the people flowing through on rubber tires? What can be learned of the modern heart from the form of the modern house, with its separate rooms for different people and different functions? Where the independent contractor sleeps. What is the resonant meaning of worldwide satellite monitoring of everything? How readily can people decide what is right and what is wrong when these decisions involve objects and systems phenomenally vast compared with a soft-skinned biped averaging 5'6" in height and weighing as much as two large boxes of books? What shall be David's strategy for the Goliath he has made?

Conclusion: Take Us to Our Leader

I have toured an immense system and commented on its power and convulsiveness. I have also sought to isolate specific elements which characterize it. Hence I moved from the oddity of literacy to the novelty of management to the ethics of shepherds to the impact of psychological tests to the exoticism of individualism to the significance of sociology to the relationship between God and evil and the core worlds of builders and soldiers. Vast, for sure. But anthropologists are accustomed to analyzing whole societies whose inhabitants consider them as complex and formidable as ours. So this study fits into a tradition, even though it is one we have imposed more on others than subjected ourselves to. Now is the time to survey ourselves with the same generous skepticism with which at best we try to understand how other people live.

Do I exaggerate the exoticism of the system I have been describing? Perhaps. But would anyone deny that industrialism is phenomenally different from other earlier systems in how and how well it produces wealth? In abundance, complexity, size, scope, force, improbability—in countless dimensions—the nature of what the system yields is extraordinary. In its extravagance, it reveals also how remarkable is the set of social arrangements of which it is formed. Nevertheless, the very extent of its accomplishment may be matched by how much it has departed from the familiar classic lines of human society. By how difficult it has made the task of noting ethically. By how difficult it has become to grasp realistically the consequences of actions which now must take place in evolutionarily novel circumstances and scale.

Yet we are all left with real ethical dilemmas to confront and solve. All members of the community are part of the broad courtroom drama. I have emphasized ethical issues. These remain at the heart of human concern. Who is good, who evil, who is the hero, who is to blame? Remember that a small-scale animal is inclined to personalize what is going on, to locate it in the actions of particular people who are well known. Life is not a general matter, not a business of impersonal systems. Social life is not an amalgam of impersonal acts. Only nature is impersonal. To deal with nature, God may be invoked, to clarify the issues and help ease the way. But there remains a distinction between the Church and the social state. Contemporary people are left with the obligation to take social actions about social nature. This depends on knowing the facts about the situation in question and appreciating the impact of whatever decision is taken.

In various organizations and professions there is renewed concern about ethics. Some ten thousand ethics courses are currently offered at colleges in the United States. My proposition has been that making ethical decisions is natural to human beings. So this suggests that the system within which these decisions must be made is in itself unnatural. Or we have lost the ethical knack. The discontinuity has to be addressed by trained people supposed to know more about conducting people's ethical lives than the people themselves.

Could this really be so? Yes. For example: there is reason to think that our broad ethical capacities were formed during a long phase of human evolution when family relations were paramount. In significant measure, right and wrong depended on the calculus of kinship. But now the world is different. I have suggested one of our ways of coping with this difference has been to elevate ideology in various forms to the moral status of kinship. Thus we may experience about ideologies many of the ethical emotions we developed for family life.

The vivid evidence of the traumatized world is that ideology is not a good basis for ethical behavior. Too readily it yields overcertainty in times of ambiguity. It stimulates overarmament when human balance is fragile. The problems to be addressed have not principally been caused by ideology. Therefore they cannot be solved by ideology. Size, scale, scope, markets, resources—these frequently salient causes of ethical dilemma are not much affected by ideology, unless it is one that in itself focuses on the size and character of social groups rather than on their beliefs, such as the "small is beautiful" initiative. The problem with ideological solutions to ethical dilemmas is that they allow—and even encourage in the name of sacred purity—decision makers to ignore often coercive empirical realities governing situations they must address.

But I have also extended the concept of ideology, to try to show that even such seemingly neutral forms of behavior as reading and making statistics contain their own surprisingly firm and unusual assumptions about social life. These in turn produce very particular kinds of social structure. The social sciences too, sociology and psychology in particular, exemplify special features of the way of life called the industrial system. Their growth and influence as much reflect cultural values of the system within which they are embedded as they are dispassionate sciences. And I tried to show how the sciences concerned with reproduction and the body helped create formidable approaches to organic realities which were sharply new and have expanded what can be done with nature.

I have tried to avoid examining these substantial issues within the well-worn frameworks of "right-wing" and "left-wing" positions, principally because neither pole has produced societies immune from the situations described here. As well, this polarization continues to produce as much intellectual banality as it does overcertainty and overarmament.

Nonetheless, it remains pertinent that the right-left dichotomy should have outburst with the industrial system. This was the system which so quickly yielded such massive personal and social change. It is also wholly understandable that the most acrimonious arguments should have accompanied such change, since there was so much misery and dislocation involved, so much wealth, so many new local and international factors to describe and understand. But just as the dichotomy appears to have resulted in a political and military impasse, so too intellectually. Time, then, to change the rules of exploration and debate. Japan conquered the industrial system without enduring the particular history that created it. It entered the game playing by different rules. Essentially preindustrial rules, with a social contract without the independent contractor. It succeeded, with sharply different social and moral rules. This is probably necessary in Euro-American societies, too. This book has examined the conditions which created the rules and some options for changing them. The schemes of shepherds and the formulae of small farmers haven't done the trick.

There is little point in concluding with an announcement of cataclysm or a bid to revise all social science. At best, some familiar elements of analysis have been brought together in a new arrangement. Perhaps some different emphasis on particular features of industrialism, such as literacy, may suggest different ways of considering these influential systems of economy. It remains essential to concentrate on the fact that critter-Man made the industrial system and that therefore critter-Man can change it. The option is as real as that. It is relevant if also sobering to acknowledge that the industrial system is as popular as it is because people like so much about it. If there is also much they do not like, then anyone interested in producing change should focus on the irritants, not the attractants. Separate out the elements, then discerningly pick and choose.

A difficulty recurs. It appears people prefer to establish connections between things. Integration remains our deep style. We are an integrating species—an aspect of our eclectic genius. A product of a small-scale scheme, we are ill at ease with shiny jump-cuts from one flavor of life to another. This means that specialists must attend to general issues since these will inevitably become salient. What happens in families affects jobs, and vice versa. Effective change demands not only revision but vision. So the trend to specialization of function that has made the system prosperous also confuses and irritates the citizenry that benefits from it. Specialization is probably not a comfortable dance. Too jerky.

Members of industrial communities have embraced a form of society phenomenally productive and luxurious for countless people. But it also makes demands apparently difficult to meet. For example, we evolved in good measure by sharpening and expanding our social skills and our capacity for emotional assessment and understanding of others. But our principal society-wide means of judging students and other candidates focuses fiercely on people's ability to perform technical tasks—calculations, making technical projections, knowing the details of physical process. Capacity for social judgment and making wide decisions need not accompany the technical requirement on the main route to entry—for example, to medical school. Later in careers, those with technical skill may take command of their workplaces without having had or developing the capacity to make good ethical decisions. And a chronic dichotomy may continue for people who take antisocial actions in public while maintaining the warmth and providence of their intimate lives—the Mafia hitman sponsoring a hearty Mother's Day feast in his home.

I needn't repeat my argument. It remains to note that the special gifts of the system correspond to what challenges it. Resolutions do not seem easy to come by. This is related to how we think. How we communicate. What we count and how. What we think people are. How we conceive of groups and their force. It is related to our estimate of the value of babies and the attraction of objects. It connects to how with astonishing restlessness we use the machines and techniques of our system to stick pins into space and confront spectacularly influential activities of forms of matter as imaginatively small as the atom. Living in a self-recreating cornucopia enhances the confidence of the residents. Dying is such an interference with the skill of the system that its existence is denied, the dead ghettoized, the mortuary industry a close ally to cartoonists; at the very end of life the pressure continues to consume wealth beyond metabolism's need.

Reality becomes a rumor of itself. A major movie actor, Charlton Heston, states he would rather play the role of a U.S. senator than contest election for a senator's seat from California. Opinion polls about today are used to create the policies of tomorrow when opinion polls will ask people to compare their present lot with yesterday's. Crisis weapons remain hidden in holes in the ground or metal submarines while the flaming imagined magic of their threat becomes the basis of expensive military diplomacy. Countries thousands of miles apart maintain the intricate enmity of reluctant in-laws sharing a dingy kitchen. An almost Buddhist embrace of epiphenomenon in the most hard-headed system of all time.

Yet at the point in the cowboy movies when the good guys win, the audience cheers. For all the drama Mephistopheles creates, the knowledge of reality's grip and of goodness's savor is shared by everyone except awkward sociopaths whose relative rarity is a reassurance. It is when organizations become sociopathological that the problem heats up. To this issue, forceful communities with large capacity for impact must turn. Not to seek individual emancipation or private salvation. But to relearn the knack of group governance. For which we've a luxurious legacy on which to draw.

Bibliography

Alonso, William, and Paul Starr. 1982. "The Political Economy of National Statistics." *Items,* Social Science Research Council 36 (Sept.):3.

American Academy of Arts and Sciences. Bulletin, XXXII (Feb. 1979):5.

AP. 1984. "Single-Parent Homes on Increase in Japan." *New York Times,* 6 May.

Ardrey, Robert. 1961. *African Genesis.* New York: Atheneum.

Arensberg, Conrad. 1980. Presidential Address to the American Anthropological Association.

Ariès, Philippe. 1962. *Centuries of Childhood.* Trans. Robert Saldick. New York: Random.

Auletta, Ken. 1981. "The Underclass." *The New Yorker* 16 Nov.

Austin, Charles. 1982. "Study of Daycare in U.S. Finds Churches Are the Main Suppliers." *New York Times,* 6 Nov.

Bandura, Albert. 1979. "Psychological Mechanisms of Aggression." In *Human Ethology: Claims and Limits of a New Discipline.* M. Cranach, et al. eds. New York: Cambridge University Press.

Bane, Mary Jo. 1976. *Here to Stay: American Families in the 20th Century.* New York: Basic Books.

Barron, James. 1984. "Urban League Cites Pressure on Black Men." *New York Times,* 1 Aug.

de Beauvoir, Simone. *The Second Sex.* 1953. New York: Knopf.

Bennett, Amanda. 1983. "China Cajoles Families and Offers Incentives to Reduce Birth Rate, but One-Child Policy Stirs Resistance, Hasn't Ended the Preference for Sons." *Wall Street Journal,* 6 July.

Berger, Peter. 1980. Foreword to *Man in the Age of Technology,* by Arnold Gehlen. Trans. Patricia Lipscomb. New York: Columbia University Press.

Berger, Peter L. 1982. "Secular Branches, Secular Roots." *Transaction/Society* 20:1.

Berger, Peter L., and Thomas Luckmann. 1967. *The Social Construction of Reality.* Garden City, NY: Anchor.ra

Bernstam, Mikhail, and Peter Swan. 1986. "The State As the Marriage Partner of Last Resort: New Findings on Minimum Wage, Youth Joblessness, Welfare, and Single Motherhood in the United States, 1960–1980." Domestic Studies Program, Hoover Institution, Stanford University, Stanford, CA.

Bettleheim, Bruno. 1969. *Children of the Dream.* London: Collier-Macmillan.

Birney, Earle. 1949. *Turvey.* Toronto: McClelland & Stewart.

Bledsoe, Caroline. 1980. *Women and Marriage in Kpelle Society.* Stanford, CA: Stanford University Press.

Boehm, Christopher. 1982. "The Evolutionary Development of Morality as Effect of Dominance Behavior and Conflict Interference." *Journal of Social and Biological Structures* 5:413–21.

Bogdan, Robert, and Margaret Ksander. 1980. "Policy Data as a Social Process: A Qualitative Approach to Quantitative Data." *Human Organization* 39 (Winter):4.

Bollinger, Dwight. 1981. "Voice Imprints." *New York Times Magazine*, 26 July.

Boswell, John. 1980. *Christianity, Social Tolerance and Homosexuality: Gay People in Western Europe from the Beginning of the Christian Era to the Fourteenth Century.* Chicago: University of Chicago Press.

Braudel, Fernand. 1977. *Afterthoughts on Material Civilization and Capitalism.* Trans. Patrial Ranum. Baltimore: Johns Hopkins University Press.

Brodsley, David. 1982. *L.A. Freeway: An Appreciative Essay.* Berkeley: University of California Press.

Brown, Harold. 1976. *Familiar Faces, Hidden Lives: The Story of Homosexual Men in America Today.* New York: Harcourt Brace Jovanovich.

Brown, Lester. 1984. "World Population Crisis . . ." *New York Times,* 8 May.

Brownmiller, Susan. 1975. *Against Our Will: Men, Women and Rape.* New York: Simon & Schuster.

Brozan, Nadine. 1983. "Daycare in New York: A Growing Need." *New York Times,* 20 July.

Burley, Nancy. 1979. "The Evolution of Concealed Ovulation." *The American Naturalist,* 114 (Dec.):6.

Burridge, Kenelm. 1979. *Someone, No One: An Essay on Individuality.* Princeton: Princeton University Press.

Chandler, Alfred. 1977. *The Visible Hand: The Managerial Hand in American Business.* Cambridge: Harvard University Press.

Chodorow, Nancy. 1978. *The Reproduction of Mothering: Psychoanalysis and the Sociology of Gender.* Berkeley: University of California Press.

Clutton-Brock, Juliet. 1981. *Domesticated Animals in Early Times.* Austin: University of Texas Press.

Coe, Christopher, et al. 1982. "Hormonal Responses Accompanying Fear and Agitation in the Squirrel Monkey." *Physiology and Behavior* 29.

Cohen, Mark N. 1977. *The Food Crisis in Prehistory: Overpopulation and the Origins of Agriculture.* New Haven: Yale University Press.

Cohen, Yehudi A. 1981. "Shrinking Households." *Society,* Jan./Feb.: 48.

Commager, Henry Steele. 1984. "How Grammar Became Glamour." *New York Times Book Review,* 26 Feb.

Cook, Alice. 1979. *The Working Mother: A Survey of Problems and Programs in Nine Countries.* Ithaca, NY: ILR Press.

Daly, Martin, and Margo Wilson. 1982. "Whom Are Newborns Said to Resemble?" *Ethology and Sociobiology* 3:2.

Daniels, Denise. 1983. "The Evolution of Concealed Ovulation and Self-Deception." *Ethology and Sociobiology* 4:2.

Daniels, Lee. 1982. "New York: A City of Renters in Small Households." *New York Times,* 5 March.

Darling-Hammond, Linda. 1984. "Mad-Hatter Test of Good Teaching." *New York Times Educational Supplement,* 8 Jan.

Darwin, Charles. 1974. *The Early Writings of Charles Darwin: Metaphysics, Materialism and the Evolution of Mind.* Paul H. Barrett, ed. Chicago: University of Chicago Press.

Dawkins, Richard. 1979. "Twelve Misunderstandings of Kin Selection." *Zeitschrift für Tierpsychologie* 51:184–200.

Decter, Midge. 1980. "The Boys on the Beach." *Commentary,* Sept.

Donzelot, Jacques. 1974. *The Policing of Families.* Trans. Robert Hurley. New York: Pantheon.

Dowd, Maureen. 1983. "Many Women in Poll Value Jobs as Much as Family Life." *New York Times,* 4 Dec.

Bibliography

Dumont, Louis. 1970. *Homo Hierarchicus: The Caste System and Its Implications*. Chicago: University of Chicago Press.

Dunn, Michael C. 1982. "Plus ça change, plus c'est la même chose." *Defence and Foreign Affairs*, May.

Durkheim, Emile. 1938. *The Rules of Sociological Method*. Glencoe, IL: Free Press.

———. 1952. *Suicide: A Study in Sociology*. Trans. G. Simpson. Glencoe, IL: Free Press.

———. 1972. *Selected Writings*. Anthony Giddens, ed. Cambridge: Cambridge University Press.

Ehrenreich, Barbara. 1983. *The Hearts of Men: American Dreams and the Flight from Commitment*. Garden City, NY: Doubleday.

———. 1984. "A Feminist's View of the New Man." *New York Times Magazine*, 20 May.

Elshtain, Jean Bethke. 1979. "Feminists Against the Family." *The Nation*, 17 Nov.

———. 1981. *Public Man, Private Woman: Women in Social and Political Thought*. Princeton: Princeton University Press.

Erik, John. 1982. "China's Policy on Births." *New York Times*, 3 Jan.

Ettore, E. M. 1980. *Lesbians, Women and Society*. London: Routledge and Keegan Paul.

Eysenck, Hans J. 1975. *The Inequality of Man*. London: Fontana.

Fallaci, Oriana. 1980. "Iranians Are Our Brothers: An Interview with Colonel Mummar el-Qaddafi of Libya by Oriana Fallaci." *New York Times Magazine*.

Farley, Jennie. 1983. *The Woman in Management: Career and Family Issues*. Ithaca, NY: ILR Press.

Feaver, George. 1969. *From Status to Contract: A Biography of Sir Henry Maine 1822–1888*. London: Longmans.

Firestone, Shulamith. 1972. *The Dialectic of Sex*. New York: Bantam.

Fiske, Edward. 1979. "Finding Fault with the Testers." *New York Times Magazine*, 18 Nov.

———. 1983. "Test Misuse Is Charged." *New York Times*, 29 Nov.

Fox, Robin. 1967. *Kinship and Marriage: An Anthropological Perspective*. Harmondsworth: Penguin.

———. 1979. "Kinship Categories as Natural Categories." In *Evolutionary Biology and Human Social Behavior: An Anthropological Perspective*. N. Chagnon and W. Irons, eds. North Scituate, MA: Duxbury Press.

———. 1980. *The Red Lamp of Incest*. New York: Dutton.

———. 1982. "Inhuman Nature and Unnatural Rights." *Society* 20:1.

Fraker, Susan. 1984. "Why Qualified Women Aren't Getting to the Top." *Fortune*, 16 April.

Freeman, Derek. 1983. *Margaret Mead and Samoa*. Cambridge: Harvard University Press.

Friedan, Betty. 1981. *The Second Stage*. New York: Summit Books.

Friedman, Thomas. 1982. "Hawking Arms Overseas." *New York Times International Economic Survey*, 14 Feb.

Frisch, Karl von. 1974. *Animal Architecture*. New York: Harcourt Brace Jovanovich.

Frisch, Rose. 1982. "Demographic Implications of the Biological Determinants of Female Fecundity." *Social Biology* 29 (Spring–Summer):1–2.

Frye, Northrop. 1981. "The Bridge of Language." *Science* 212 (10 April):4491.

Fuchs, Victor. 1983. "Divorce Rate's Fiscal Impact." *New York Times*, 7 Sept.

Galbraith, John Kenneth. 1971. *Economics, Peace, and Laughter*. New York: Signet.

Gallup, George G., Jr., and Susan D. Suarez. 1983. "Homosexuality as a By-product of Selection for Optimal Heterosexual Strategies." *Perspectives in Biology and Medicine* 26 (Winter):2.

Gay, Peter. 1983. *The Education of the Senses*. New York: Oxford University Press.

Gehlen, Arnold. 1980. *Man in the Age of Technology*. Trans. Patricia Lipscomb. New York: Columbia University Press.

Göllner, Ernest. 1965. *Thought and Change*. London: Weidenfeld and Nicolson.

——. 1974. *Legitimation of Belief*. Cambridge: Cambridge University Press.

Giedion, Siegfried. 1969. *Mechanization Takes Command*. New York: Norton.

Gilder, George. 1981. *Men and Marriage*. Gretna, LA: Pelican Publishing.

——. 1982. "But What About Welfare's Grim Side?" *New York Times*, 22 April.

Gilligan, Carol. 1982. *In a Different Voice: Psychological Theory and Women's Development*. Cambridge: Harvard University Press.

Gilman, Charlotte Perkins. 1898, 1966. In *Women and Economics: A Study of the Economic Relation Between Men and Women as a Factor in Social Evolution*. C. Degler, ed. New York: Harper & Row.

Gladue, Briand A. 1983. "Hormones, Psychosexuality and Reproduction: Biology, Brain and Behavior." *Politics and the Life Sciences* 2 (Aug.):1.

Godelier, Maurice. 1972. *Rationality and Irrationality in Economics*. Trans. Brian Pearce. New York: Monthly Review Press.

Goffman, Erving. 1956. *The Presentation of Self in Everyday Life*. Edinburgh: University of Edinburgh. Monograph #2.

——. 1963. *Stigma: Notes on the Management of Spoiled Identity*. Englewood Cliffs, NJ: Prentice-Hall.

——. 1978. "Gender Advertisements." In *Female Hierarchies*. L. Tiger and H. Fowler, eds. Chicago: Aldine.

Goldberg, Steven. 1974. *The Inevitability of Patriarchy*. New York: Morrow.

Goleman, Daniel. 1984. "Psychology Is Revising Its View of Women." *New York Times*, 20, March.

Gottschalk, Earl, Jr. 1981. "Maternity Leave." *Wall Street Journal*, 20 July.

Gould, Stephen J. 1984. "Similarities Between the Sexes." *New York Times Book Review*, 17 Aug.

Greer, Germaine. 1980. *The Female Eunuch*. London: MacGibbon and Kee.

——. 1984. *Sex and Destiny*. New York: Harper & Row.

Gregerson, Edgar. 1983. *Sexual Practices: The Story of Human Sexuality*. New York: Franklin Watts.

Hacker, Andrew. 1982. "Farewell to the Family." *New York Review of Books*, 18 March.

Haddad, Helen. 1981. "On to the Second Stage with Betty Friedan." *Smith College Quarterly*.

Hamburg, David. 1963. "Emotions in Perspective of Human Evolution." In *Expression of Emotions in Man*. P. Knapp, ed. New York: International University Press.

Hareven, Tamara K. 1982. *Family Time and Industrial Time*. Cambridge: Cambridge University Press.

Harris, Adrienne. "The Rationalization of Infancy." Unpublished.

Hartley, Shirley Foster. 1975. *Illegitimacy*. Berkeley: University of California Press.

Hawkes, Kristen, and James F. O'Connell. 1981. "Affluent Hunters? Some Comments in Light of the Alyawara Case." *American Anthropologist* 83.

Headrick, Daniel. 1981. *The Tools of Empire, Technology and European Imperialism in the Nineteenth Century*. New York: Oxford University Press.

Hernnstein, Richard. 1982. "IQ Testing and the Media." *Atlantic Monthly*, Aug.

Heyer, Paul. 1982. *Nature, Human Nature, and Society*. Westport, CT: Greenwood.

Hrdy, Sarah Blaffer. 1977. *The Langurs of Abu*. Cambridge: Harvard University Press.

——. 1979. "Infanticide Among Animals: A Review, Classification, and Ex-

Bibliography

amination of the Implications for the Reproductive Strategies of Females." *Ethology and Sociobiology* 1.

―――. 1981. *The Women That Never Evolved.* Cambridge: Harvard University Press.

Huxtable, Ada Louise. 1981. "Is Modern Architecture Dead?" *New York Review of Books*, 10 July.

Jacobs, Jane. 1984. Quoted in Roger Scruton, "Public Space and the Classical Vernacular." *The Public Interest* 74 (Winter): 9.

Kadish, Mortimer, and Sanford Kadish. 1973. *Discretion to Disobey: A Study of Lawful Departures from Legal Rules.* Stanford: Stanford University Press.

Kakar, Sudhir. 1970. *Frederick Taylor: A Study in Personality and Innovation.* Cambridge: MIT Press.

Kaldor, Mary. 1983. "Technology and the Arms Race." *The Nation*, 9 April, 240.

Konner, Melvin. 1982. *The Tangled Wing.* New York: Holt.

Kunz, Phillip R., Merlin B. Brinkerhoff, and Vicke Hundley. 1973. "Relation of Income and Childlessness." *Social Biology* XX (June).

Kurland, Jeffrey, and Steven Gaulin. "The Evolution of Male Parental Invest-ment: Effects of Genetic Relatedness and Feeding Ecology on the Allocation of Reproductive Effort." Unpublished.

Lakoff, Robin. 1975. *Language and Women's Place.* New York: Harper & Row.

Lamb, Michael. 1982. "Why Swedish Fathers Aren't Liberated." *Psychology Today*, Oct.

Lamming, George. 1981. Introduction to *A History of the Guyanese Working People, 1881–1905*, by Walter Rodney. Baltimore: Johns Hopkins University Press.

Landes, David. 1983. *Revolution in Time: Clocks and the Making of the Modern World.* Cambridge: Harvard University Press.

Lapidus, Gail Warshofsky. 1978. Women in Soviet Society: Equality, Develop-ment and Social Change. Berkeley: University of California Press.

Lasch, Christopher. 1977. *Haven in a Heartless World: The Family Besieged.* New York: Norton.

Laslett, Peter, Karla Oosterveen, and Richard Smith. 1980. *Bastardy and Its Comparative History: Studies in the History of Illegitimacy and Marital Noncon-formism in Britain, France, Germany, Sweden, North America, Jamaica and Japan.* Cambridge: Harvard University Press.

Leibnitz, G. W. 1951. *Selections.* Philip Weiner, ed. New York: Scribner.

Le Goff, Jacques. 1980. *Time, Work and Culture in the Middle Ages.* Trans. A. Goldhammer. Chicago: University of Chicago Press.

Leontief, Wassily. 1982. "Academic Economics." *Science* 217, 9 July.

Lewin, Roger. 1983. "Were Lucy's Feet Made for Walking?" *Science* 220 (13 May):4598.

Lewin, Tamar. 1983. "Sex Differentials in Insurance: Bills Propose Equal Rates." *New York Times*, 2 May.

―――. 1984. "Maternity Leave: Is It Leave, Indeed?" *New York Times*, 22 July.

C. S. Lewis. 1944. *The Problem of Pain.* New York: Macmillan.

Lewontin, Richard. 1982. "The Inferiority Complex." *New York Review of Books*, 22 Oct.

Lewontin, R., Rose S., and Kamin L. 1984 *Not in Our Genes: Biology, Ideology, and Human Nature.* New York: Pantheon.

Lothstein, Leslie M. 1982. "Sex Reassignment Surgery." *American Journal of Psychiatry* 139 (April):4.

Lukes, Steven. 1983. "From Reportage to Evaluation." *Times Literary Supple-ment* 4192, 5 Aug.

Luker, Kristin. 1975. *Taking Chances: Abortion and the Decision Not to Con-tracept.* Berkeley: University of California Press.

Macfarlane, Alan. 1979. *The Origins of English Individualism: The Family, Property, and Social Transition.* Cambridge: Cambridge University Press.

McGuire, Michael, and Susan Essock-Vitale. 1982. "Self-Deception in Social-

Support Networks: Possible Influence of Kinship, Wealth, and Reproductive Success." Ninth International Primatological Congress, Atlanta, August.

McGuire, Michael, M. J. Raleigh, and C. Johnson. 1983. "Social Dominance in Adult Male Vervet Monkeys: Behavioral-Biochemical Relationships." *Social Science Information* 22:2.

Macpherson, C. B. 1962. *The Political Theory of Political Individualism.* London: Penguin.

Madsen, Douglas. 1985. "A Biochemical Property Relating to Power Seeking in Humans." *American Political Science Review* 79:448–57.

Maittal, Schlomo. 1982. *Minds, Markets and Money: Psychological Foundations of Economic Behavior.* New York: Basic Books.

Malinowski, Bronislaw. 1929. *The Sexual Life of Savages in Northwest Malanesia.* London: Routledge.

Mannoni, O. 1956. *Prospero and Caliban: The Psychology of Colonization.* Trans. Pamela Powesland. London: Methuen.

Marx, Karl. 1979. *The Letters of Karl Marx.* Sel. and Trans. by Saul K. Padover. Englewood Cliffs, NJ: Prentice-Hall.

Matarazzo, Joseph D. 1983. "Computerized Psychological Testing." *Science* 221 (22 July):4608.

Mello, Nancy, et al. 1983. "Alcohol Self-Stimulation Disrupts Reproductive Function in Female Macaque Monkeys." *Science* 221 (12 Aug.).

Millett, Kate. 1970. *Sexual Politics.* Garden City, NY: Doubleday.

Miyazaki, Ichismaya. 1981. *China's Examination Hell.* Trans. Conrad Schirokauer. New Haven: Yale University Press.

Moffatt, Michael. 1979. *An Untouchable Community in South India: Structure and Consensus.* Princeton: Princeton University Press.

Morris, Jan. 1984. "Gender Mercies." *Vanity Fair,* June.

Moynihan, Daniel Patrick. 1981. "Books Floccinaucinihilipilificationism." *The New Yorker,* 19 Aug.

Murphy, Michael R., Paul D. MacLean, and Sue C. Hamilton. 1981. "Species-Typical Behavior of Hamsters Deprived from Birth of the Neocortex." *Science* 213.

Nairn, Allan, et al. 1980. *The Reign of ETS: The Corporation That Makes Up Minds.* Washington, DC: Learning Research Project.

Newton, Esther. 1972. *Mother Camp: Female Impersonators in America.* Englewood Cliffs, NJ: Prentice-Hall.

New York Times. 1981. "India's Population Growth Unchecked in Ten Years." *New York Times,* 19 March.

————. 1982. "1.55 Million Abortions Reported in 1980." *New York Times,* 23 Feb.

O'Flaherty, Wendy Doniger. 1976. *The Origins of Evil in Hindu Mythology.* Berkeley: University of California Press.

Ong, Walter. 1977. *Interfaces of the Word: Studies in the Evolution of Consciousness and Culture.* Ithaca, NY: Cornell University Press.

————. 1982. *Orality and Literacy: The Technologizing of the Word.* New York: Methuen.

Ortega y Gasset, José. 1972. *Meditations on Hunting.* New York: Scribner.

Oxenham, John. 1980. *Literacy; Reading, Writing and Social Organization.* London: Routledge and Kegan Paul.

Pacey, Arnold. 1983. *The Culture of Technology.* Cambridge: MIT Press.

Penman, Robyn, Russell Meares, Kay Baker, and Jeanette Milgrom-Friedman. 1983. "Synchrony in Mother-Infant Interaction: A Possible Neurophysiological Base." *Journal of Medical Psychology* 56:1–7.

Pfeiffer, John. 1977. *The Emergence of Society: A Prehistory of the Establishment.* New York: McGraw-Hill.

————. 1982. *The Creative Explosion: An Inquiry into the Origins of Art and Religion.* New York: Harper & Row.

Piatelli-Palmerini, Massimo. 1980. Foreword to *Language and Learning: The*

Bibliography

Debate Between Jean Piaget and Noam Chomsky. Piatelli-Palmerini, ed. Cambridge: Harvard University Press.

Pollack, Andrew. 1982. "Testing People by Computer." *New York Times,* 8 April.

Prial, Frank J. 1981. "Birth Control Ads Make Debut on French TV." *New York Times,* 29 Nov.

Pritchett, V. S. 1983. "The Last Victorian." *The New Yorker,* 22 Aug. 89.

Raleigh, M. T., M. McGuire, G. Brammer, and A. Yuwiler. 1984. "Social Status and Whole Blood Serotonin in Vervets." *Archives of General Psychiatry.*

Reed, James. 1983. *The Birth Control Movement in American Society.* Princeton: Princeton University Press.

Reinisch, J. M. 1976. "Effect of Prenatal Hormone Exposure on Physical and Psychological Development in Humans and Animals: With a Note on the State of the Field." In *Hormones and Psychopathology.* E. Sachar, ed. New York: Raven Press.

Reinisch, J. M., and S. A. Sanders. 1982. "Early Barbiturate Exposure. The Brain, Sexually Dimorphic Behavior and Learning." *Neuroscience and Biobehavioral Reviews* 6:311–19.

Remoff, Heather S. 1984. *Female Choice.* New York: Norton.

Richard, Michel, and Jean-Sebastian Stehli. 1983. "Orthographie en Ruine." *Le Point* 552 (18 April).

Richards, Audrey I. 1969. "Characteristics of Ethical Systems in Primitive Human Society." In *Biology and Ethics.* F. J. Ebling, ed. New York: Academic Press.

Rosenblum, Leonard, and Gayle Paulley. 1984. "The Effects of Varying Environmental Demands on Maternal and Infant Behavior." *Child Development* 55.

Rukang, Wu, and Lin Shenglon. 1983. "Peking Man." *Scientific American* 248 (June).

Samuels, Dorothy, and Norman Rollins. 1982. "Lie Detectors Lie." *New York Times,* 17 Feb.

Scherer, Klaus. 1982. "The Nature and Function of Emotions." *Social Science Information* 21 (4/5):507.

Scruton, Roger. 1984. "Public Space and the Cassical Vernacular." *The Public Interest* 74 (Winter): 9.

Sennett, Richard. 1978. *The Fall of Public Man.* New York: Vintage.

Serrin, William. 1984. "The Way That Works at Lincoln." *New York Times,* 15 Jan.

Sheppard, Nathaniel. 1982. "Single Parent." *New York Times,* 14 Oct.

Sherman, Mark. 1984. "The College Board Joins Publishers of SAT 'Cram' Books." *New York Times Educational Supplement,* 8 Jan.

Sherrill, Robert. 1983. "The Zany Sport of Liberal Fratricide: Firing on Our Own Troops." *The Nation* 15 Jan.

Short, R. V. 1984. "Breast Feeding." *Scientific American* 250 (April):4.

Shorter, Edward. 1983. *A History of Women's Bodies.* New York: Basic Books.

Silk, Leonard. 1984. "The Politics of the Budget." *New York Times,* 3 Feb.

Silverstein, Pam, and Josetta Srb. 1979. *Flexitime: Where, When and How?* Ithaca, NY: ILR Press.

Simmel, Georg. 1950. *The Sociology of Georg Simmel.* Trans. Kurt H. Wolf. Glencoe, IL: Fress Press.

———. 1978. *The Philosophy of Money.* Trans. Tom Bottomore and David Frisby. London, Boston: Routledge and Kegan Paul.

Sivard, Ruth. 1980. *World Military and Social Expenditures 1980.* Leesburg, VA: World Priorities, p. 5.

Skinner, B. F. 1983. "Origins of a Behaviorist." *Psychology Today,* Sept.: 24.

Smith, Adam. 1966. *The Theory of Moral Sentiments.* New York: Kelley.

Smithson, Alison, ed. 1968. *Team Ten Primer.* Cambridge: MIT Press.

Solomon, Robert J. 1981. "Truth-in-Testing Is (A) (B) (C)." *New York Times,* 10 March.

335

Sorokin, Pitirim. 1963. Foreword to *Community and Society*, by Ferdinand Tonnies. Loomis and McKinney, eds. New York: Harper & Row.

Spiro, Melford E. 1958. *Children of the Kibbutz*. Cambridge: Harvard University Press.

———. 1958. *Kibbutz, Venture in Utopia*. Cambridge: Harvard University Press.

———. 1979. *Gender and Culture: Kibbutz Women Revisted*. Durham, NC: Duke University Press.

Stebbins, G. Ledyard. 1982. *Darwin to DNA: Molecules to Humanity*. San Francisco: Freeman, pp. 372–78.

Stecklis, H. D., et al. 1983. "Progesterone and Socio-sexual Behavior in Stumptailed Macaques (*Macacca Arctoides*): Hormonal and Socio-environmental Interactions." In *Hormones, Drugs, and Social Behavior in Primates*. H. D. Stecklis and A. S. Kling, eds. N.Y. Spectrum.

Stern, Robert A. M. 1981. "Giedion's Ghost." *Skyline*, Oct.: 22.

Strenio, A. J. 1981. *The Testing Trap*. New York: Rawson.

Sulzberger, A. O., Jr. 1981. "A Third of New York Births in '80 Were to the Unmarried." *New York Times*, 18 Oct.

Tafuri, Manfredo. 1979. *Theories and History of Architecture*. New York: Harper & Row, p. 185.

Thurow, Lester. 1983. *Dangerous Currents: The State of Economics*. New York: Random.

Tiger, Lionel. 1969. *Men in Groups*. New York: Random.

———. 1975. "Somatic Factors and Social Behaviour." In *Biosocial Anthropology*. R. Fox, ed. London: Melody Press.

———. 1979. *Optimism: The Biology of Hope*. New York: Simon & Shuster.

———. 1984. *Men in Groups*. London, New York: Marion Boyars.

Tiger, Lionel, and Robin Fox. 1970. *The Imperial Animal*. New York: Holt.

Tonnies, Ferdinand. 1963. *Community and Society*. Loomis and McKinney, eds. New York: Harper & Row.

Trucco, Terry. 1983. "In Japan, Problems of Working Women." *New York Times*, 19 June.

UPI. 1981. "U.S. Census Bureau Says Divorces and Unmarried Couples Increased in 70's." *New York Times*, 19 Oct.

———. 1983. "Infertility Increases in Young Women." *New York Times*, 10 Feb.

Vogt, Jerry, and Seymour Levine. 1980. "Response of Mother and Infant Squirrel Monkeys to Separation and Disturbance." *Physiology and Behavior* 24:829–32.

Von Lang, Jochen, and Claus Sibyll, eds. 1984. *Eichmann Interrogated*. New York: Random.

Washburn, Sherwood. 1978. "Human Behavior and the Behavior of other Animals." *American Psychologist* 33:405–18.

Wasser, Samuel, and David Barash. 1983. "Reproductive Suppression Among Female Mammals: Implications for Bio-medicine and Sexual Selection Theory." *Quarterly Review of Biology* 58 (Dec.).

Weitzman, Lenore J. 1981. "The Economics of Divorce: Social and Economic Consequences of Property, Alimony, and Child Support Awards." *UCLA Law Review* 28 (Aug.):6.

Western, Jonah D., and Shirley C. Strum. 1983. "Sex, Kinship, and the Evolution of Social Manipulation." *Ethology and Sociobiology* 4:1.

Westoff, Charles, and Norman Ryder. 1977. *The Contraceptive Revolution*. Princeton: Princeton University Press.

White, Edmund. 1980. *States of Desire*. New York: Dutton.

———. 1983. "Sexual Culture." *Vanity Fair*, December.

Whymant, Robert. 1984. "Japan's High-Rolling Robot Eyes." *Sunday Times* (London), 1 July.

Whyte, William F. 1955. *Street Corner Society*. Chicago: University of Chicago Press.

Bibliography

———. 1956. *The Organization Man.* New York: Simon & Shuster.

Wilford, John Noble. 1983. "Ethiopian Bones Called Oldest Ancestor of Man." *New York Times,* 11 June.

Wilkinson, Rupert. 1964. *The Prefects: British Leadership and the Public School Tradition.* Oxford: Oxford University Press.

Willis, Ellen. 1981. "Mr. Right Is Dead." *The Nation,* 14 Nov.

Wilson, E. O. 1978. "For Sociobiology." In *The Sociobiology Debate.* Arthur Caplan, ed. New York: Harper & Row.

Winner, Langdon. 1977. *Autonomous Technology: Technics Out of Control as a Theme in Political Thought.* Cambridge: MIT Press.

Wren, Daniel. 1979. *The Evolution of Management Thought.* New York: Wiley.

Zalesnik, Abraham. 1970. Foreword to *Frederick Taylor: A Study in Personality and Innovation.* Sudhir Kakar, ed. Cambridge: MIT Press.

Zuckerman, Solly. 1982. "Arming for Armageddon: Defence Scientists—Not Generals—Set the Pace." *The Sciences,* March.

Zumwalt, Rosemary. 1982. "Arnold van Gennep: The Hermit of Bourg-La-Reine." *American Anthropologist* 84:2.

Acknowledgments

Despite the fact that writing a book all-too-readily comes to seem the same challenge as living a life, there are nonetheless some people and organizations to whom I am grateful for their contribution to this project. They are responsible only for their goodwill and professionalism, not my use or abuse of their generosity.

Rutgers University provided a Faculty Leave at a most opportune time, and was in general a deft and supportive provider of an academic home. Edwina Segledi and Janet Bascom of the Department of Anthropology have been capably helpful.

During the initial years of this project, the Harry Frank Guggenheim Foundation provided decisive financial and logistical support. I am grateful for this, and want to note the graciousness of its Chairman Peter Lawson-Johnston, and in particular the effectiveness and warmth of its Executive Director George Fontaine. Paul Parren and Joe Koenigsberger unobtrusively managed the details of administering the support I received.

Karen Colvard, program officer of the Foundation, was as intelligently helpful as she was cheerful during preparation of much of the manuscript. I owe her a sizable debt.

The late Baroness Minda de Gunzburg and the ASDA Foundation provided valued help during the latter phases of the project.

I had the good fortune of capable research assistance from a number of Rutgers graduate students, including Daniel Fernando, Dr. Renate Fernandez, Dr. Linda Marchant, Dr. Tom Melchionne, and Rita Srivistava.

A large number of colleagues in the quizzical trades have been generous with their time, and patient to boot, as I insisted on talking about this book. The names of some of the more highly victimized are: Gabriel Paes de Carvalho, Vladimir Denisov, Barbaralee Diamonstein, Robin Fox, Robert Gersin, Oscar Hechter, Mario Laserna, Michael Lax, Wassily Leontief, Robert J. Lifton, Alice Morton, Sam Nillson, Massimo Piatelli-Palmerini, Barbara Radice, Dieter Rams, Joe Slater, Ettore Sottsass, Massimo Vignelli, E. O. Wilson, Shoshanah Zuboff.

Alan U. Schwartz has been both protective and effective. Michael and Cornelia Bessie have been extraordinarily constructive and understanding in working with this book and its author. An advantage of taking substantial time over a book is that there is time to gain new friends. At Harper & Row, Ann Volpe and Brooke Drysdale have been smoothly efficient while Ann Simon and Ann Edelman made the often-trying process of copyediting a professional pleasure.

My son Sebastian has been helpful in countless ways and rewarding in even more.

Index

Index

Index

About The Author

Lionel Tiger was born in Montreal and studied at McGill University there and for his doctorate at the London School of Economics and Political Science. He has taught at McGill, the University of Ghana, the University of British Columbia in Vancouver and since 1969 at Rutgers University in New Jersey where he is Professor of Anthropology. From 1972 to 1984 he was Research Director of the Harry Frank Guggenheim Foundation, and has received among others fellowships from the John Simon Guggenheim and Rockefeller Foundations and the Canada Council. He is currently Chairman of the Board of Social Scientists of *U.S. News and World Report*.

Since 1965 he has been interested in the relationship of the social and natural sciences and wrote that year with Robin Fox of the University of London an impudent article subsequently published in the *Journal of the Royal Anthropological Institute* and called "The Zoological Perspective in Social Science." In 1969 he published *Men in Groups* which brought his concept of "male bonding" to public attention and two years later *The Imperial Animal* with Robin Fox. He has also published books on three generations of women in the Israeli kibbutz movement, on the biology of human optimism, and on the food of China. His books have been translated into eight languages and he has addressed academic, business, and government organizations in an adequate array of countries and situations. He was a "Literary Lion" of the New York Public Library in 1981 and has been Secretary and a Board Member of American PEN since 1980. He lives in New York City and his son is a high school student.

1846 SOC